NAOKI URASAWA'S 20th CENTURY BOYS

VOL 21
ARRIVAL OF THE SPACE ALIENS

Story & Art by
NAOKI URASAWA

With the cooperation of
Takashi NAGASAKI

PROFILES

NAOKI URASAWA'S 20th CENTURY BOYS

As the Friend moves forward with his plan to annihilate humanity, will tomorrow ever come for the world...?!

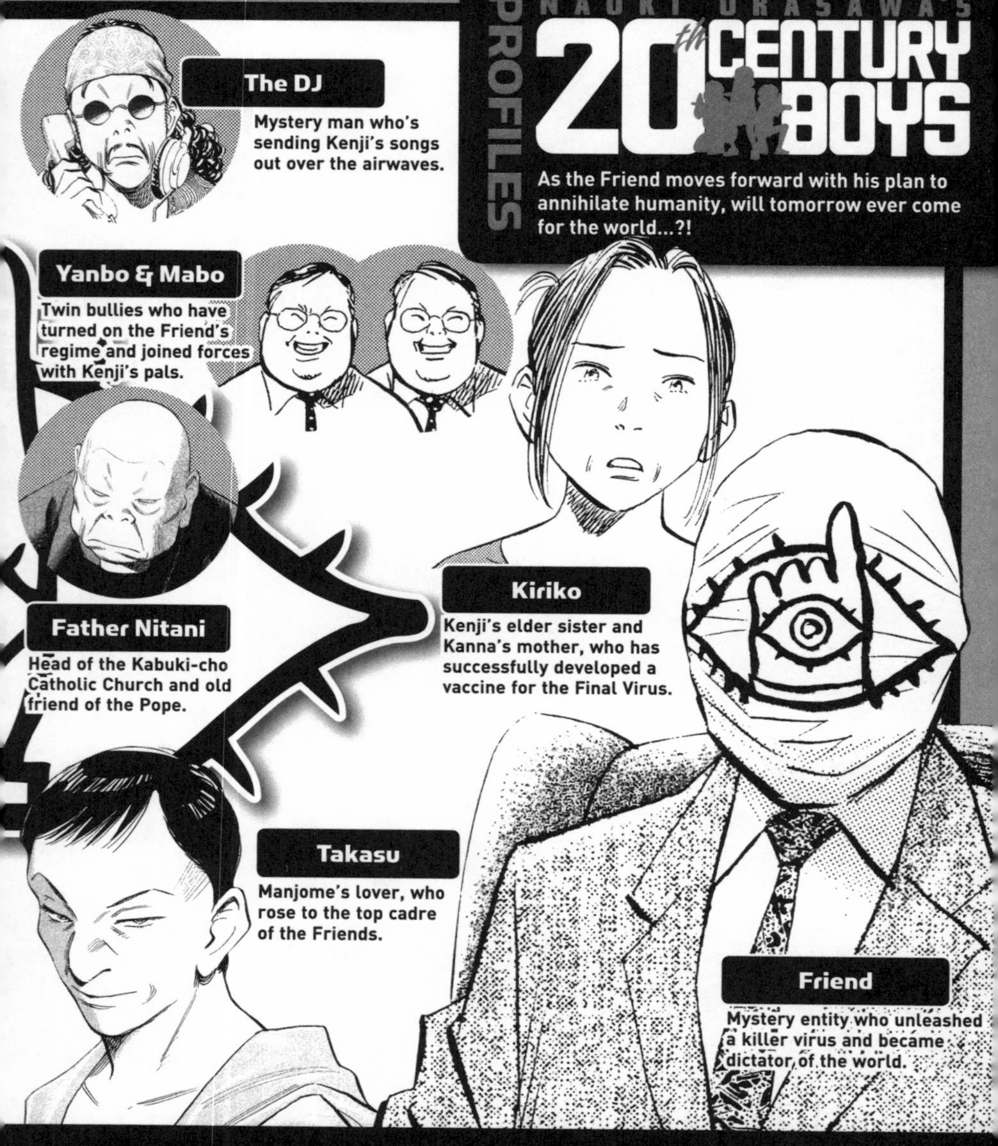

The DJ

Mystery man who's sending Kenji's songs out over the airwaves.

Yanbo & Mabo

Twin bullies who have turned on the Friend's regime and joined forces with Kenji's pals.

Father Nitani

Head of the Kabuki-cho Catholic Church and old friend of the Pope.

Kiriko

Kenji's elder sister and Kanna's mother, who has successfully developed a vaccine for the Final Virus.

Takasu

Manjome's lover, who rose to the top cadre of the Friends.

Friend

Mystery entity who unleashed a killer virus and became dictator of the world.

The Friend then became leader of the world, but is assassinated in 2015 by Yamane, a member of the Friends organization. But incredibly, the Friend comes back to life at the Expo opening ceremony, just in time to shield the Pope from an assassin's bullet. Deified by the world for this miracle, the Friend then orders the dispersal of a killer virus around the world, resulting in the destruction of the world as we know it...

And now, three years later, the Friend is President of the World, ruling Japan with an iron fist. His plans for the total annihilation of humanity are steadily moving forward, but the group of boys who'd played together almost 50 years earlier are coming together and getting ready for the final showdown. And Kenji, who'd been missing for all those years, is heading down to Tokyo!!

H CENTURY BOYS

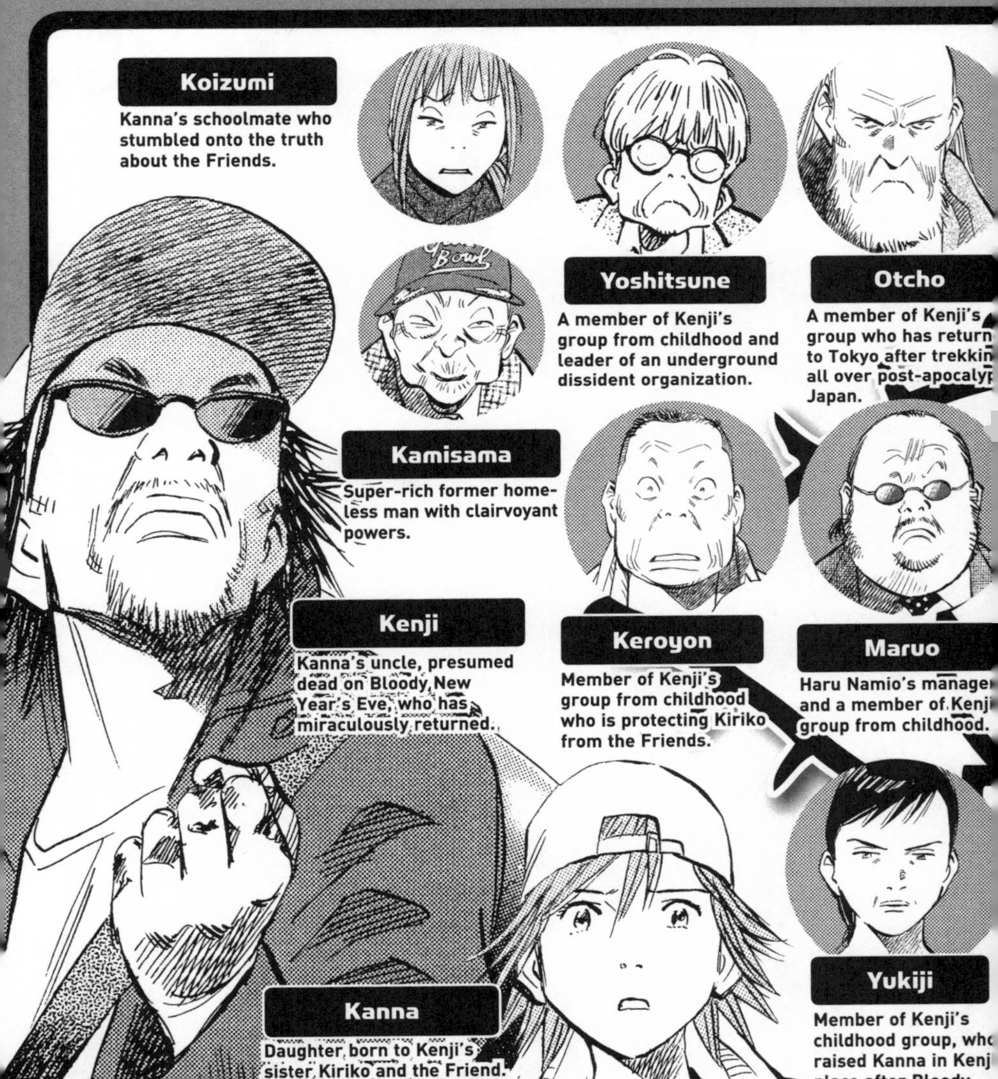
Koizumi
Kanna's schoolmate who stumbled onto the truth about the Friends.
Yoshitsune
A member of Kenji's group from childhood and leader of an underground dissident organization.
Otcho
A member of Kenji's group who has return to Tokyo after trekkin all over post-apocalyp Japan.
Kamisama
Super-rich former homeless man with clairvoyant powers.
Kenji
Kanna's uncle, presumed dead on Bloody New Year's Eve, who has miraculously returned.
Keroyon
Member of Kenji's group from childhood who is protecting Kiriko from the Friends.
Maruo
Haru Namio's manage and a member of Kenj group from childhood.
Kanna
Daughter born to Kenji's sister Kiriko and the Friend.
Yukiji
Member of Kenji's childhood group, wh raised Kanna in Kenj place after Bloody New Year's Eve.

The story so far...

In the early 1970s, Kenji and his friends were elementary schoolers who dreamed of the exciting future that awaited them in the 21st century. In their secret headquarters, out in an empty lot, they made up a ridiculous scenario about a League of Evil, whose plan to destroy the world would be thwarted by a group of heroes. They wrote this story in *The Book of Prophecy*.

Later in 1997, the adult Kenji is raising his missing sister's baby Kanna and is shocked when he realizes that a series of ominous incidents is following *The Book of Prophecy*, and that a charismatic leader known only as the Friend seems to be behind it all. On the last night of the 20th century, later known as "Bloody New Year's Eve," the Friend acts the part of the hero who saved the world and Kenji, who lost his life trying to stop him, was branded a terrorist.

A SUMMARY OF 2

NAOKI URASAWA'S

20th CENTURY BOYS

CONTENTS

VOL 21

ARRIVAL OF THE SPACE ALIENS

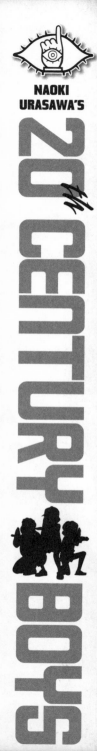

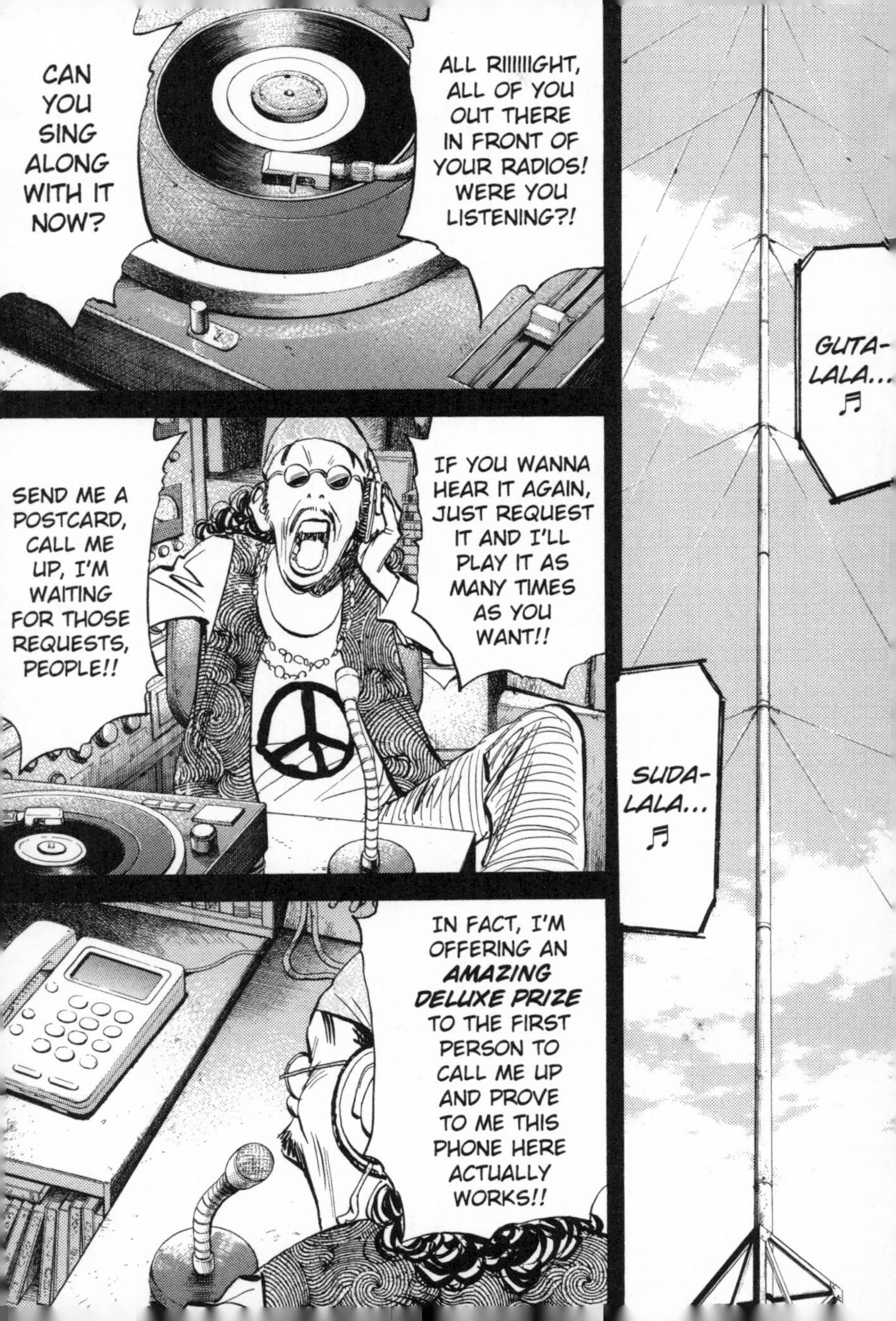
GUTA-LALA... ♬
SUDA-LALA... ♬
ALL RIIIIIGHT, ALL OF YOU OUT THERE IN FRONT OF YOUR RADIOS! WERE YOU LISTENING?!
CAN YOU SING ALONG WITH IT NOW?
IF YOU WANNA HEAR IT AGAIN, JUST REQUEST IT AND I'LL PLAY IT AS MANY TIMES AS YOU WANT!!
SEND ME A POSTCARD, CALL ME UP, I'M WAITING FOR THOSE REQUESTS, PEOPLE!!
IN FACT, I'M OFFERING AN ***AMAZING DELUXE PRIZE*** TO THE FIRST PERSON TO CALL ME UP AND PROVE TO ME THIS PHONE HERE ACTUALLY WORKS!!

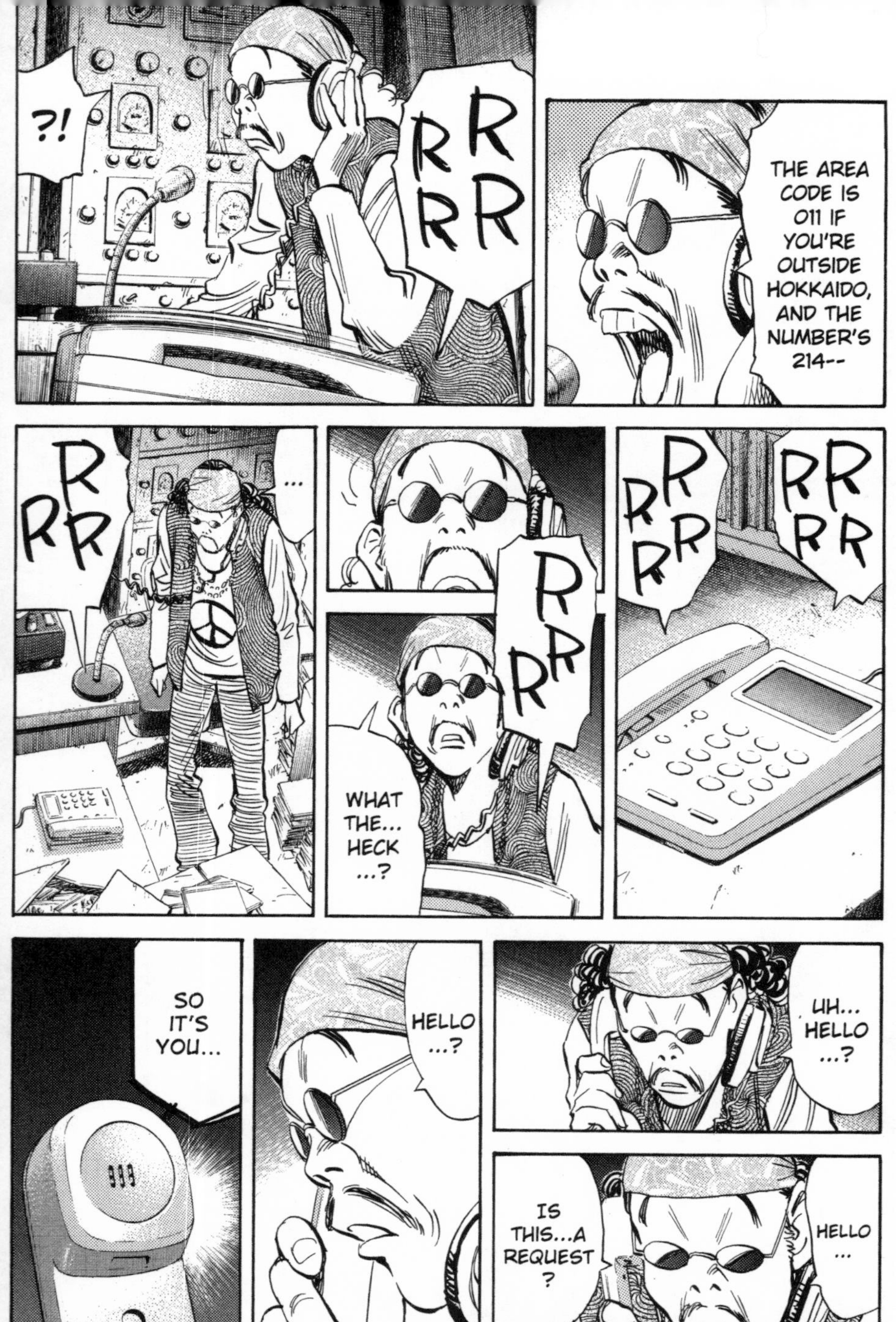
THE AREA CODE IS 011 IF YOU'RE OUTSIDE HOKKAIDO, AND THE NUMBER'S 214--
RRRR
?!
RRRR
RRRR
RRR
WHAT THE... HECK ...?
RRR
...
UH... HELLO ...?
HELLO ...
IS THIS...A REQUEST ?
HELLO ...?
SO IT'S YOU...

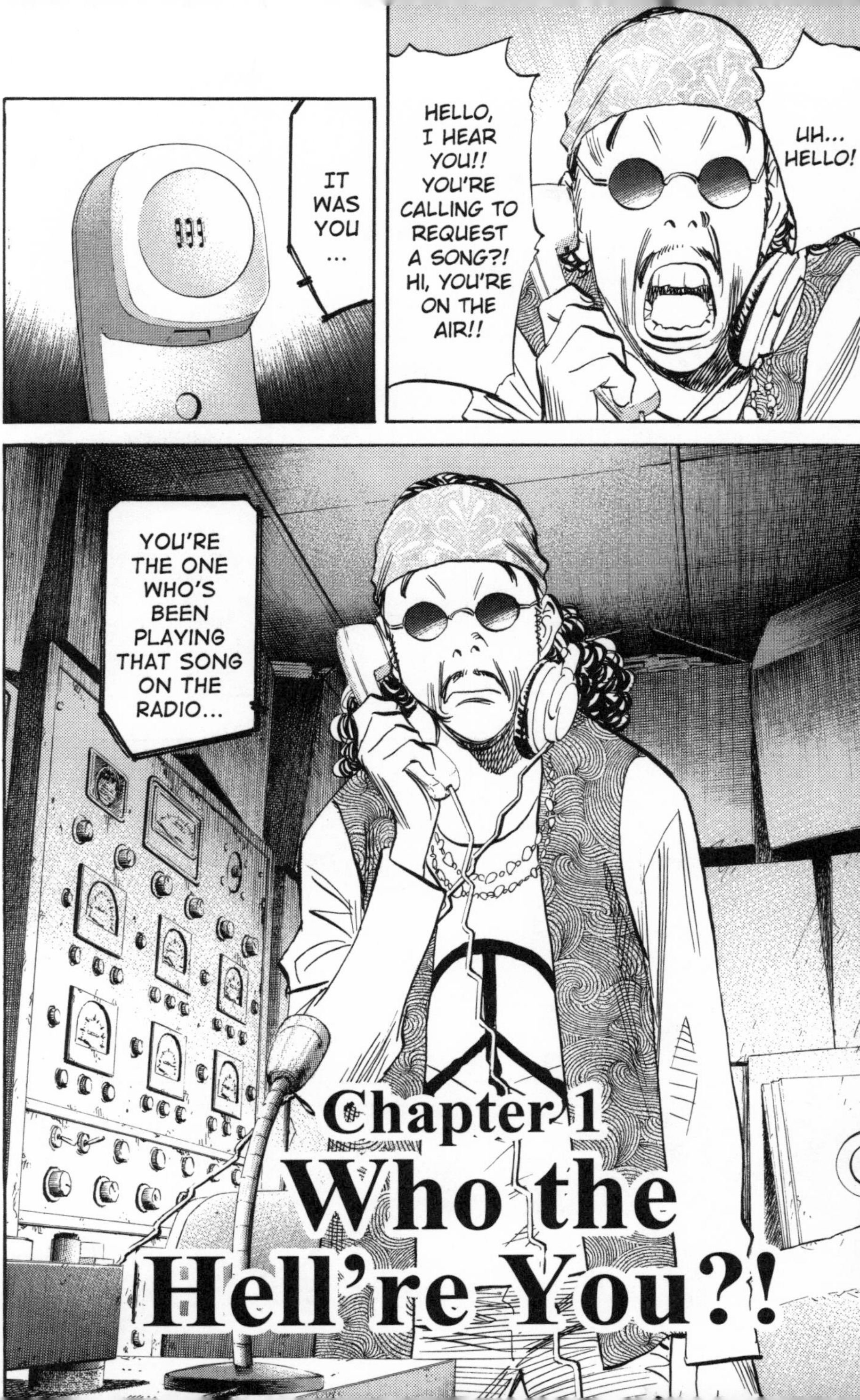
UH... HELLO!
HELLO, I HEAR YOU!! YOU'RE CALLING TO REQUEST A SONG?! HI, YOU'RE ON THE AIR!!
IT WAS YOU ...
YOU'RE THE ONE WHO'S BEEN PLAYING THAT SONG ON THE RADIO...
Chapter 1
Who the Hell're You?!

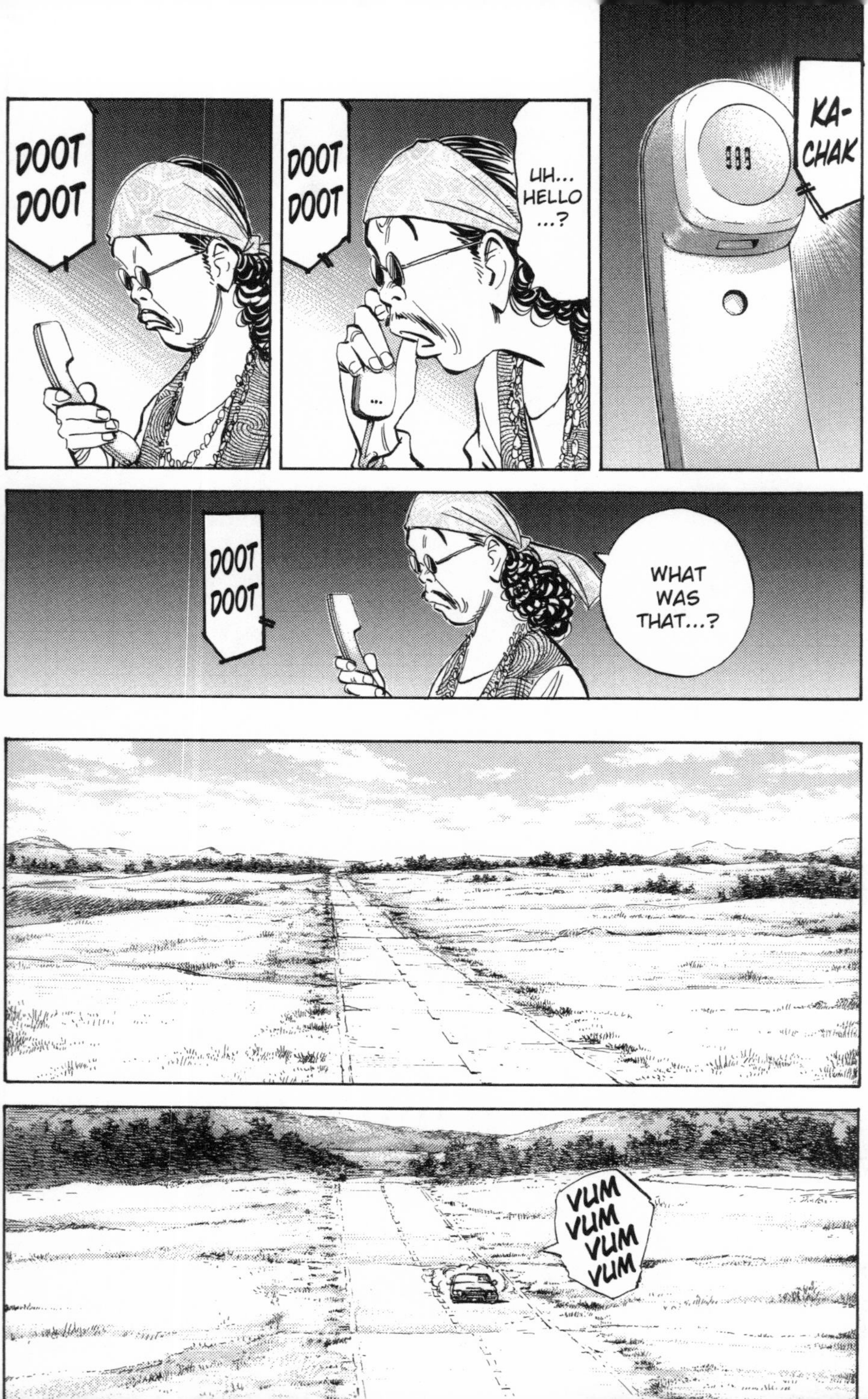
KA-CHAK
UH... HELLO ...?
DOOT DOOT
DOOT DOOT
WHAT WAS THAT...?
DOOT DOOT
VUM VUM VUM VUM

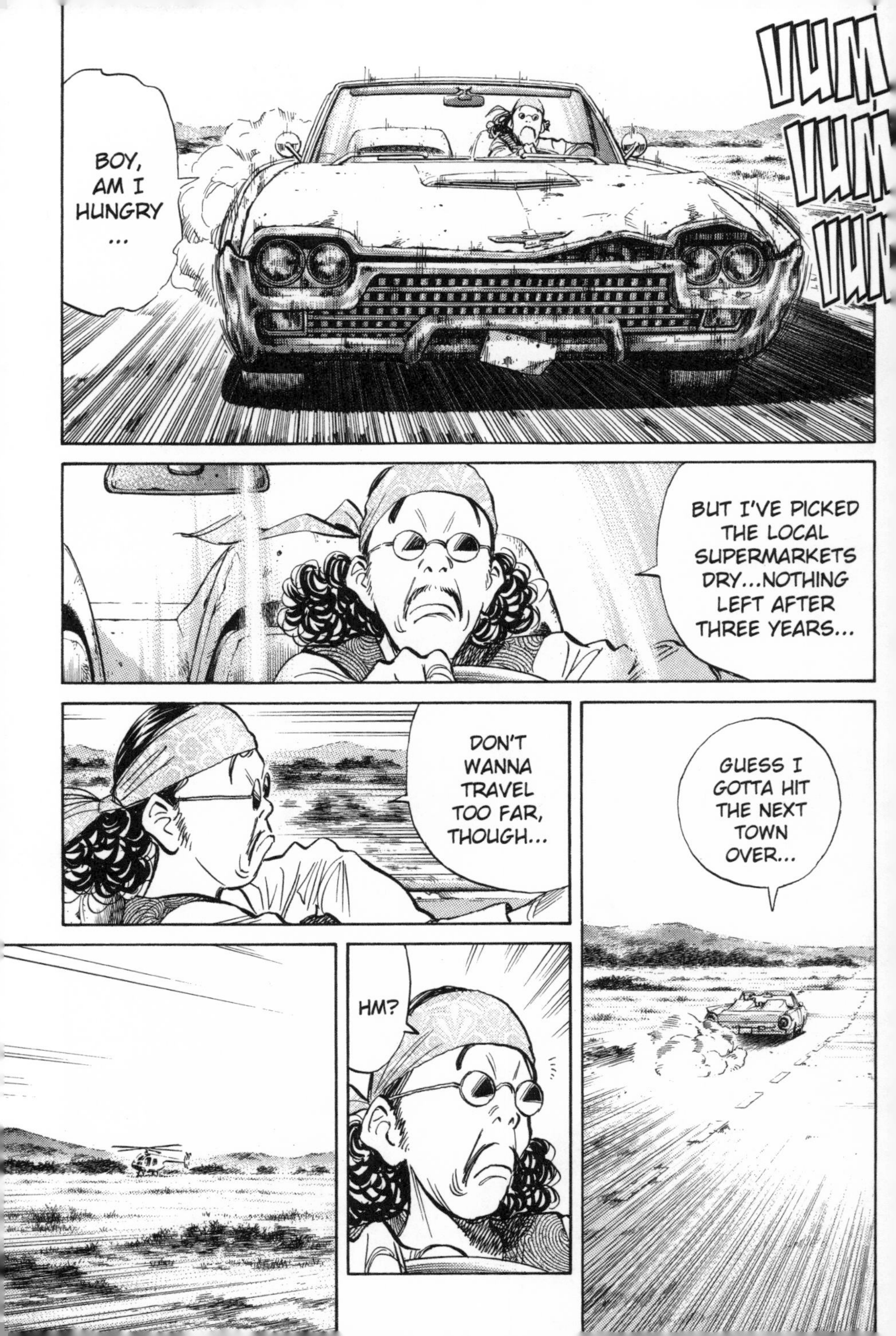
VUM
VUM
VUM
BOY, AM I HUNGRY ...
BUT I'VE PICKED THE LOCAL SUPERMARKETS DRY...NOTHING LEFT AFTER THREE YEARS...
GUESS I GOTTA HIT THE NEXT TOWN OVER...
DON'T WANNA TRAVEL TOO FAR, THOUGH...
HM?

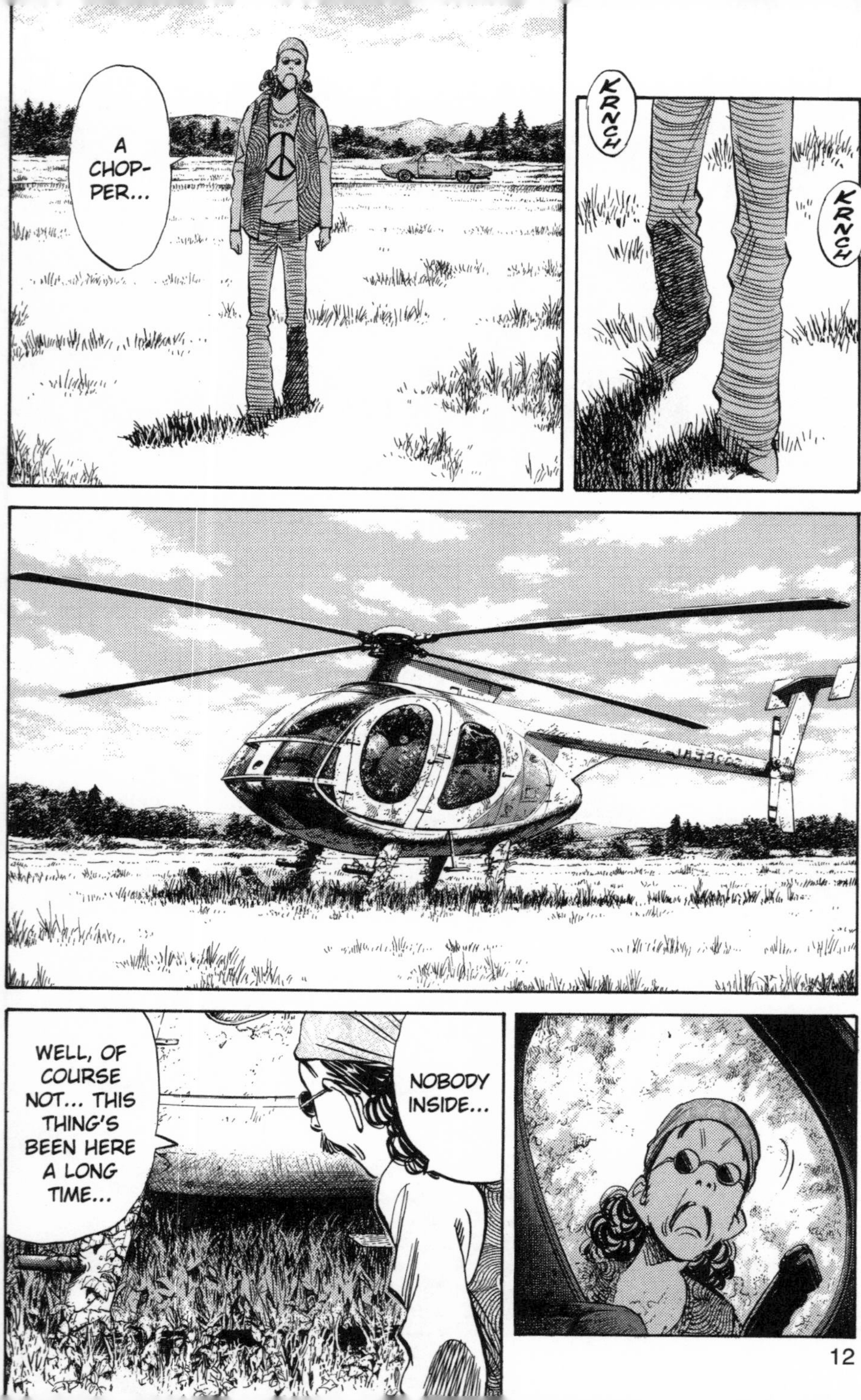
KRNCH
KRNCH
A CHOP-PER...
NOBODY INSIDE...
WELL, OF COURSE NOT... THIS THING'S BEEN HERE A LONG TIME...

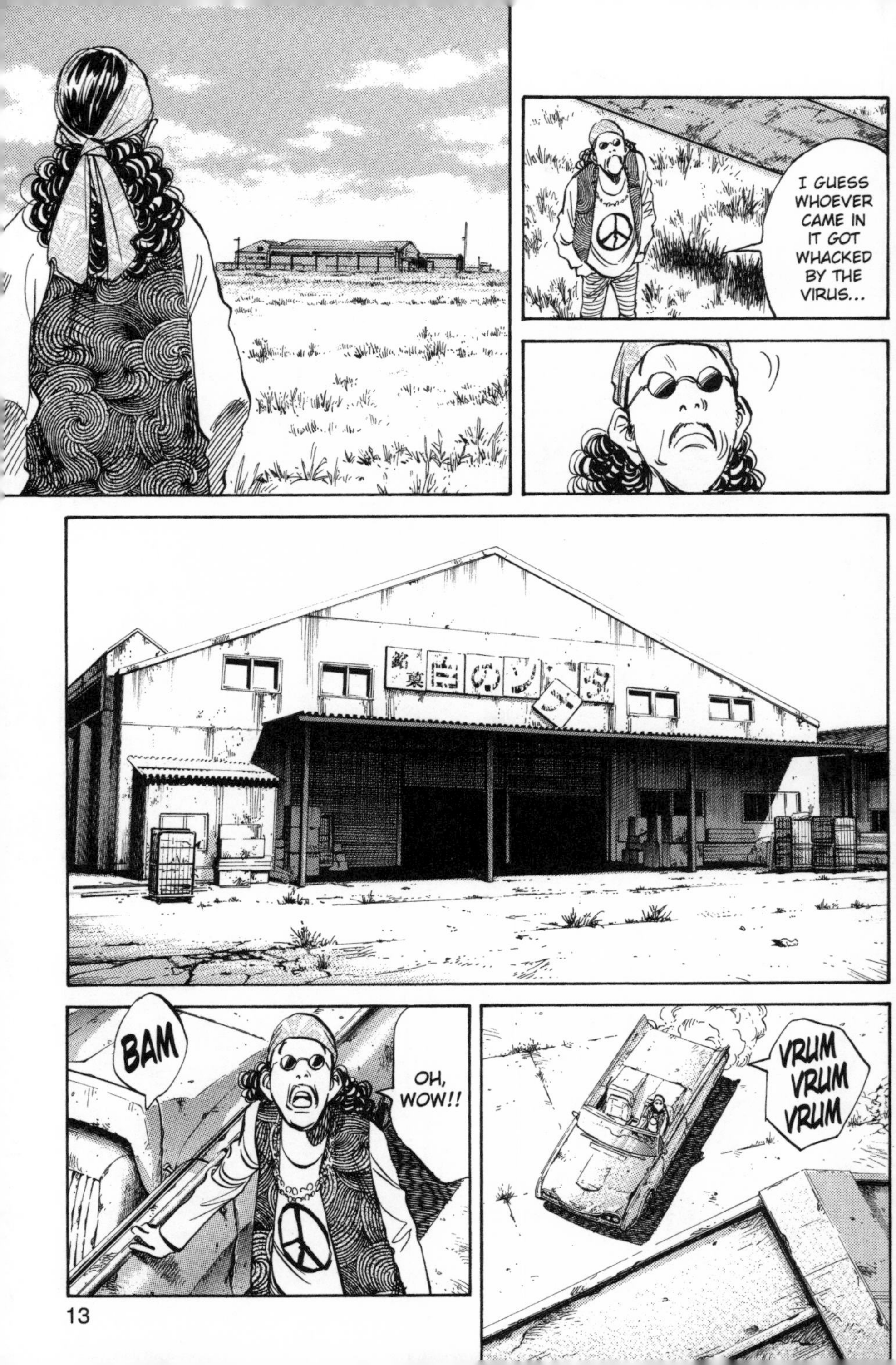
I GUESS WHOEVER CAME IN IT GOT WHACKED BY THE VIRUS...
VRUM VRUM VRUM
BAM
OH, WOW!!

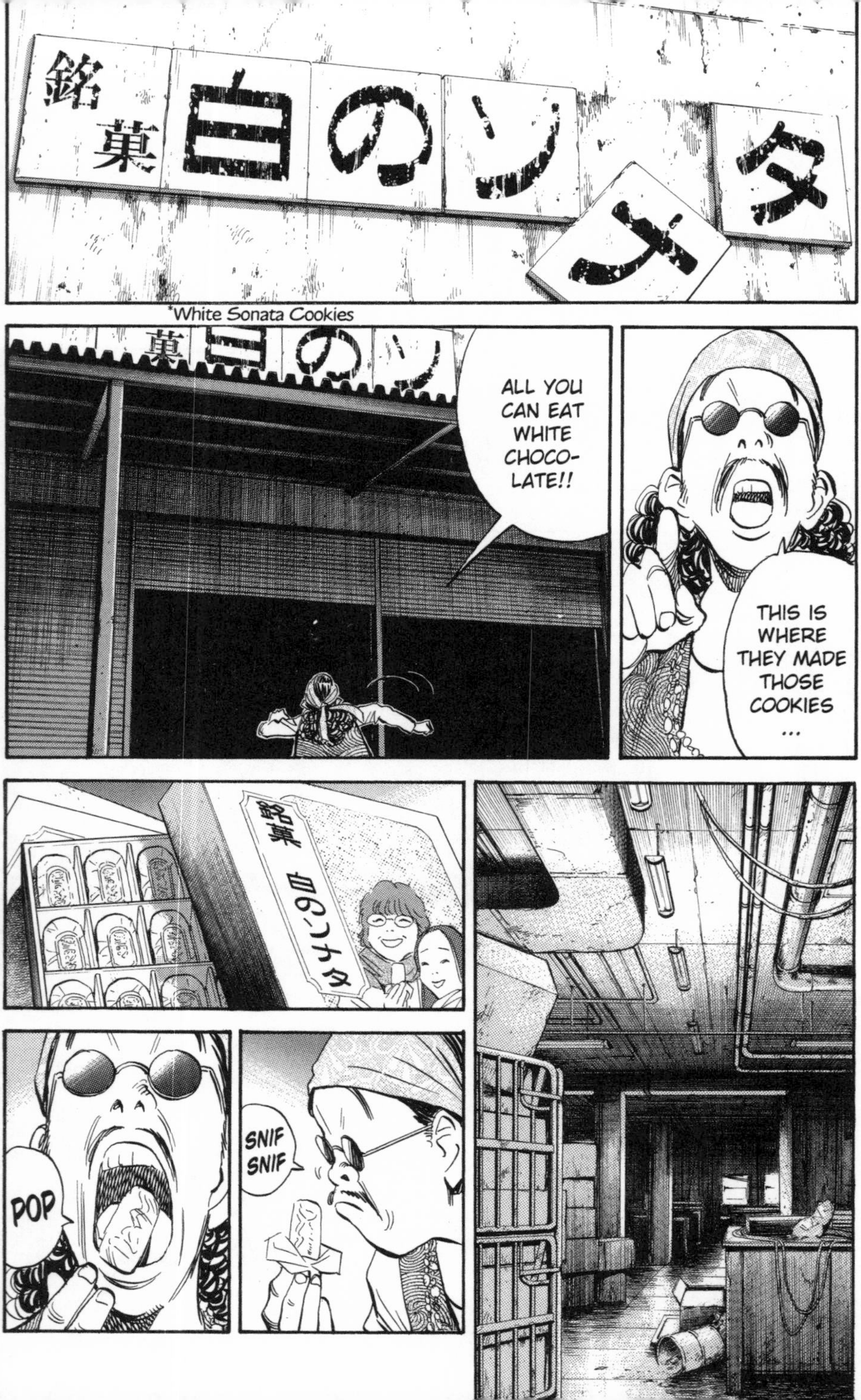
銘菓 白のソナタ
*White Sonata Cookies
THIS IS WHERE THEY MADE THOSE COOKIES ...
ALL YOU CAN EAT WHITE CHOCOLATE!!
銘菓 白のソナタ
SNIF SNIF
POP

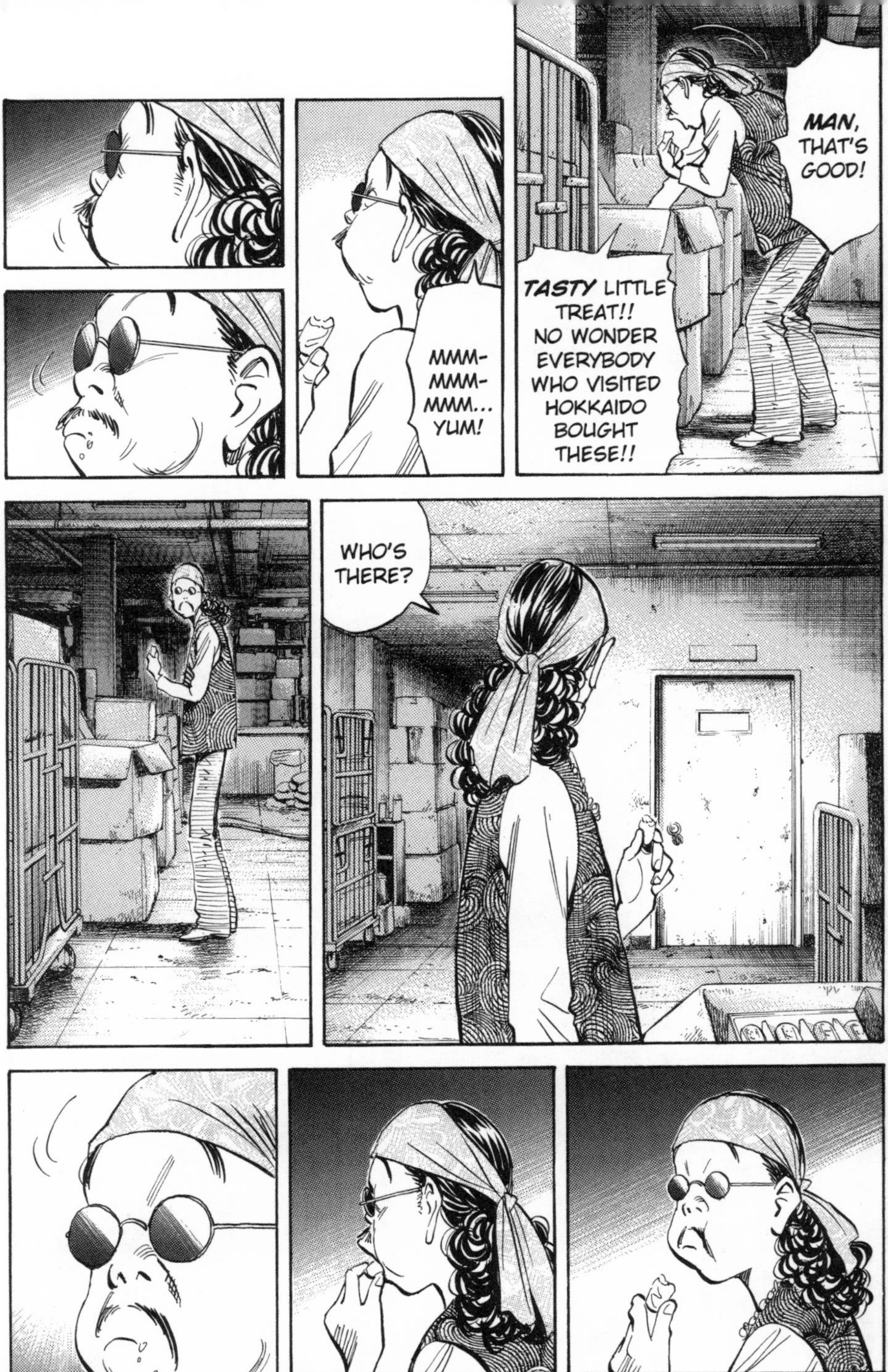

MAN, THAT'S GOOD!
TASTY LITTLE TREAT!! NO WONDER EVERYBODY WHO VISITED HOKKAIDO BOUGHT THESE!!
MMM-MMM-MMM... YUM!
WHO'S THERE?

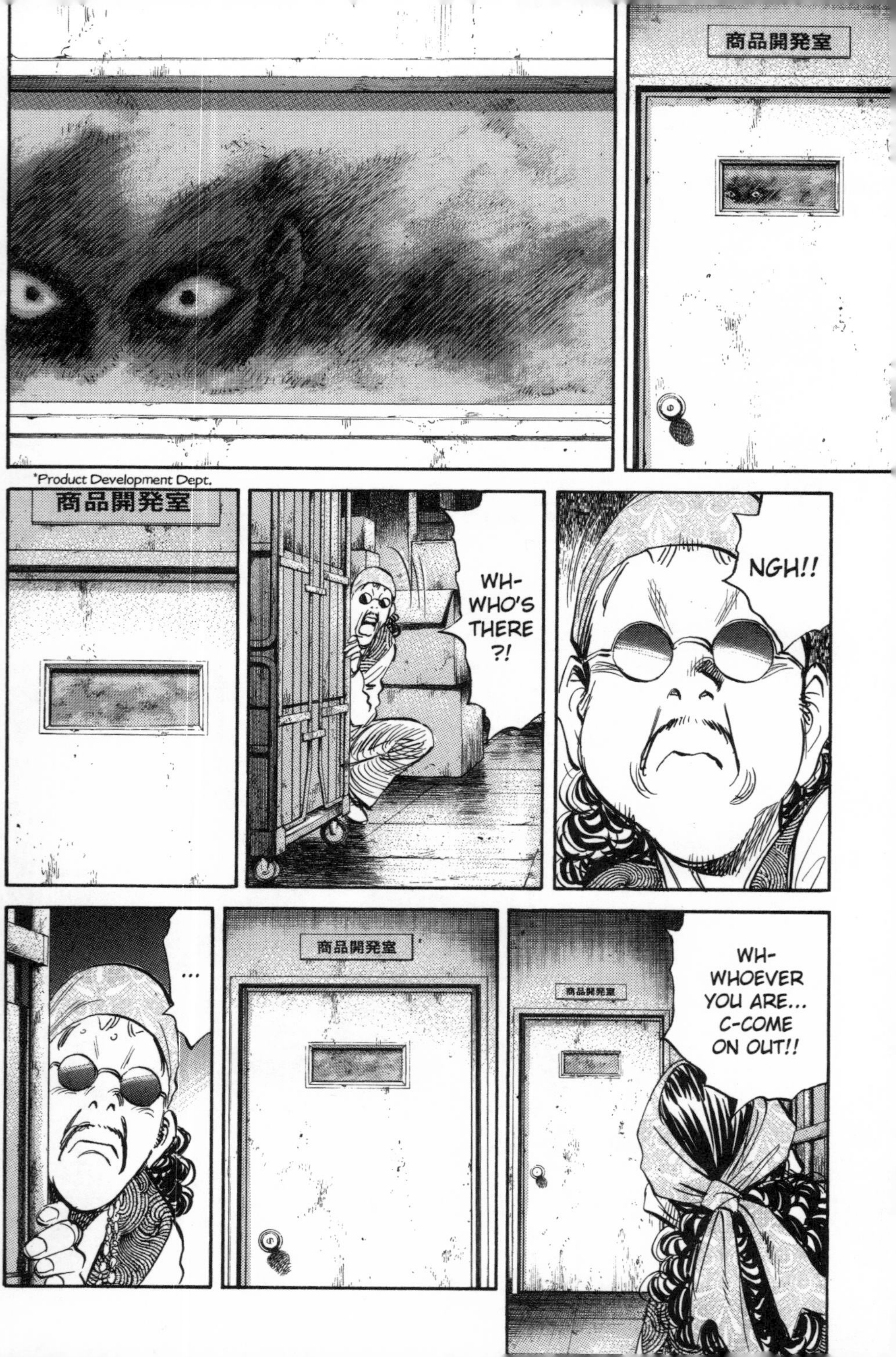

商品開発室
*Product Development Dept.
NGH!!
WH-
WHO'S
THERE
?!
商品開発室
WH-
WHOEVER
YOU ARE...
C-COME
ON OUT!!
商品開発室
商品開発室
...

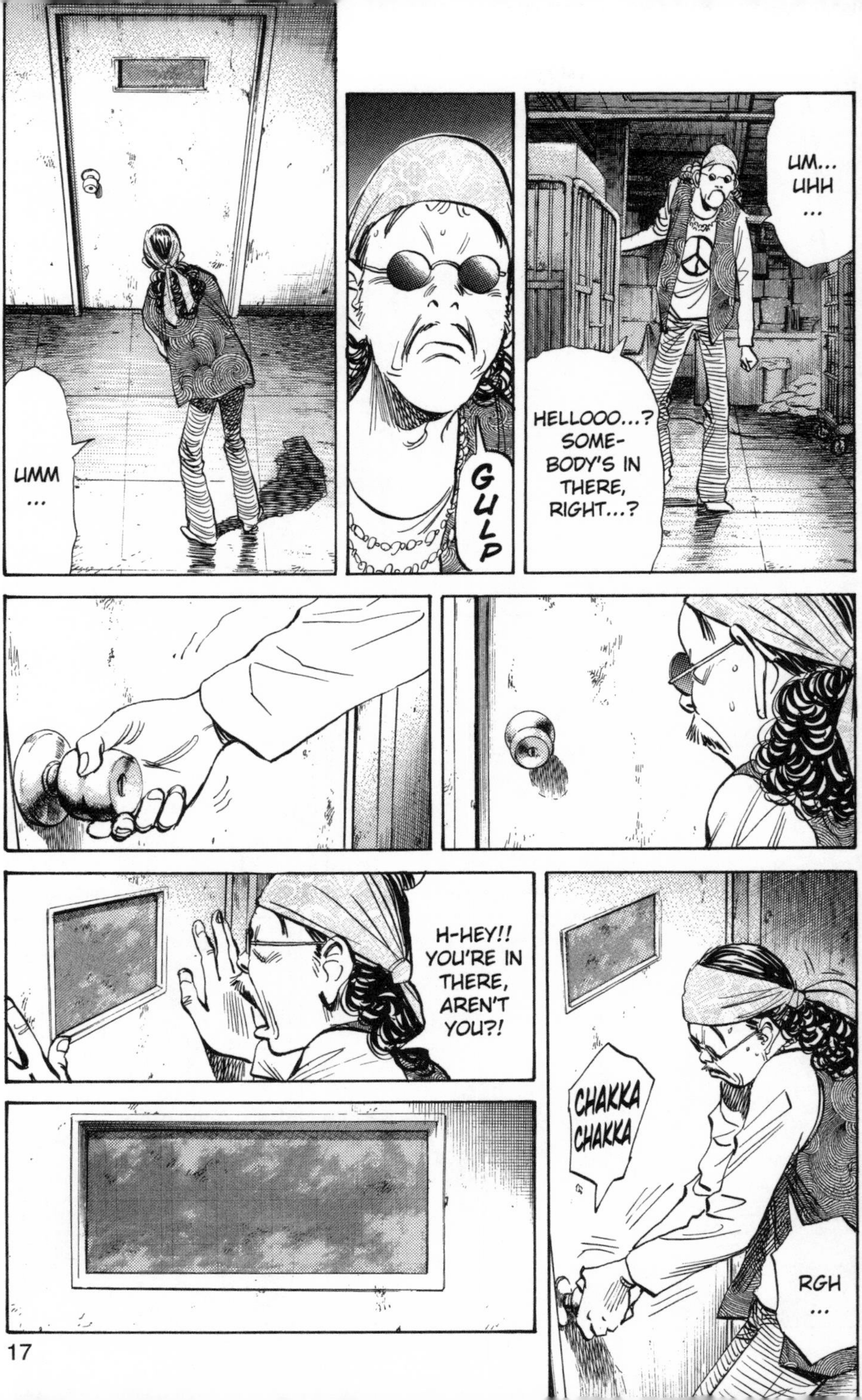
UM... UHH ...
HELLOOO...? SOME-BODY'S IN THERE, RIGHT...?
GULP
UMM ...
CHAKKA CHAKKA
RGH ...
H-HEY!! YOU'RE IN THERE, AREN'T YOU?!

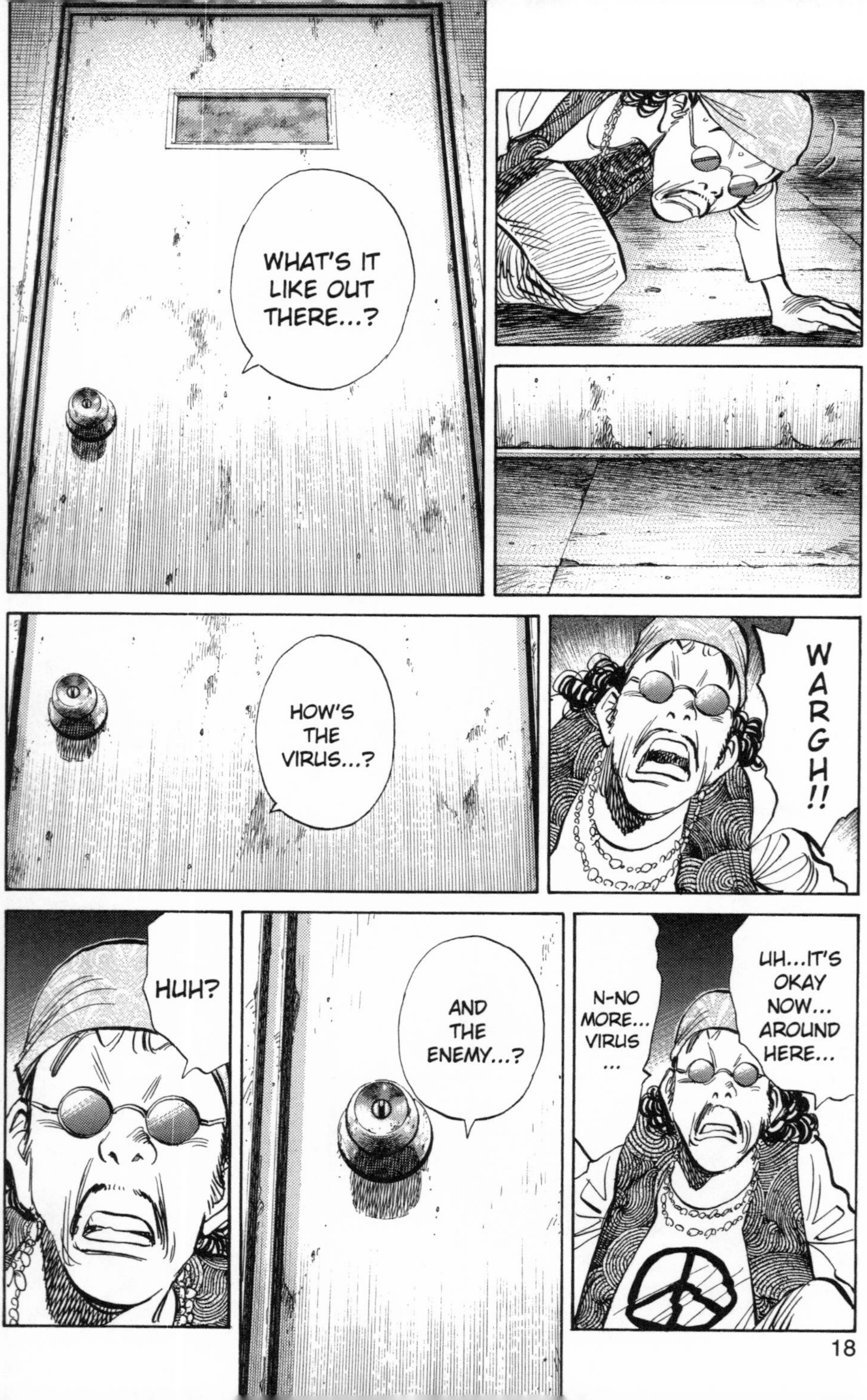
WHAT'S IT LIKE OUT THERE...?
WARGH!!
HOW'S THE VIRUS...?
UH...IT'S OKAY NOW... AROUND HERE...
N-NO MORE... VIRUS ...
AND THE ENEMY...?
HUH?

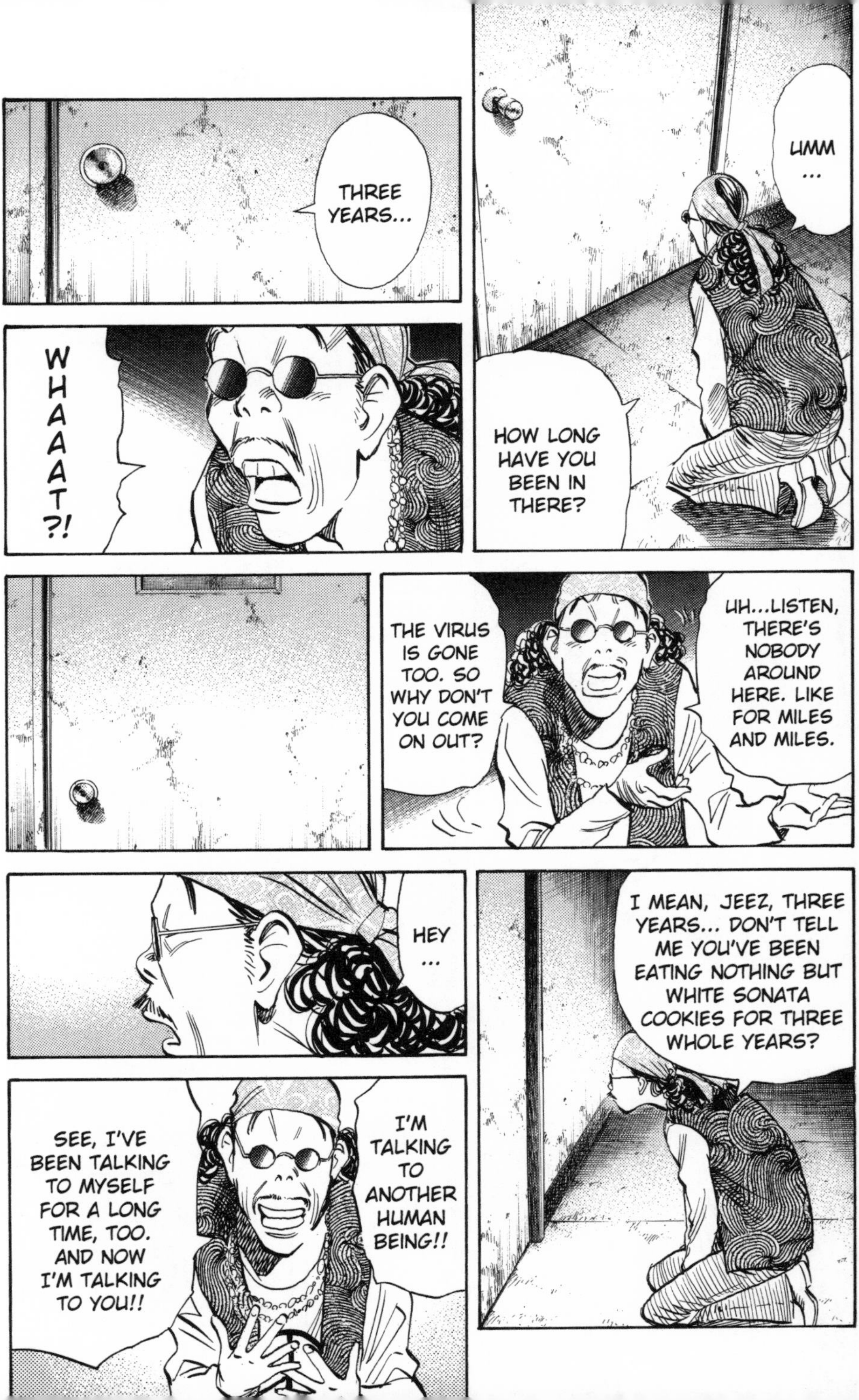
UMM...
HOW LONG HAVE YOU BEEN IN THERE?
THREE YEARS...
WHAAAAT?!
UH...LISTEN, THERE'S NOBODY AROUND HERE. LIKE FOR MILES AND MILES.
THE VIRUS IS GONE TOO. SO WHY DON'T YOU COME ON OUT?
I MEAN, JEEZ, THREE YEARS... DON'T TELL ME YOU'VE BEEN EATING NOTHING BUT WHITE SONATA COOKIES FOR THREE WHOLE YEARS?
HEY...
I'M TALKING TO ANOTHER HUMAN BEING!!
SEE, I'VE BEEN TALKING TO MYSELF FOR A LONG TIME, TOO. AND NOW I'M TALKING TO YOU!!

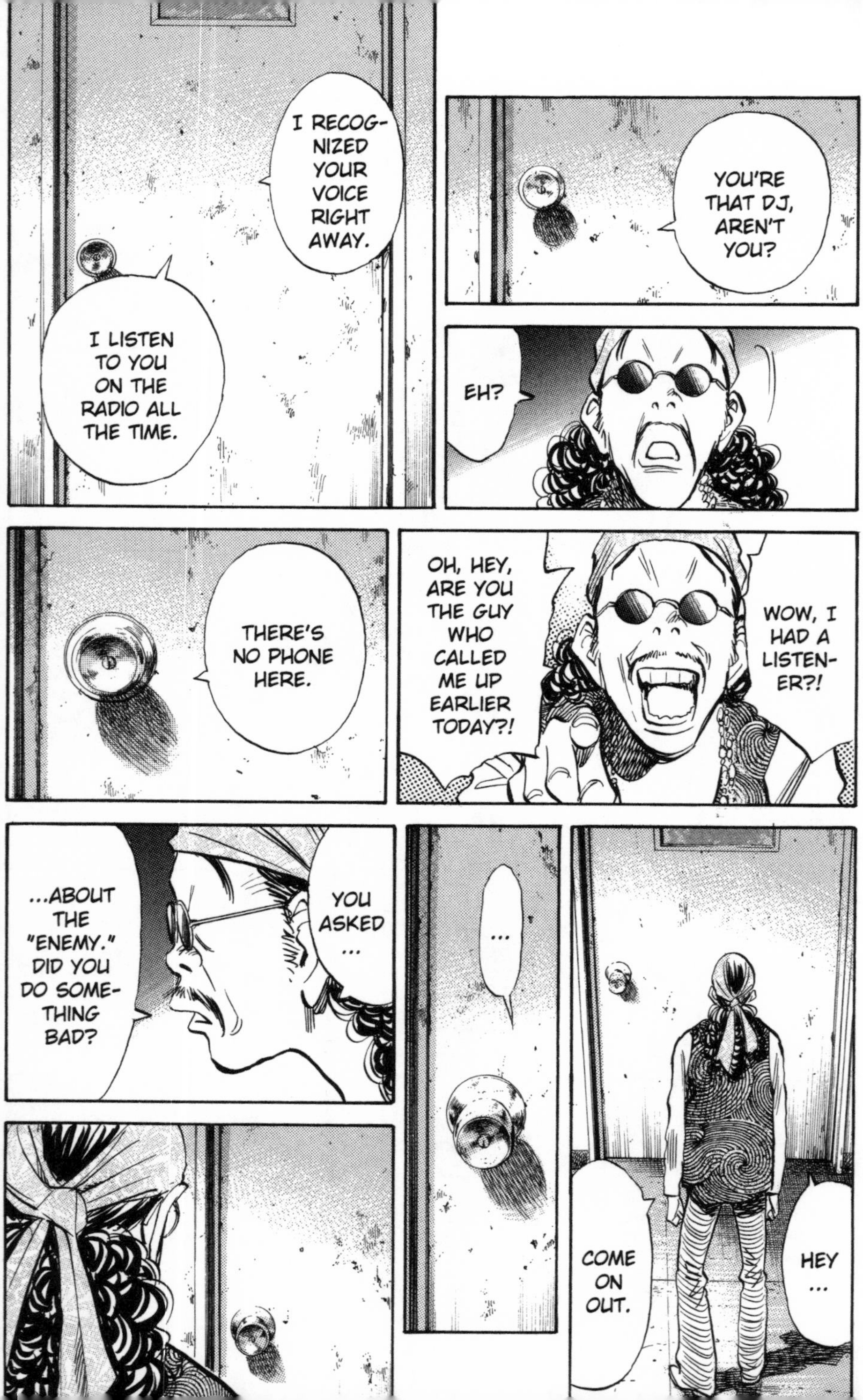
YOU'RE THAT DJ, AREN'T YOU?
EH?
I RECOG-NIZED YOUR VOICE RIGHT AWAY.
I LISTEN TO YOU ON THE RADIO ALL THE TIME.
WOW, I HAD A LISTEN-ER?!
OH, HEY, ARE YOU THE GUY WHO CALLED ME UP EARLIER TODAY?!
THERE'S NO PHONE HERE.
HEY...
COME ON OUT.
...
YOU ASKED...
...ABOUT THE "ENEMY." DID YOU DO SOME-THING BAD?

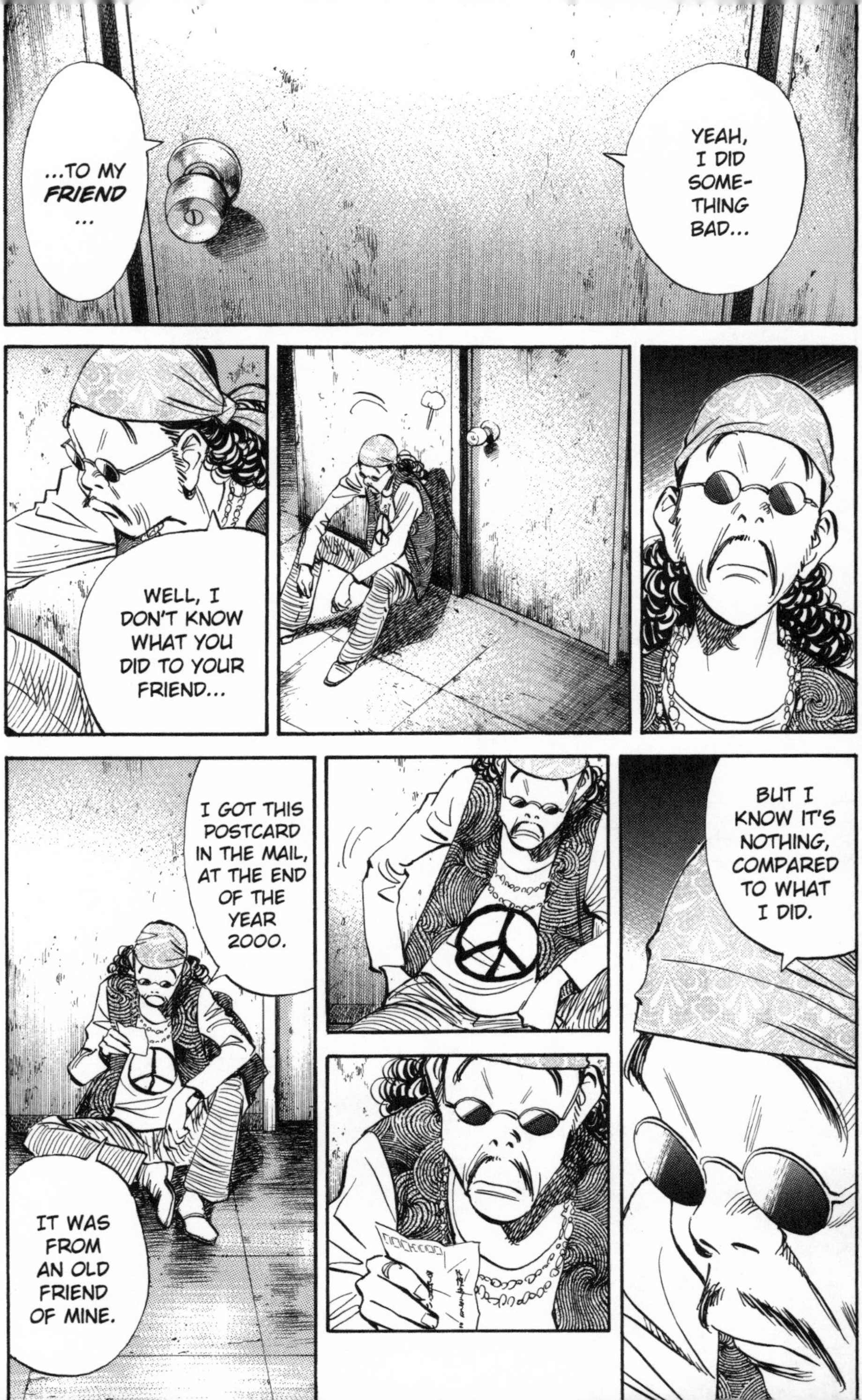
YEAH, I DID SOMETHING BAD...
...TO MY FRIEND ...
WELL, I DON'T KNOW WHAT YOU DID TO YOUR FRIEND...
BUT I KNOW IT'S NOTHING, COMPARED TO WHAT I DID.
I GOT THIS POSTCARD IN THE MAIL, AT THE END OF THE YEAR 2000.
IT WAS FROM AN OLD FRIEND OF MINE.

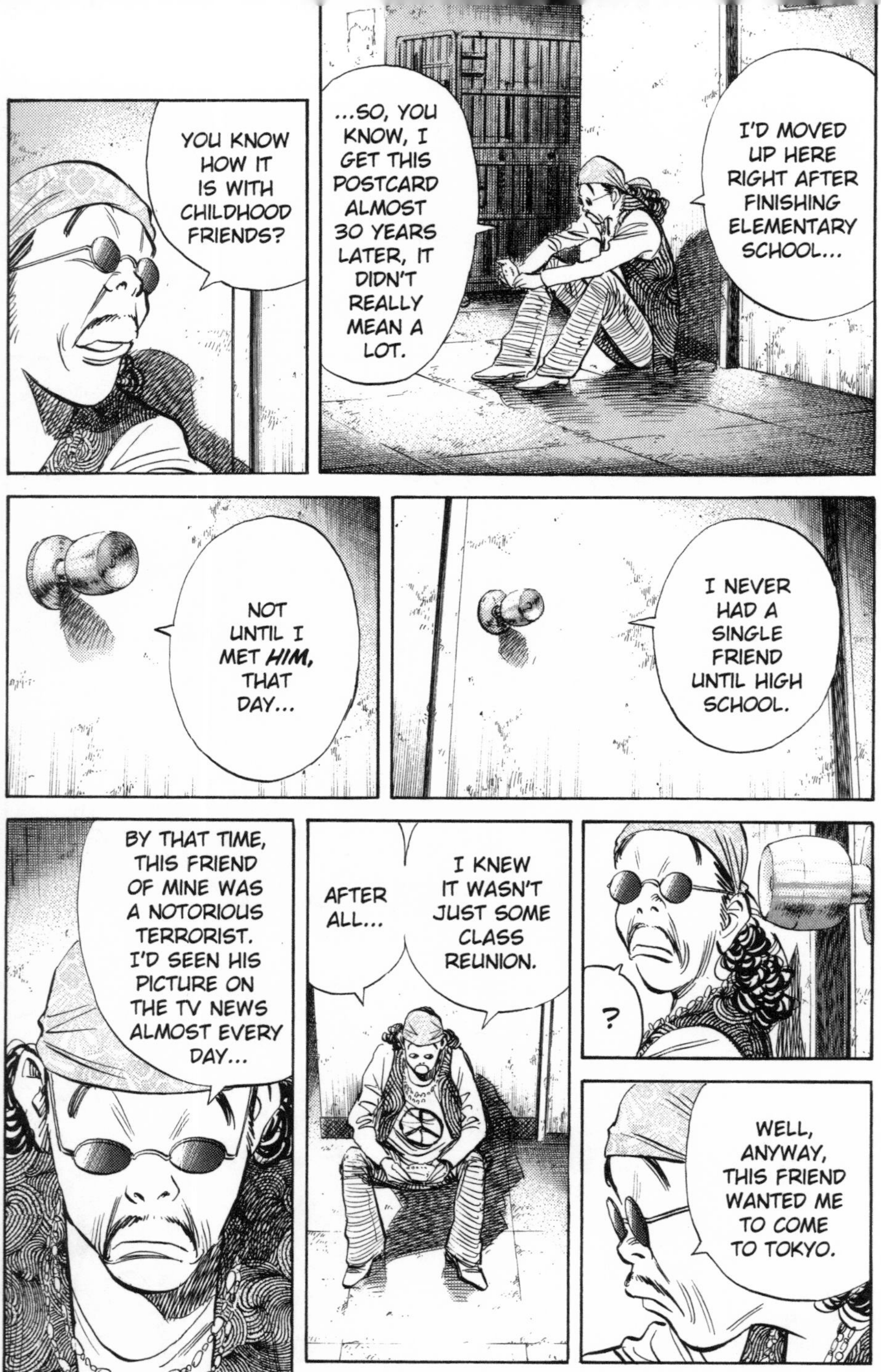
I'D MOVED UP HERE RIGHT AFTER FINISHING ELEMENTARY SCHOOL...
...SO, YOU KNOW, I GET THIS POSTCARD ALMOST 30 YEARS LATER, IT DIDN'T REALLY MEAN A LOT.
YOU KNOW HOW IT IS WITH CHILDHOOD FRIENDS?
I NEVER HAD A SINGLE FRIEND UNTIL HIGH SCHOOL.
NOT UNTIL I MET *HIM*, THAT DAY...
?
WELL, ANYWAY, THIS FRIEND WANTED ME TO COME TO TOKYO.
I KNEW IT WASN'T JUST SOME CLASS REUNION.
AFTER ALL...
BY THAT TIME, THIS FRIEND OF MINE WAS A NOTORIOUS TERRORIST. I'D SEEN HIS PICTURE ON THE TV NEWS ALMOST EVERY DAY...

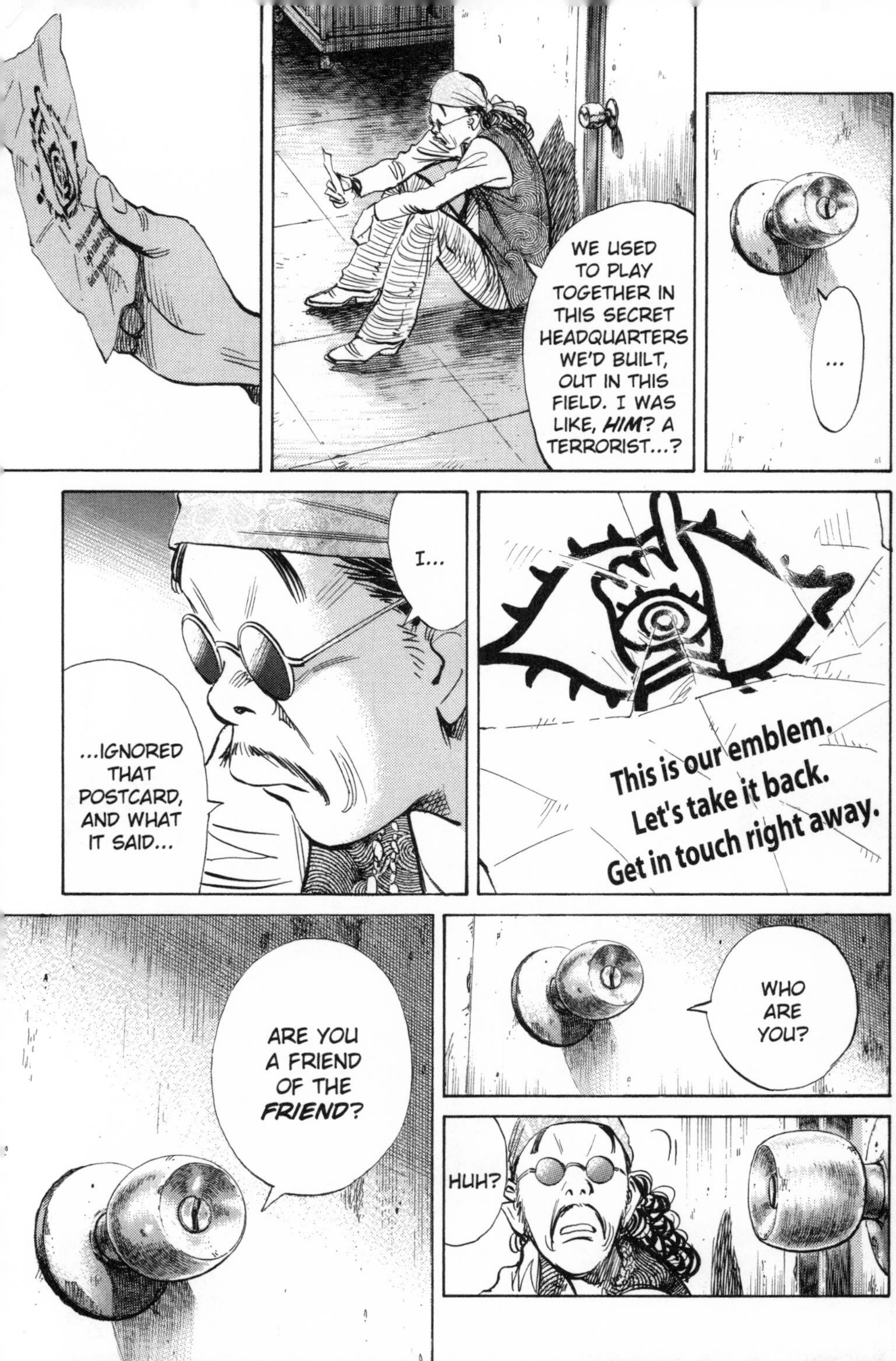
...
WE USED TO PLAY TOGETHER IN THIS SECRET HEADQUARTERS WE'D BUILT, OUT IN THIS FIELD. I WAS LIKE, *HIM*? A TERRORIST...?
This is our emblem.
Let's take it back.
Get in touch right away.
I...
...IGNORED THAT POSTCARD, AND WHAT IT SAID...
WHO ARE YOU?
HUH?
ARE YOU A FRIEND OF THE *FRIEND*?

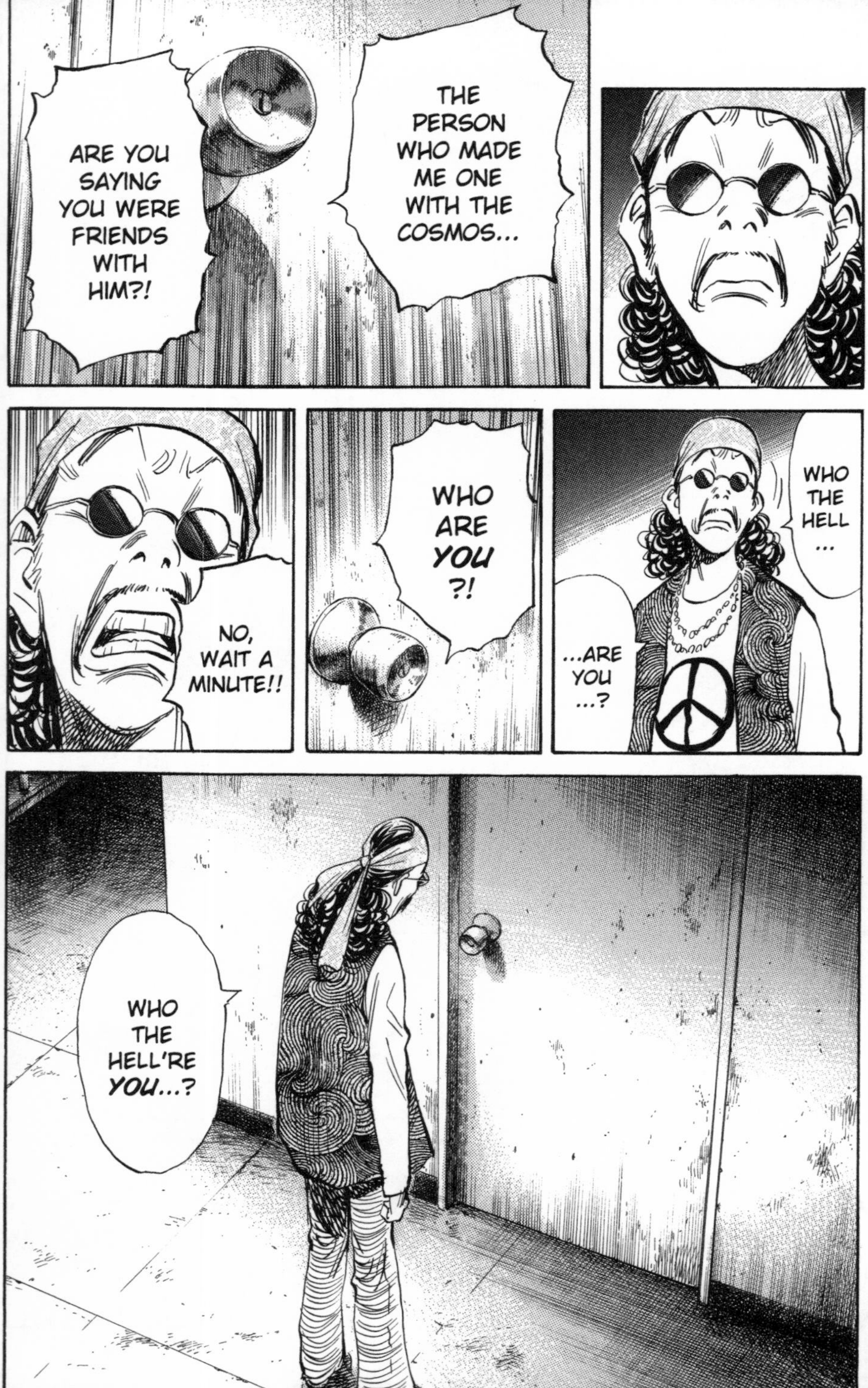
THE PERSON WHO MADE ME ONE WITH THE COSMOS...
ARE YOU SAYING YOU WERE FRIENDS WITH HIM?!
WHO THE HELL...
...ARE YOU...?
WHO ARE *YOU*?!
NO, WAIT A MINUTE!!
WHO THE HELL'RE *YOU*...?

Chapter 2 Hide-and-Seek

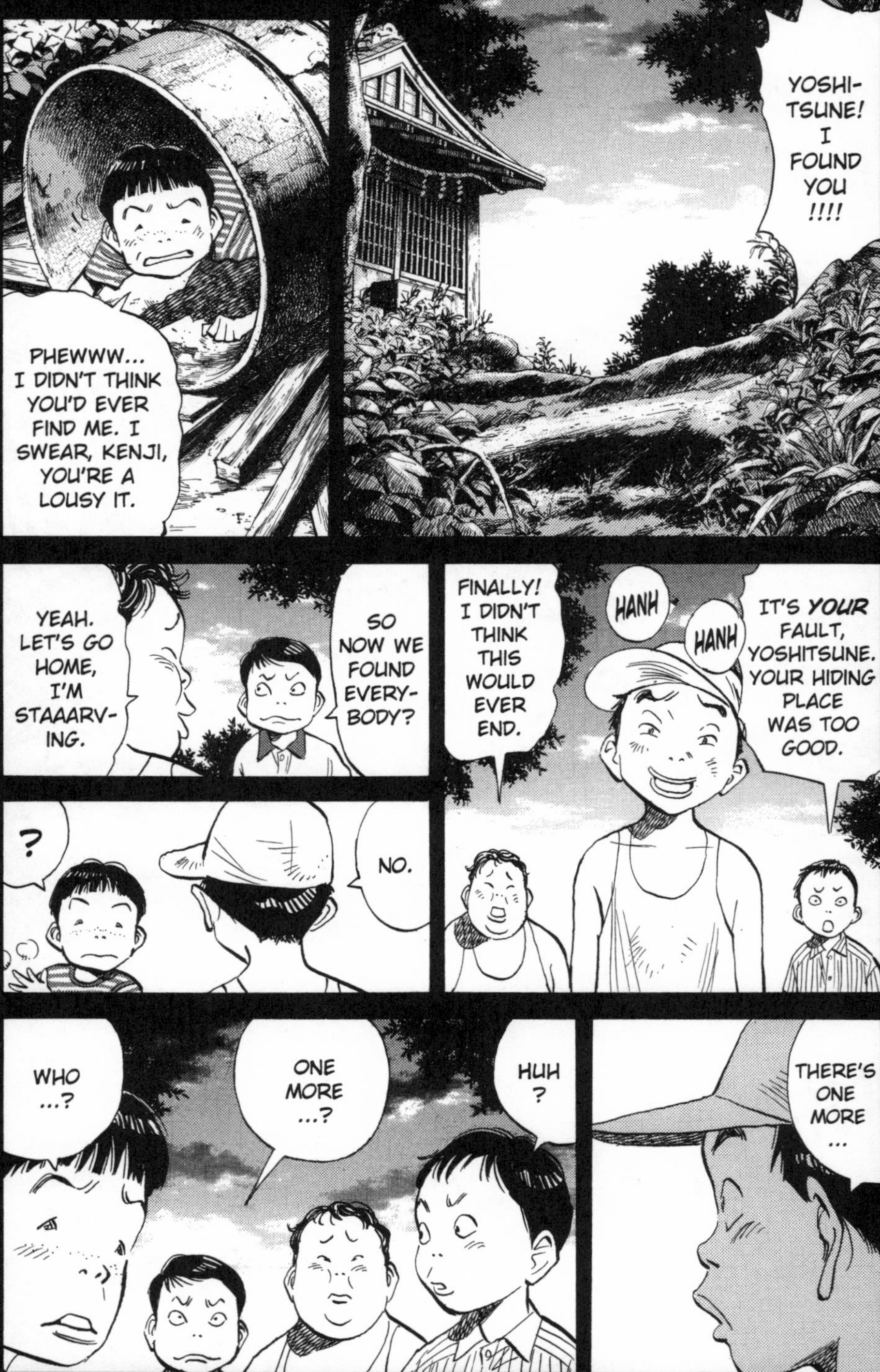
YOSHI-TSUNE! I FOUND YOU !!!!
PHEWWW... I DIDN'T THINK YOU'D EVER FIND ME. I SWEAR, KENJI, YOU'RE A LOUSY IT.
IT'S *YOUR* FAULT, YOSHITSUNE. YOUR HIDING PLACE WAS TOO GOOD.
HANH
HANH
FINALLY! I DIDN'T THINK THIS WOULD EVER END.
SO NOW WE FOUND EVERY-BODY?
YEAH. LET'S GO HOME, I'M STAAARV-ING.
NO.
?
THERE'S ONE MORE ...
HUH ?
ONE MORE ...?
WHO ...?

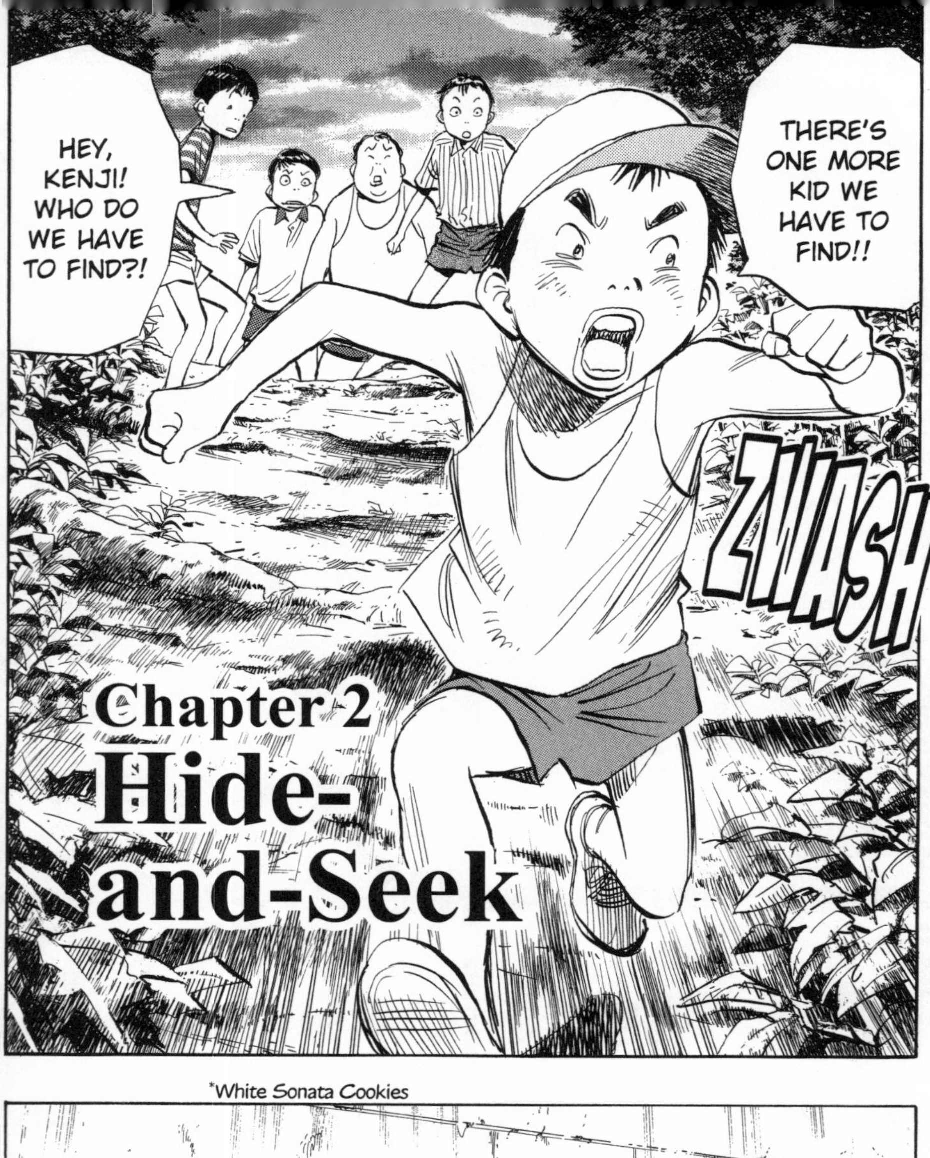
THERE'S ONE MORE KID WE HAVE TO FIND!!
HEY, KENJI! WHO DO WE HAVE TO FIND?!
ZWASH

Chapter 2 Hide-and-Seek

*White Sonata Cookies

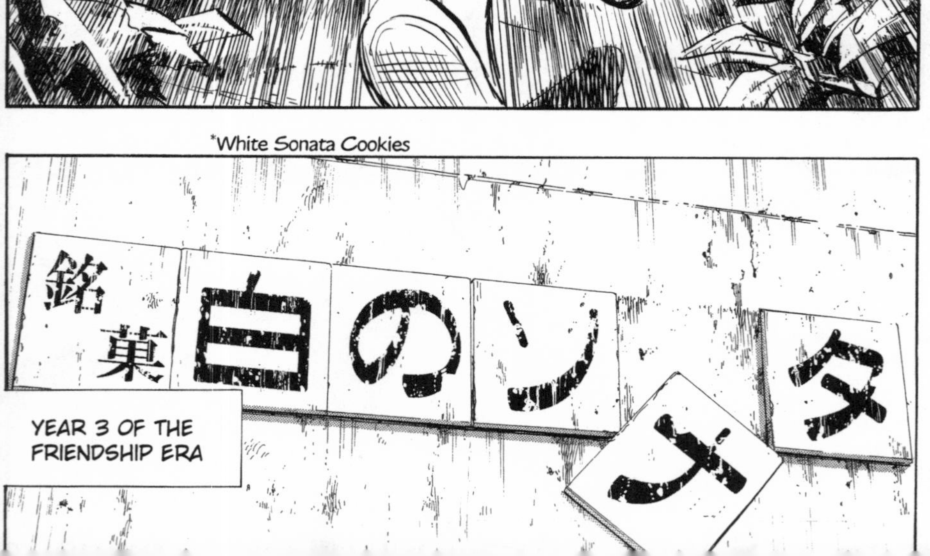
銘菓
白のソナタ
YEAR 3 OF THE FRIENDSHIP ERA

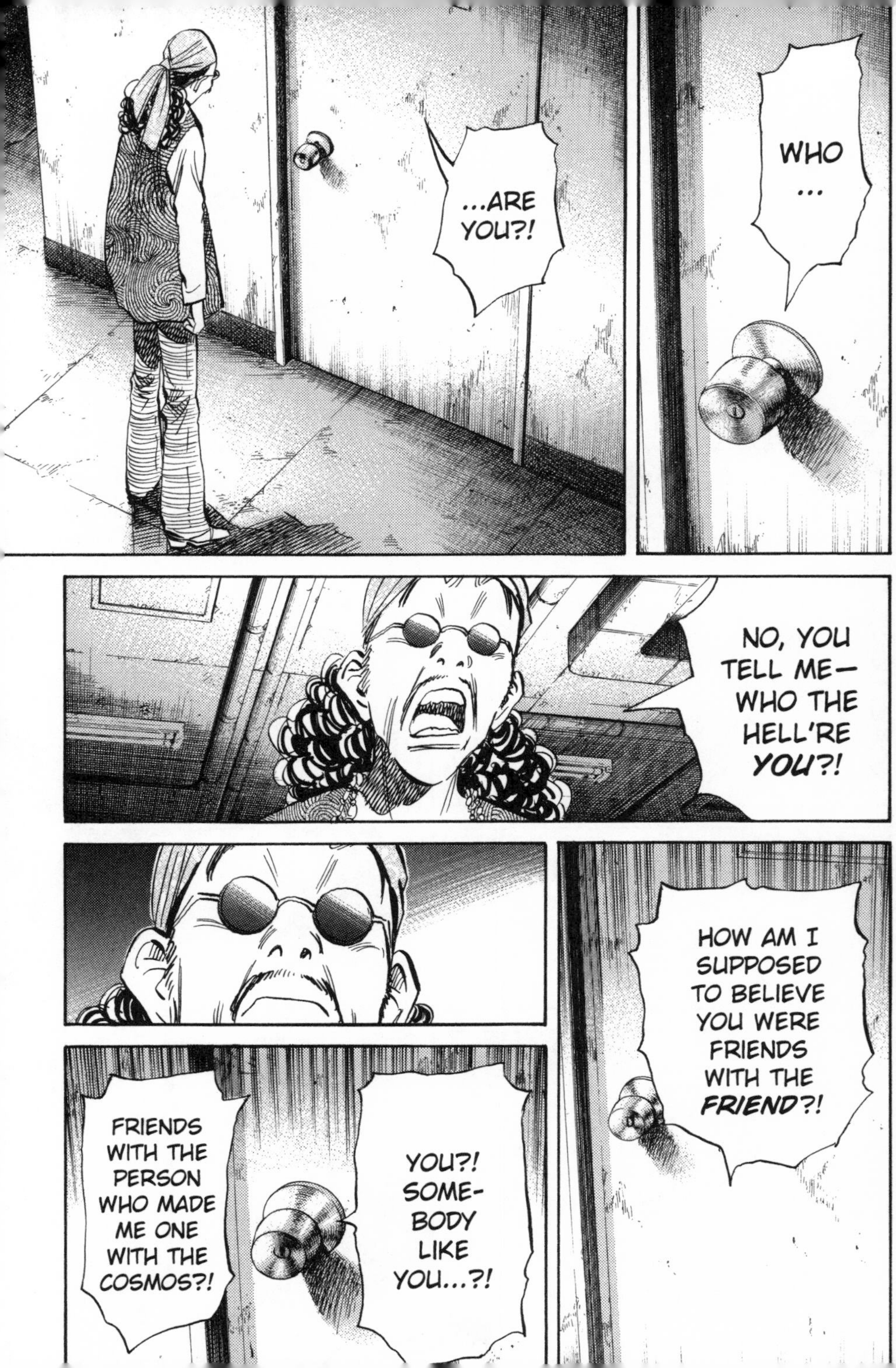
WHO ...
...ARE YOU?!
NO, YOU TELL ME— WHO THE HELL'RE *YOU*?!
HOW AM I SUPPOSED TO BELIEVE YOU WERE FRIENDS WITH THE *FRIEND*?!
YOU?! SOME-BODY LIKE YOU...?!
FRIENDS WITH THE PERSON WHO MADE ME ONE WITH THE COSMOS?!

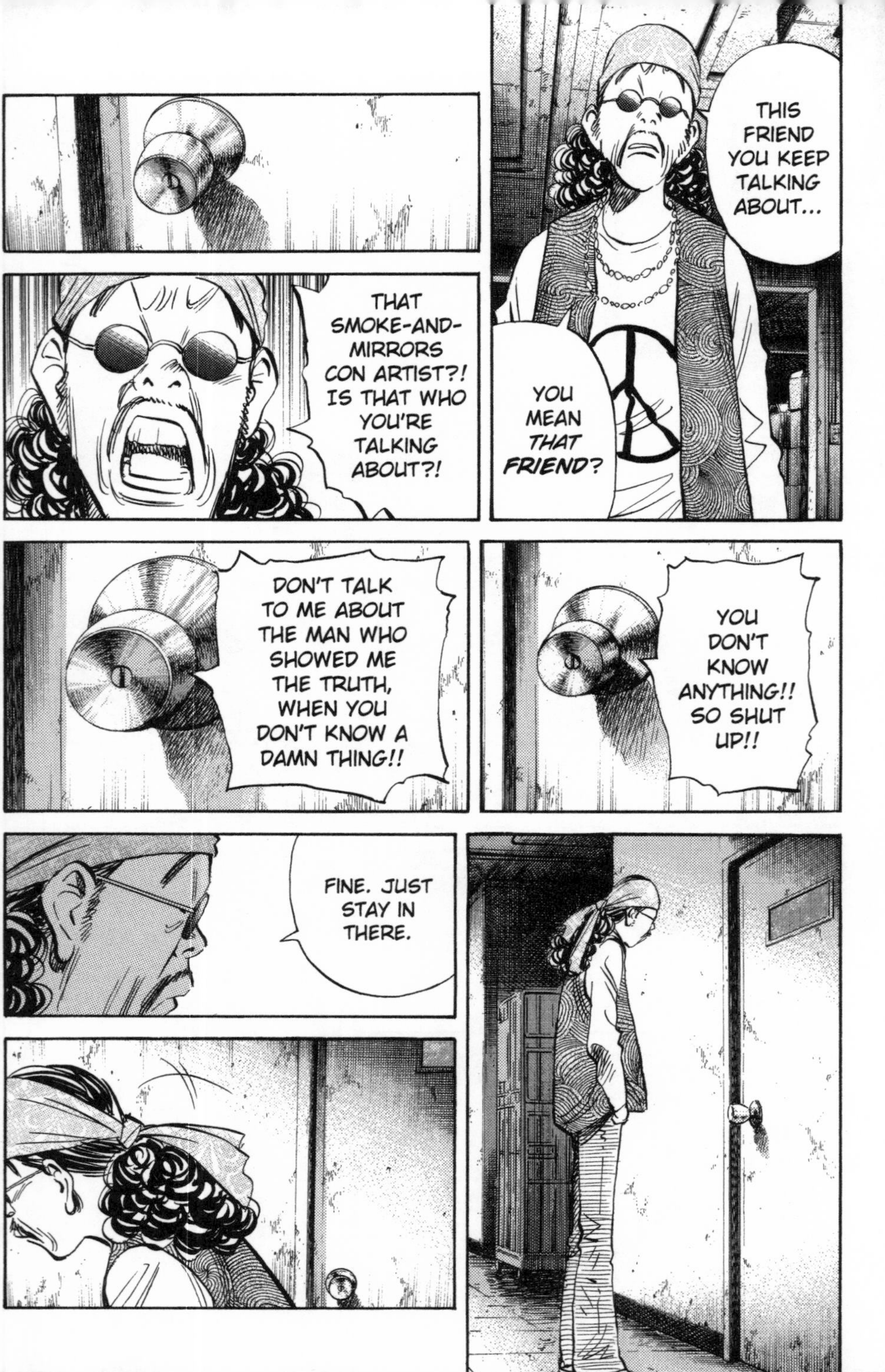
THIS FRIEND YOU KEEP TALKING ABOUT...
YOU MEAN *THAT FRIEND*?
THAT SMOKE-AND-MIRRORS CON ARTIST?! IS THAT WHO YOU'RE TALKING ABOUT?!
YOU DON'T KNOW ANYTHING!! SO SHUT UP!!
DON'T TALK TO ME ABOUT THE MAN WHO SHOWED ME THE TRUTH, WHEN YOU DON'T KNOW A DAMN THING!!
FINE. JUST STAY IN THERE.

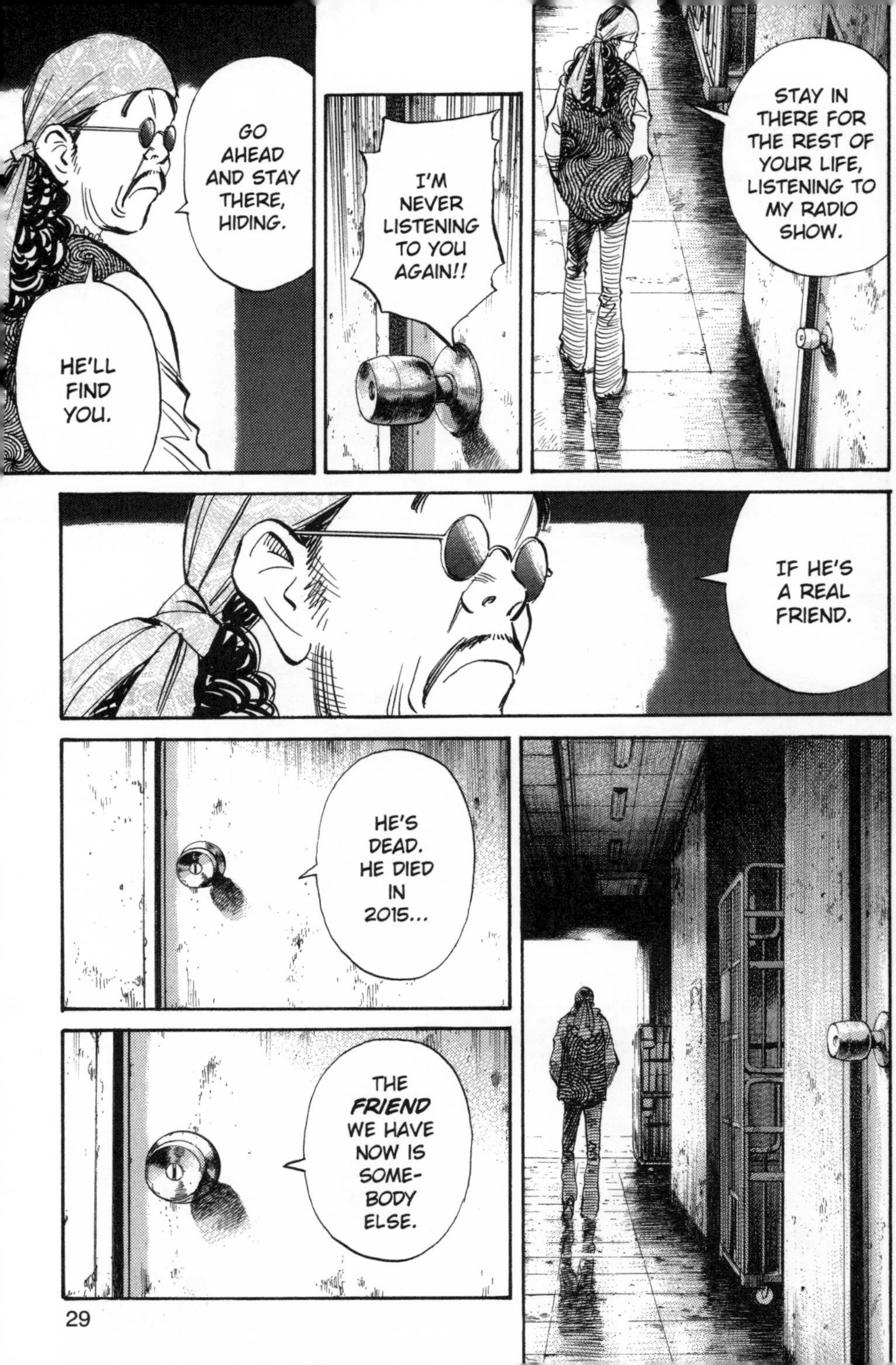
STAY IN THERE FOR THE REST OF YOUR LIFE, LISTENING TO MY RADIO SHOW.
I'M NEVER LISTENING TO YOU AGAIN!!
GO AHEAD AND STAY THERE, HIDING.
HE'LL FIND YOU.
IF HE'S A REAL FRIEND.
HE'S DEAD. HE DIED IN 2015...
THE *FRIEND* WE HAVE NOW IS SOME-BODY ELSE.

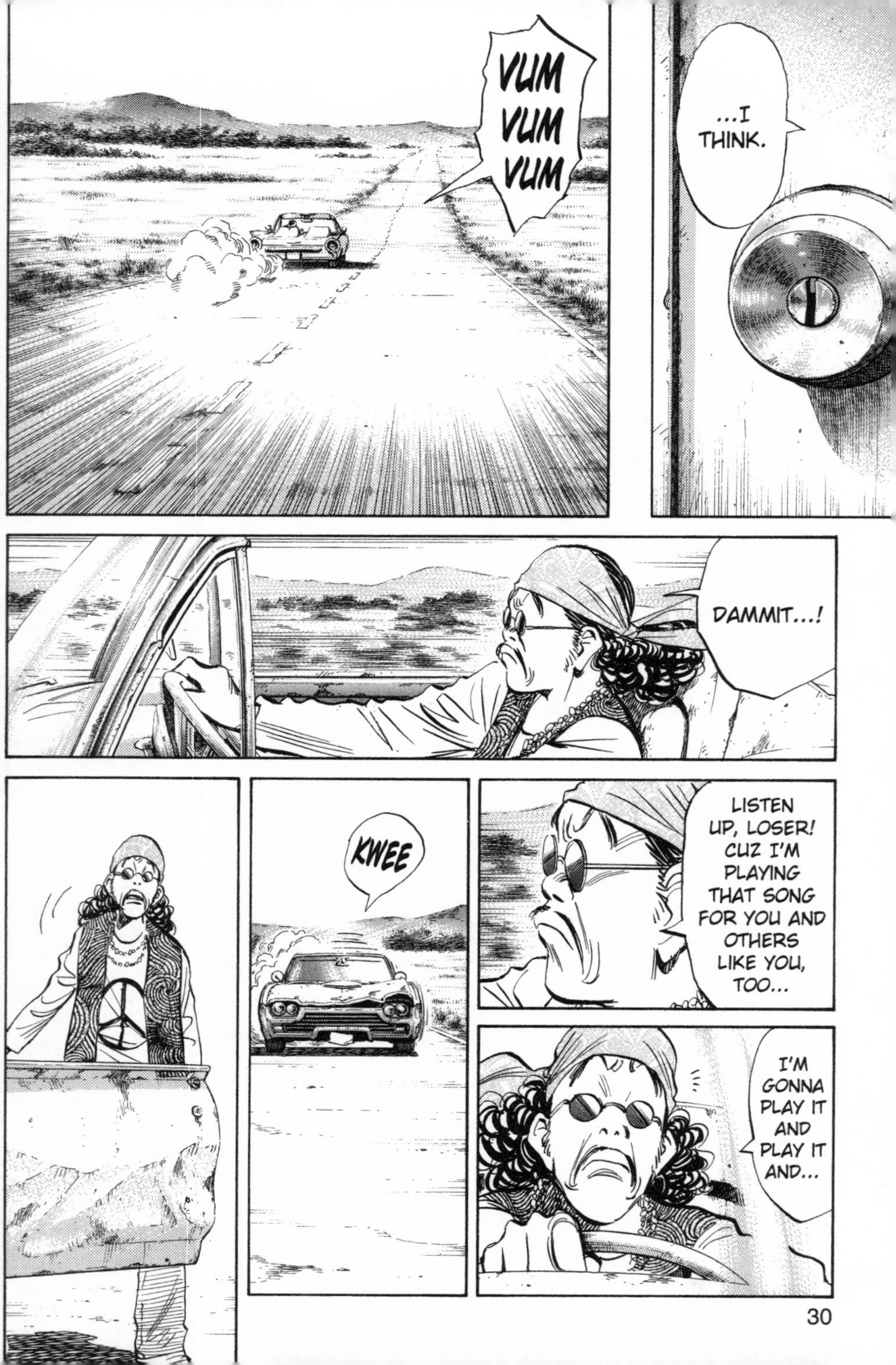
...I THINK.
VUM VUM VUM
DAMMIT...!
LISTEN UP, LOSER! CUZ I'M PLAYING THAT SONG FOR YOU AND OTHERS LIKE YOU, TOO...
I'M GONNA PLAY IT AND PLAY IT AND...
KWEE

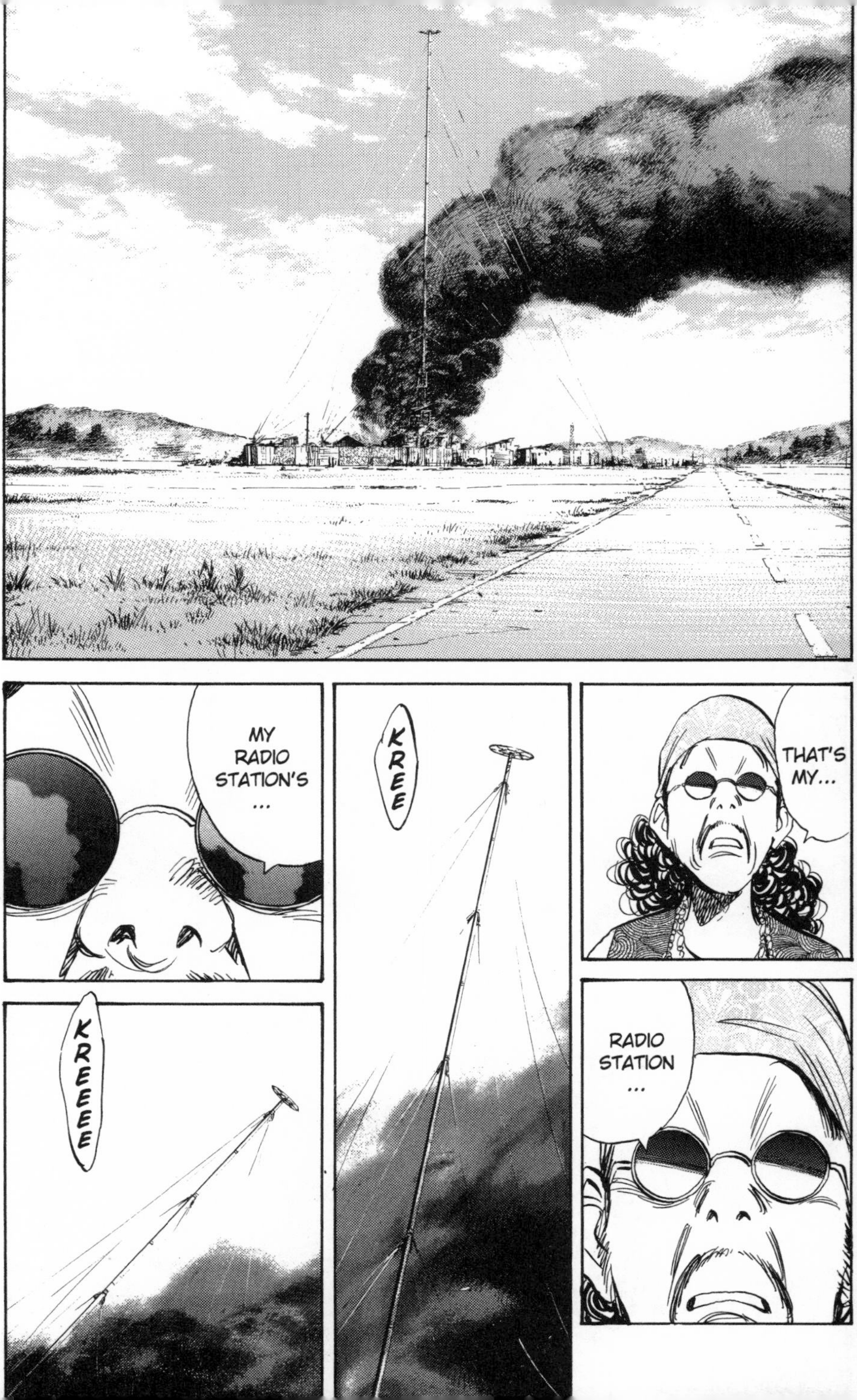
THAT'S MY...
RADIO STATION ...
KREE
MY RADIO STATION'S ...
KREEEEE

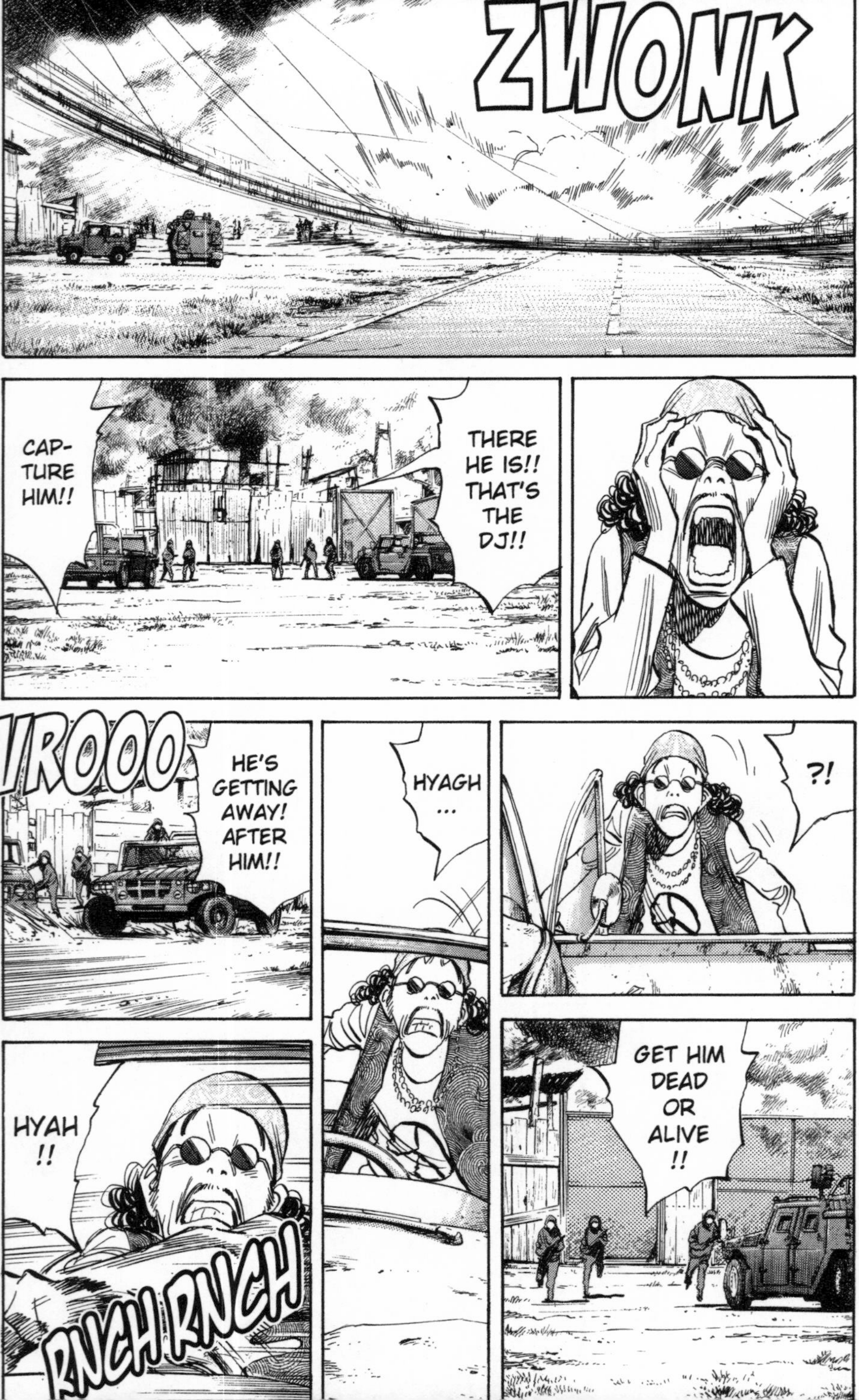
ZWONK
THERE HE IS!! THAT'S THE DJ!!
CAP-TURE HIM!!
?!
GET HIM DEAD OR ALIVE!!
HYAGH ...
VROOO
HE'S GETTING AWAY! AFTER HIM!!
HYAH !!
RNCH RNCH

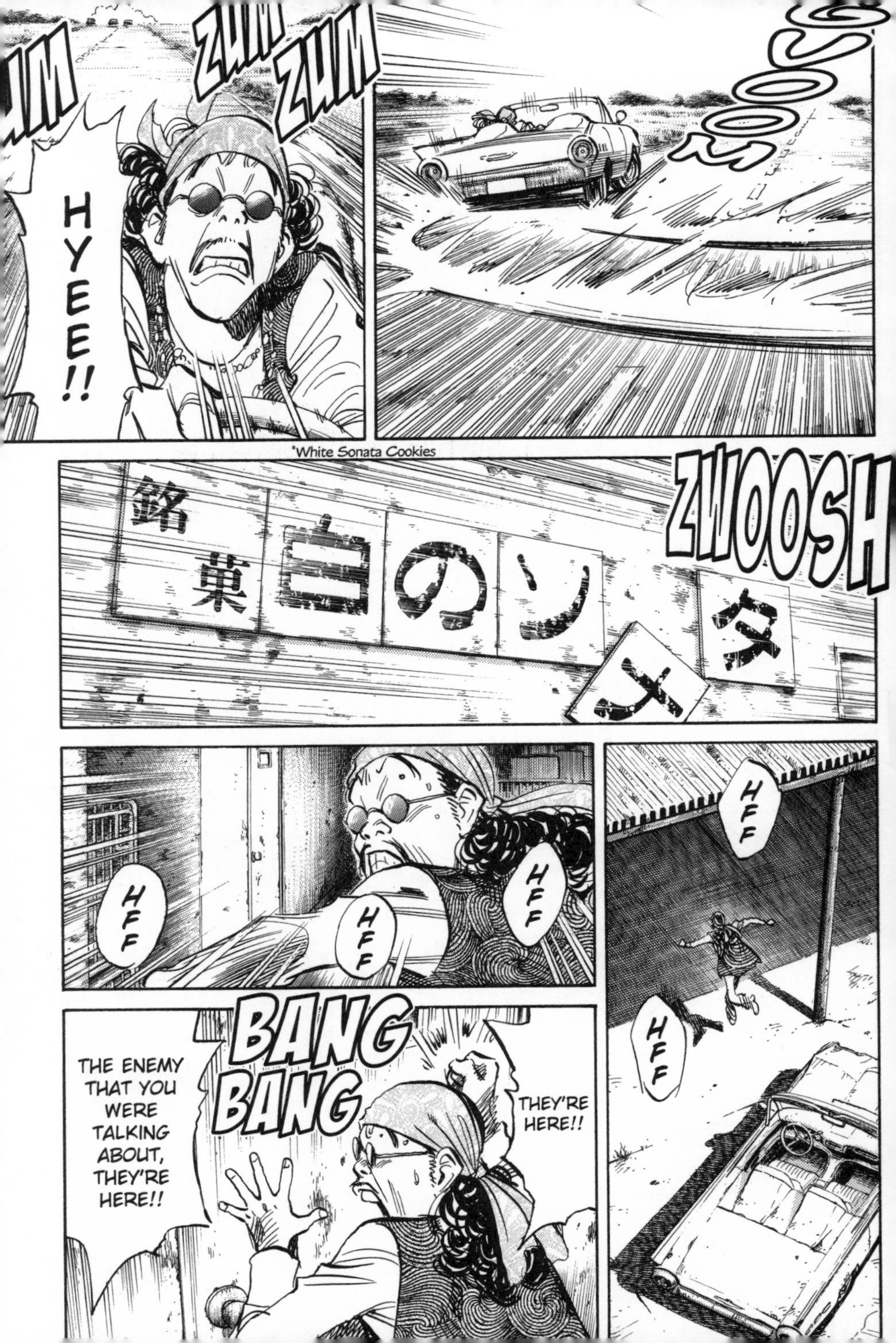
ZUM
ZUM
ZUM
HYEEE!!
*White Sonata Cookies
ZWOOSH
銘菓
白のソナタ
HFF
HFF
HFF
HFF
HFF
BANG
BANG
THEY'RE HERE!!
THE ENEMY THAT YOU WERE TALKING ABOUT, THEY'RE HERE!!

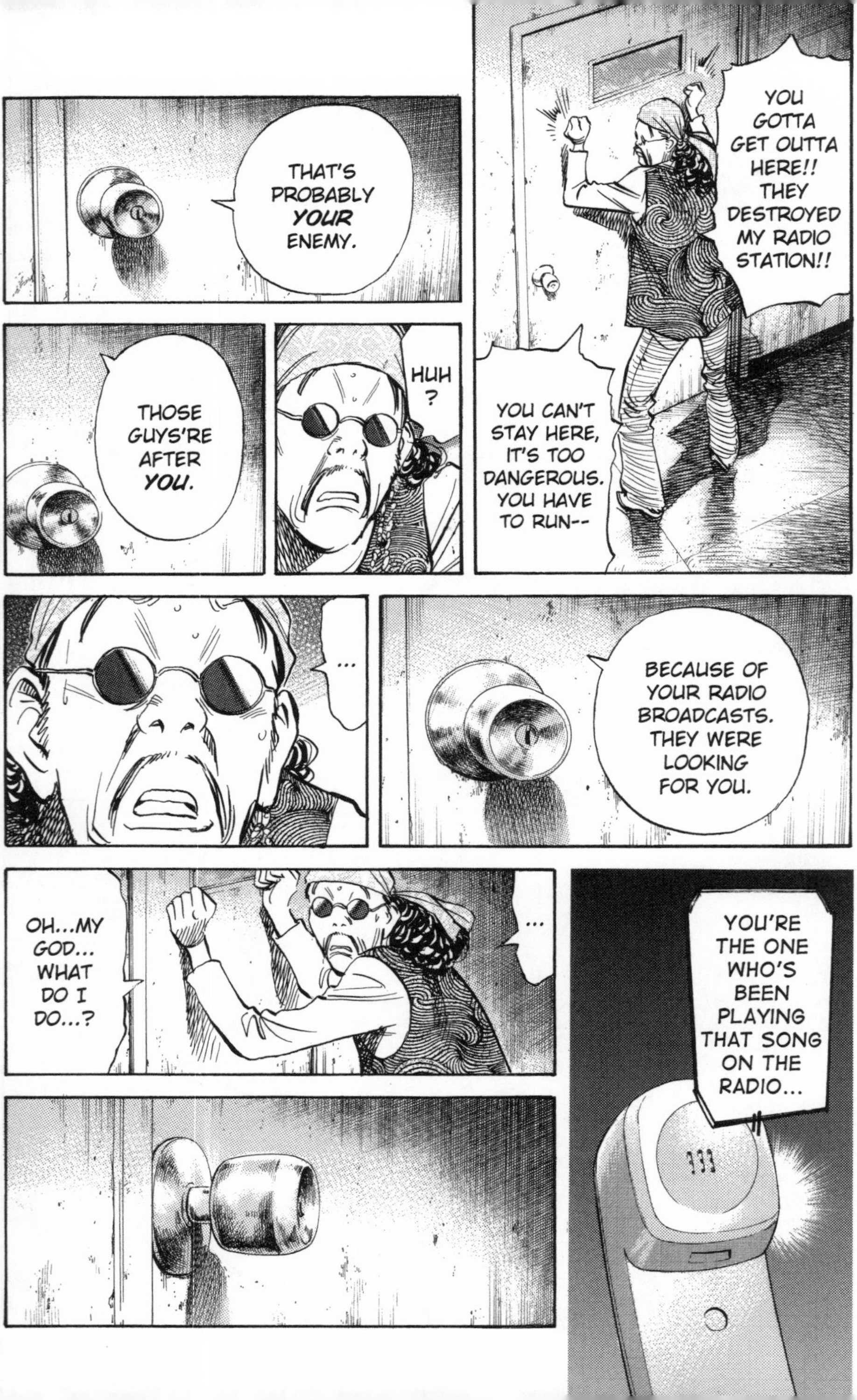
YOU GOTTA GET OUTTA HERE!! THEY DESTROYED MY RADIO STATION!!
YOU CAN'T STAY HERE, IT'S TOO DANGEROUS. YOU HAVE TO RUN--
THAT'S PROBABLY *YOUR* ENEMY.
HUH?
THOSE GUYS'RE AFTER *YOU*.
BECAUSE OF YOUR RADIO BROADCASTS. THEY WERE LOOKING FOR YOU.
...
YOU'RE THE ONE WHO'S BEEN PLAYING THAT SONG ON THE RADIO...
...
OH...MY GOD... WHAT DO I DO...?

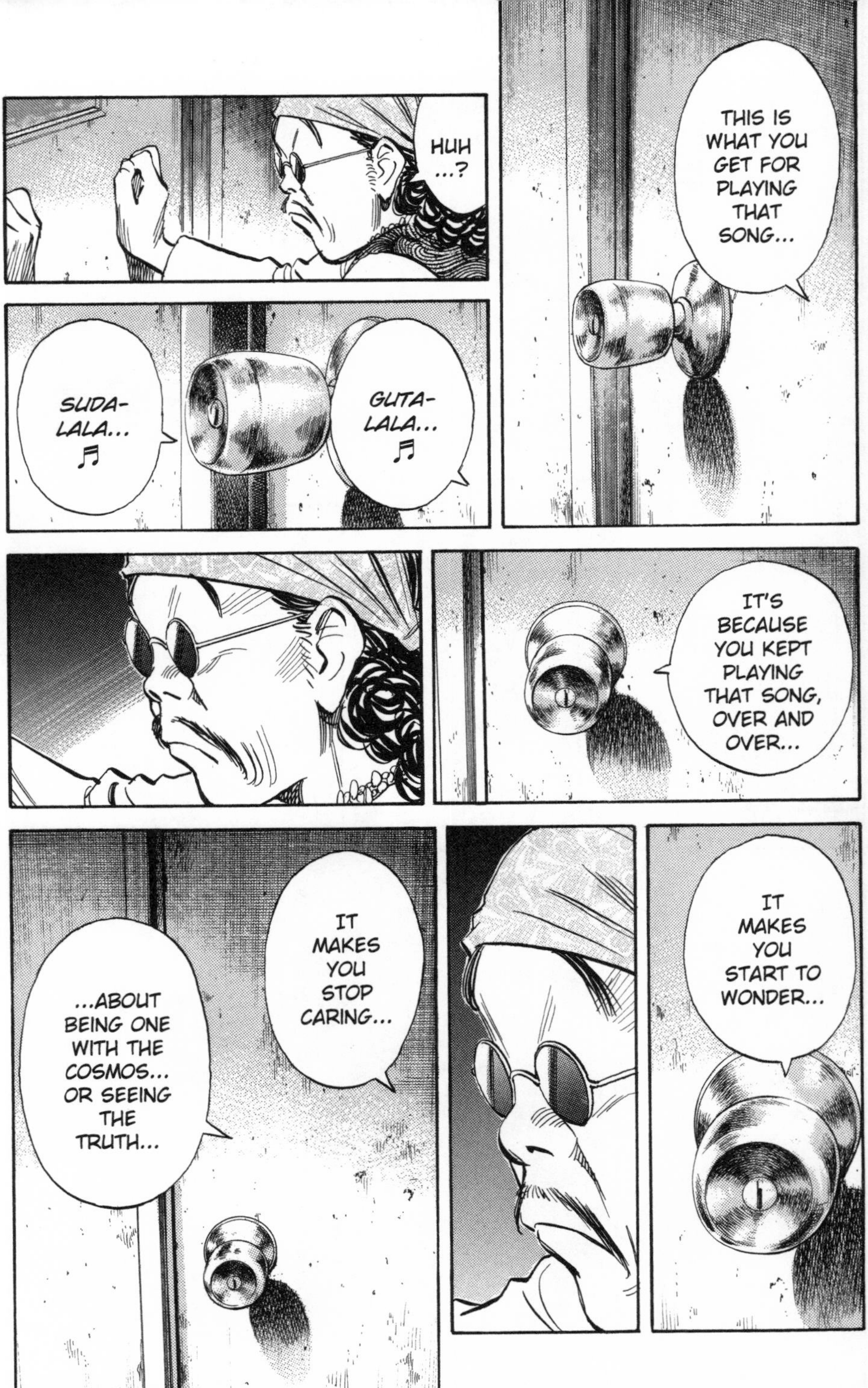
THIS IS WHAT YOU GET FOR PLAYING THAT SONG...
HUH ...?
GUTA-LALA... ♬
SUDA-LALA... ♬
IT'S BECAUSE YOU KEPT PLAYING THAT SONG, OVER AND OVER...
IT MAKES YOU START TO WONDER...
IT MAKES YOU STOP CARING...
...ABOUT BEING ONE WITH THE COSMOS... OR SEEING THE TRUTH...

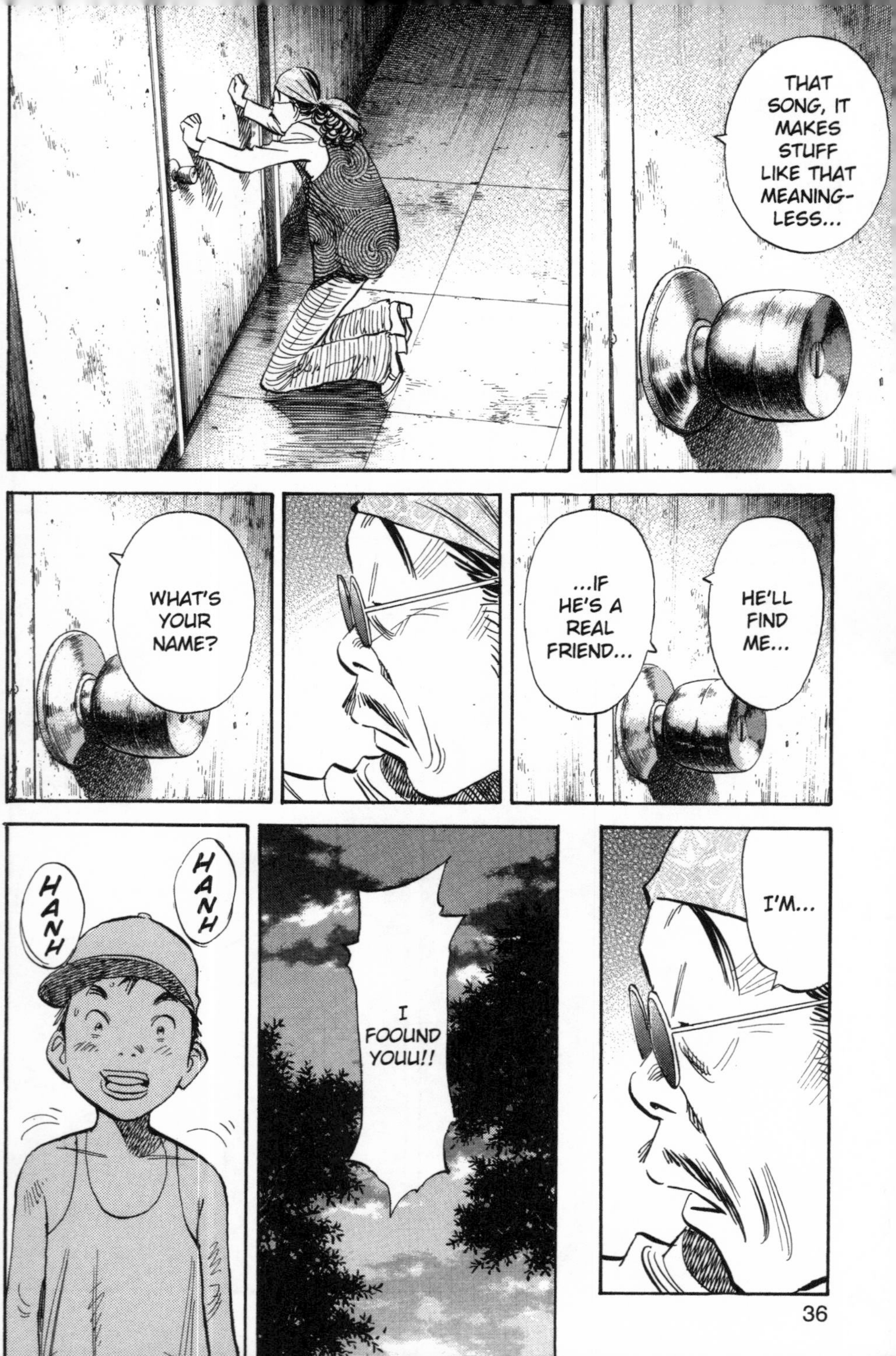
THAT SONG, IT MAKES STUFF LIKE THAT MEANING-LESS...
HE'LL FIND ME...
...IF HE'S A REAL FRIEND...
WHAT'S YOUR NAME?
I'M...
I FOOUND YOUU!!
HANH
HANH

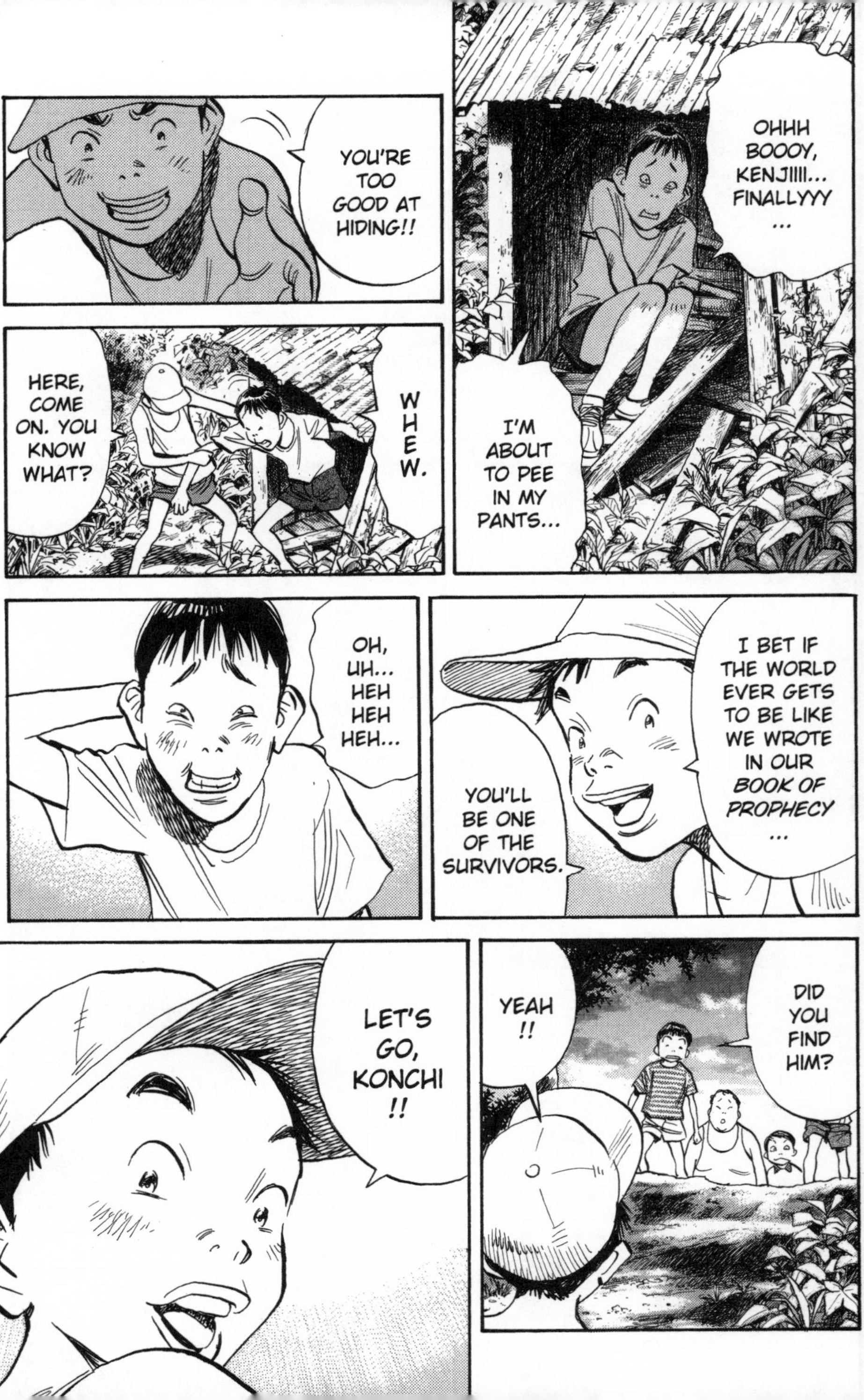
OHHH BOOOY, KENJIIII... FINALLYYY ...
I'M ABOUT TO PEE IN MY PANTS...
YOU'RE TOO GOOD AT HIDING!!
HERE, COME ON. YOU KNOW WHAT?
WHEW.
I BET IF THE WORLD EVER GETS TO BE LIKE WE WROTE IN OUR *BOOK OF PROPHECY* ...
YOU'LL BE ONE OF THE SURVIVORS.
OH, UH... HEH HEH HEH...
DID YOU FIND HIM?
YEAH !!
LET'S GO, KONCHI !!

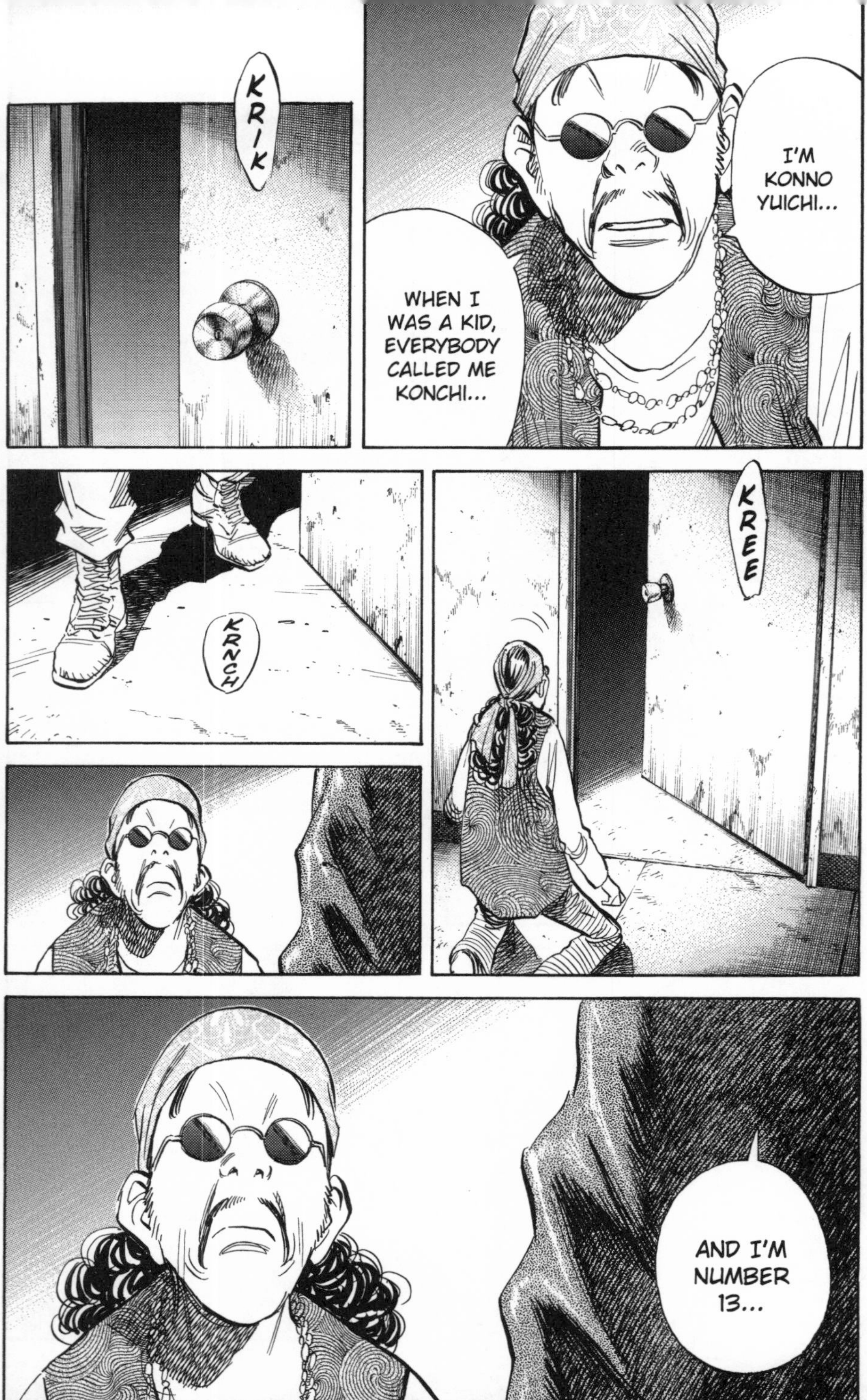
I'M KONNO YUICHI...
WHEN I WAS A KID, EVERYBODY CALLED ME KONCHI...
KRIK
KREE
KRNCH
AND I'M NUMBER 13...

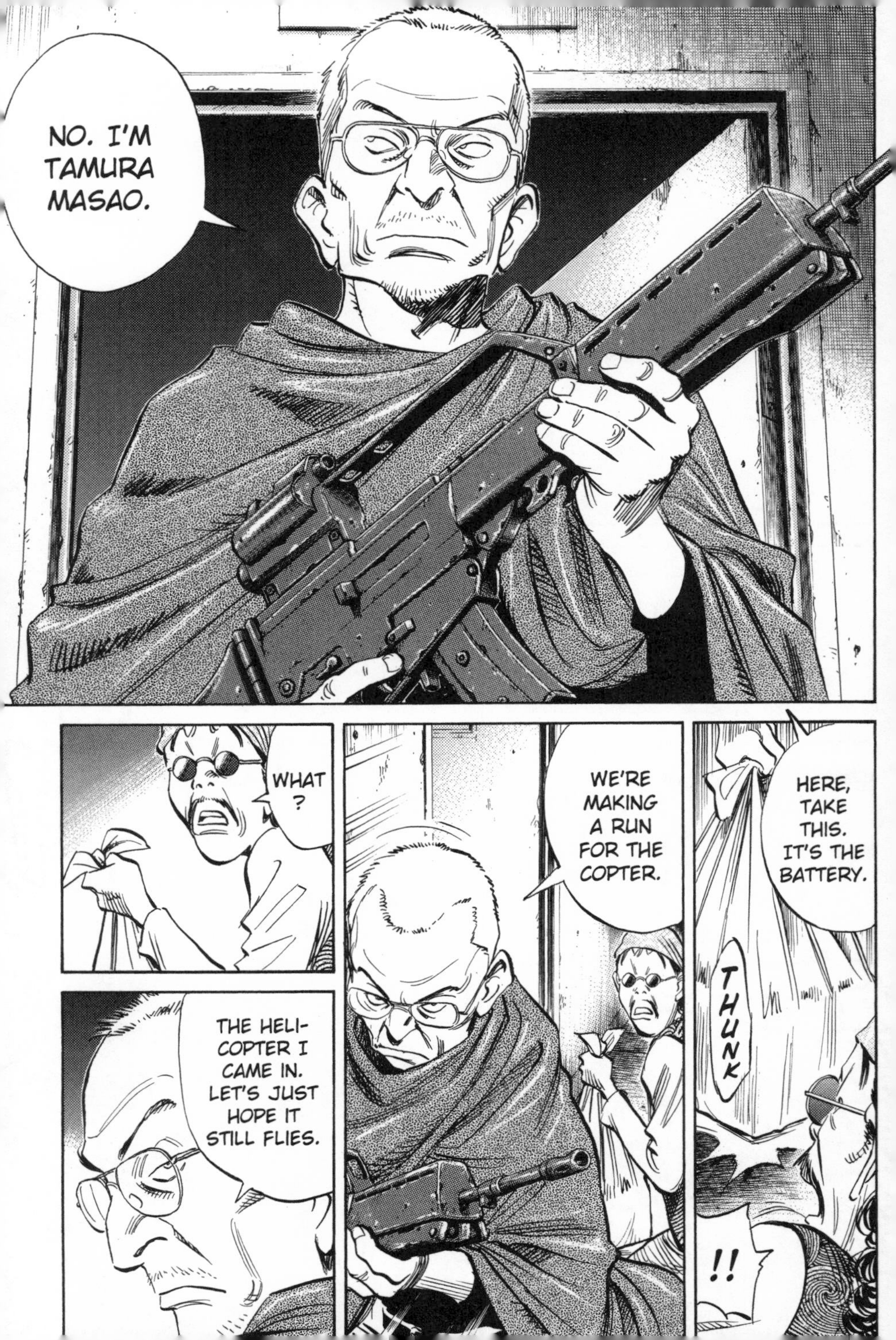
NO. I'M TAMURA MASAO.
HERE, TAKE THIS. IT'S THE BATTERY.
THUNK
!!
WE'RE MAKING A RUN FOR THE COPTER.
WHAT?
THE HELI-COPTER I CAME IN. LET'S JUST HOPE IT STILL FLIES.

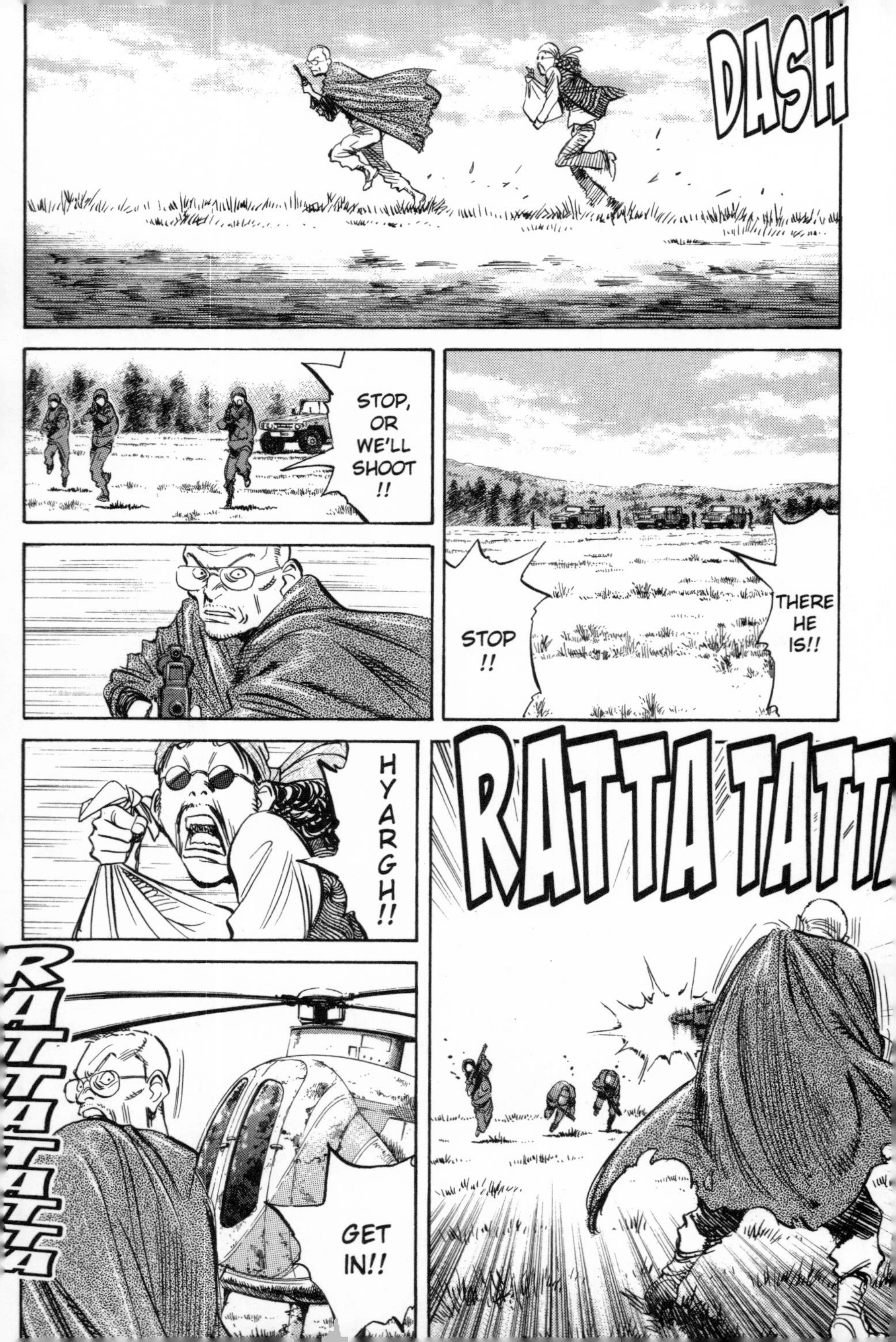
DASH
THERE HE IS!!
STOP!!
STOP, OR WE'LL SHOOT!!
RATTA TATT
HYARGH!!
RATTATATTA
GET IN!!

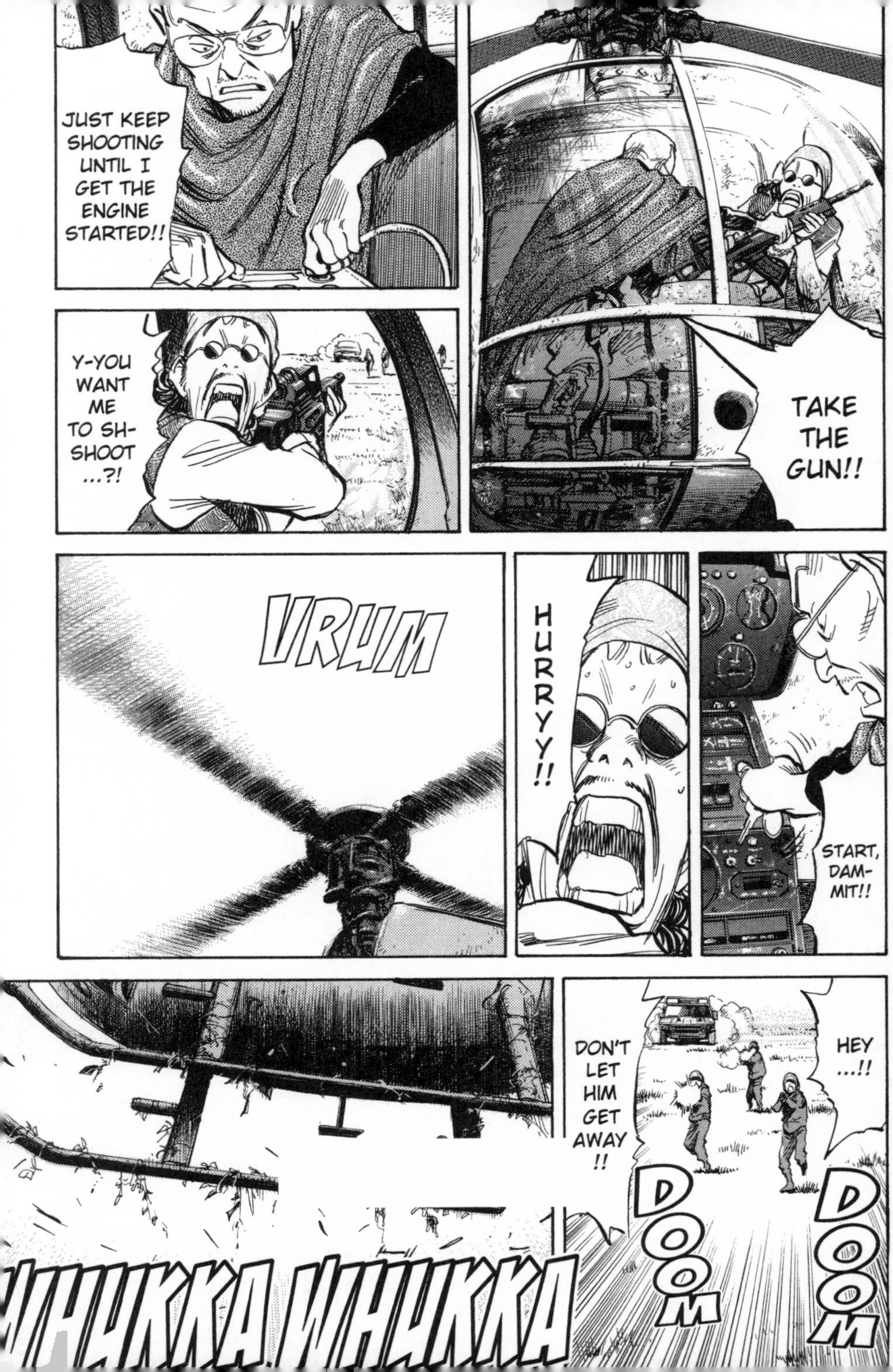
TAKE THE GUN!!
JUST KEEP SHOOTING UNTIL I GET THE ENGINE STARTED!!
Y-YOU WANT ME TO SH-SHOOT ...?!
START, DAM-MIT!!
HURRYY!!
VRUM
HEY ...!!
DON'T LET HIM GET AWAY !!
DOOM
DOOM
WHUKKA WHUKKA

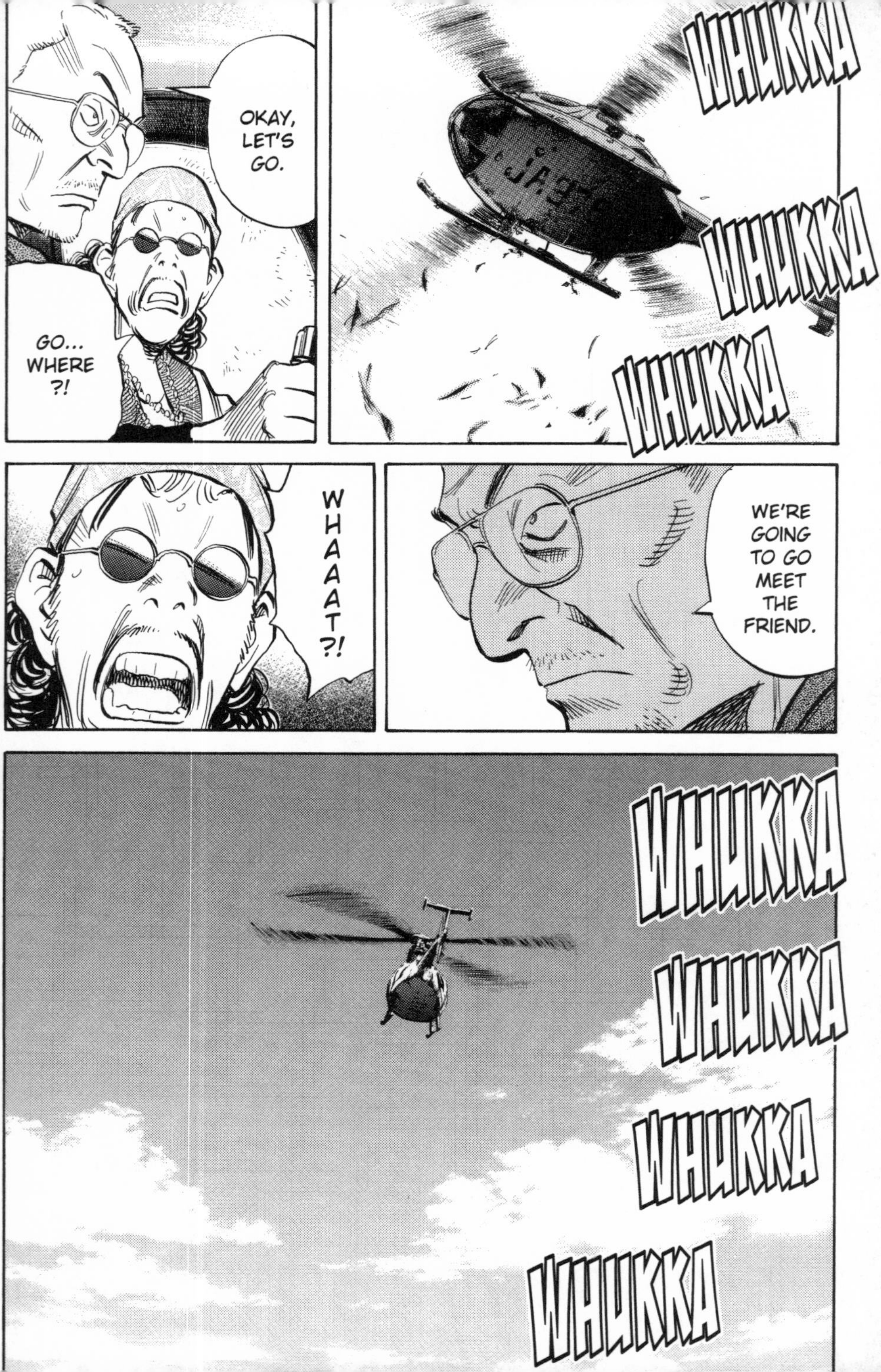
WHUKKA
WHUKKA
WHUKKA
OKAY, LET'S GO.
GO... WHERE ?!
WE'RE GOING TO GO MEET THE FRIEND.
WHAAAAT?!
WHUKKA
WHUKKA
WHUKKA
WHUKKA

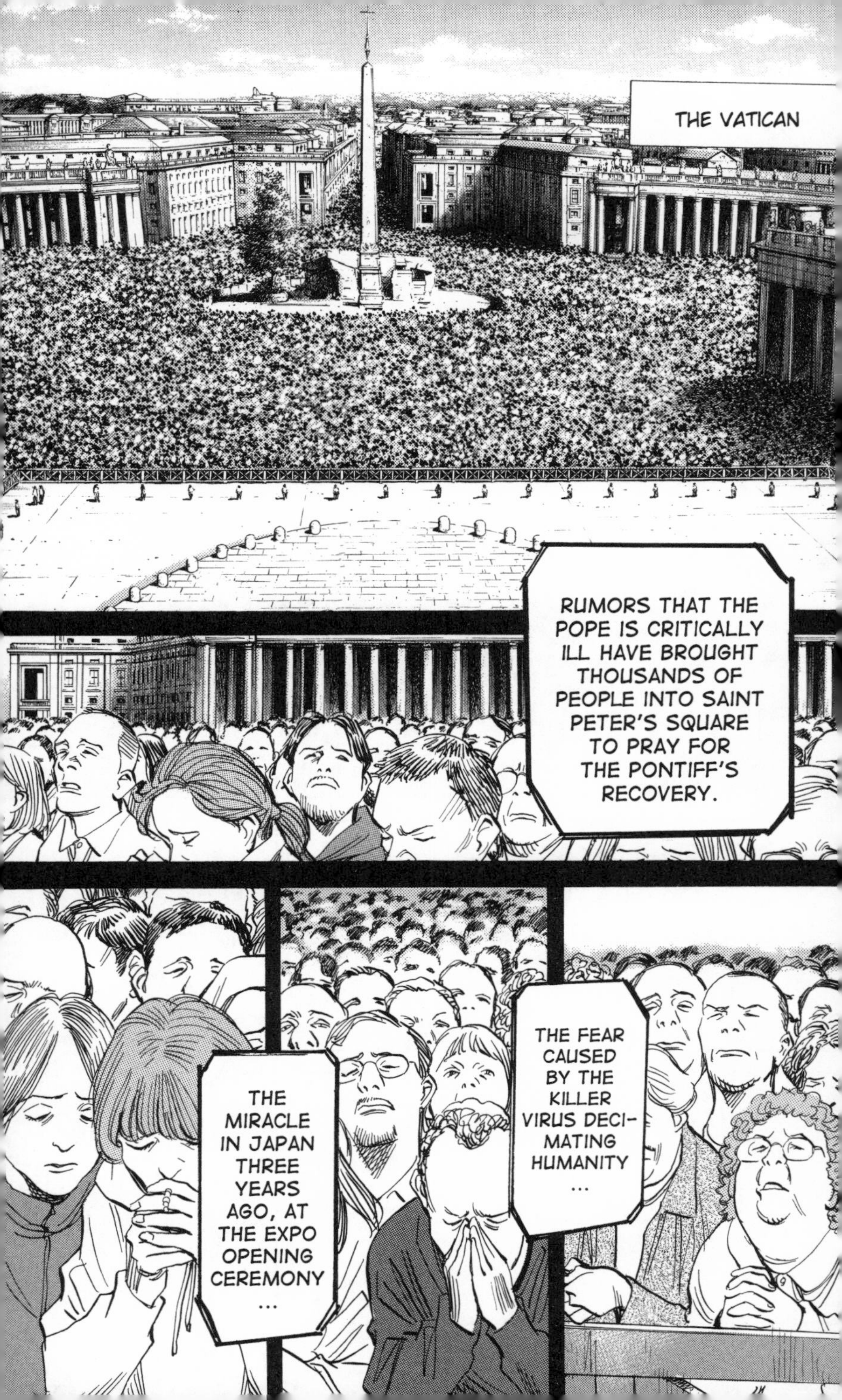
THE VATICAN
RUMORS THAT THE POPE IS CRITICALLY ILL HAVE BROUGHT THOUSANDS OF PEOPLE INTO SAINT PETER'S SQUARE TO PRAY FOR THE PONTIFF'S RECOVERY.
THE FEAR CAUSED BY THE KILLER VIRUS DECI-MATING HUMANITY ...
THE MIRACLE IN JAPAN THREE YEARS AGO, AT THE EXPO OPENING CEREMONY ...

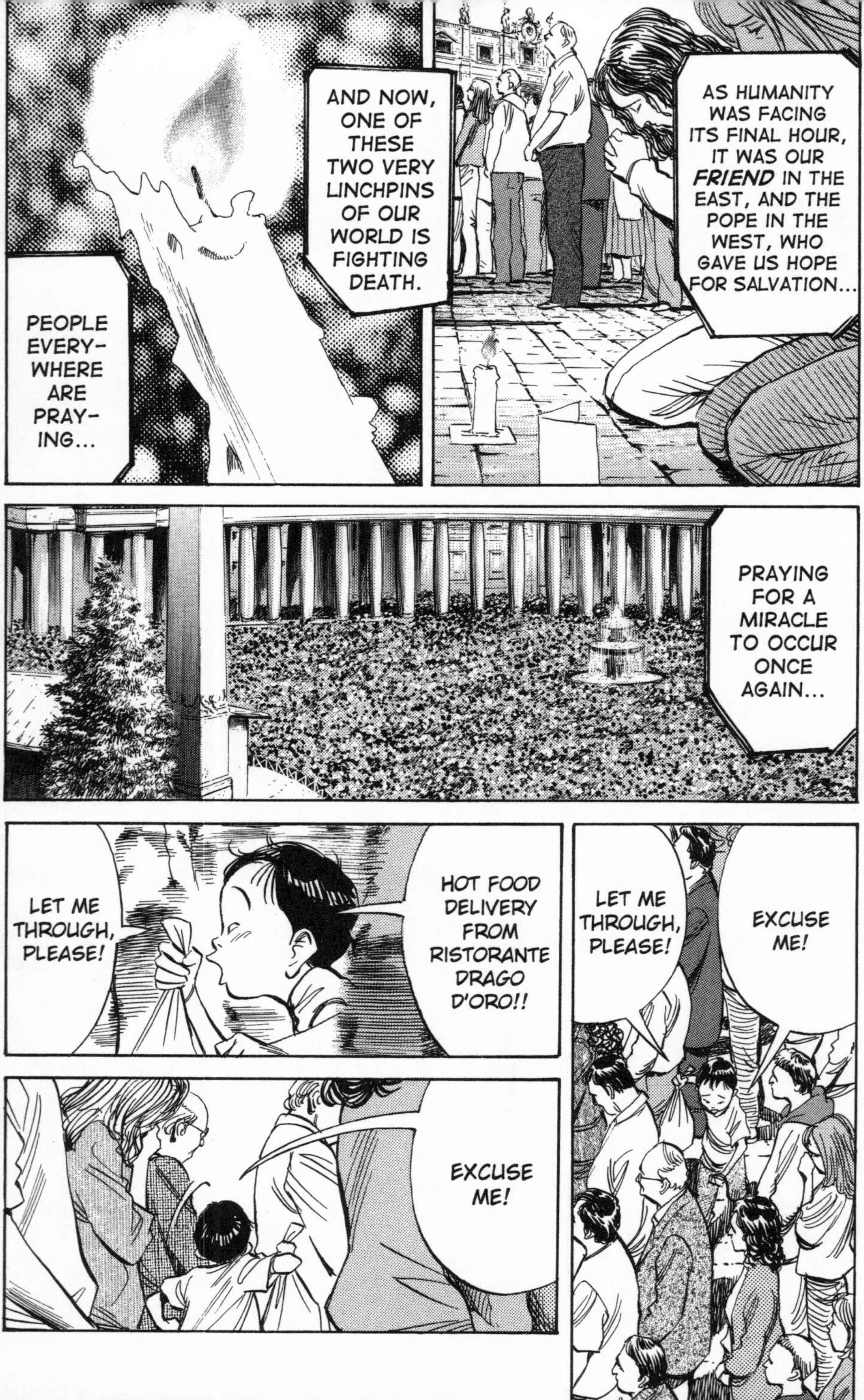
AS HUMANITY WAS FACING ITS FINAL HOUR, IT WAS OUR *FRIEND* IN THE EAST, AND THE POPE IN THE WEST, WHO GAVE US HOPE FOR SALVATION...
AND NOW, ONE OF THESE TWO VERY LINCHPINS OF OUR WORLD IS FIGHTING DEATH.
PEOPLE EVERY-WHERE ARE PRAY-ING...
PRAYING FOR A MIRACLE TO OCCUR ONCE AGAIN...
EXCUSE ME!
LET ME THROUGH, PLEASE!
HOT FOOD DELIVERY FROM RISTORANTE DRAGO D'ORO!!
LET ME THROUGH, PLEASE!
EXCUSE ME!

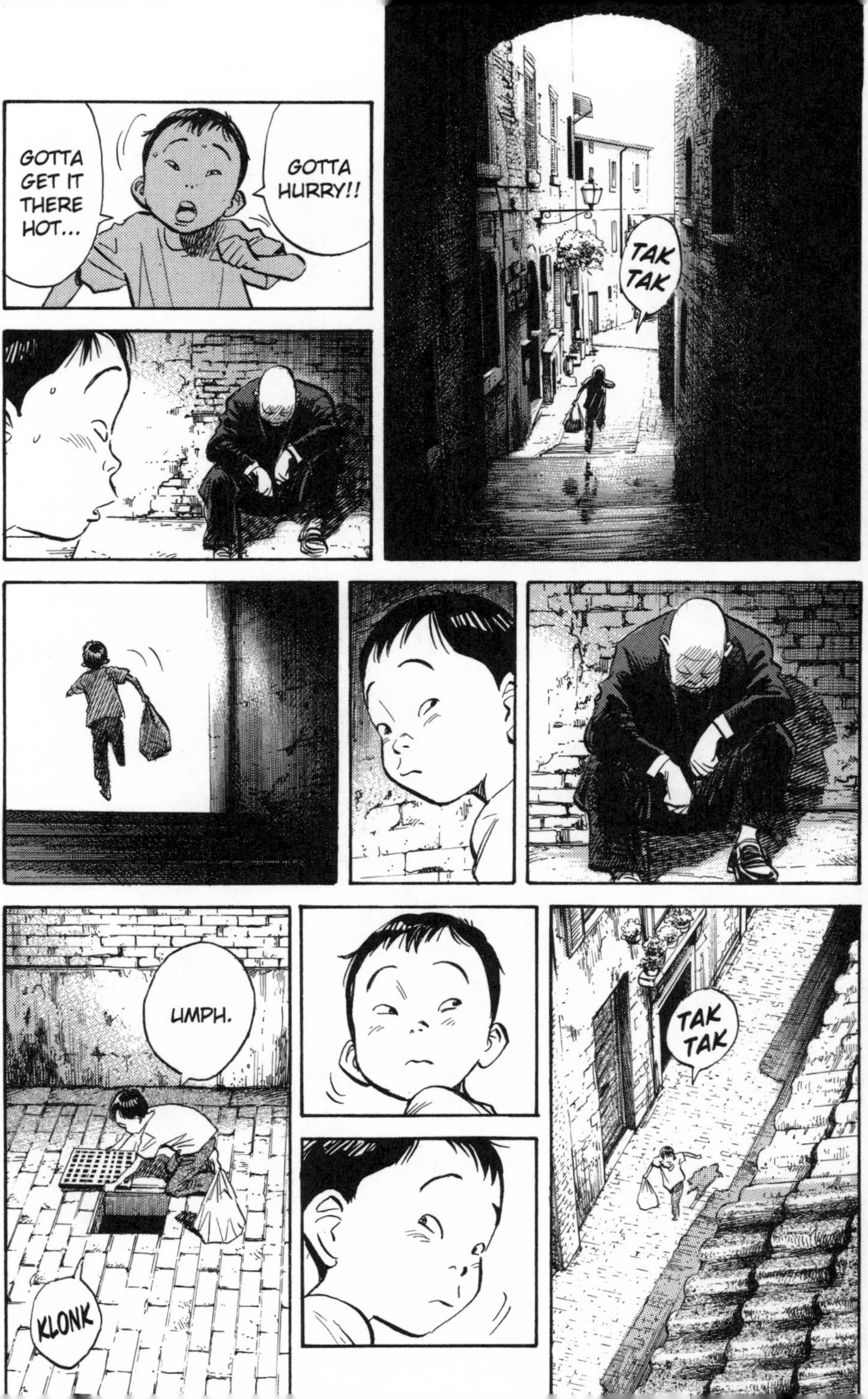
TAK TAK
GOTTA HURRY!!
GOTTA GET IT THERE HOT...
TAK TAK
UMPH.
KLONK

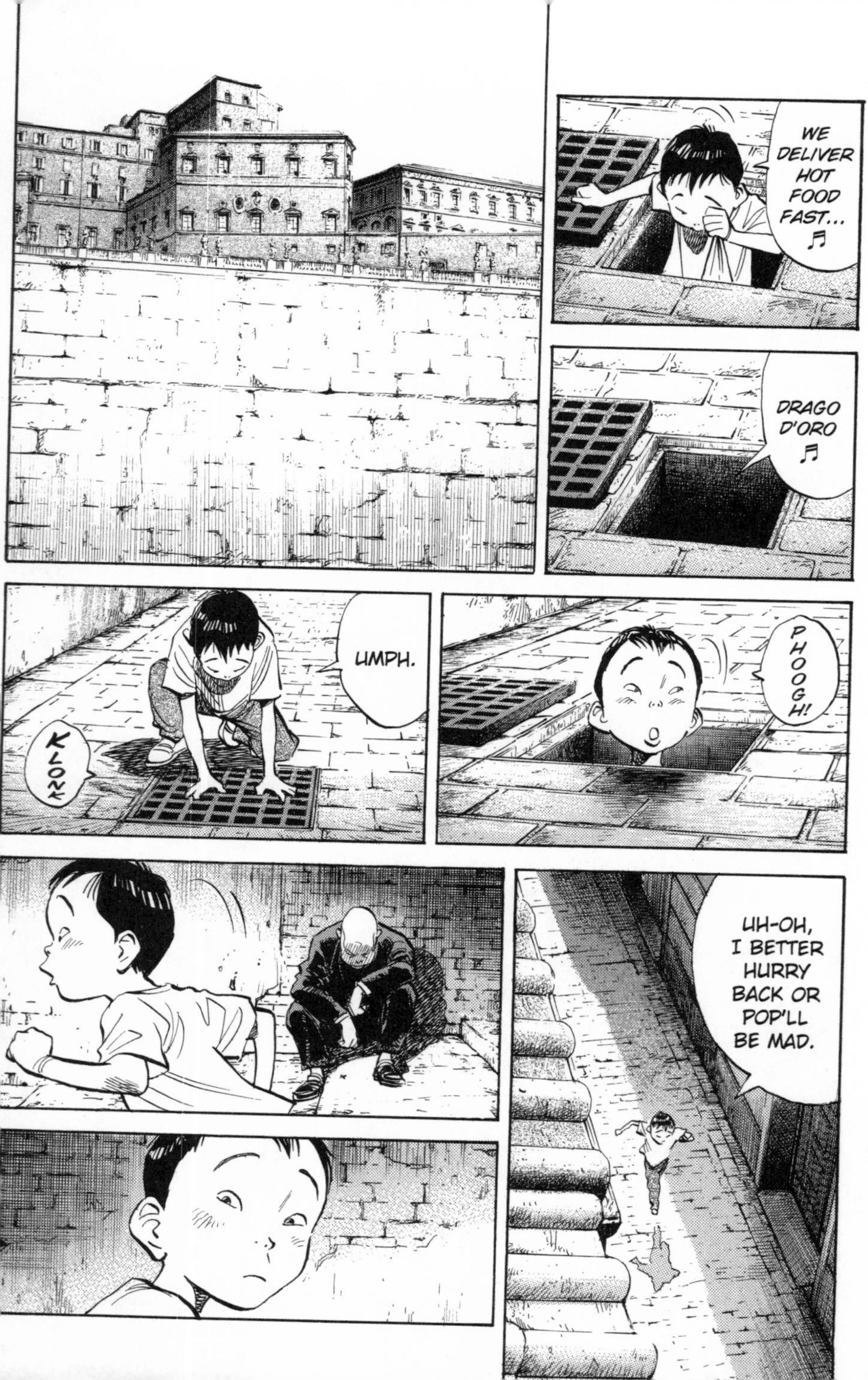
WE DELIVER HOT FOOD FAST... ♬
DRAGO D'ORO ♬
PHOOOGH!
UMPH.
KLONK
UH-OH, I BETTER HURRY BACK OR POP'LL BE MAD.

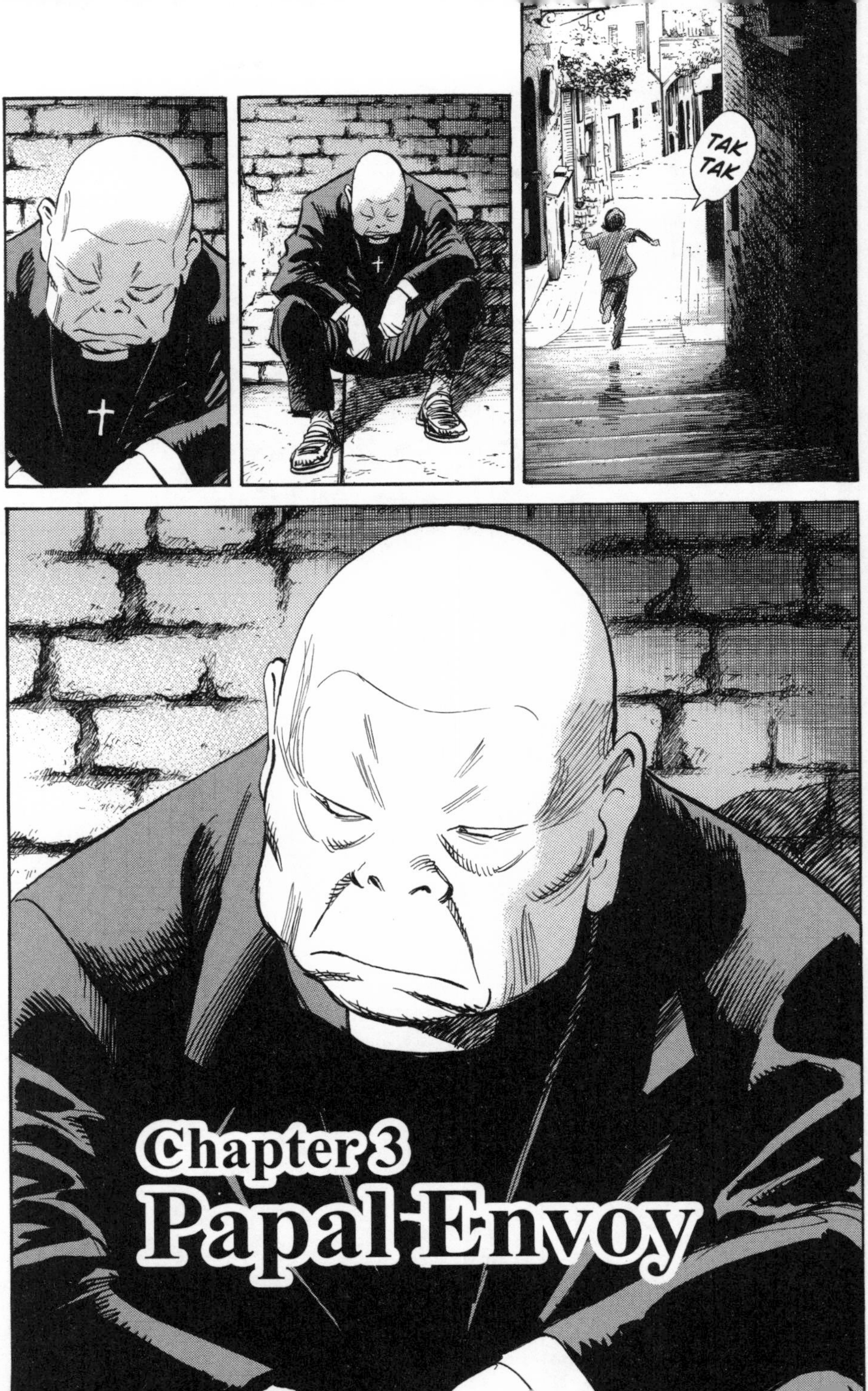
TAK TAK
Chapter 3
Papal Envoy

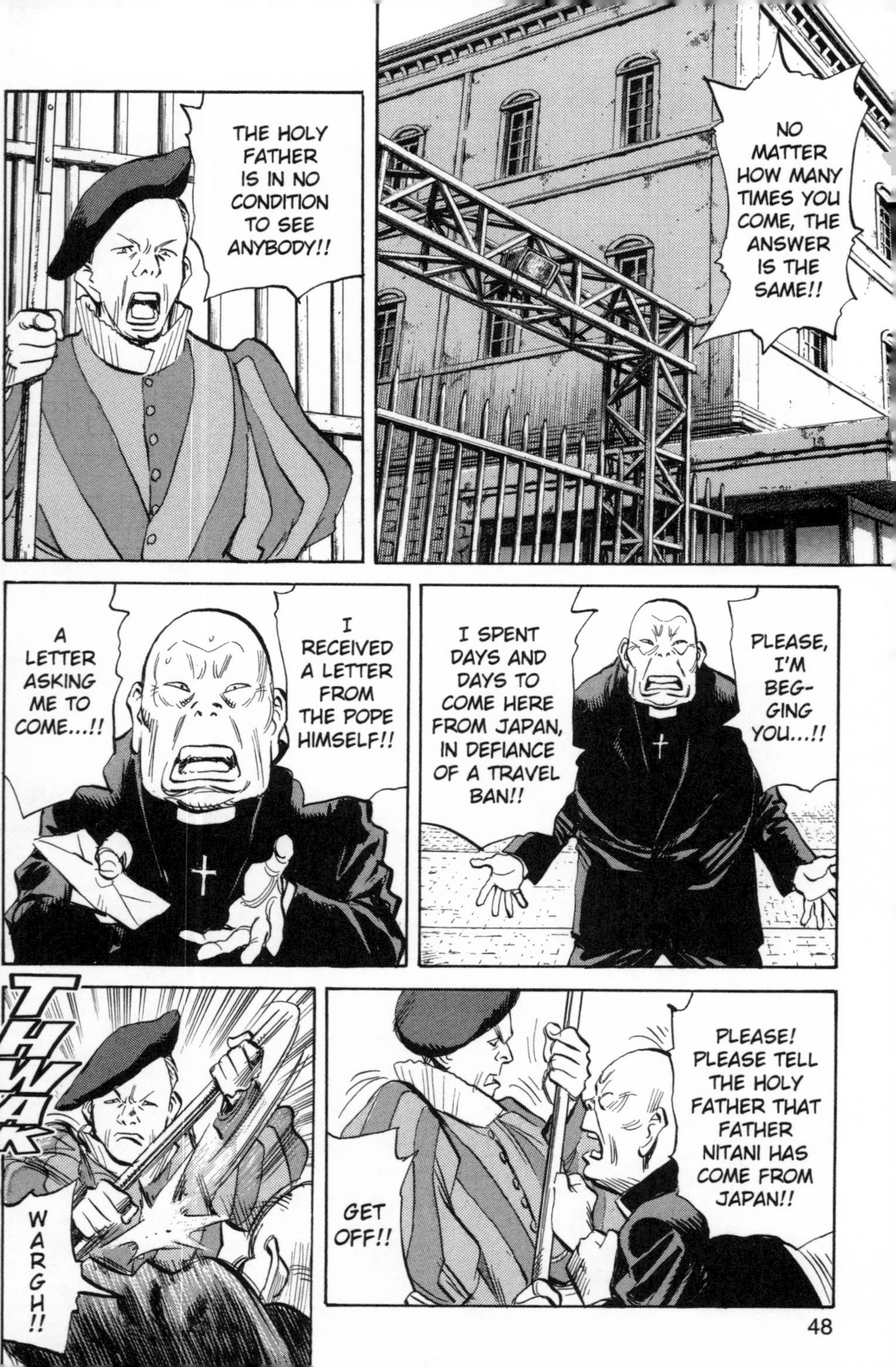
NO MATTER HOW MANY TIMES YOU COME, THE ANSWER IS THE SAME!!
THE HOLY FATHER IS IN NO CONDITION TO SEE ANYBODY!!
PLEASE, I'M BEG-GING YOU...!!
I SPENT DAYS AND DAYS TO COME HERE FROM JAPAN, IN DEFIANCE OF A TRAVEL BAN!!
I RECEIVED A LETTER FROM THE POPE HIMSELF!!
A LETTER ASKING ME TO COME...!!
PLEASE! PLEASE TELL THE HOLY FATHER THAT FATHER NITANI HAS COME FROM JAPAN!!
GET OFF!!
THWAK
WARGH!!

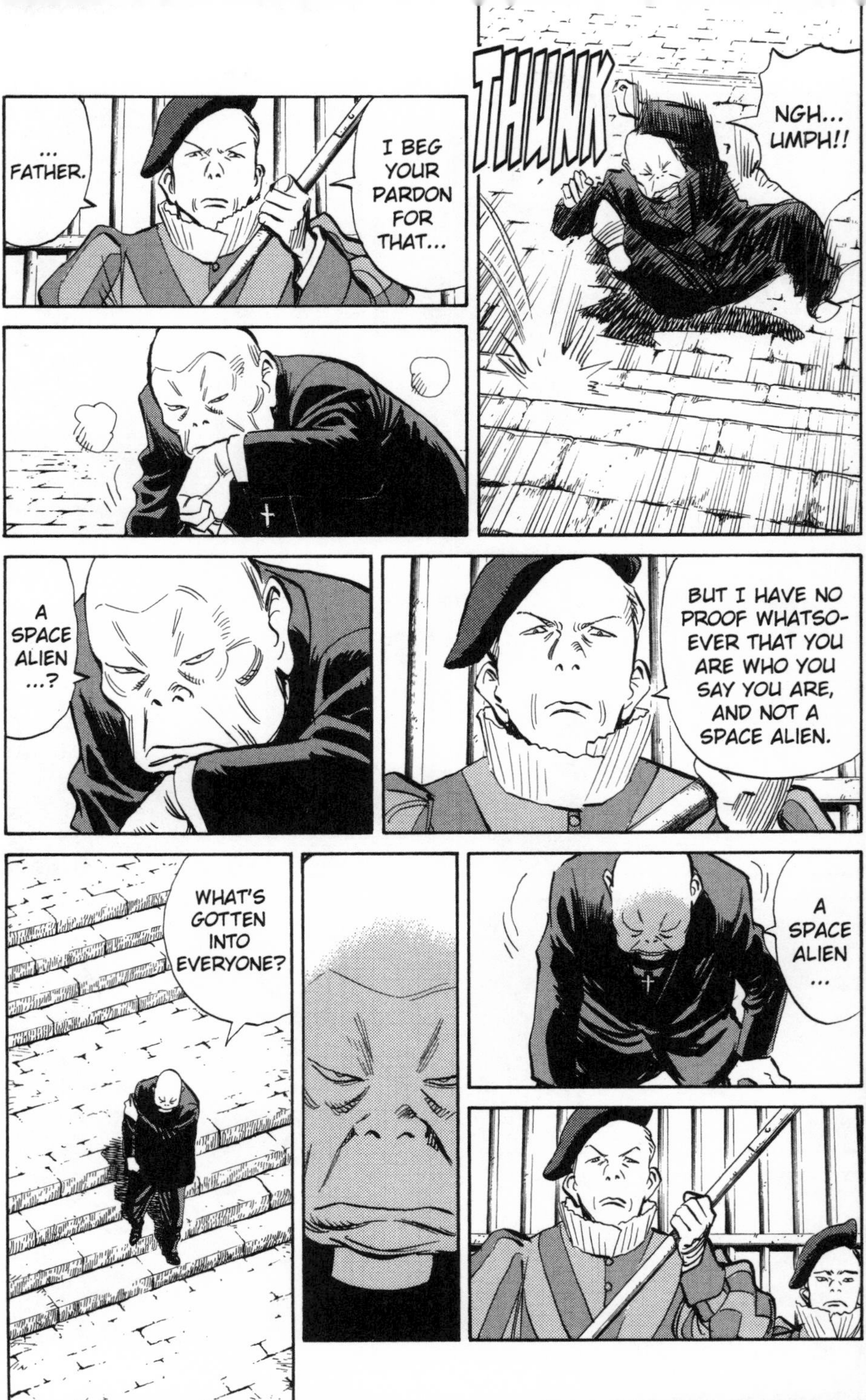
THUNK
NGH... UMPH!!
I BEG YOUR PARDON FOR THAT...
... FATHER.
BUT I HAVE NO PROOF WHATSO-EVER THAT YOU ARE WHO YOU SAY YOU ARE, AND NOT A SPACE ALIEN.
A SPACE ALIEN ...?
A SPACE ALIEN ...
WHAT'S GOTTEN INTO EVERYONE?

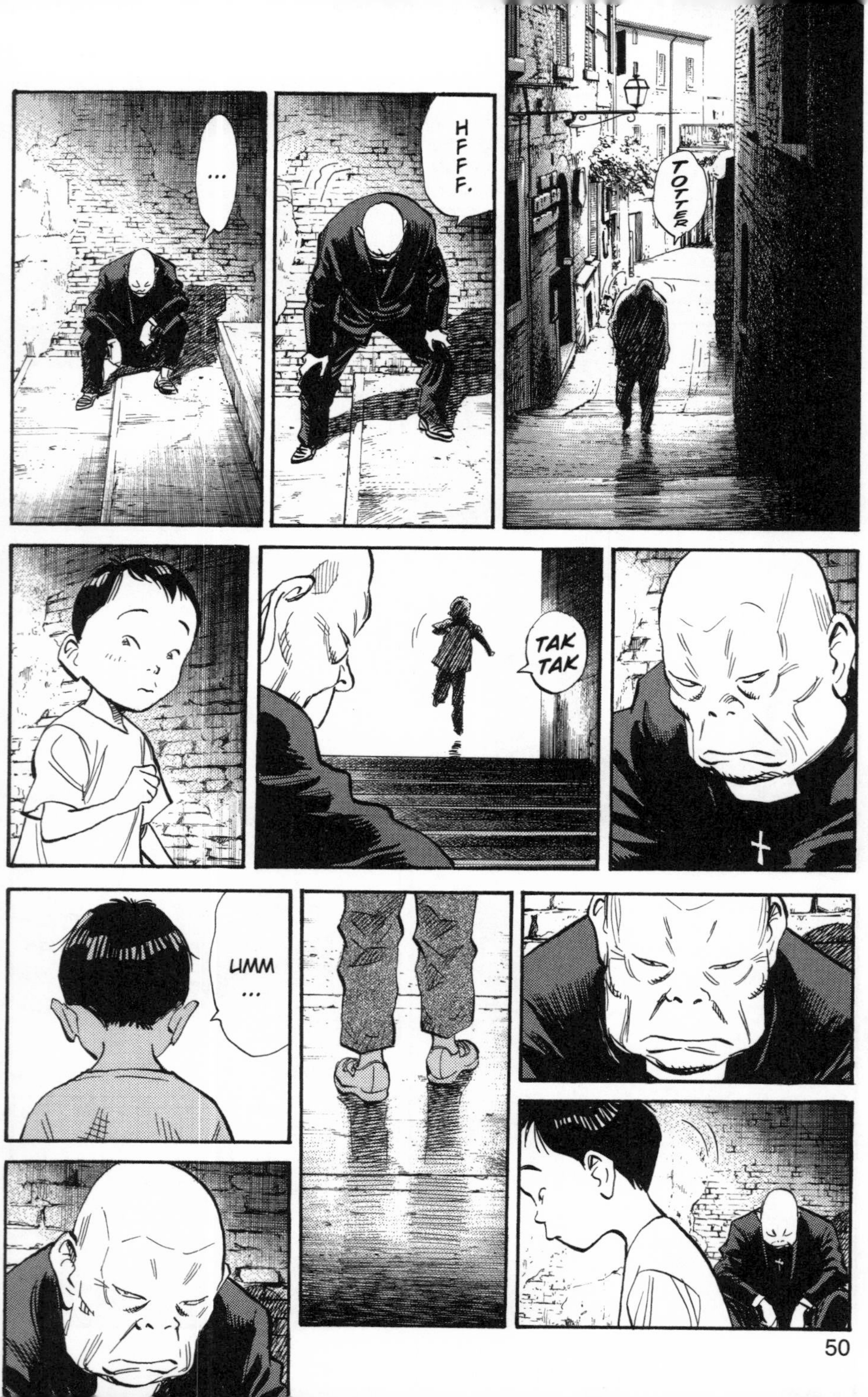
TOTTER
HFFF.
...
TAK TAK
UMM ...

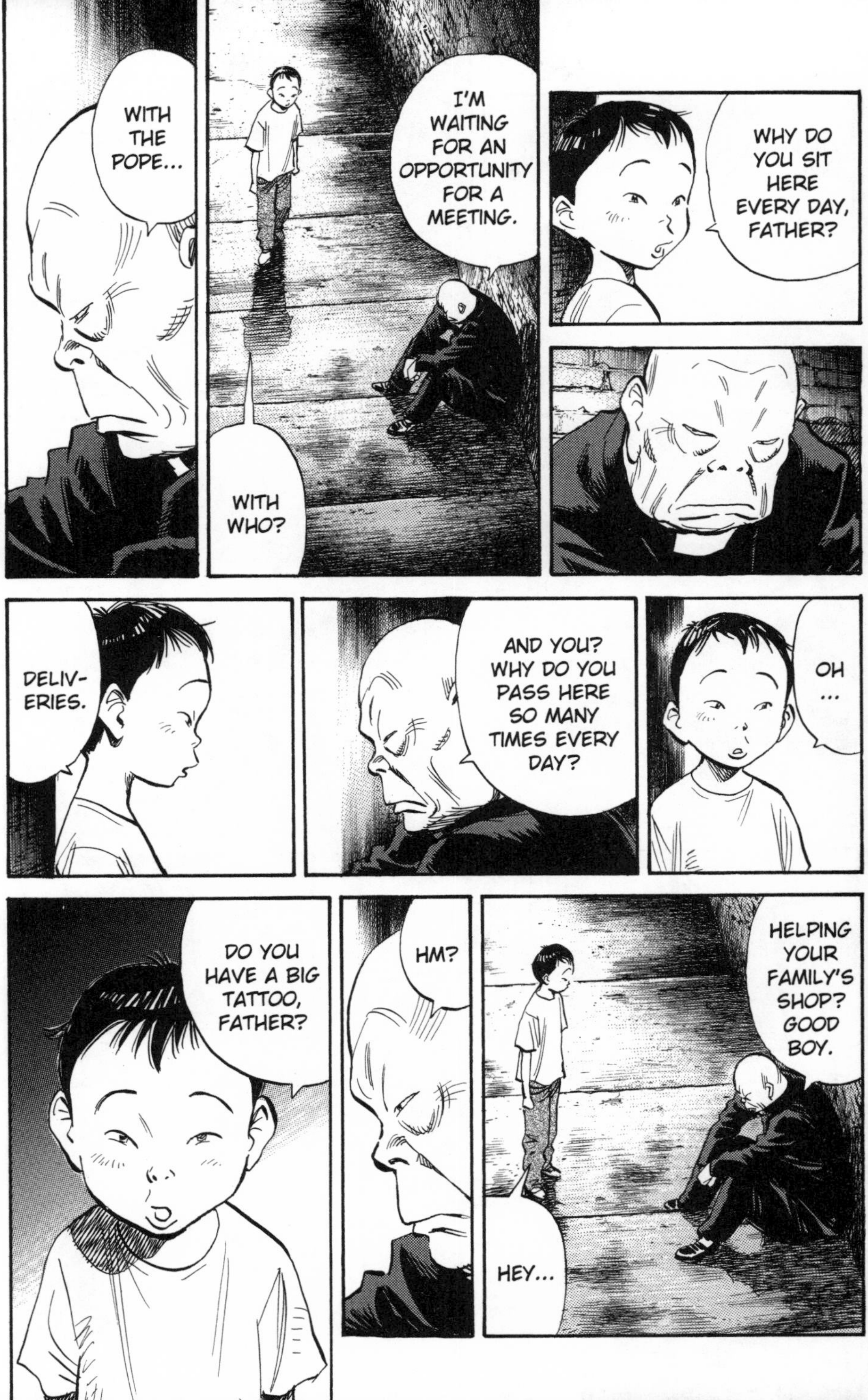
WHY DO YOU SIT HERE EVERY DAY, FATHER?
I'M WAITING FOR AN OPPORTUNITY FOR A MEETING.
WITH WHO?
WITH THE POPE...
OH ...
AND YOU? WHY DO YOU PASS HERE SO MANY TIMES EVERY DAY?
DELIV-ERIES.
HELPING YOUR FAMILY'S SHOP? GOOD BOY.
HEY...
HM?
DO YOU HAVE A BIG TATTOO, FATHER?

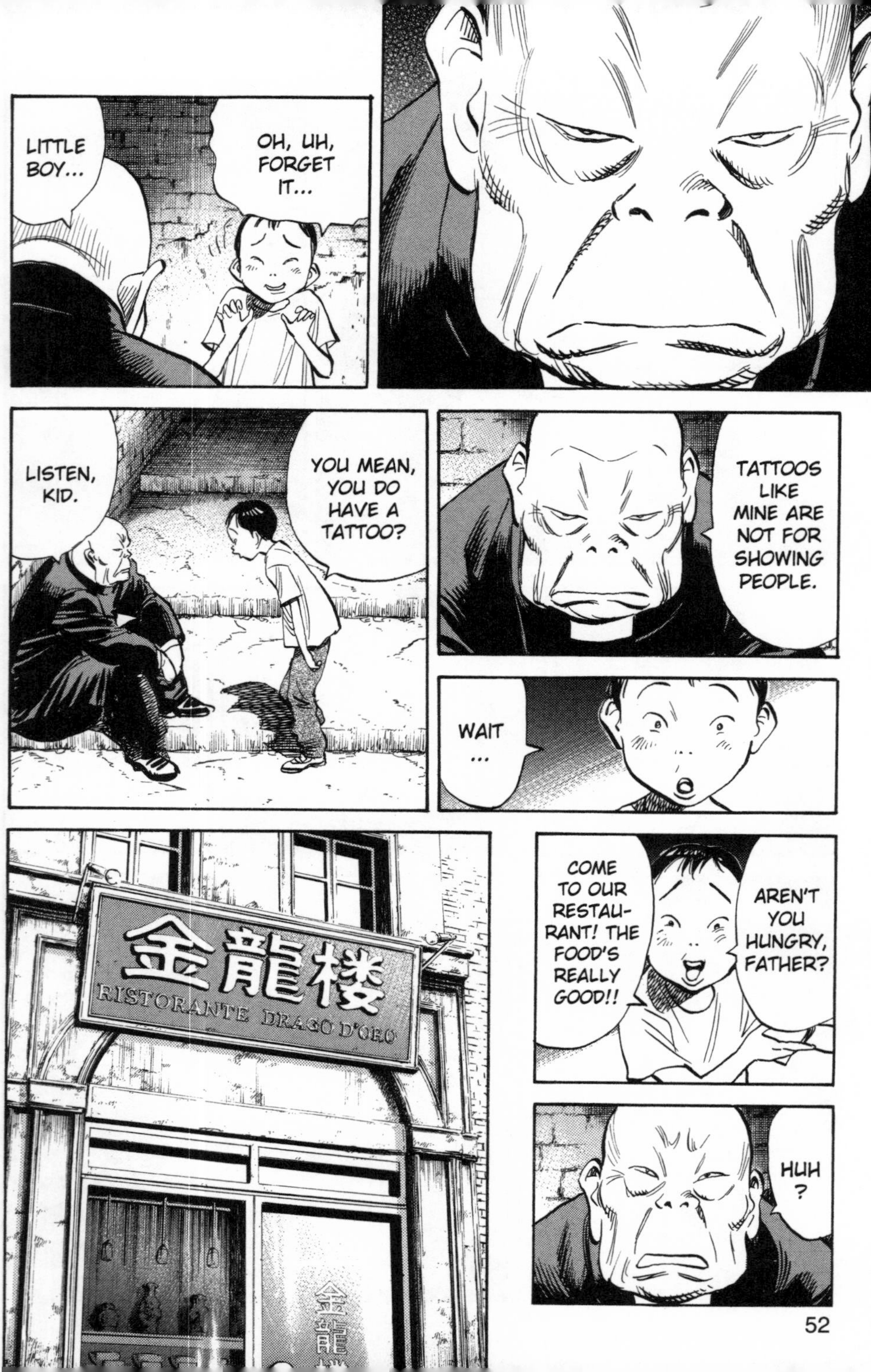
OH, UH, FORGET IT...
LITTLE BOY...
TATTOOS LIKE MINE ARE NOT FOR SHOWING PEOPLE.
WAIT ...
YOU MEAN, YOU DO HAVE A TATTOO?
LISTEN, KID.
AREN'T YOU HUNGRY, FATHER?
COME TO OUR RESTAU-RANT! THE FOOD'S REALLY GOOD!!
HUH ?
金龍楼
RISTORANTE DRAGO D'ORO
金龍

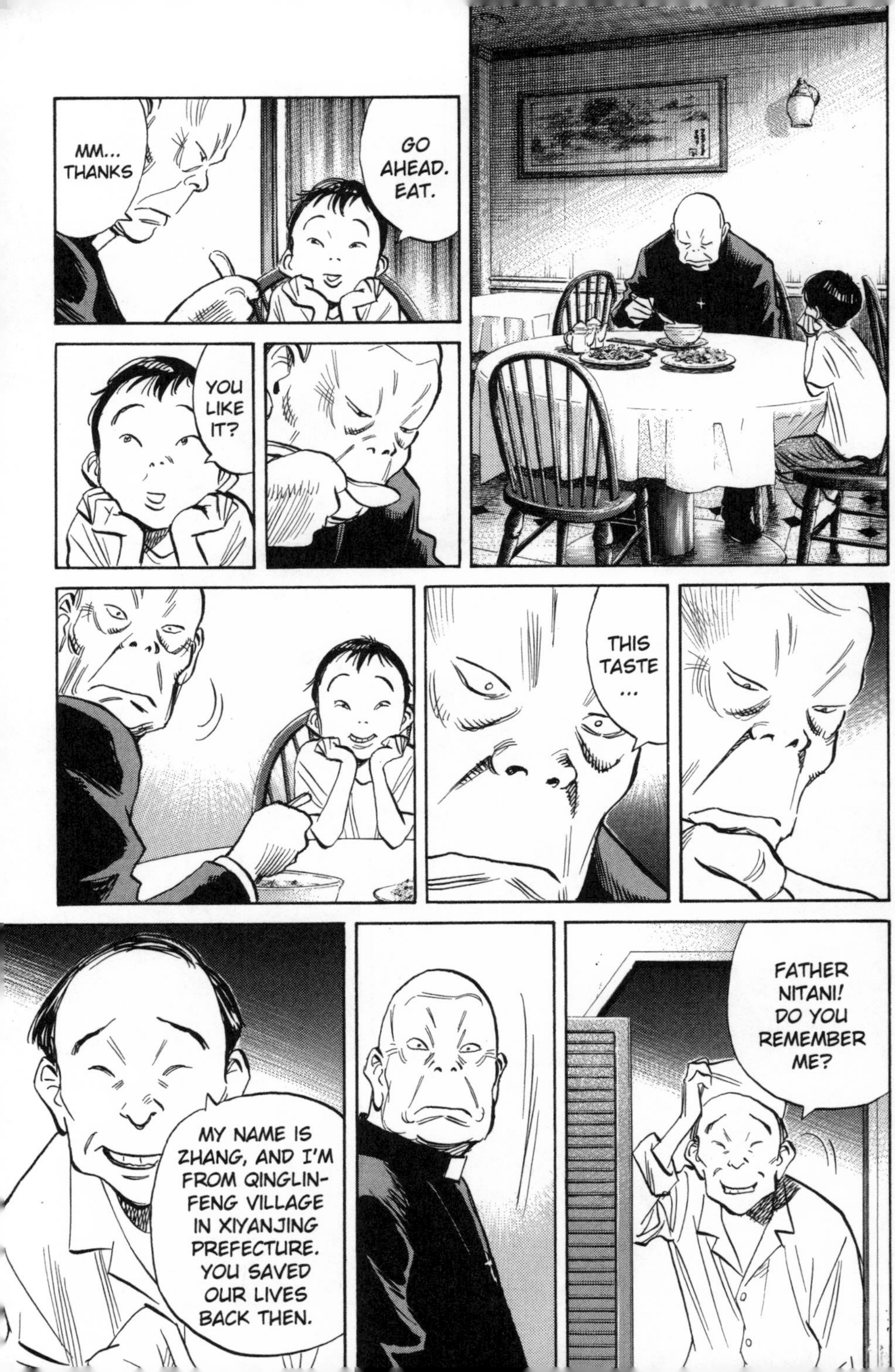
GO AHEAD. EAT.
MM... THANKS
YOU LIKE IT?
THIS TASTE ...
FATHER NITANI! DO YOU REMEMBER ME?
MY NAME IS ZHANG, AND I'M FROM QINGLIN-FENG VILLAGE IN XIYANJING PREFECTURE. YOU SAVED OUR LIVES BACK THEN.

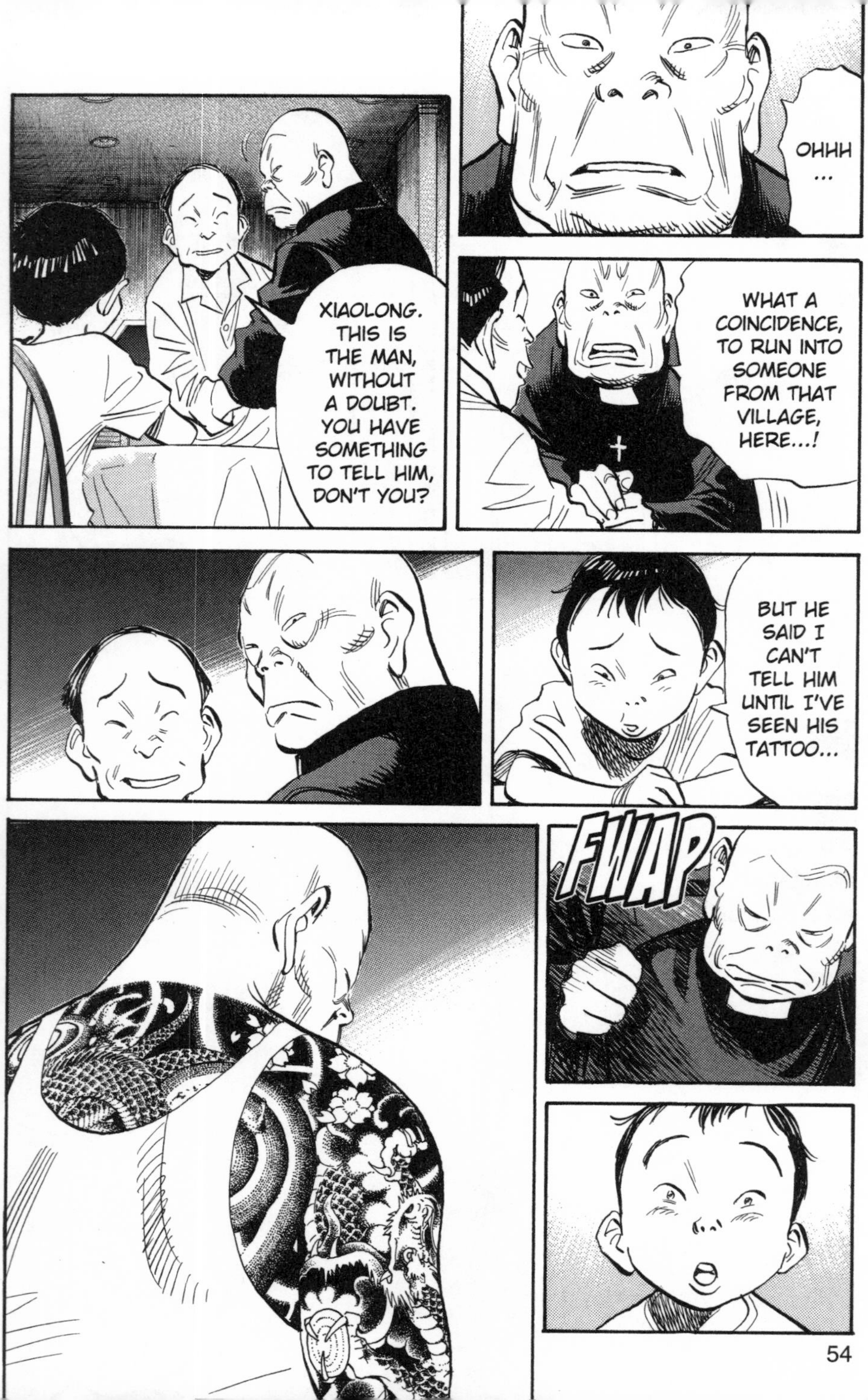
OHHH ...
WHAT A COINCIDENCE, TO RUN INTO SOMEONE FROM THAT VILLAGE, HERE...!
XIAOLONG. THIS IS THE MAN, WITHOUT A DOUBT. YOU HAVE SOMETHING TO TELL HIM, DON'T YOU?
BUT HE SAID I CAN'T TELL HIM UNTIL I'VE SEEN HIS TATTOO...
FWAP

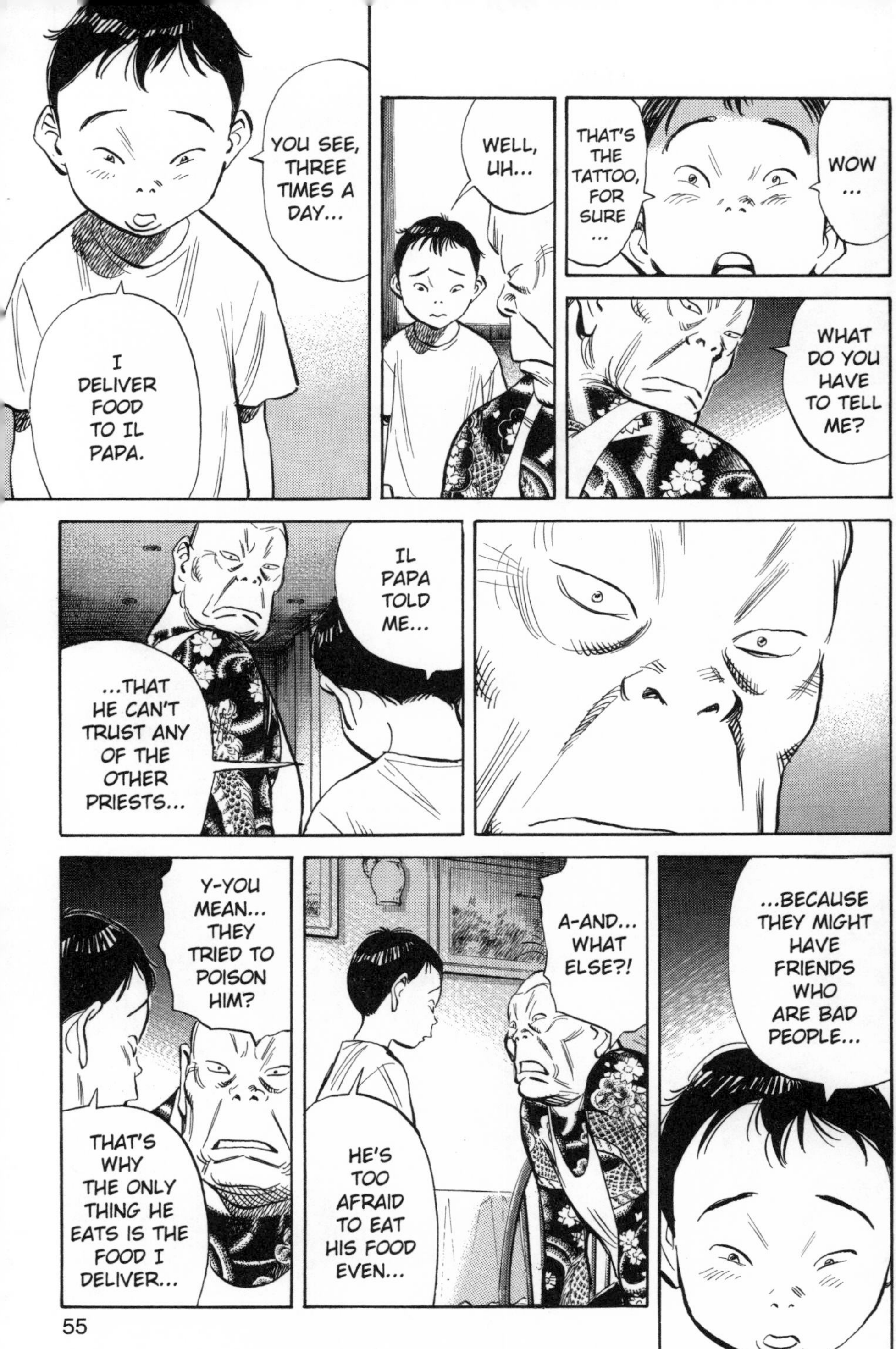
WOW ...
THAT'S THE TATTOO, FOR SURE ...
WHAT DO YOU HAVE TO TELL ME?
WELL, UH...
YOU SEE, THREE TIMES A DAY...
I DELIVER FOOD TO IL PAPA.
IL PAPA TOLD ME...
...THAT HE CAN'T TRUST ANY OF THE OTHER PRIESTS...
...BECAUSE THEY MIGHT HAVE FRIENDS WHO ARE BAD PEOPLE...
A-AND... WHAT ELSE?!
HE'S TOO AFRAID TO EAT HIS FOOD EVEN...
Y-YOU MEAN... THEY TRIED TO POISON HIM?
THAT'S WHY THE ONLY THING HE EATS IS THE FOOD I DELIVER...

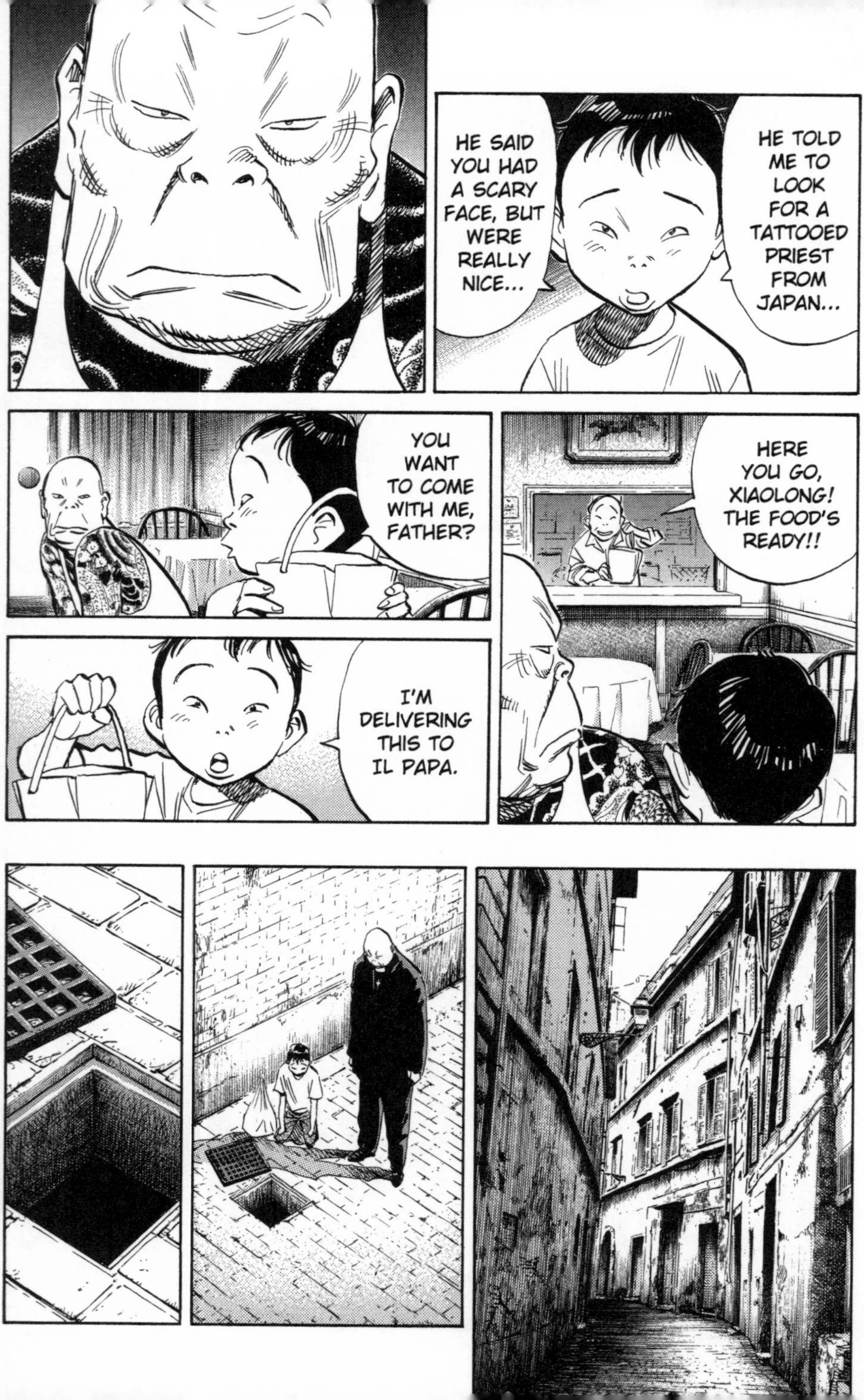
HE TOLD ME TO LOOK FOR A TATTOOED PRIEST FROM JAPAN...
HE SAID YOU HAD A SCARY FACE, BUT WERE REALLY NICE...
HERE YOU GO, XIAOLONG! THE FOOD'S READY!!
YOU WANT TO COME WITH ME, FATHER?
I'M DELIVERING THIS TO IL PAPA.

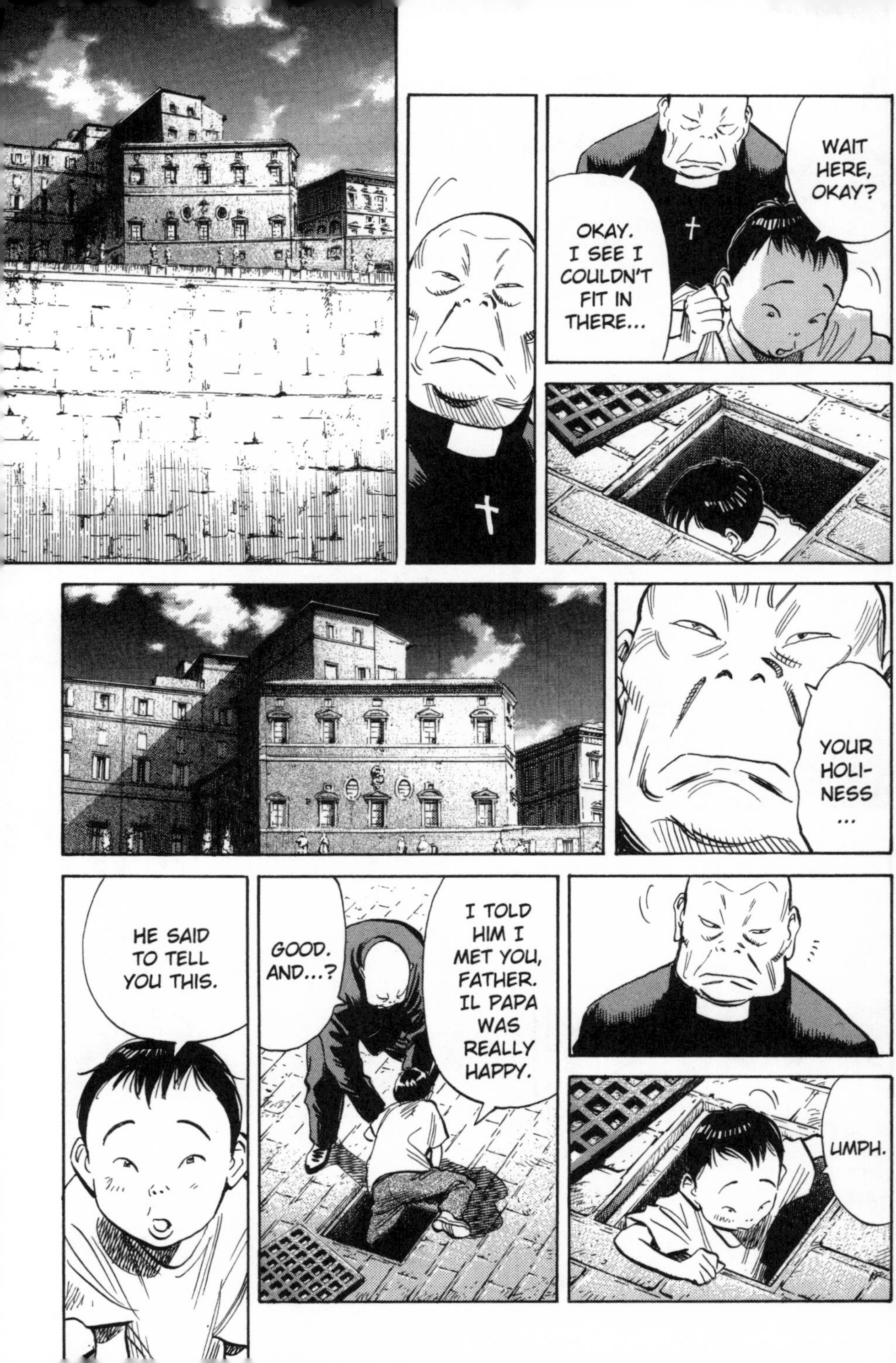
WAIT HERE, OKAY?
OKAY. I SEE I COULDN'T FIT IN THERE...
YOUR HOLI-NESS ...
UMPH.
I TOLD HIM I MET YOU, FATHER. IL PAPA WAS REALLY HAPPY.
GOOD. AND...?
HE SAID TO TELL YOU THIS.

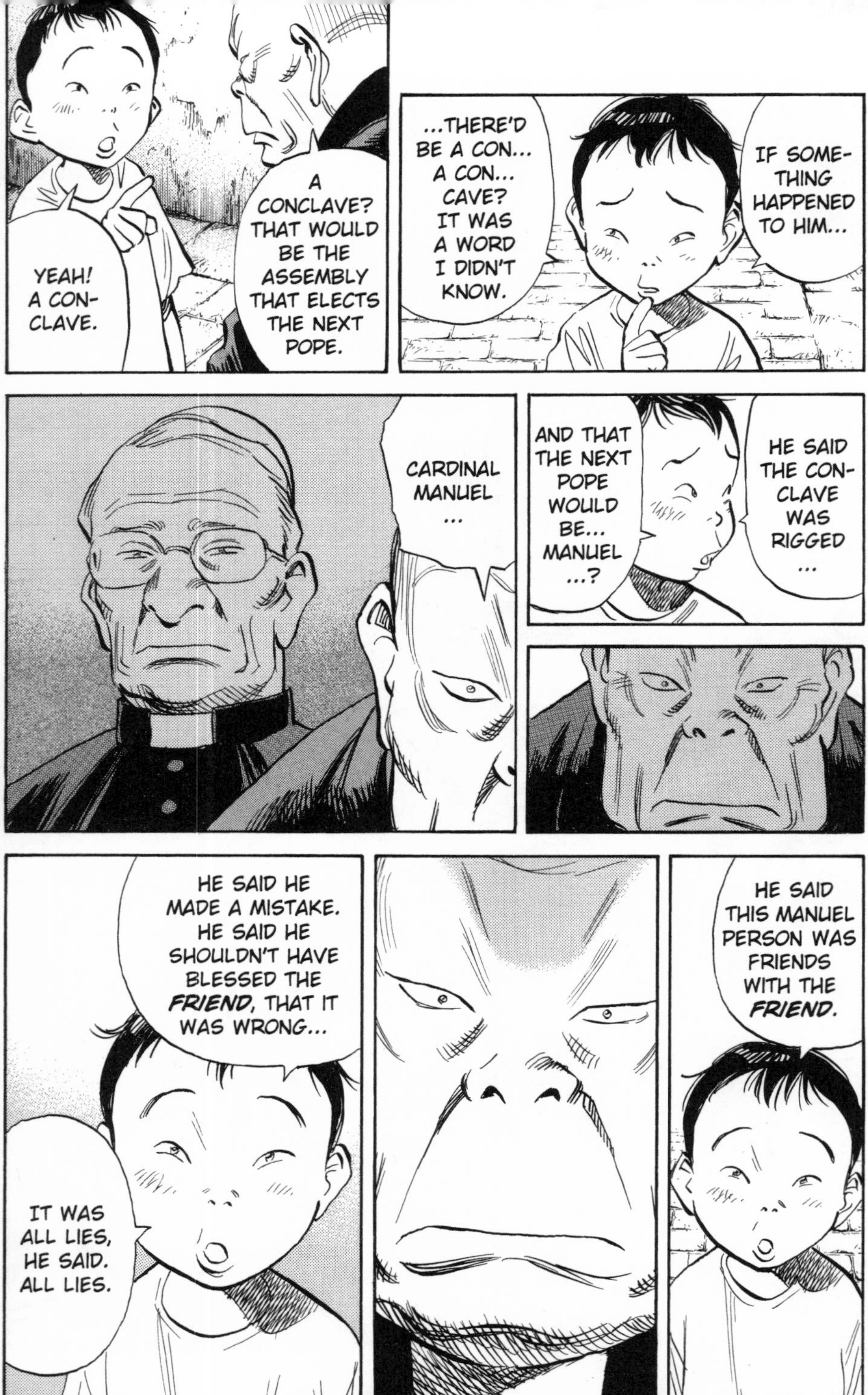
IF SOMETHING HAPPENED TO HIM...
...THERE'D BE A CON... A CON... CAVE? IT WAS A WORD I DIDN'T KNOW.
A CONCLAVE? THAT WOULD BE THE ASSEMBLY THAT ELECTS THE NEXT POPE.
YEAH! A CONCLAVE.
HE SAID THE CONCLAVE WAS RIGGED...
AND THAT THE NEXT POPE WOULD BE... MANUEL...?
CARDINAL MANUEL...
HE SAID THIS MANUEL PERSON WAS FRIENDS WITH THE ***FRIEND***.
HE SAID HE MADE A MISTAKE. HE SAID HE SHOULDN'T HAVE BLESSED THE ***FRIEND***, THAT IT WAS WRONG...
IT WAS ALL LIES, HE SAID. ALL LIES.

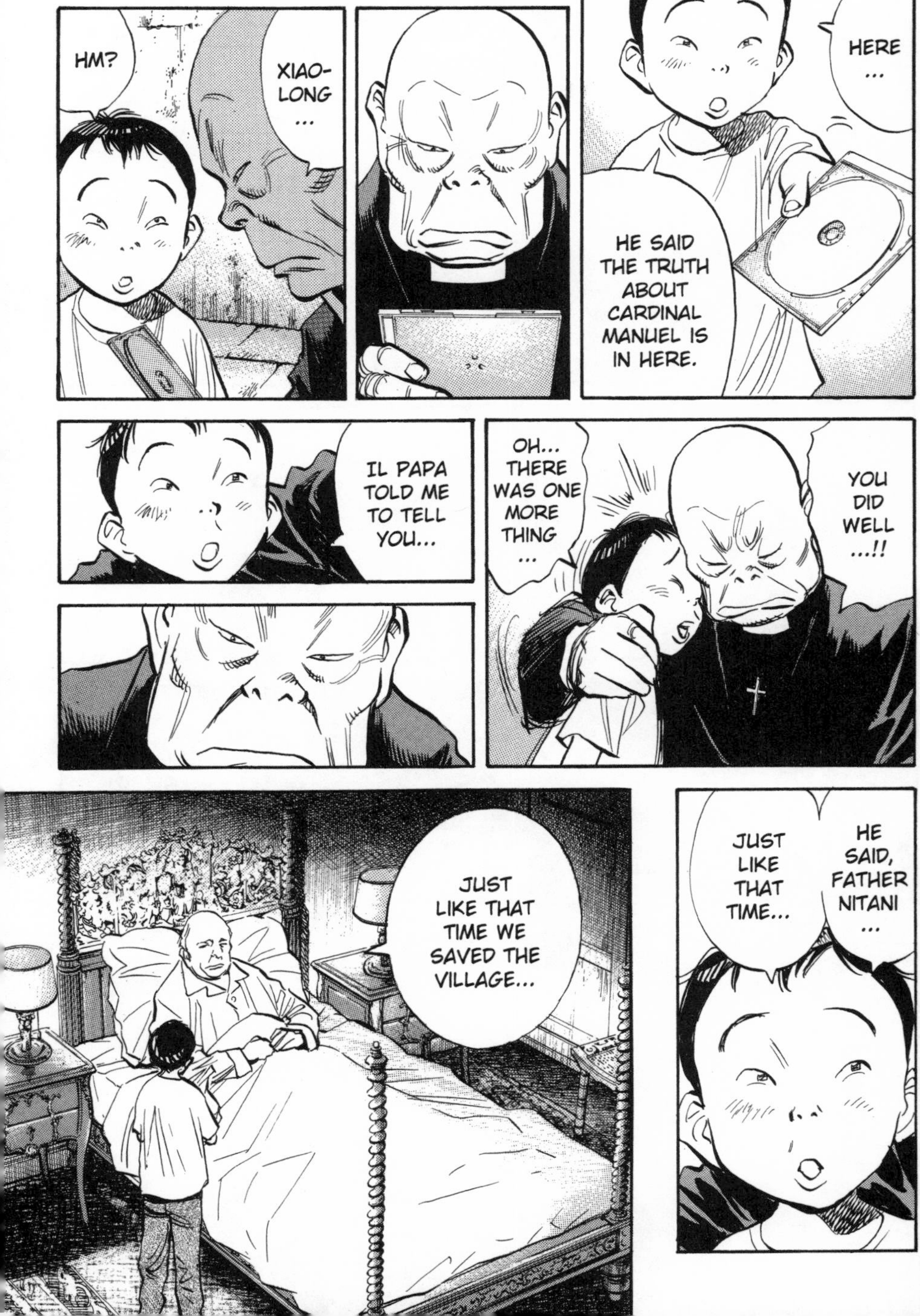
HERE ...
HE SAID THE TRUTH ABOUT CARDINAL MANUEL IS IN HERE.
XIAO-LONG ...
HM?
YOU DID WELL ...!!
OH... THERE WAS ONE MORE THING ...
IL PAPA TOLD ME TO TELL YOU...
HE SAID, FATHER NITANI ...
JUST LIKE THAT TIME...
JUST LIKE THAT TIME WE SAVED THE VILLAGE...

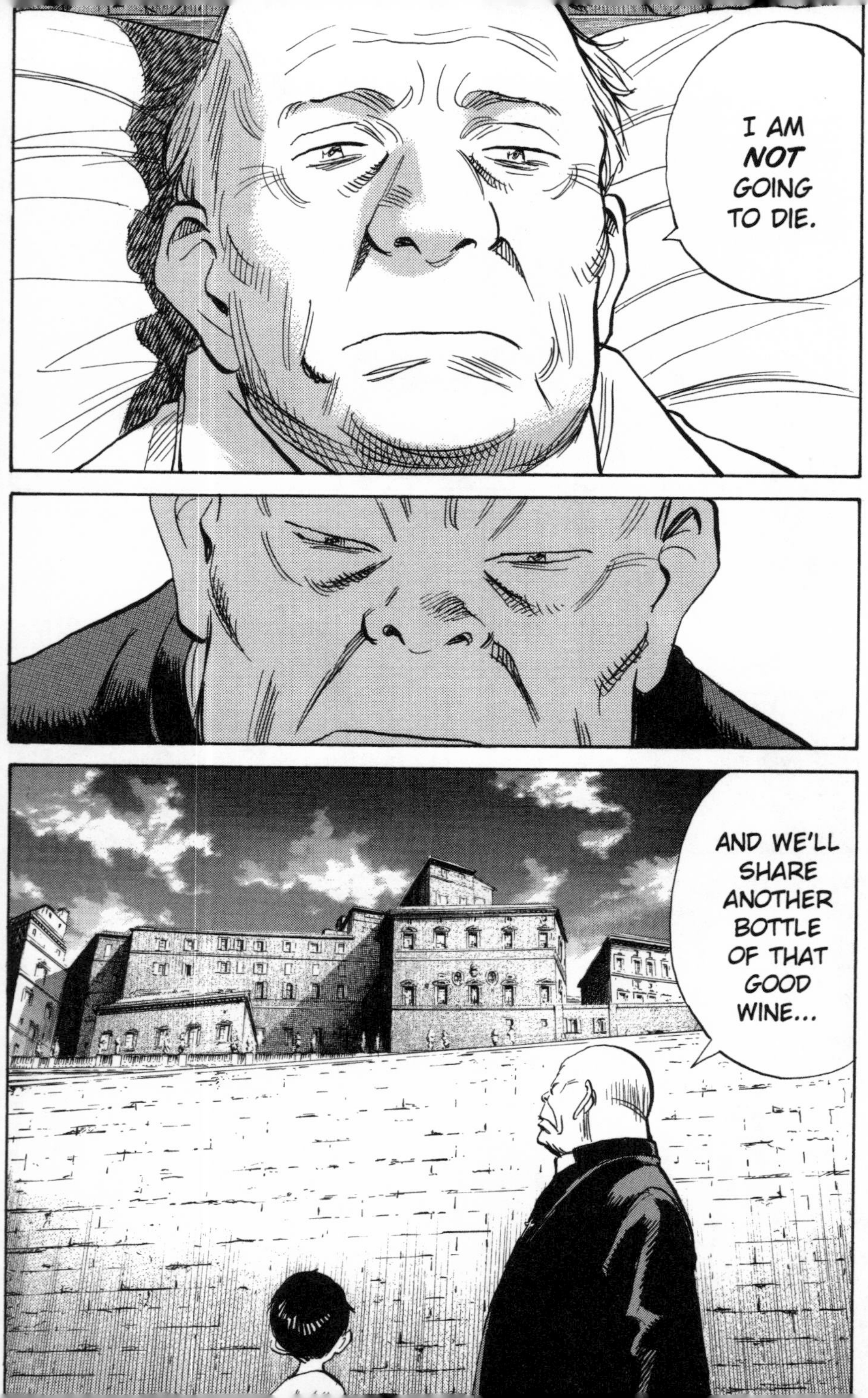
I AM NOT GOING TO DIE.
AND WE'LL SHARE ANOTHER BOTTLE OF THAT GOOD WINE...

Chapter 4 Let's Play

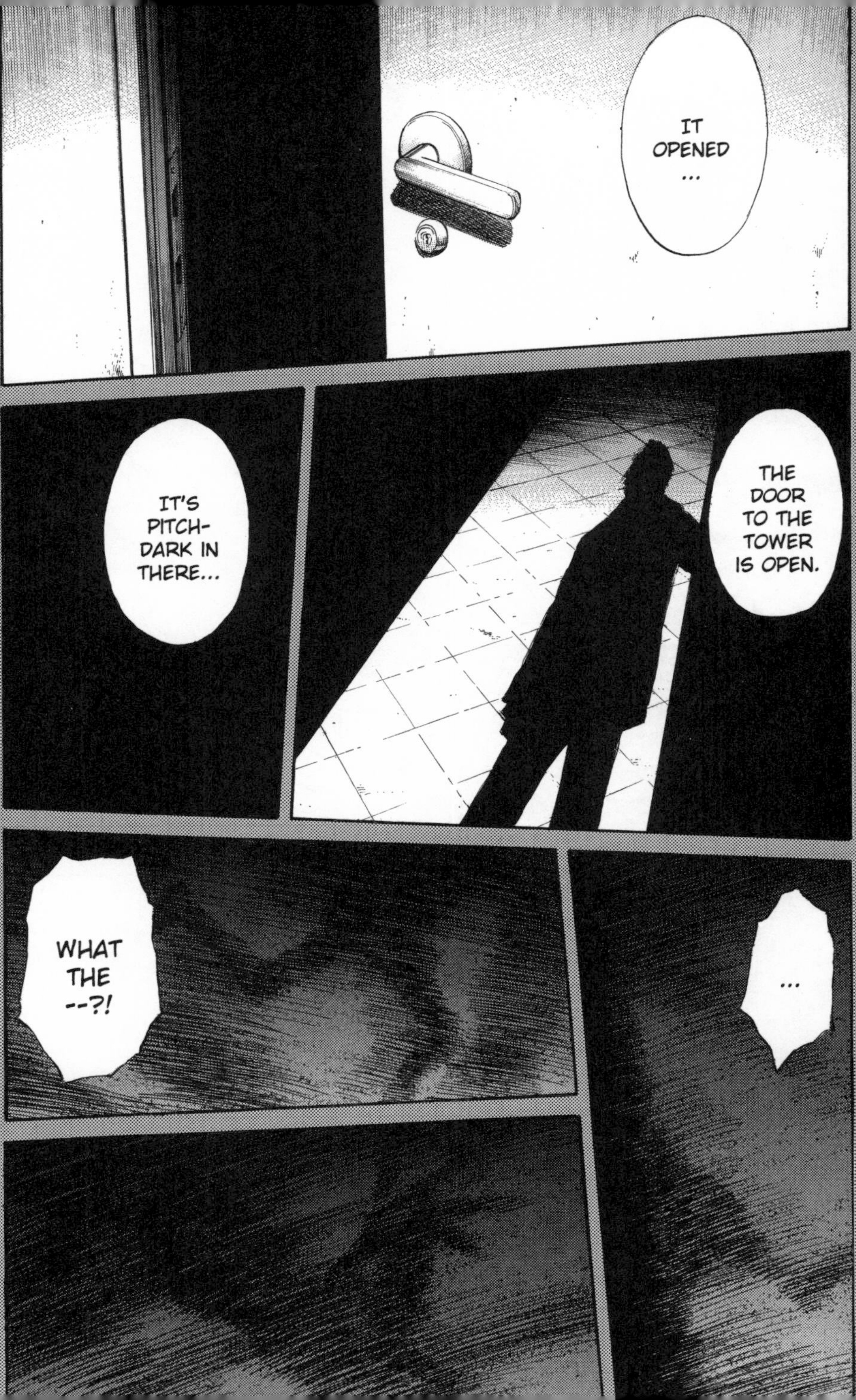
IT OPENED ...
THE DOOR TO THE TOWER IS OPEN.
IT'S PITCH-DARK IN THERE...
...
WHAT THE --?!

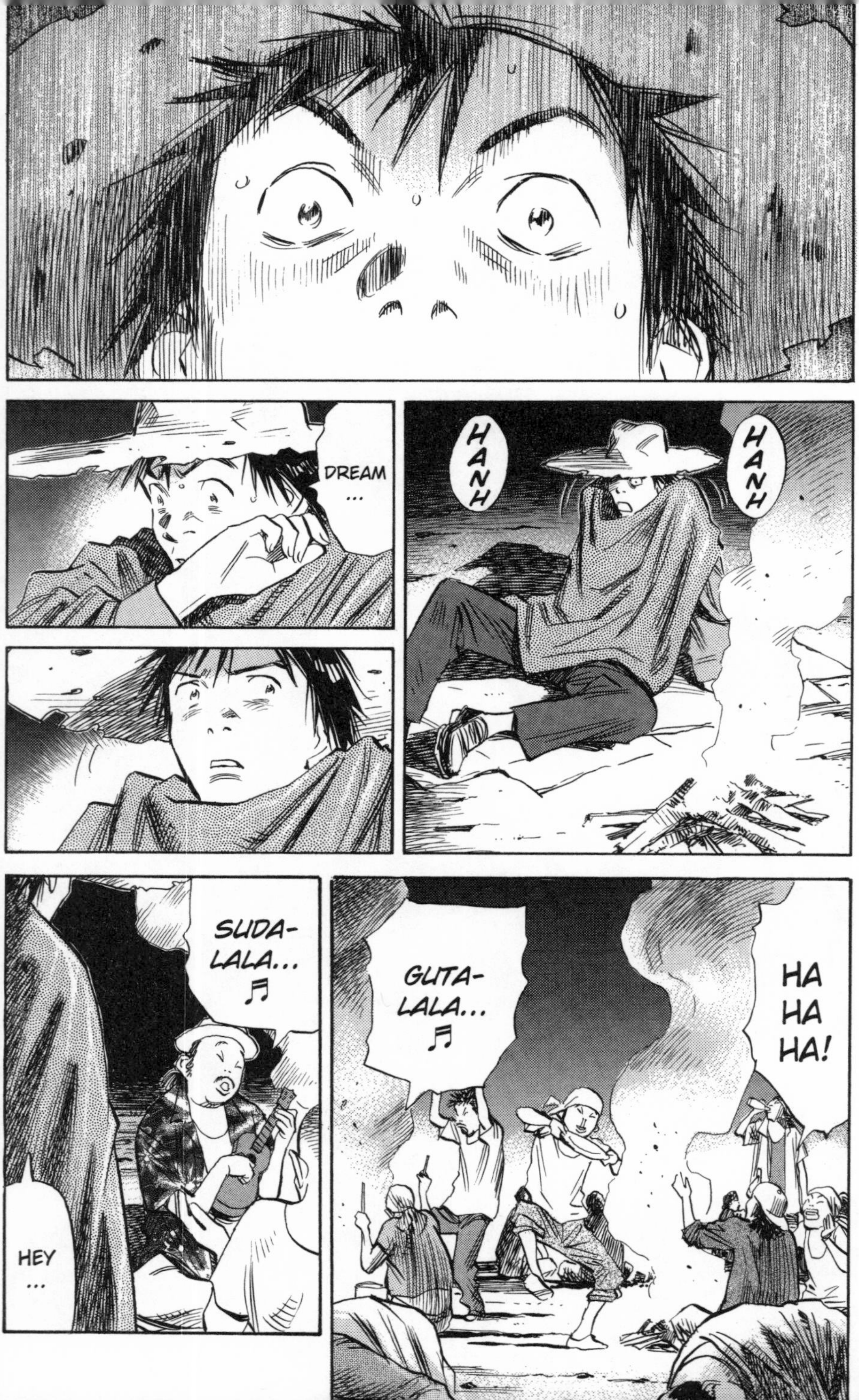
HANH
HANH
DREAM ...
HA HA HA!
GUTA-LALA... ♬
SUDA-LALA... ♬
HEY ...

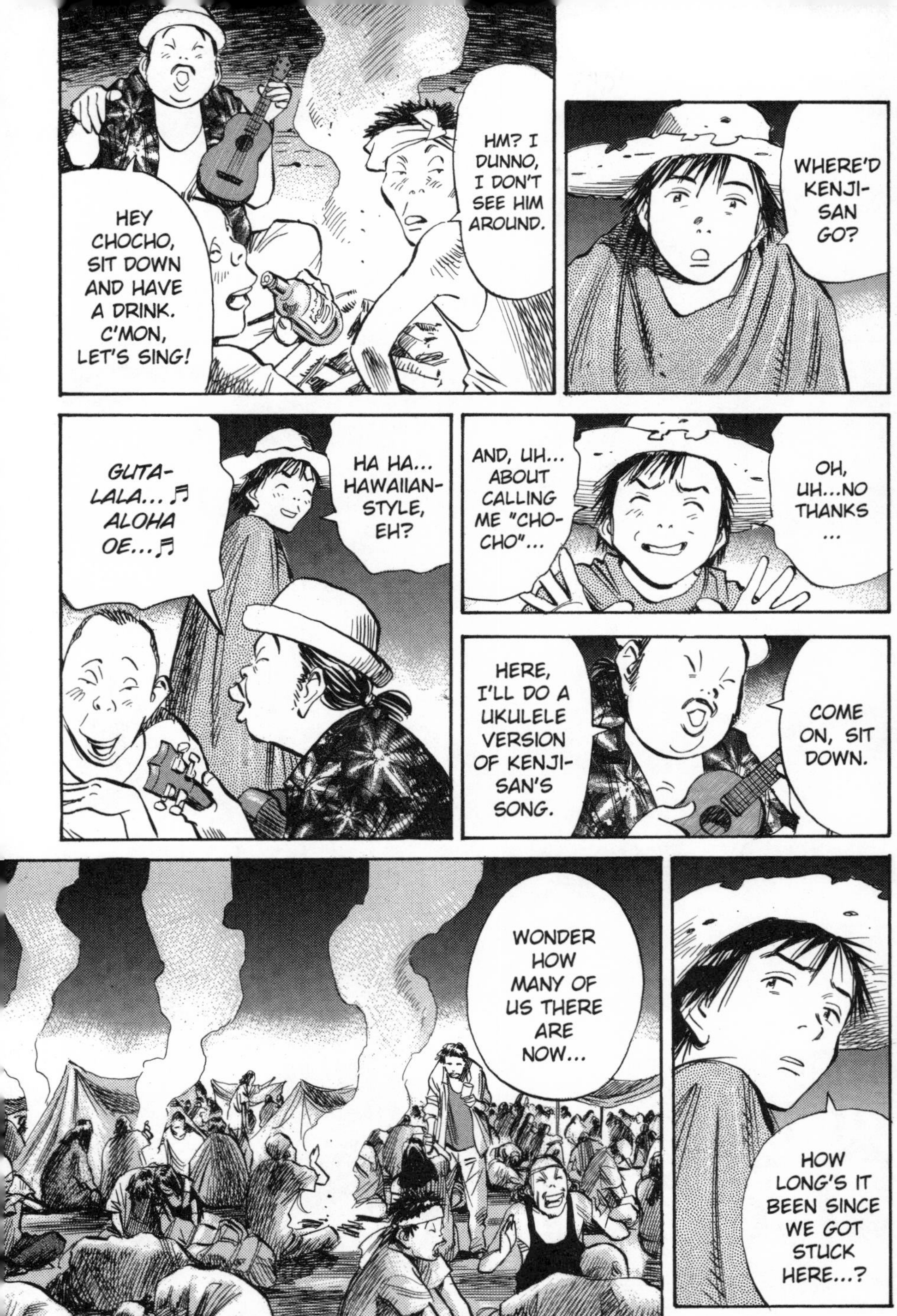
WHERE'D KENJI-SAN GO?
HM? I DUNNO, I DON'T SEE HIM AROUND.
HEY CHOCHO, SIT DOWN AND HAVE A DRINK. C'MON, LET'S SING!
OH, UH...NO THANKS ...
AND, UH... ABOUT CALLING ME "CHO-CHO"...
COME ON, SIT DOWN.
HERE, I'LL DO A UKULELE VERSION OF KENJI-SAN'S SONG.
HA HA... HAWAIIAN-STYLE, EH?
GUTA-LALA... ♫ ALOHA OE... ♫
HOW LONG'S IT BEEN SINCE WE GOT STUCK HERE...?
WONDER HOW MANY OF US THERE ARE NOW...

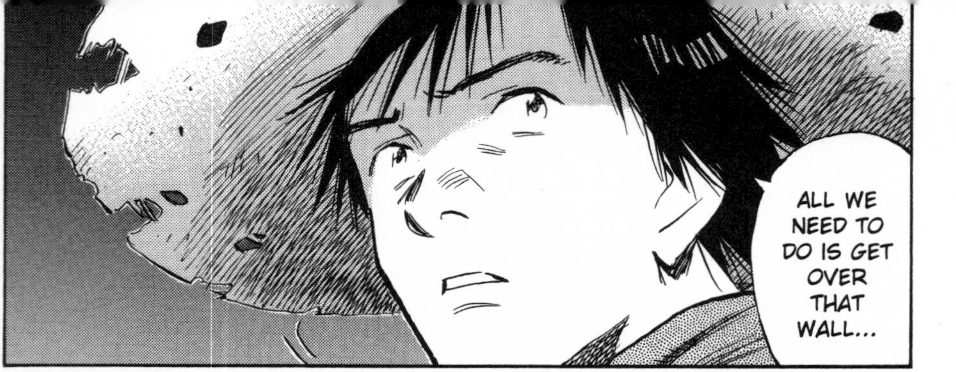
ALL WE NEED TO DO IS GET OVER THAT WALL...

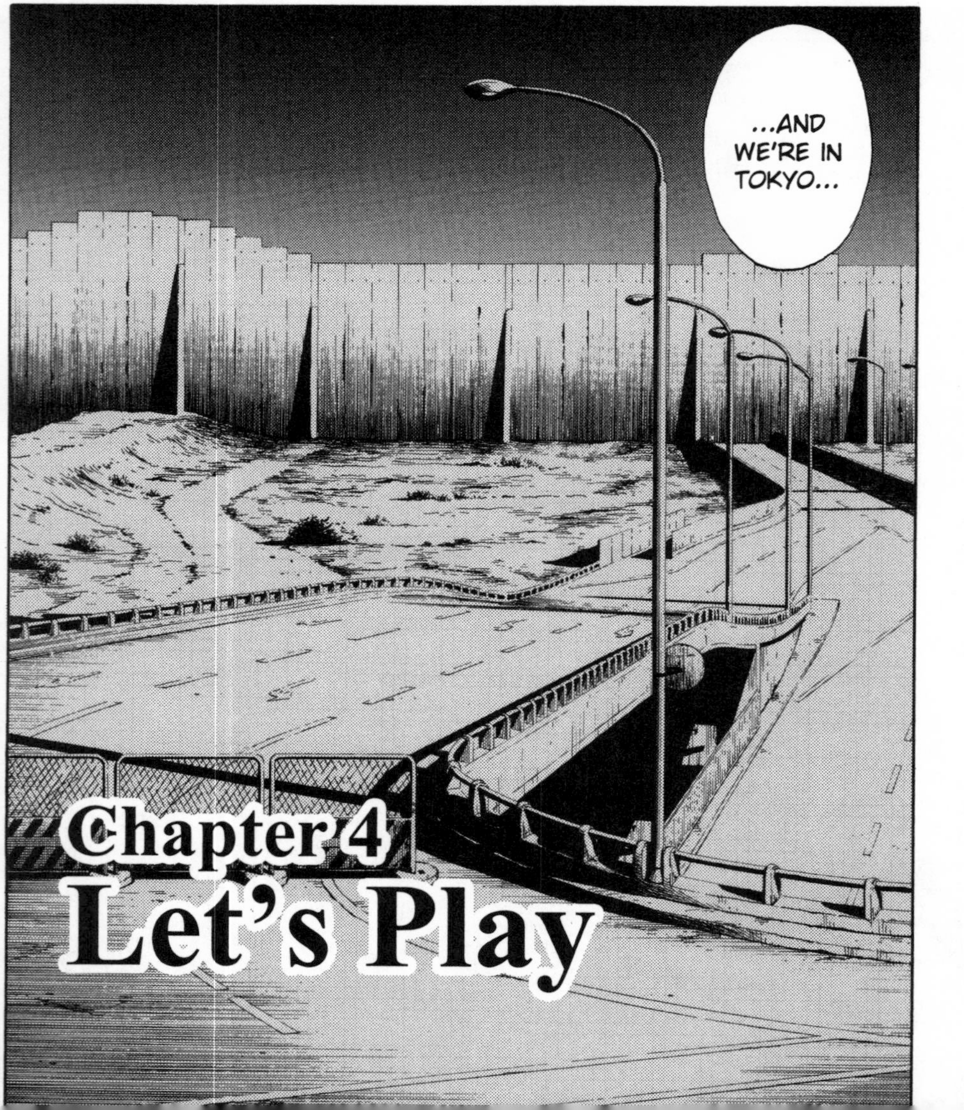
...AND WE'RE IN TOKYO...
Chapter 4
Let's Play

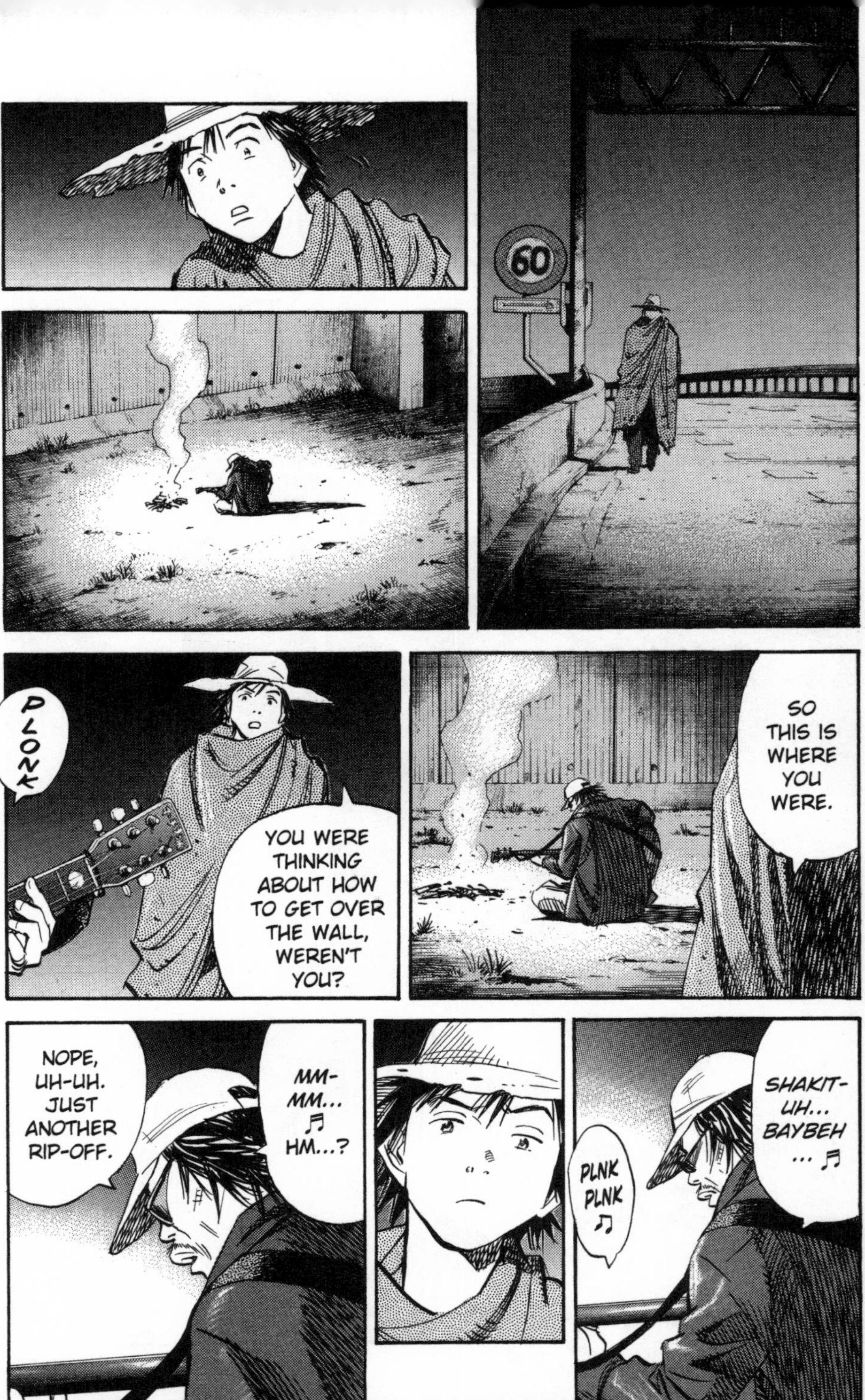
SO THIS IS WHERE YOU WERE.
YOU WERE THINKING ABOUT HOW TO GET OVER THE WALL, WEREN'T YOU?
PLONK
SHAKIT-UH... BAYBEH ... ♬
PLNK PLNK ♫
MM-MM... ♬ HM...?
NOPE, UH-UH. JUST ANOTHER RIP-OFF.

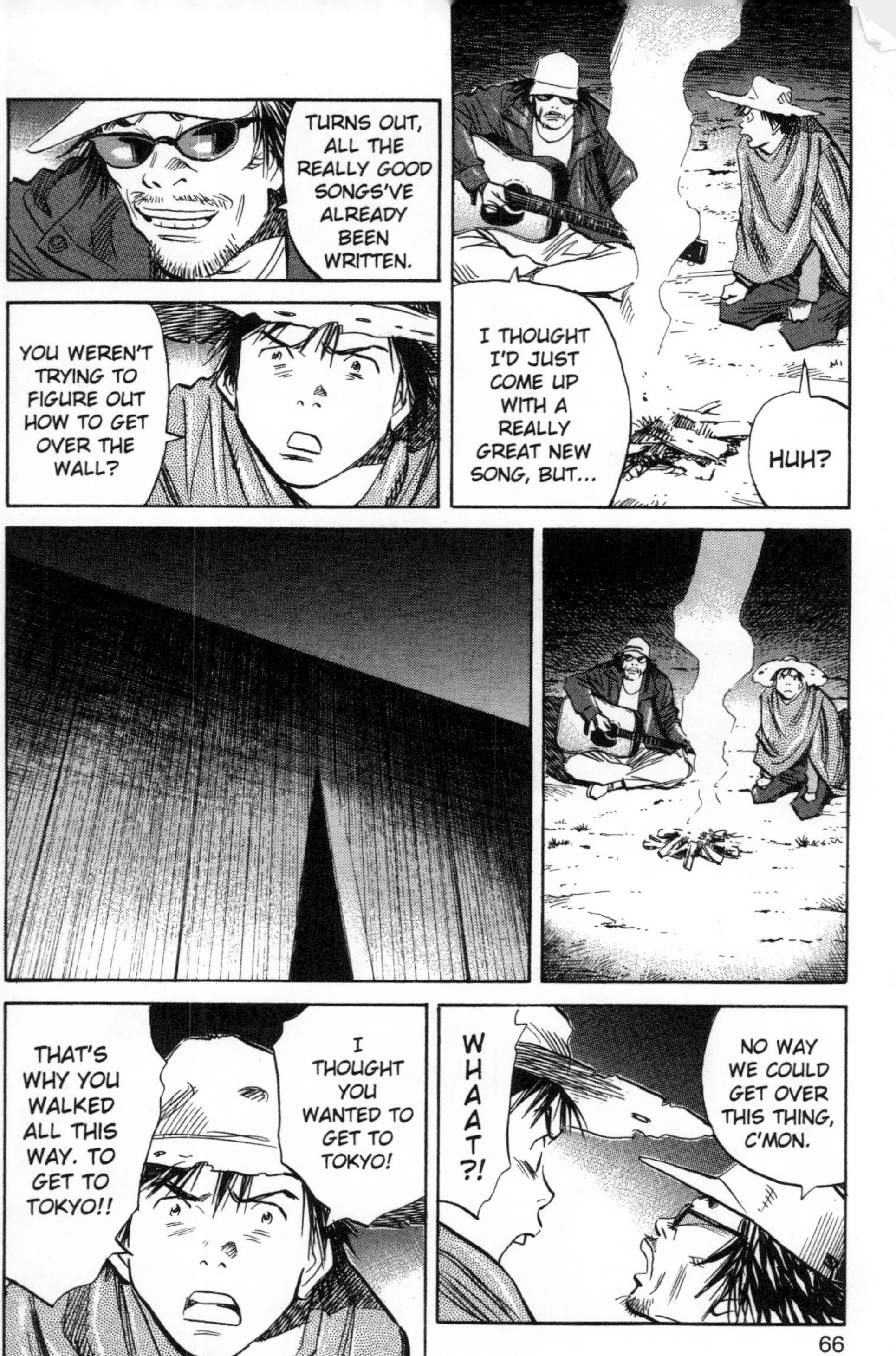
I THOUGHT I'D JUST COME UP WITH A REALLY GREAT NEW SONG, BUT...
HUH?
TURNS OUT, ALL THE REALLY GOOD SONGS'VE ALREADY BEEN WRITTEN.
YOU WEREN'T TRYING TO FIGURE OUT HOW TO GET OVER THE WALL?
NO WAY WE COULD GET OVER THIS THING, C'MON.
WHAAAT?!
I THOUGHT YOU WANTED TO GET TO TOKYO!
THAT'S WHY YOU WALKED ALL THIS WAY. TO GET TO TOKYO!!

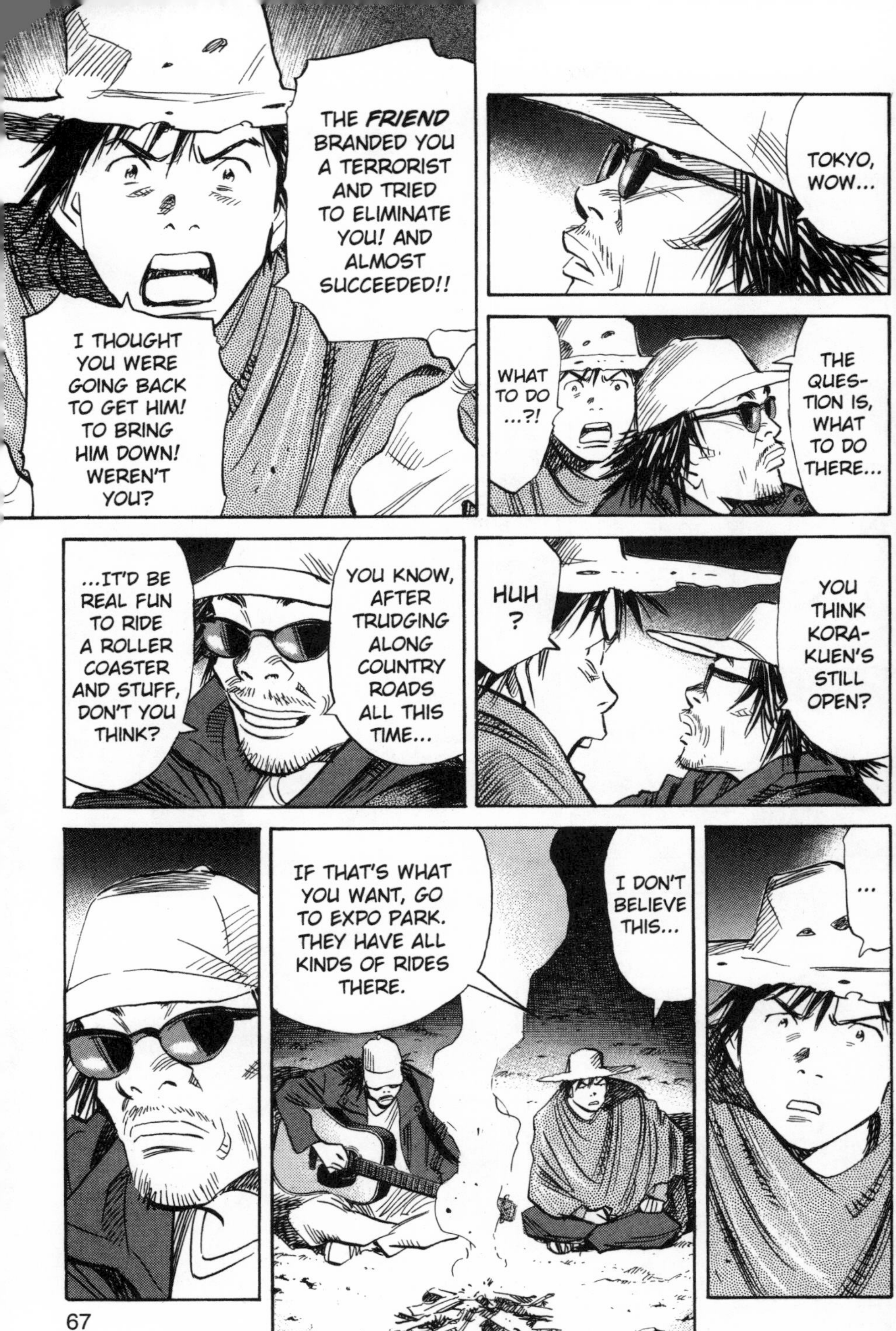
TOKYO, WOW...
THE QUESTION IS, WHAT TO DO THERE...
WHAT TO DO ...?!
THE *FRIEND* BRANDED YOU A TERRORIST AND TRIED TO ELIMINATE YOU! AND ALMOST SUCCEEDED!!
I THOUGHT YOU WERE GOING BACK TO GET HIM! TO BRING HIM DOWN! WEREN'T YOU?
YOU THINK KORAKUEN'S STILL OPEN?
HUH ?
YOU KNOW, AFTER TRUDGING ALONG COUNTRY ROADS ALL THIS TIME...
...IT'D BE REAL FUN TO RIDE A ROLLER COASTER AND STUFF, DON'T YOU THINK?
...
I DON'T BELIEVE THIS...
IF THAT'S WHAT YOU WANT, GO TO EXPO PARK. THEY HAVE ALL KINDS OF RIDES THERE.

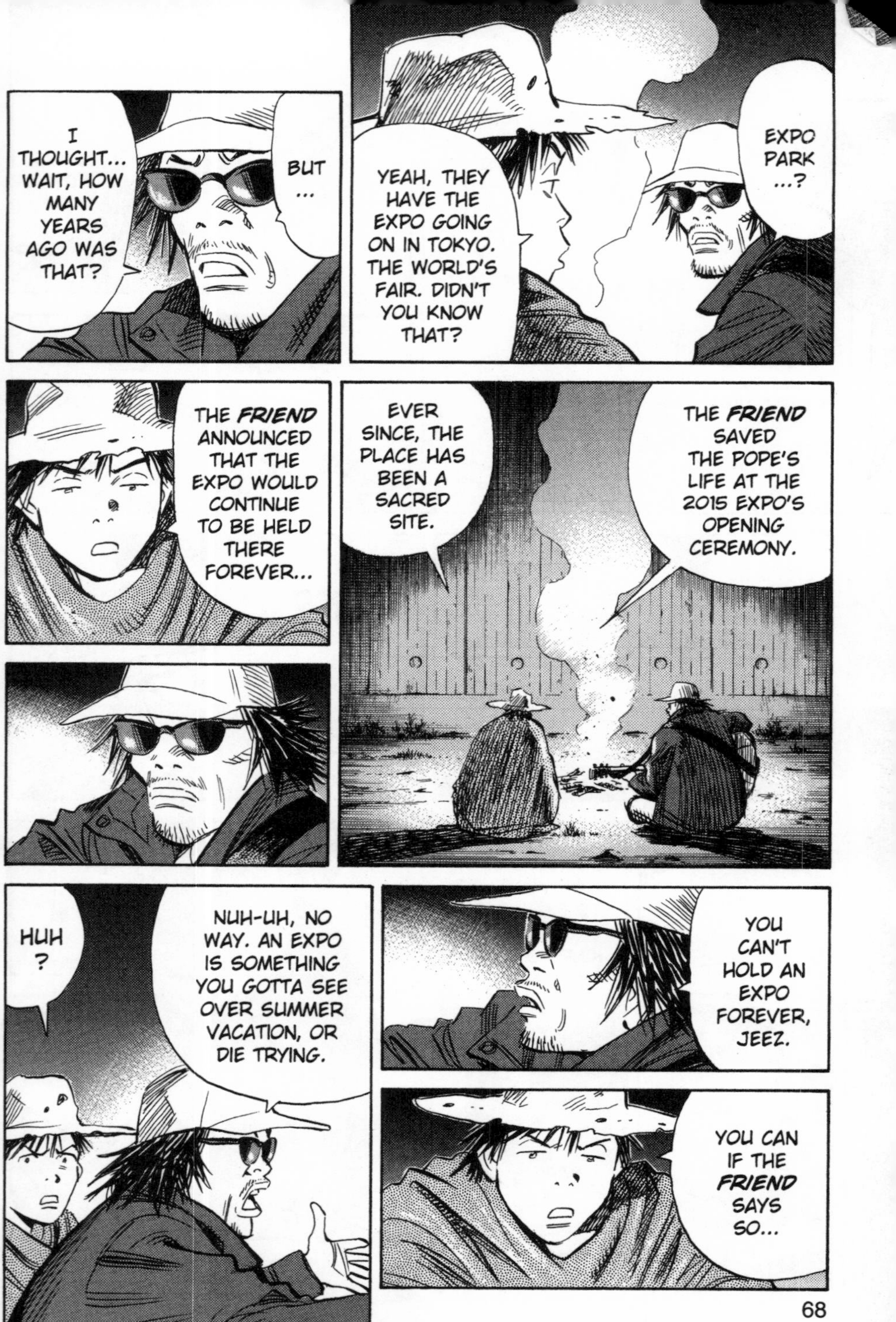
EXPO PARK ...?
YEAH, THEY HAVE THE EXPO GOING ON IN TOKYO. THE WORLD'S FAIR. DIDN'T YOU KNOW THAT?
BUT ...
I THOUGHT... WAIT, HOW MANY YEARS AGO WAS THAT?
THE *FRIEND* SAVED THE POPE'S LIFE AT THE 2015 EXPO'S OPENING CEREMONY.
EVER SINCE, THE PLACE HAS BEEN A SACRED SITE.
THE *FRIEND* ANNOUNCED THAT THE EXPO WOULD CONTINUE TO BE HELD THERE FOREVER...
YOU CAN'T HOLD AN EXPO FOREVER, JEEZ.
YOU CAN IF THE *FRIEND* SAYS SO...
NUH-UH, NO WAY. AN EXPO IS SOMETHING YOU GOTTA SEE OVER SUMMER VACATION, OR DIE TRYING.
HUH ?

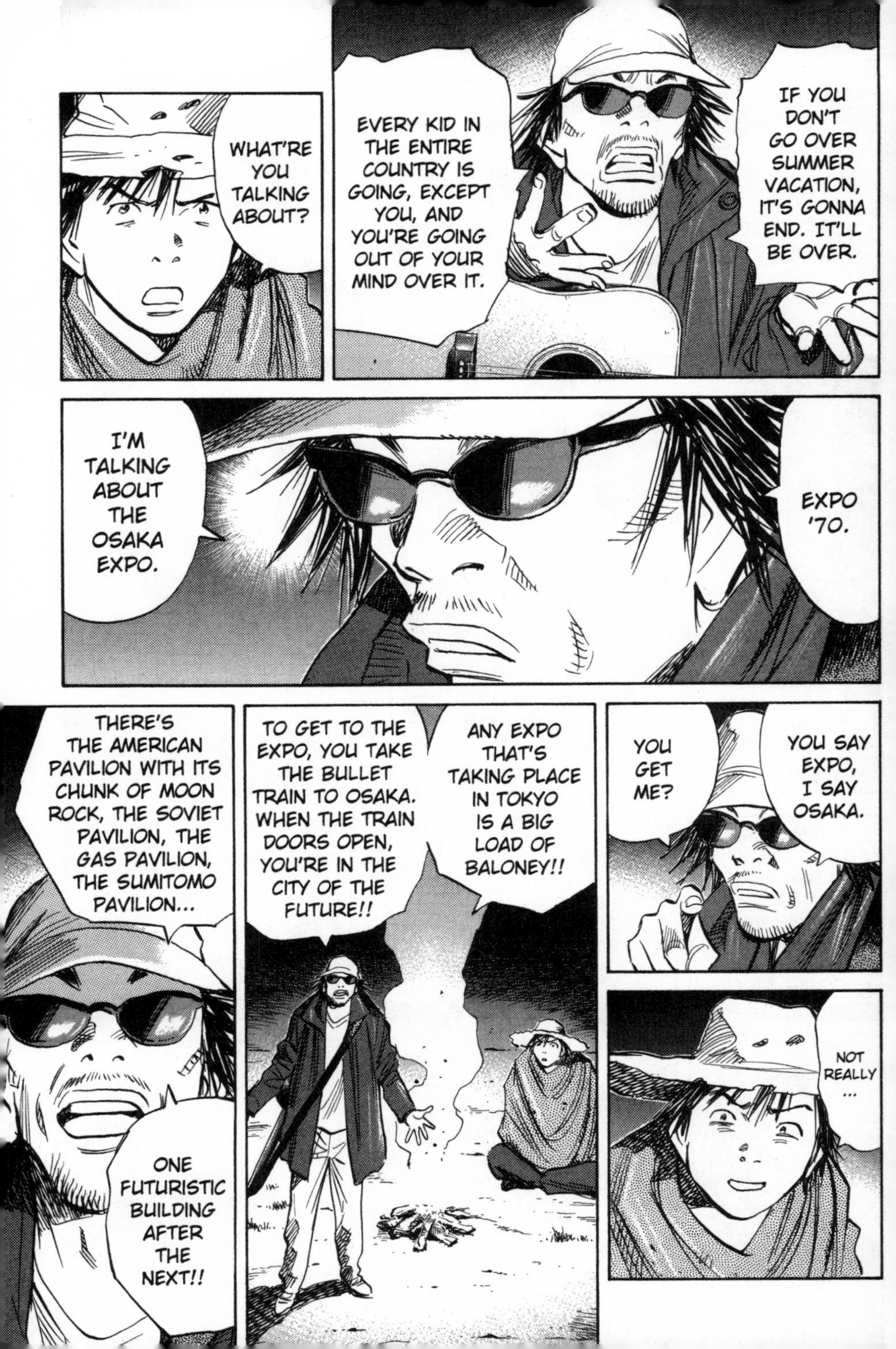
IF YOU DON'T GO OVER SUMMER VACATION, IT'S GONNA END. IT'LL BE OVER.
EVERY KID IN THE ENTIRE COUNTRY IS GOING, EXCEPT YOU, AND YOU'RE GOING OUT OF YOUR MIND OVER IT.
WHAT'RE YOU TALKING ABOUT?
EXPO '70.
I'M TALKING ABOUT THE OSAKA EXPO.
YOU SAY EXPO, I SAY OSAKA.
YOU GET ME?
NOT REALLY ...
ANY EXPO THAT'S TAKING PLACE IN TOKYO IS A BIG LOAD OF BALONEY!!
TO GET TO THE EXPO, YOU TAKE THE BULLET TRAIN TO OSAKA. WHEN THE TRAIN DOORS OPEN, YOU'RE IN THE CITY OF THE FUTURE!!
THERE'S THE AMERICAN PAVILION WITH ITS CHUNK OF MOON ROCK, THE SOVIET PAVILION, THE GAS PAVILION, THE SUMITOMO PAVILION...
ONE FUTURISTIC BUILDING AFTER THE NEXT!!

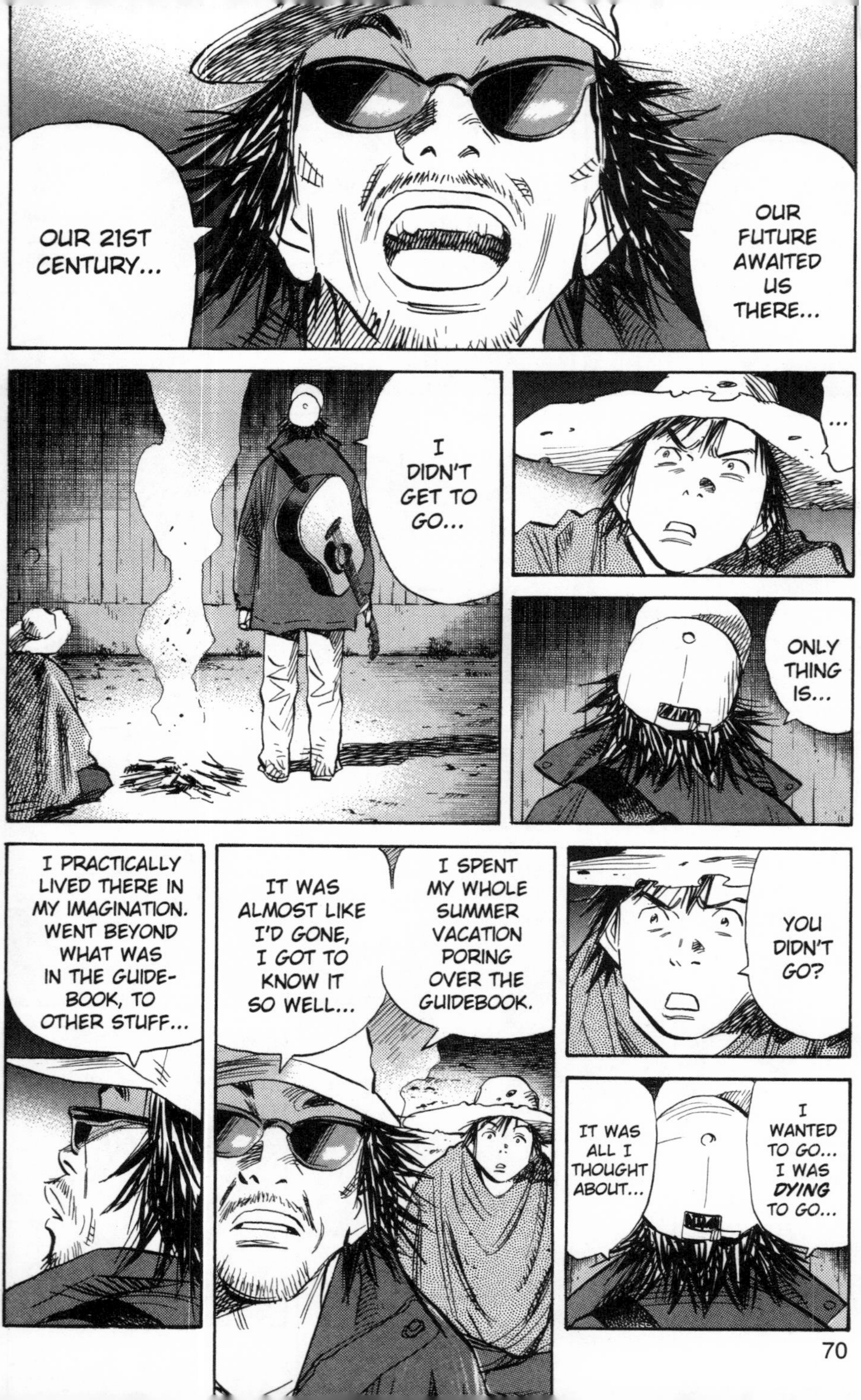
OUR FUTURE AWAITED US THERE...
OUR 21ST CENTURY...
...
ONLY THING IS...
I DIDN'T GET TO GO...
YOU DIDN'T GO?
I WANTED TO GO... I WAS *DYING* TO GO...
IT WAS ALL I THOUGHT ABOUT...
I SPENT MY WHOLE SUMMER VACATION PORING OVER THE GUIDEBOOK.
IT WAS ALMOST LIKE I'D GONE, I GOT TO KNOW IT SO WELL...
I PRACTICALLY LIVED THERE IN MY IMAGINATION. WENT BEYOND WHAT WAS IN THE GUIDE-BOOK, TO OTHER STUFF...

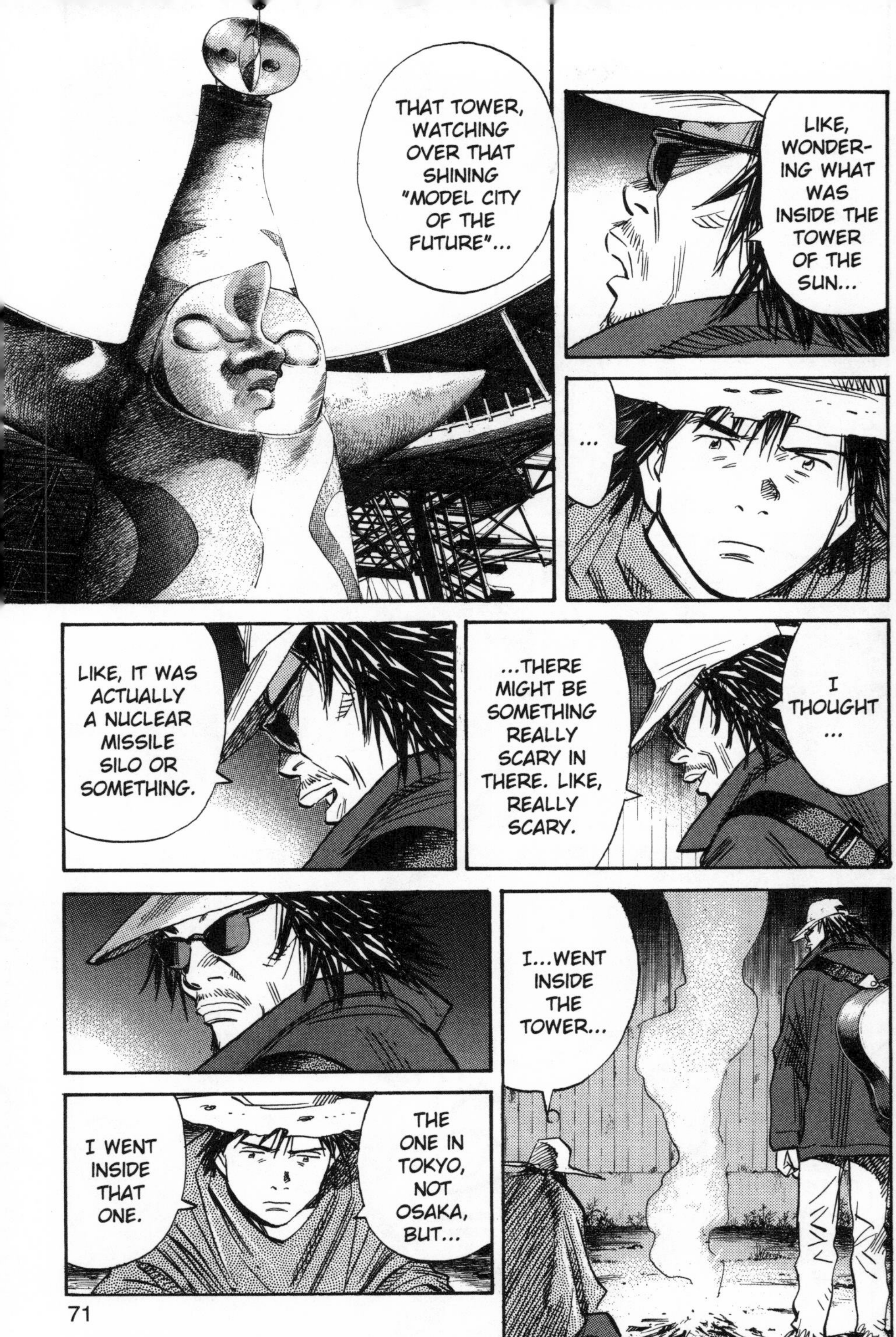
LIKE, WONDERING WHAT WAS INSIDE THE TOWER OF THE SUN...
...
THAT TOWER, WATCHING OVER THAT SHINING "MODEL CITY OF THE FUTURE"...
I THOUGHT...
...THERE MIGHT BE SOMETHING REALLY SCARY IN THERE. LIKE, REALLY SCARY.
LIKE, IT WAS ACTUALLY A NUCLEAR MISSILE SILO OR SOMETHING.
I...WENT INSIDE THE TOWER...
THE ONE IN TOKYO, NOT OSAKA, BUT...
I WENT INSIDE THAT ONE.

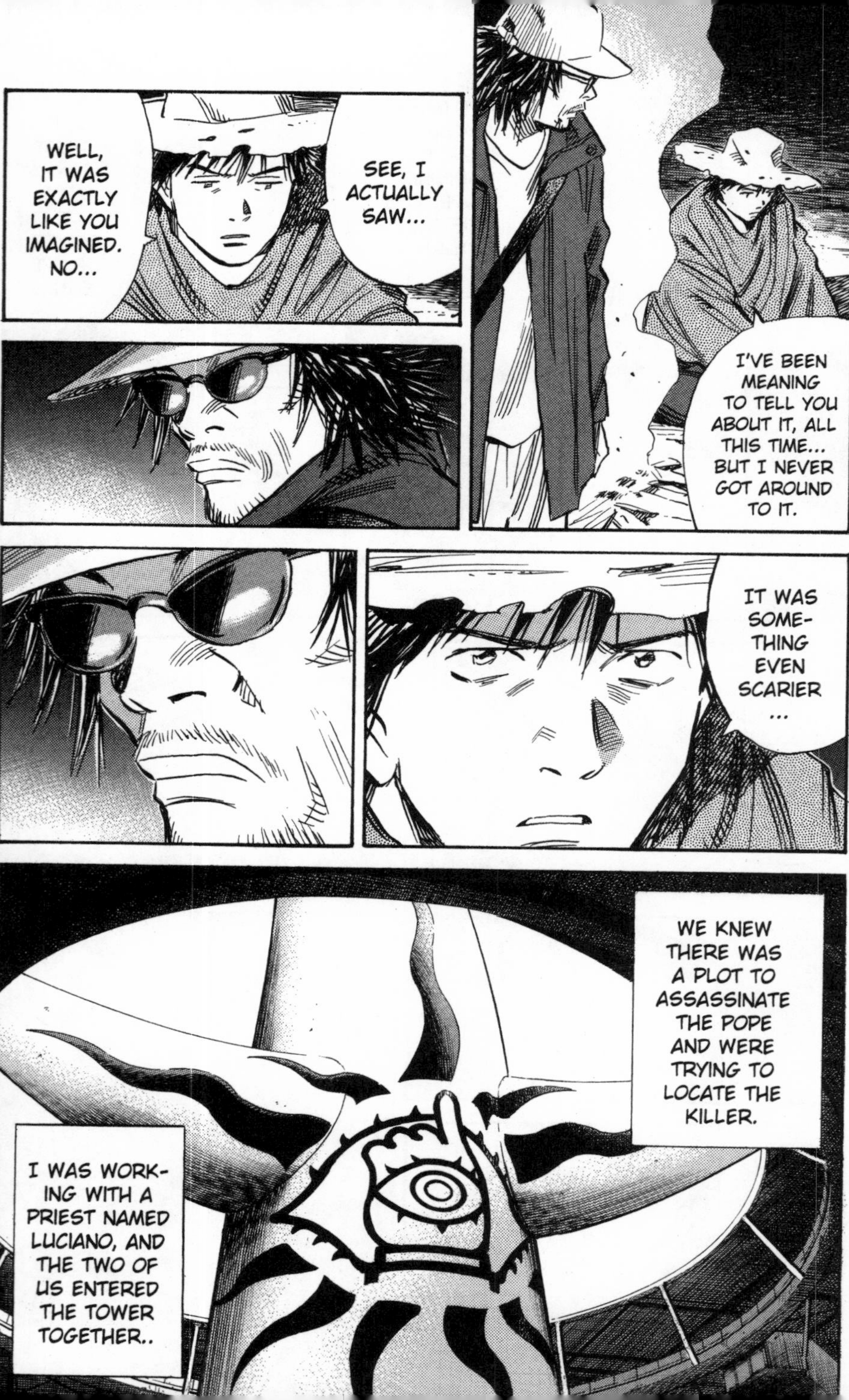
I'VE BEEN MEANING TO TELL YOU ABOUT IT, ALL THIS TIME... BUT I NEVER GOT AROUND TO IT.
SEE, I ACTUALLY SAW...
WELL, IT WAS EXACTLY LIKE YOU IMAGINED. NO...
IT WAS SOME-THING EVEN SCARIER ...
WE KNEW THERE WAS A PLOT TO ASSASSINATE THE POPE AND WERE TRYING TO LOCATE THE KILLER.
I WAS WORK-ING WITH A PRIEST NAMED LUCIANO, AND THE TWO OF US ENTERED THE TOWER TOGETHER..

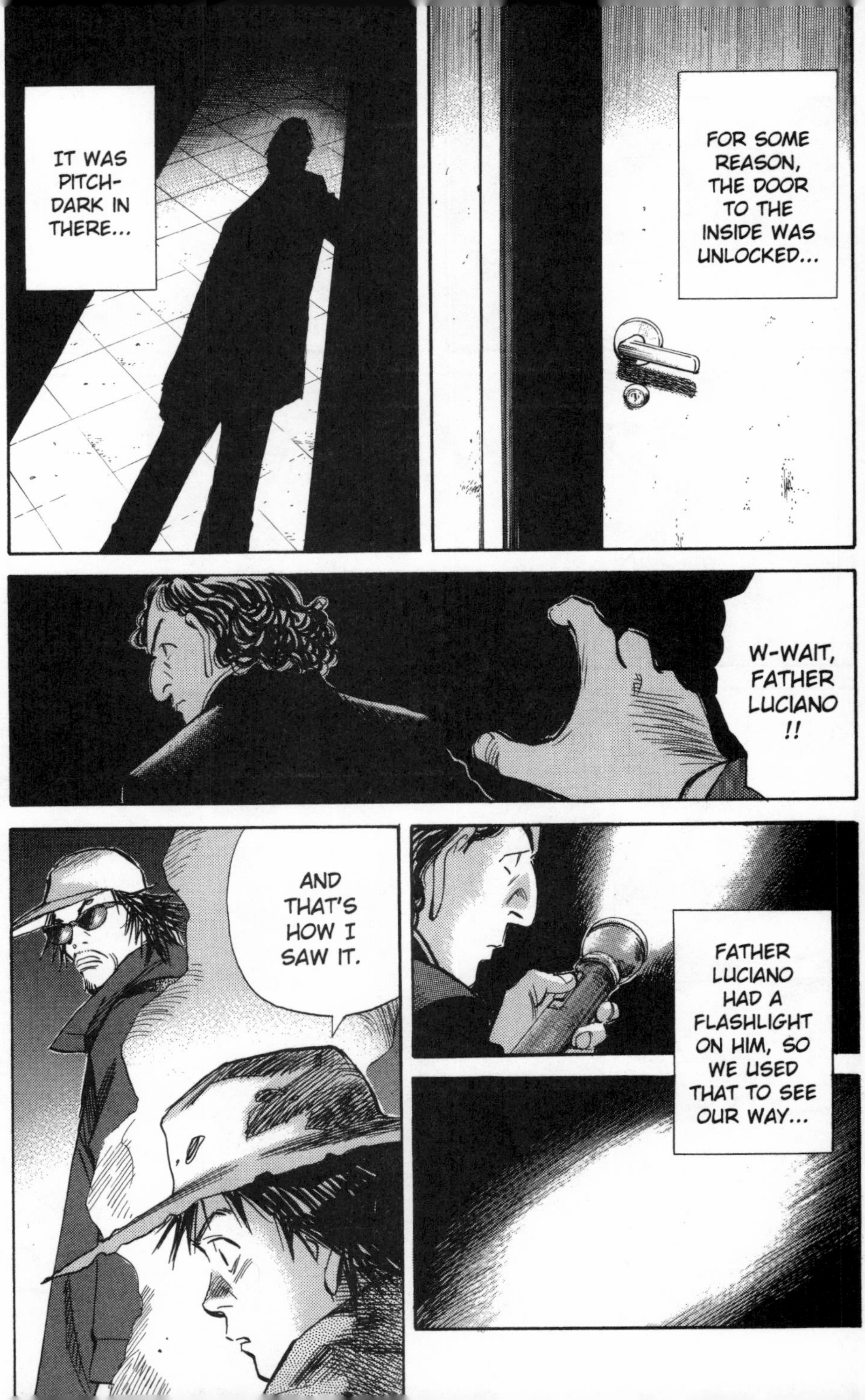
FOR SOME REASON, THE DOOR TO THE INSIDE WAS UNLOCKED...
IT WAS PITCH-DARK IN THERE...
W-WAIT, FATHER LUCIANO !!
FATHER LUCIANO HAD A FLASHLIGHT ON HIM, SO WE USED THAT TO SEE OUR WAY...
AND THAT'S HOW I SAW IT.

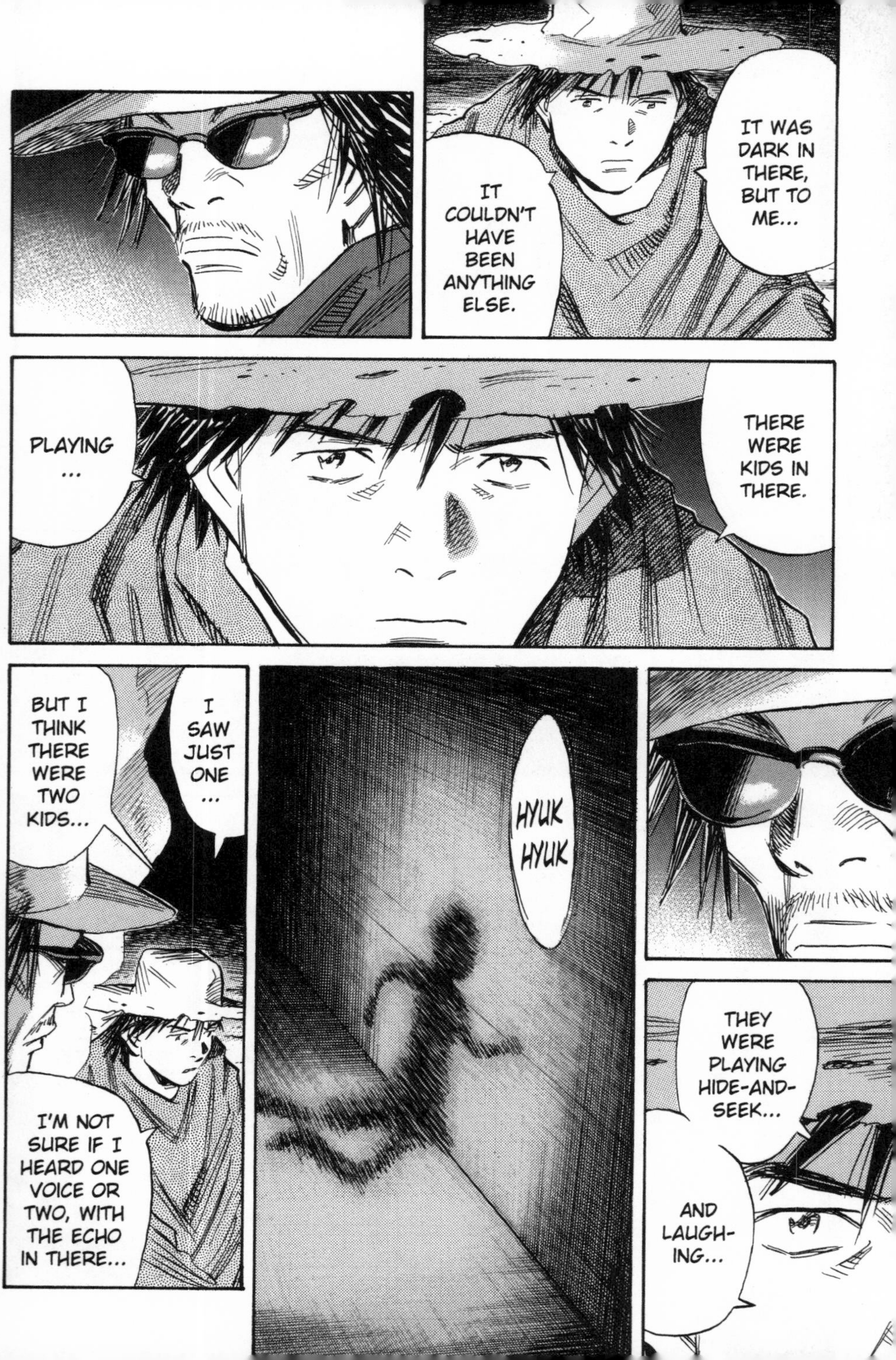
IT WAS DARK IN THERE, BUT TO ME...
IT COULDN'T HAVE BEEN ANYTHING ELSE.
THERE WERE KIDS IN THERE.
PLAYING ...
THEY WERE PLAYING HIDE-AND-SEEK...
AND LAUGH-ING...
HYUK HYUK
I SAW JUST ONE ...
BUT I THINK THERE WERE TWO KIDS...
I'M NOT SURE IF I HEARD ONE VOICE OR TWO, WITH THE ECHO IN THERE...

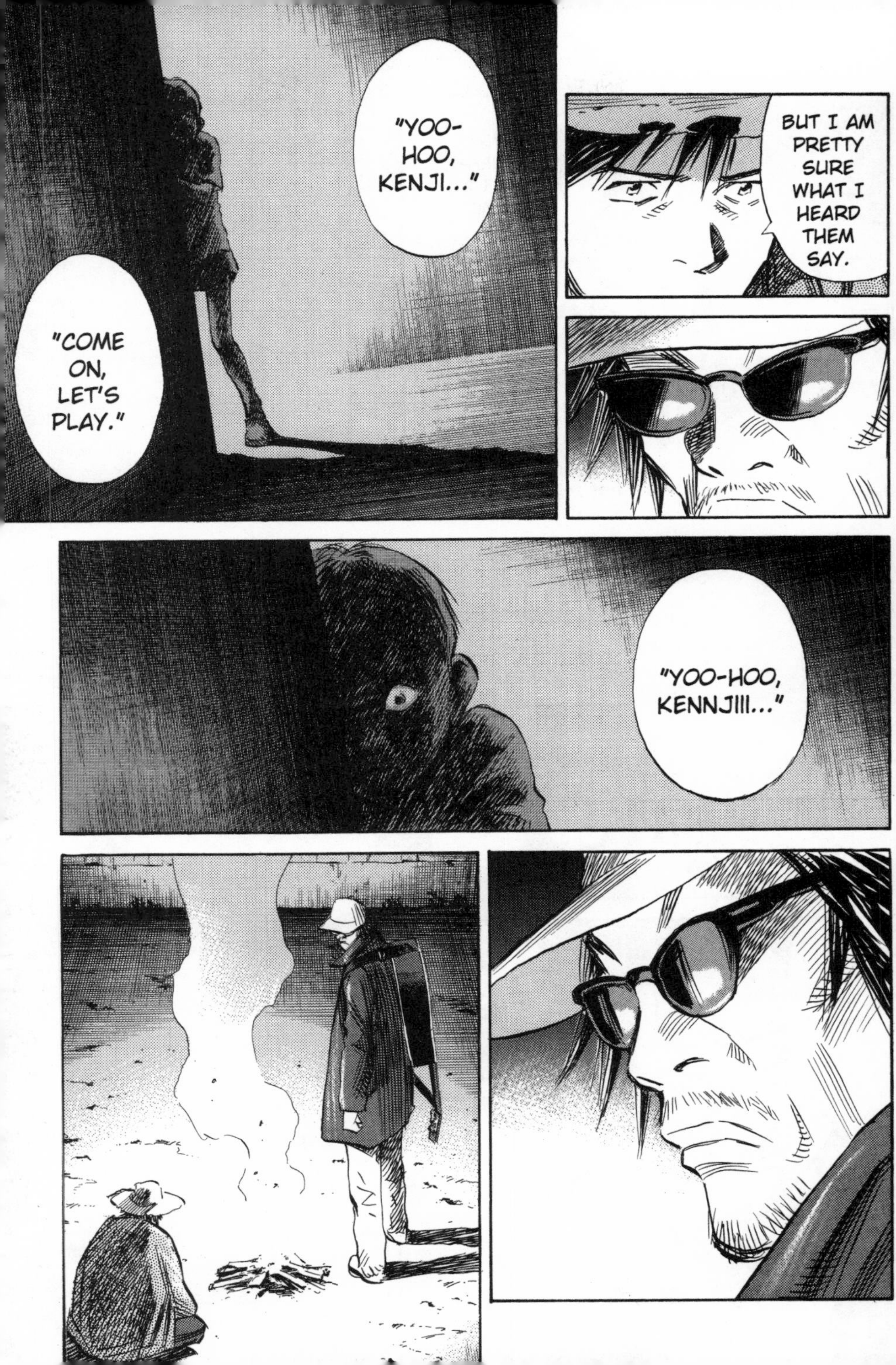
BUT I AM PRETTY SURE WHAT I HEARD THEM SAY.
"YOO-HOO, KENJI..."
"COME ON, LET'S PLAY."
"YOO-HOO, KENNJIII..."

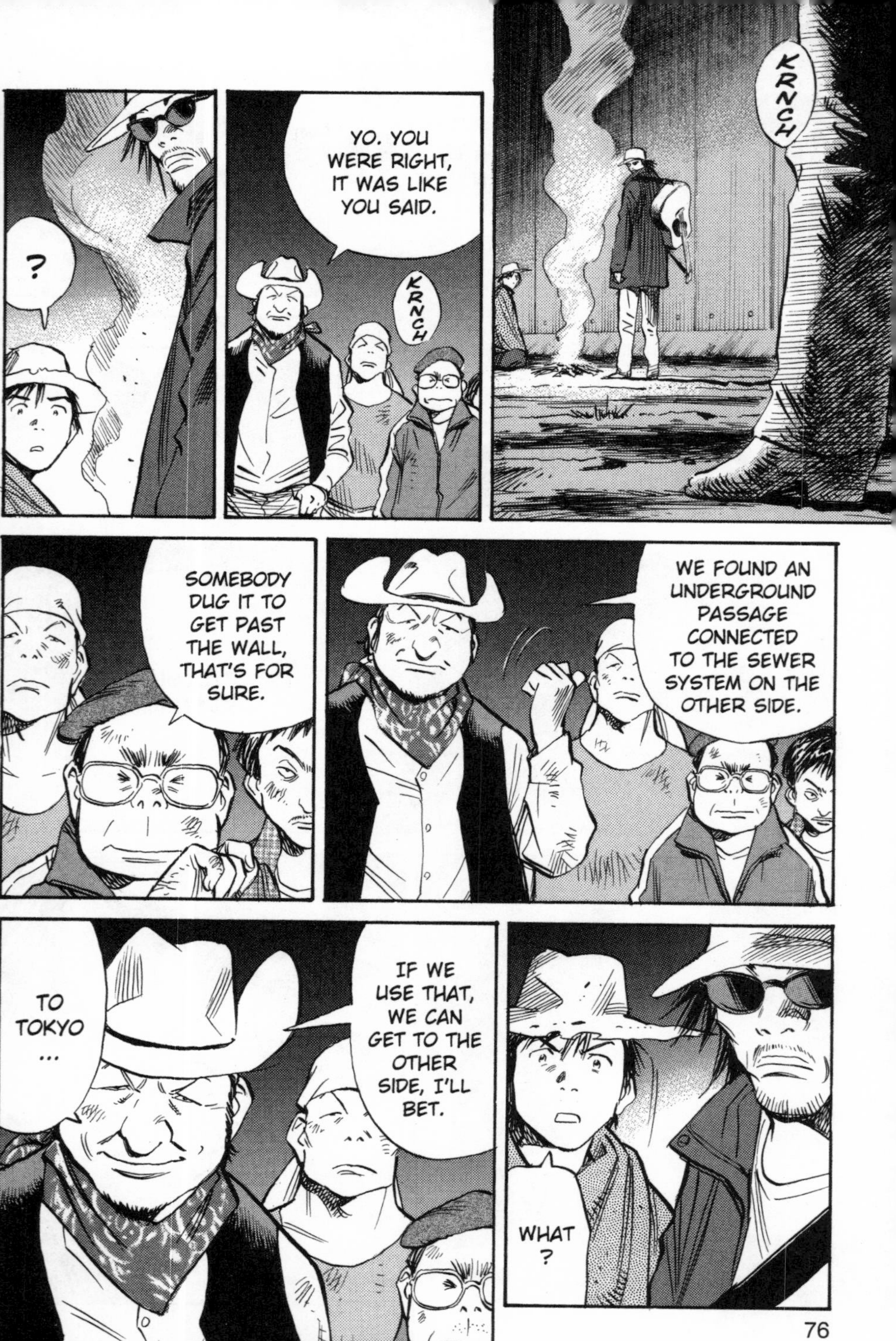
KRNCH
YO. YOU WERE RIGHT, IT WAS LIKE YOU SAID.
KRNCH
?
WE FOUND AN UNDERGROUND PASSAGE CONNECTED TO THE SEWER SYSTEM ON THE OTHER SIDE.
SOMEBODY DUG IT TO GET PAST THE WALL, THAT'S FOR SURE.
WHAT ?
IF WE USE THAT, WE CAN GET TO THE OTHER SIDE, I'LL BET.
TO TOKYO ...

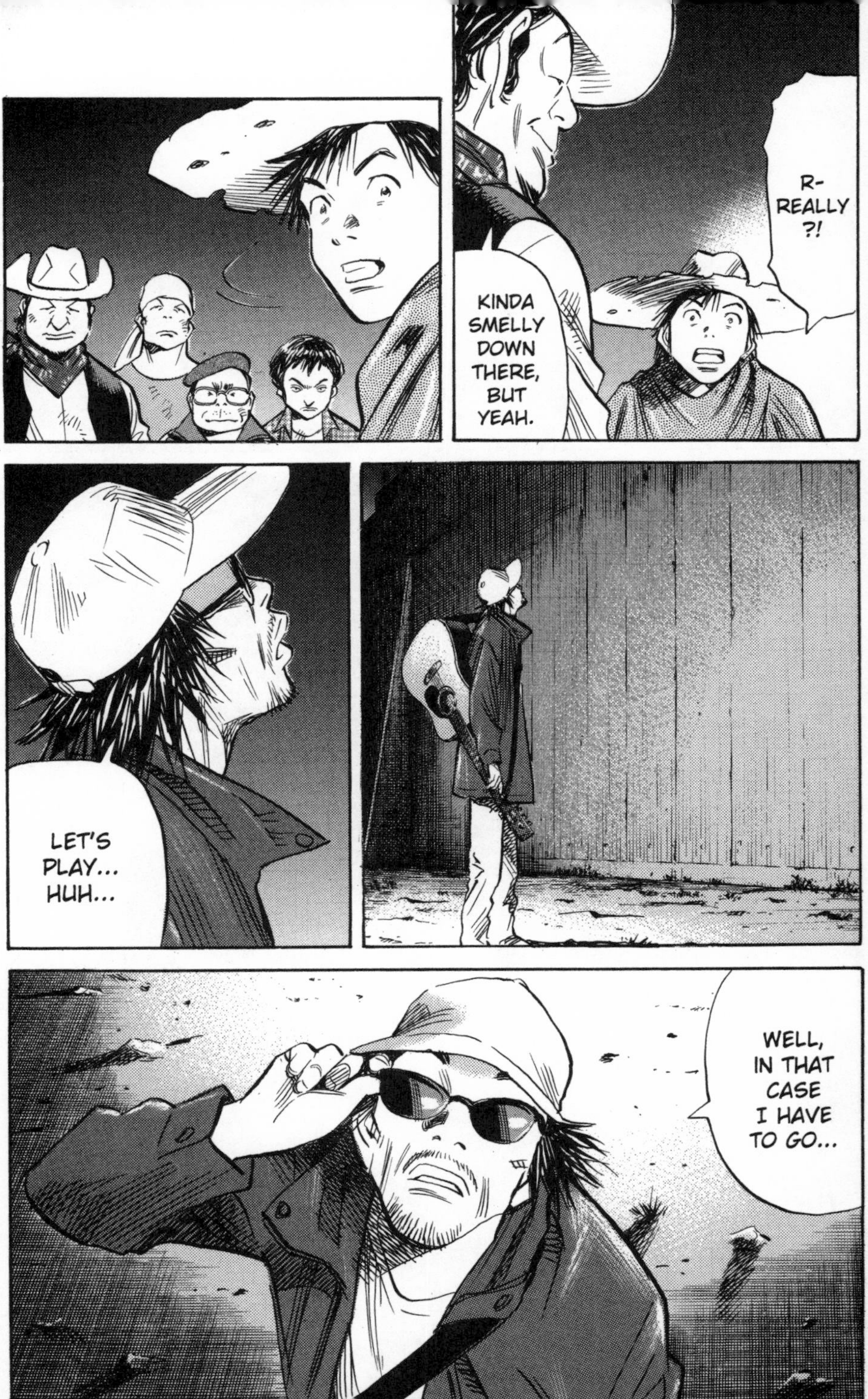
R-REALLY?!
KINDA SMELLY DOWN THERE, BUT YEAH.
LET'S PLAY... HUH...
WELL, IN THAT CASE I HAVE TO GO...

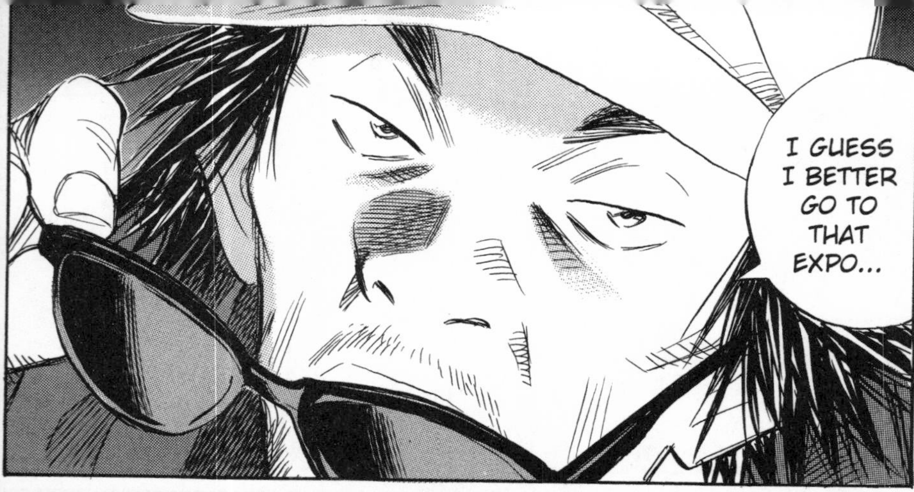
I GUESS I BETTER GO TO THAT EXPO...
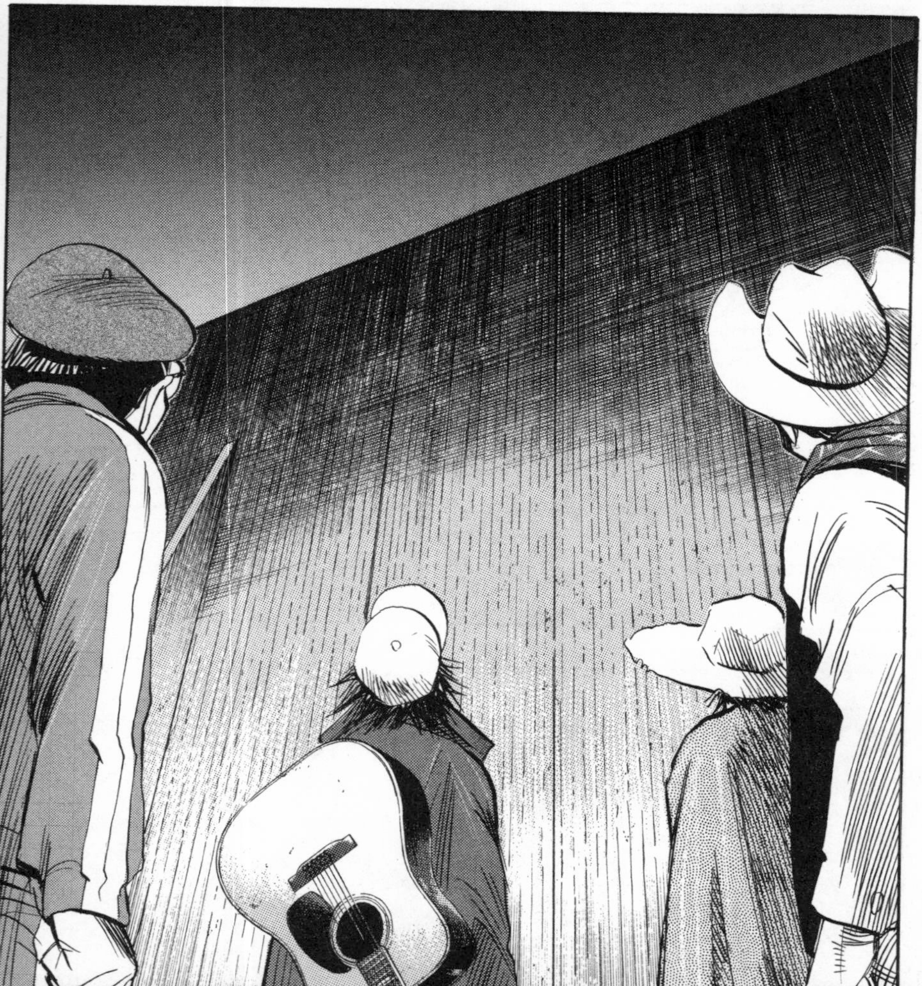

Chapter 5 Arrival of the Space Aliens

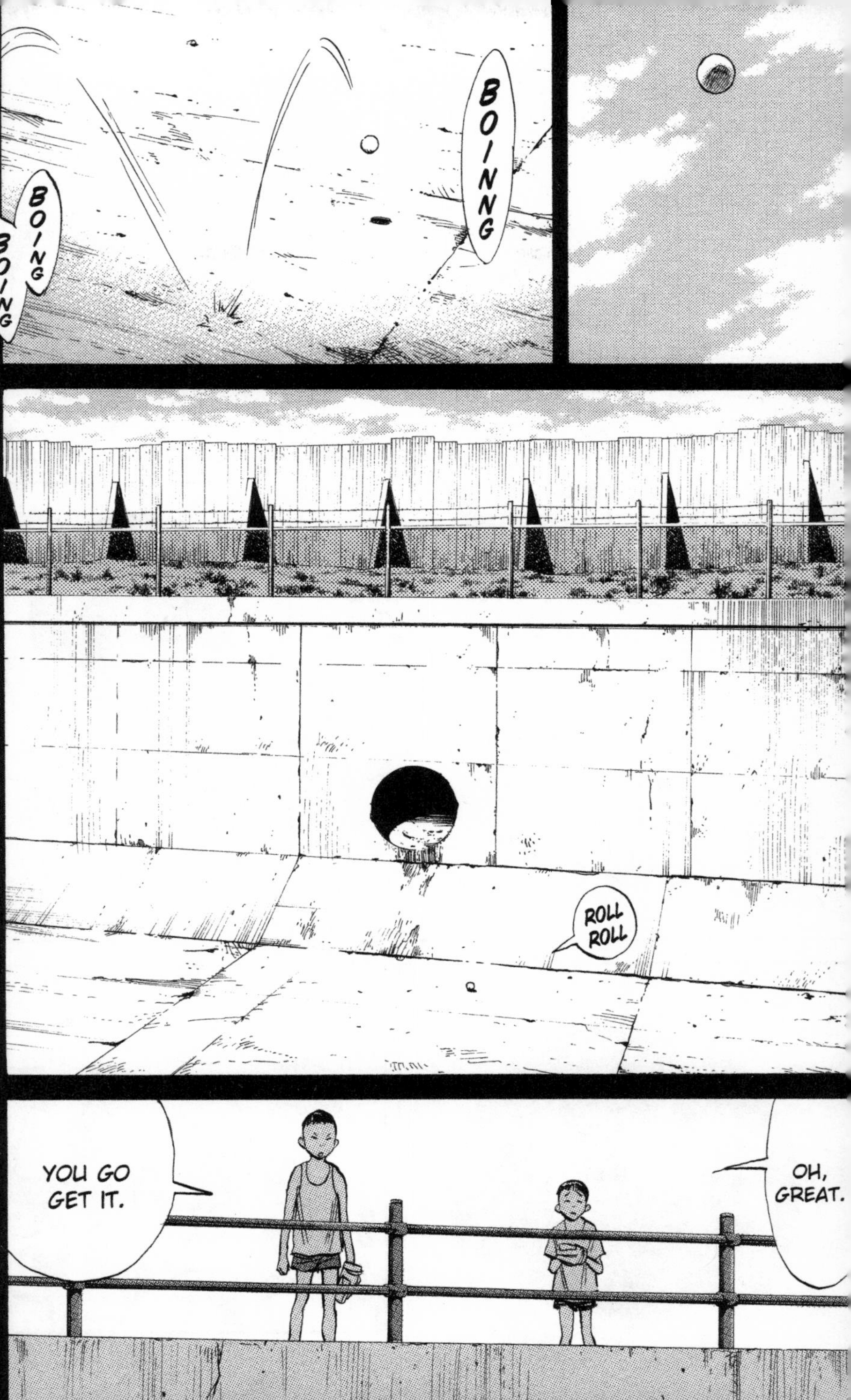
BOINNG
BOING
BOING
ROLL ROLL
OH, GREAT.
YOU GO GET IT.

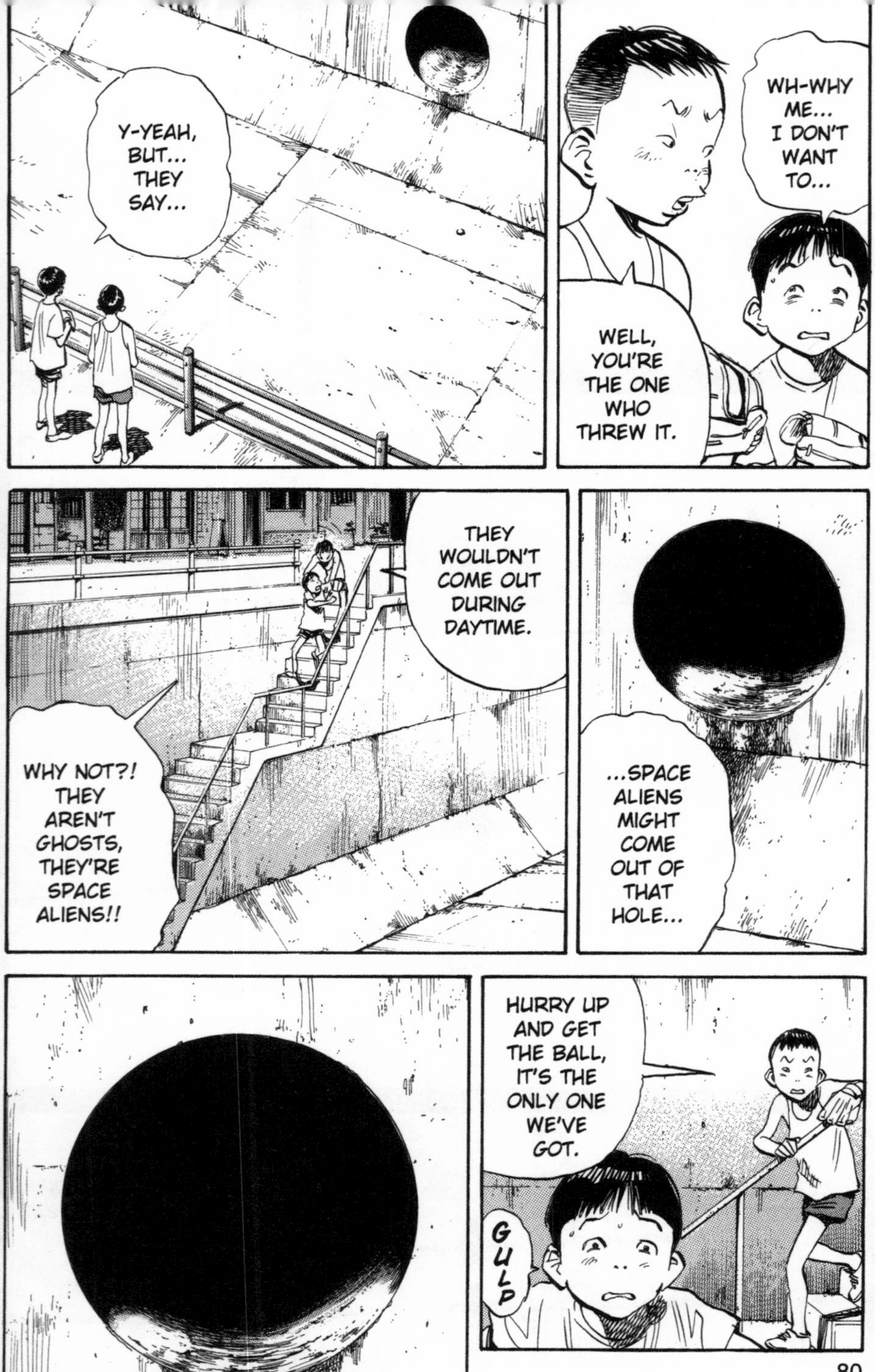
WH-WHY ME... I DON'T WANT TO...
WELL, YOU'RE THE ONE WHO THREW IT.
Y-YEAH, BUT... THEY SAY...
...SPACE ALIENS MIGHT COME OUT OF THAT HOLE...
THEY WOULDN'T COME OUT DURING DAYTIME.
WHY NOT?! THEY AREN'T GHOSTS, THEY'RE SPACE ALIENS!!
HURRY UP AND GET THE BALL, IT'S THE ONLY ONE WE'VE GOT.
GULP

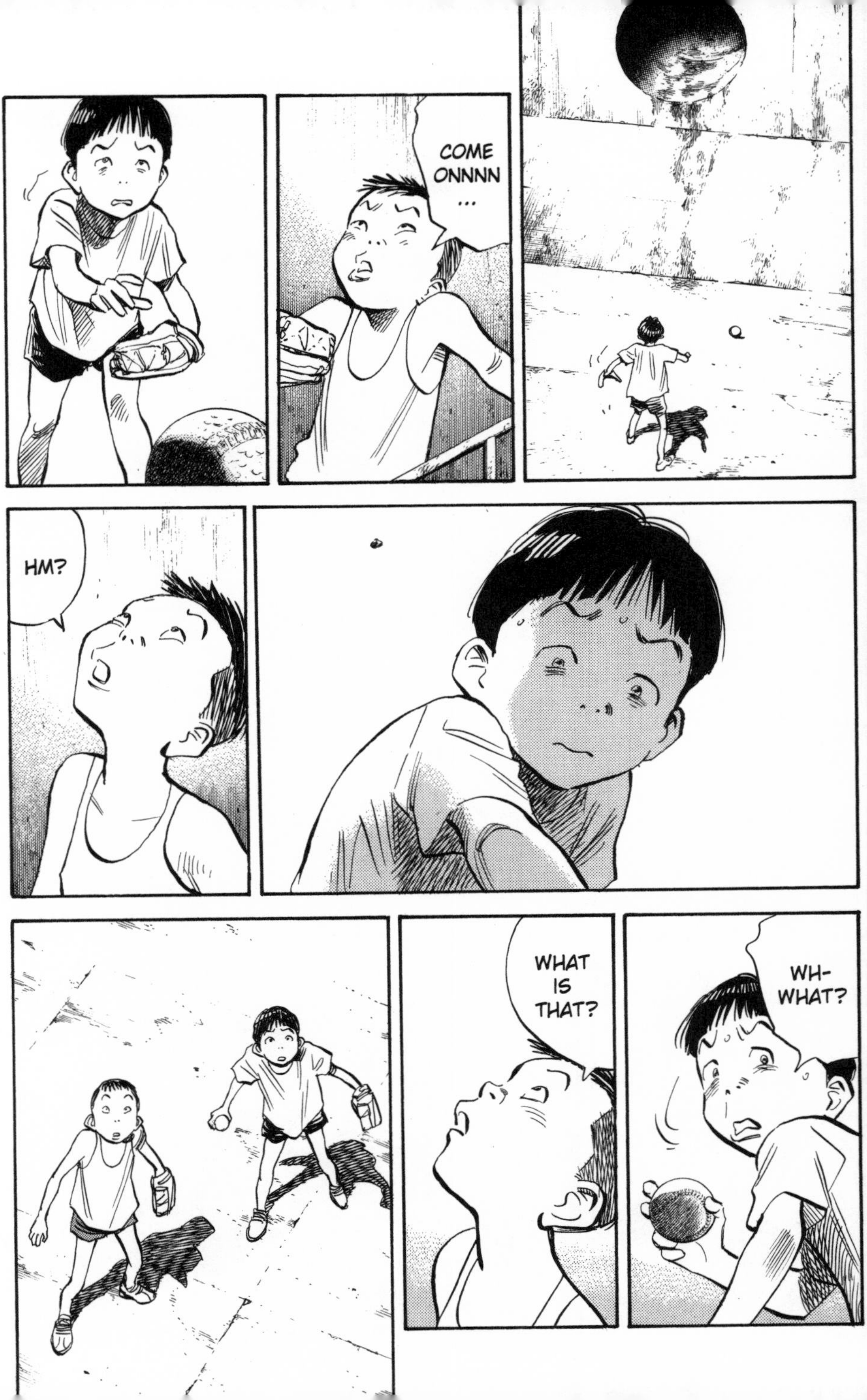
COME ONNNN ...
HM?
WH- WHAT?
WHAT IS THAT?

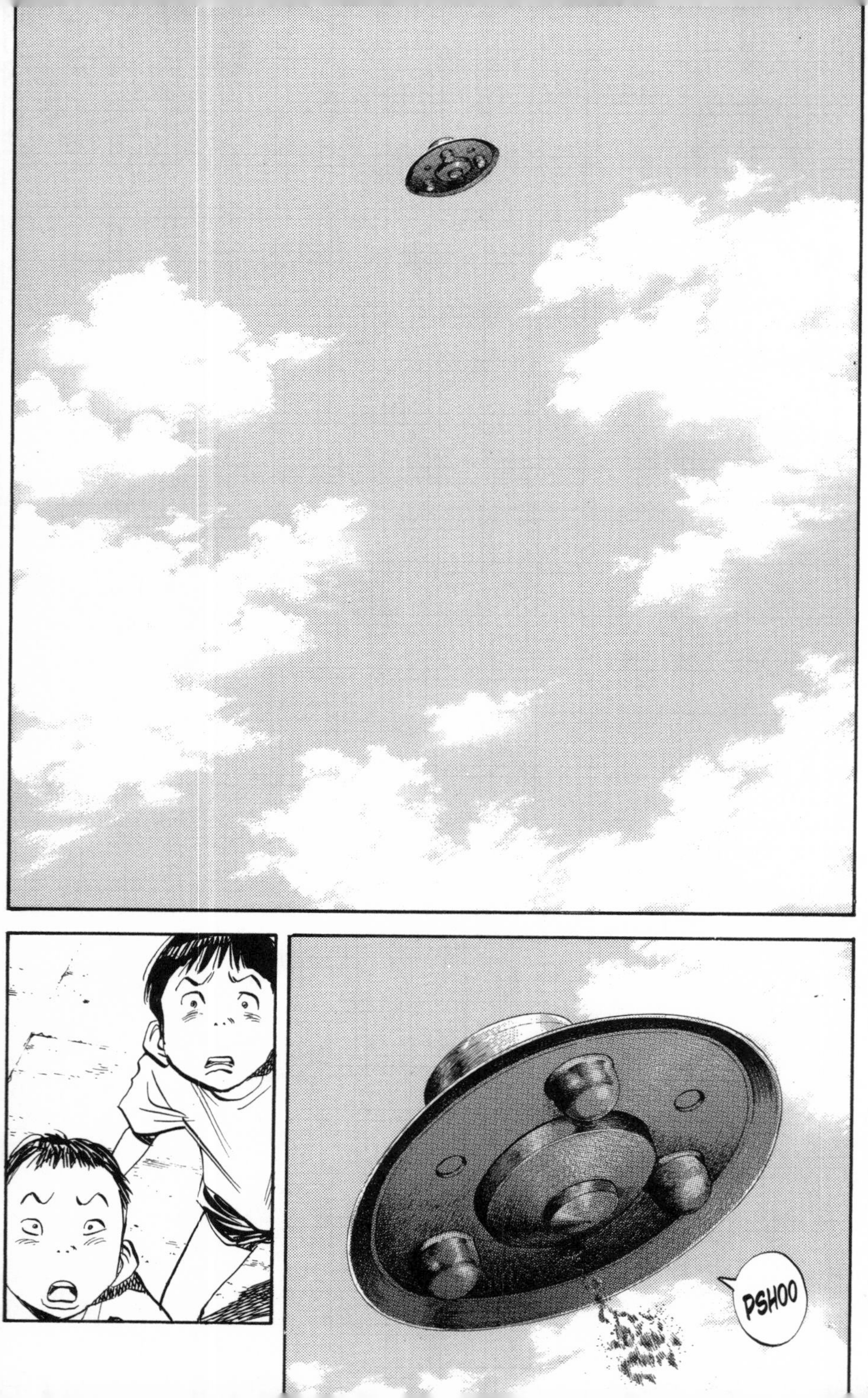
PSHOO

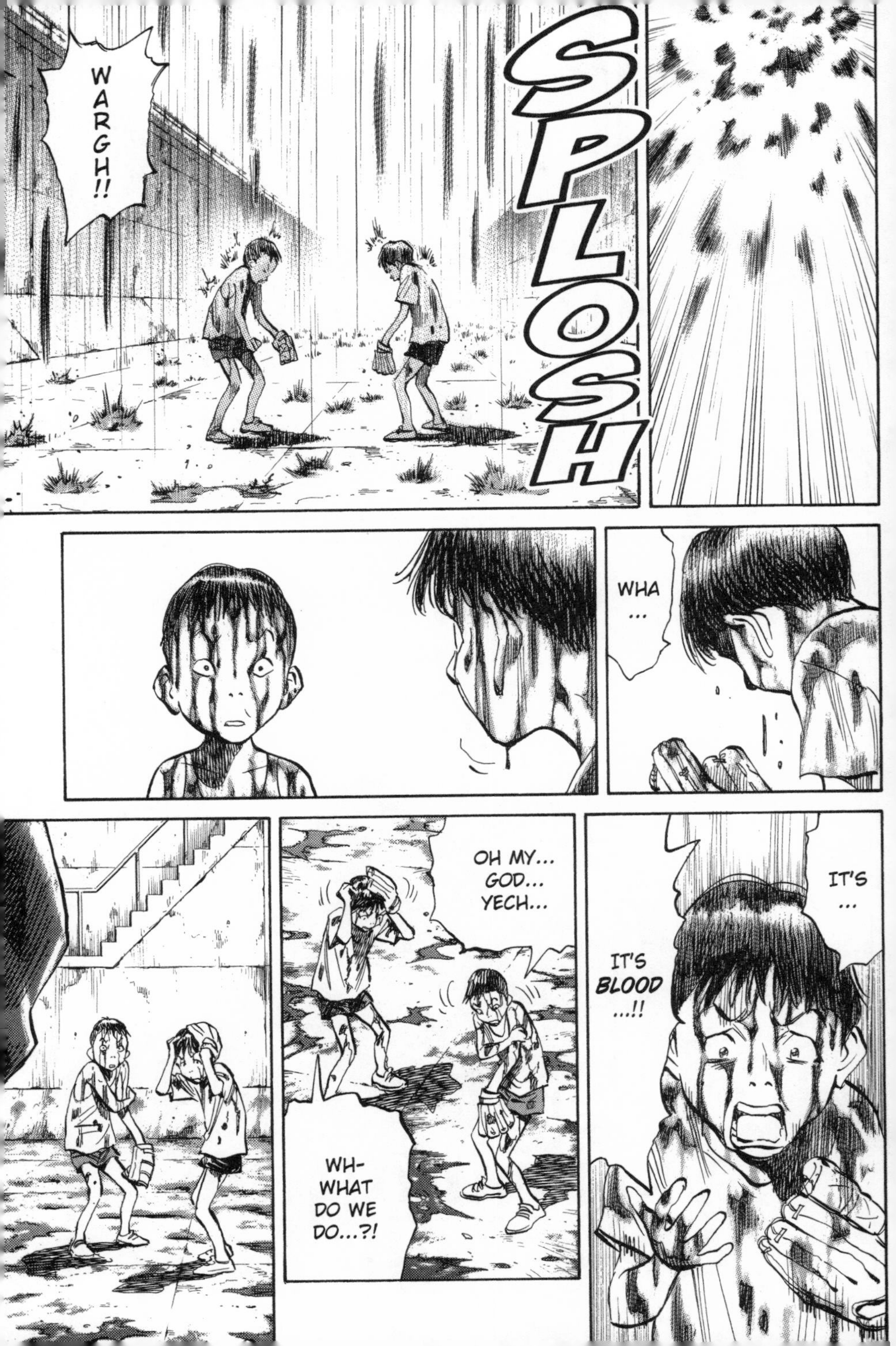
SPLOSH
WARGH!!
WHA...
IT'S...
IT'S BLOOD...!!
OH MY... GOD... YECH...
WH- WHAT DO WE DO...?!

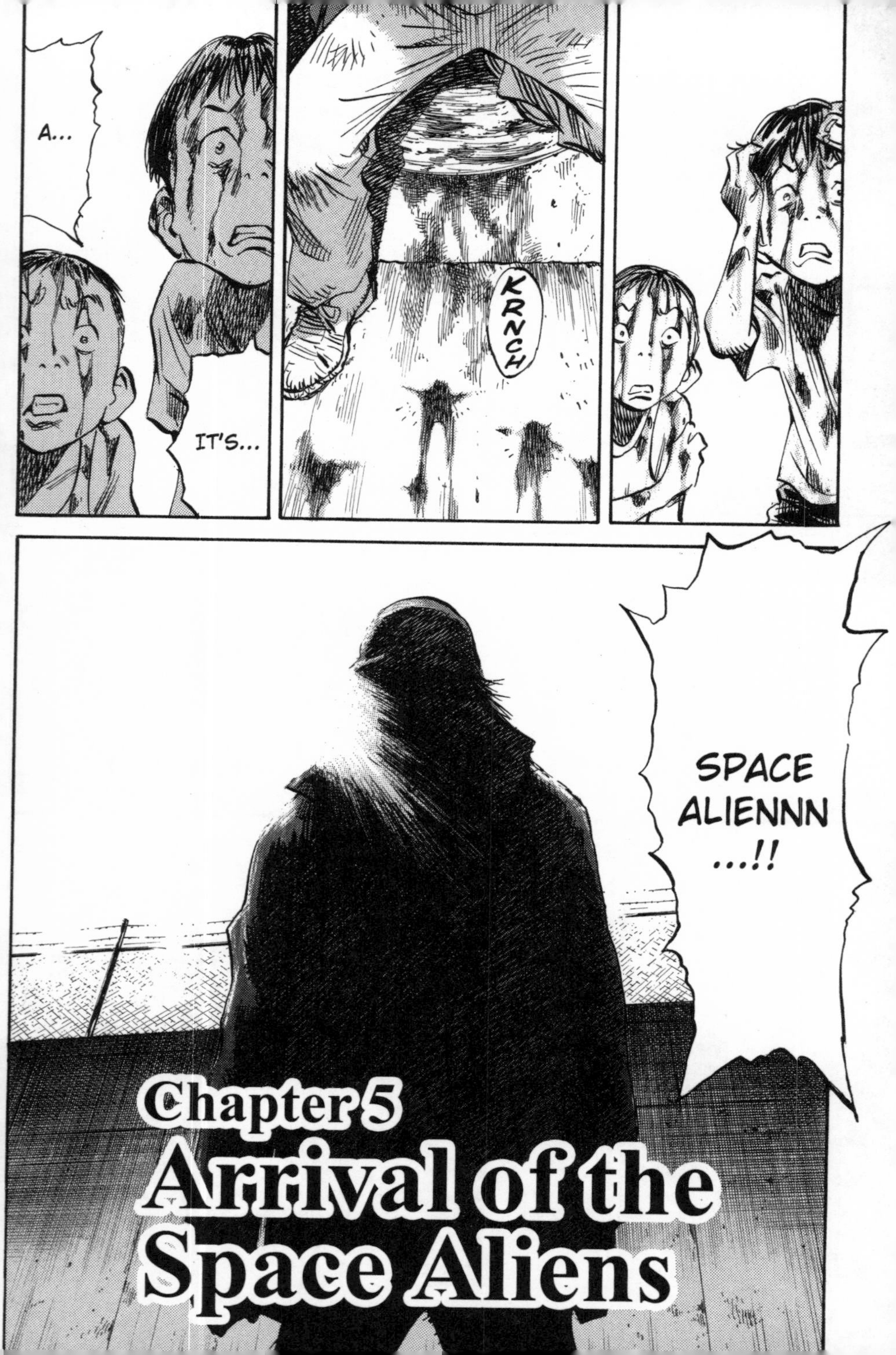
KRNCH
A...
IT'S...
SPACE ALIENNN ...!!

Chapter 5
Arrival of the Space Aliens

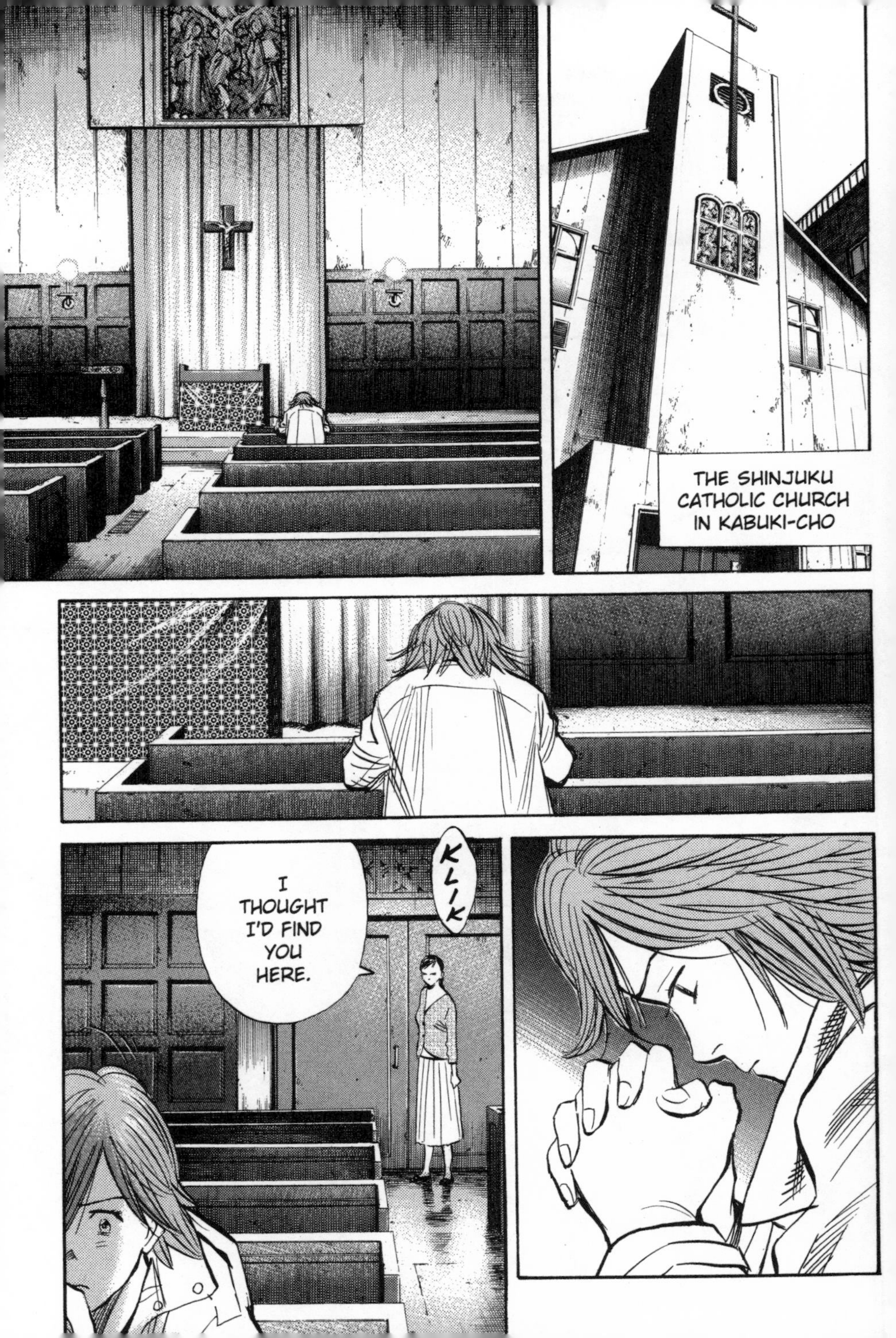
THE SHINJUKU CATHOLIC CHURCH IN KABUKI-CHO
KLIK
I THOUGHT I'D FIND YOU HERE.

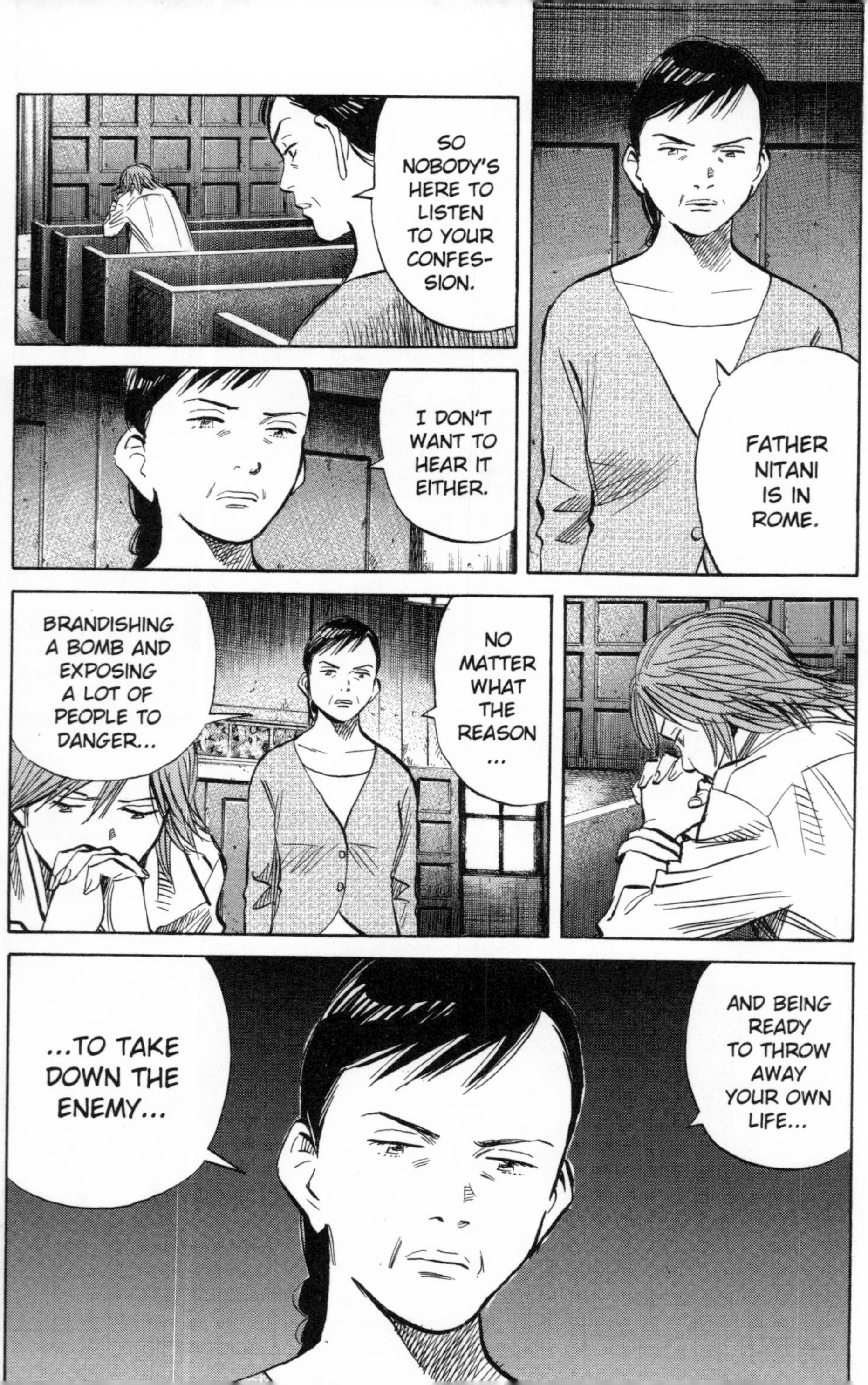
FATHER NITANI IS IN ROME.
SO NOBODY'S HERE TO LISTEN TO YOUR CONFES-SION.
I DON'T WANT TO HEAR IT EITHER.
NO MATTER WHAT THE REASON ...
BRANDISHING A BOMB AND EXPOSING A LOT OF PEOPLE TO DANGER...
AND BEING READY TO THROW AWAY YOUR OWN LIFE...
...TO TAKE DOWN THE ENEMY...

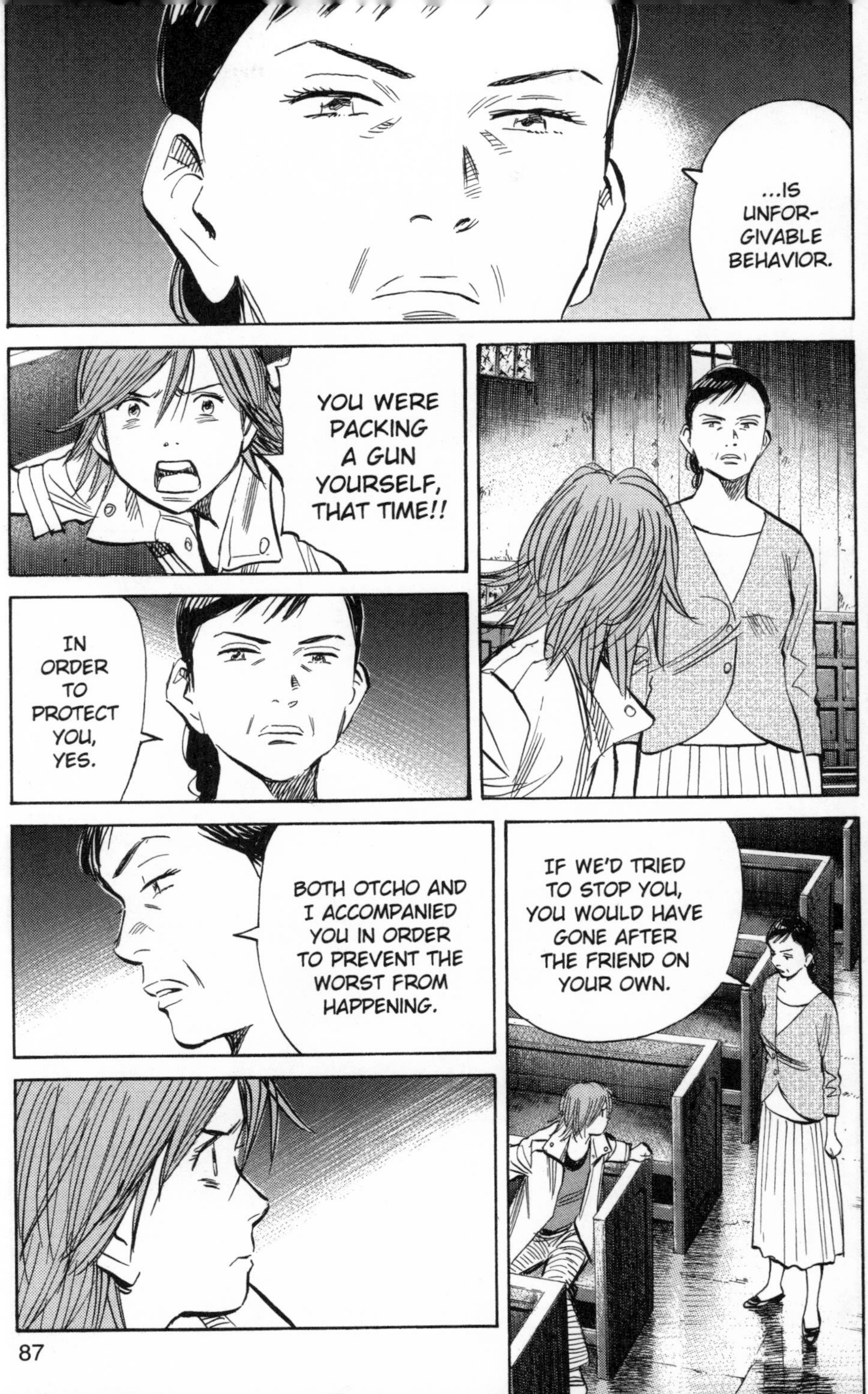
...IS UNFORGIVABLE BEHAVIOR.
YOU WERE PACKING A GUN YOURSELF, THAT TIME!!
IN ORDER TO PROTECT YOU, YES.
IF WE'D TRIED TO STOP YOU, YOU WOULD HAVE GONE AFTER THE FRIEND ON YOUR OWN.
BOTH OTCHO AND I ACCOMPANIED YOU IN ORDER TO PREVENT THE WORST FROM HAPPENING.

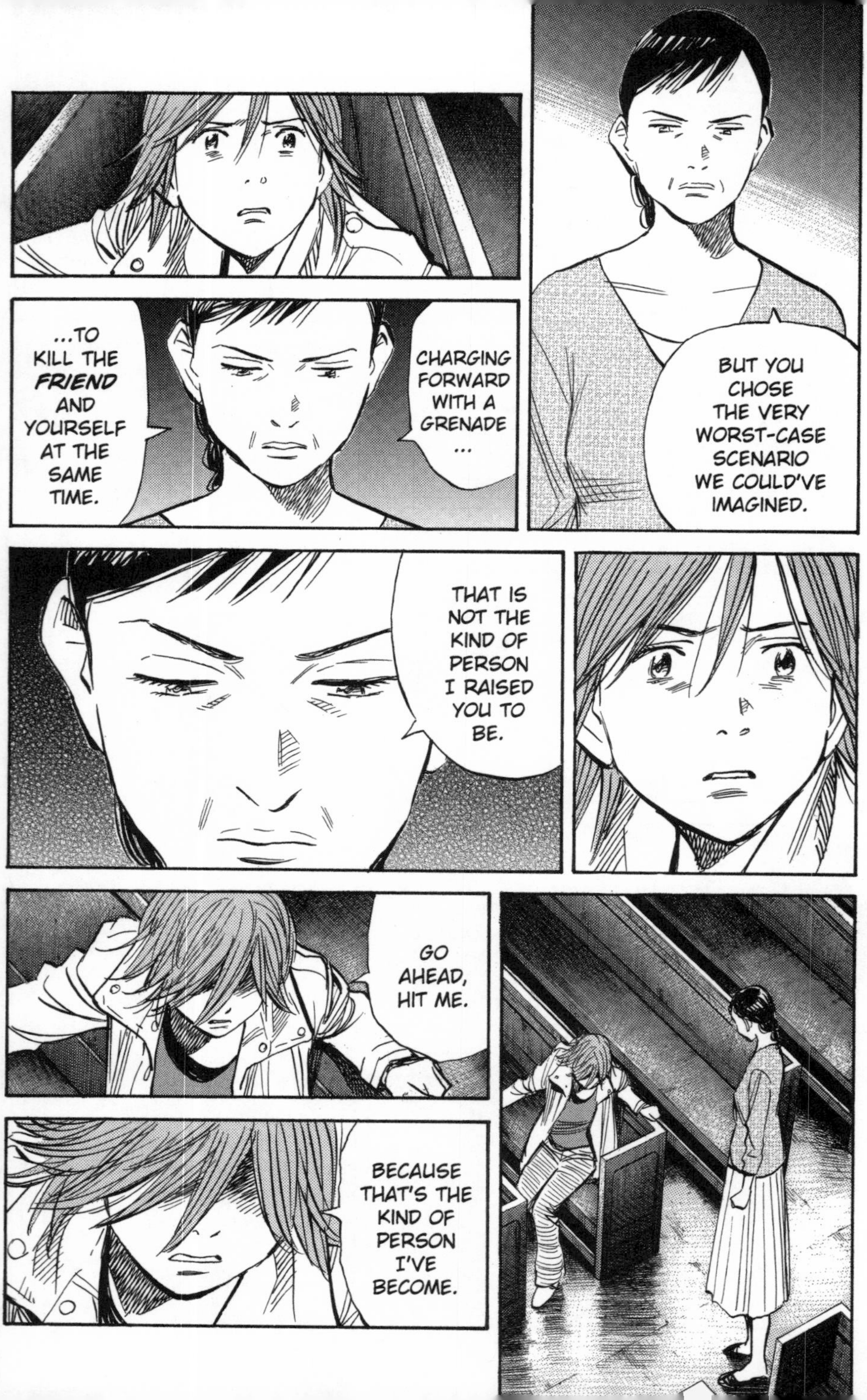
BUT YOU CHOSE THE VERY WORST-CASE SCENARIO WE COULD'VE IMAGINED.
CHARGING FORWARD WITH A GRENADE ...
...TO KILL THE *FRIEND* AND YOURSELF AT THE SAME TIME.
THAT IS NOT THE KIND OF PERSON I RAISED YOU TO BE.
GO AHEAD, HIT ME.
BECAUSE THAT'S THE KIND OF PERSON I'VE BECOME.

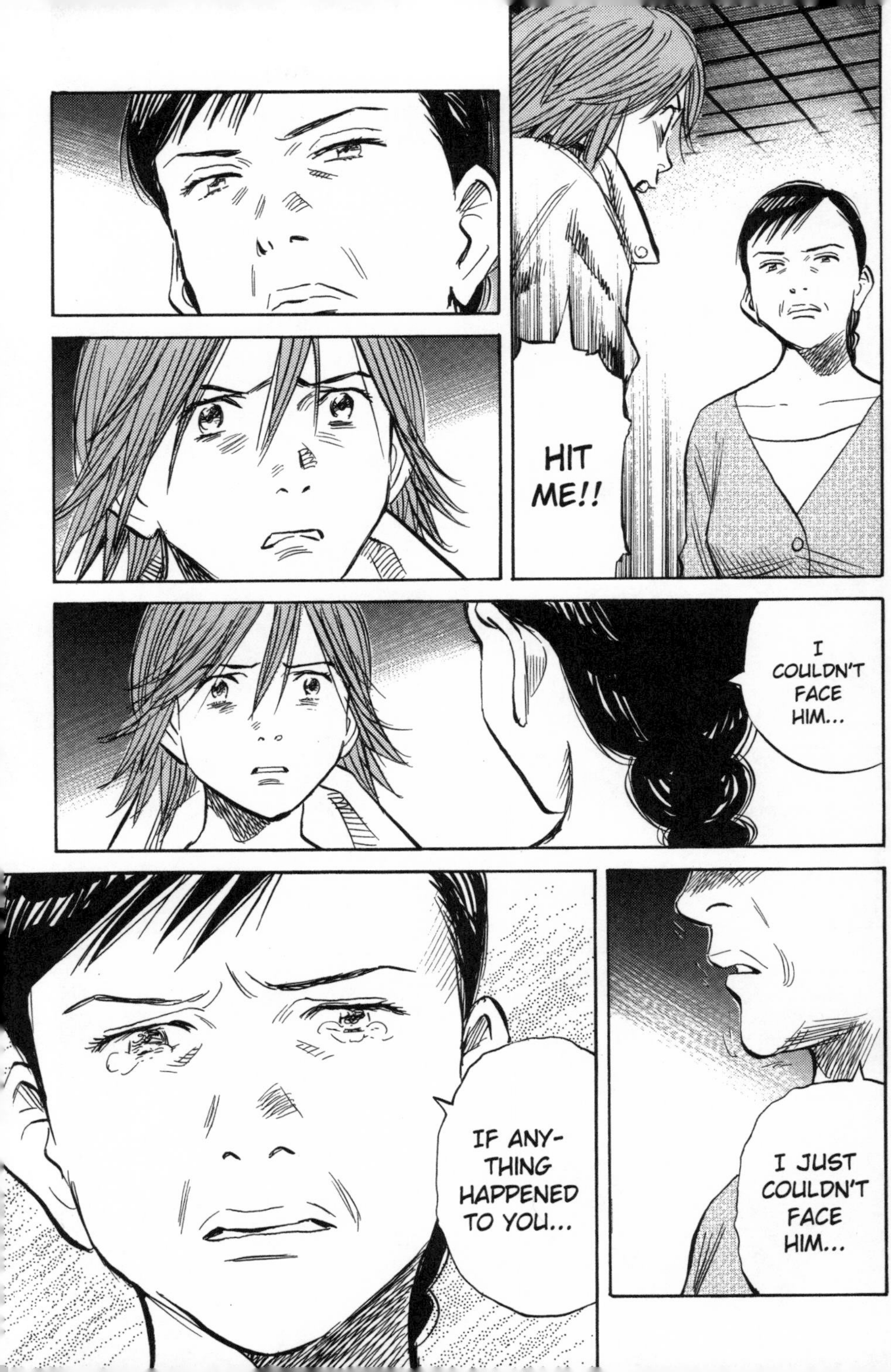
HIT ME!!
I COULDN'T FACE HIM...
I JUST COULDN'T FACE HIM...
IF ANY-THING HAPPENED TO YOU...

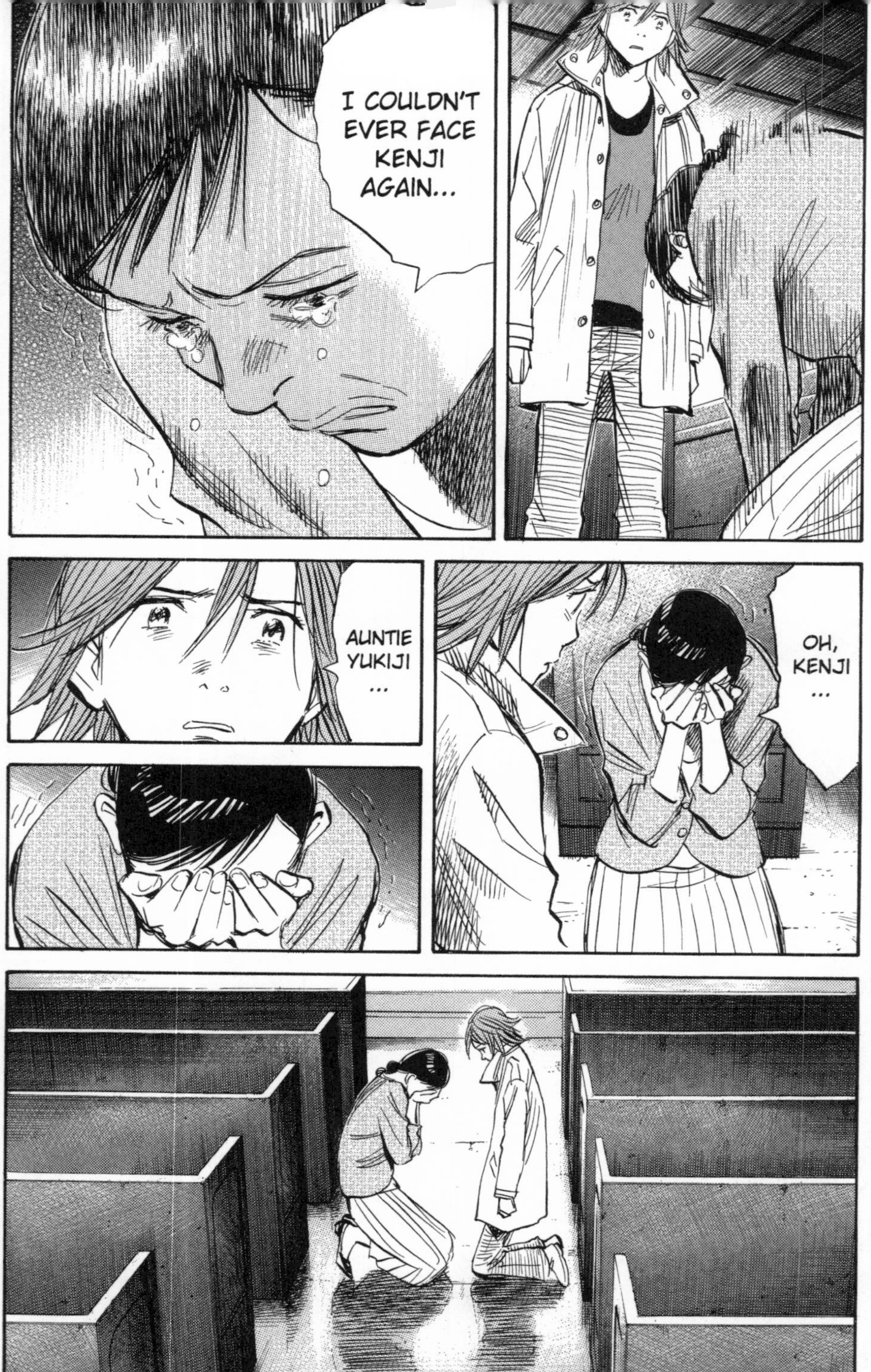
I COULDN'T EVER FACE KENJI AGAIN...
OH, KENJI ...
AUNTIE YUKIJI ...

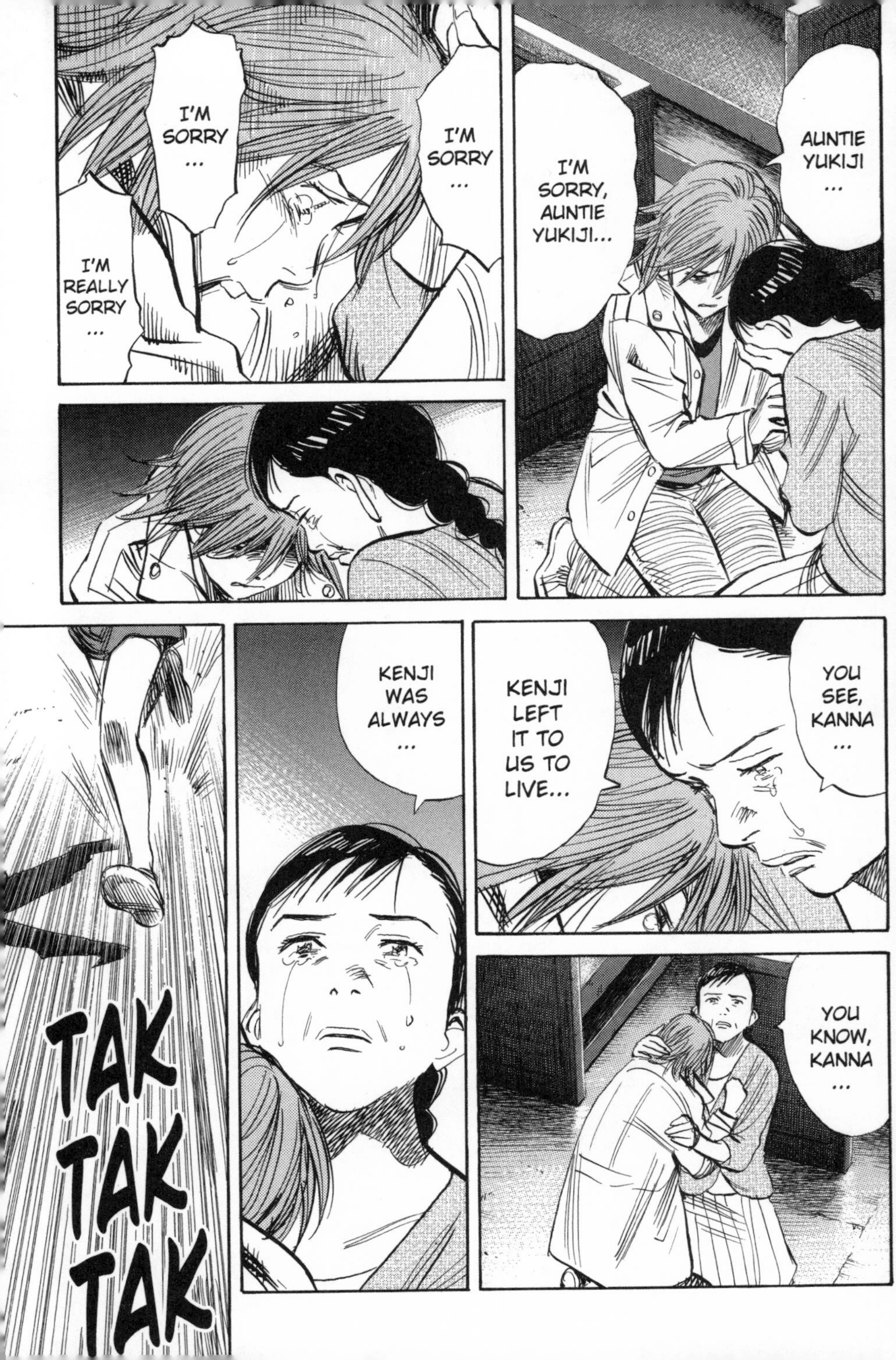
AUNTIE YUKIJI ...
I'M SORRY, AUNTIE YUKIJI...
I'M SORRY ...
I'M SORRY ...
I'M REALLY SORRY ...
YOU SEE, KANNA ...
KENJI LEFT IT TO US TO LIVE...
YOU KNOW, KANNA ...
KENJI WAS ALWAYS ...
TAK TAK TAK

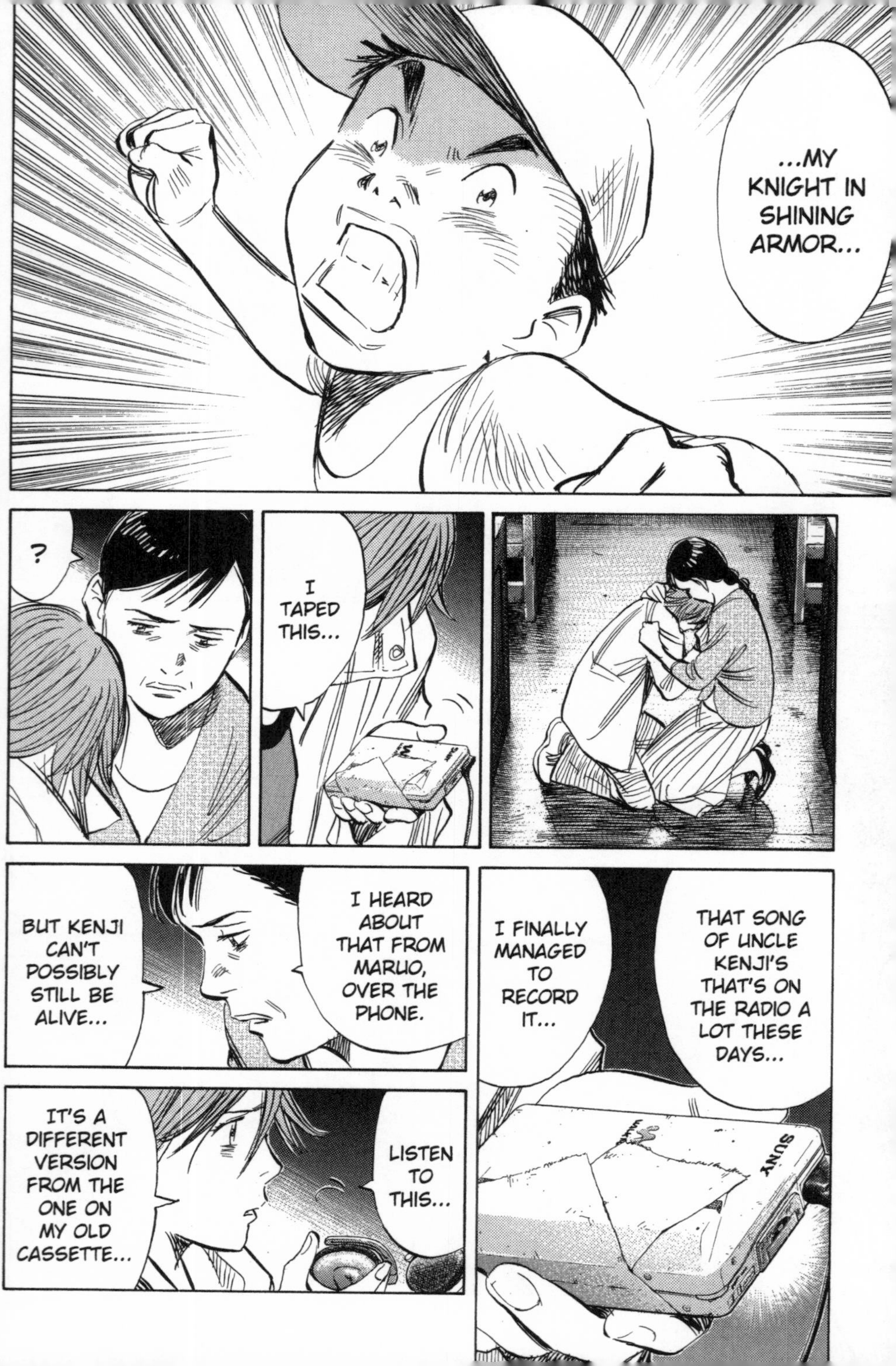
...MY KNIGHT IN SHINING ARMOR...
I TAPED THIS...
?
THAT SONG OF UNCLE KENJI'S THAT'S ON THE RADIO A LOT THESE DAYS...
I FINALLY MANAGED TO RECORD IT...
SUNY
I HEARD ABOUT THAT FROM MARUO, OVER THE PHONE.
BUT KENJI CAN'T POSSIBLY STILL BE ALIVE...
LISTEN TO THIS...
IT'S A DIFFERENT VERSION FROM THE ONE ON MY OLD CASSETTE...

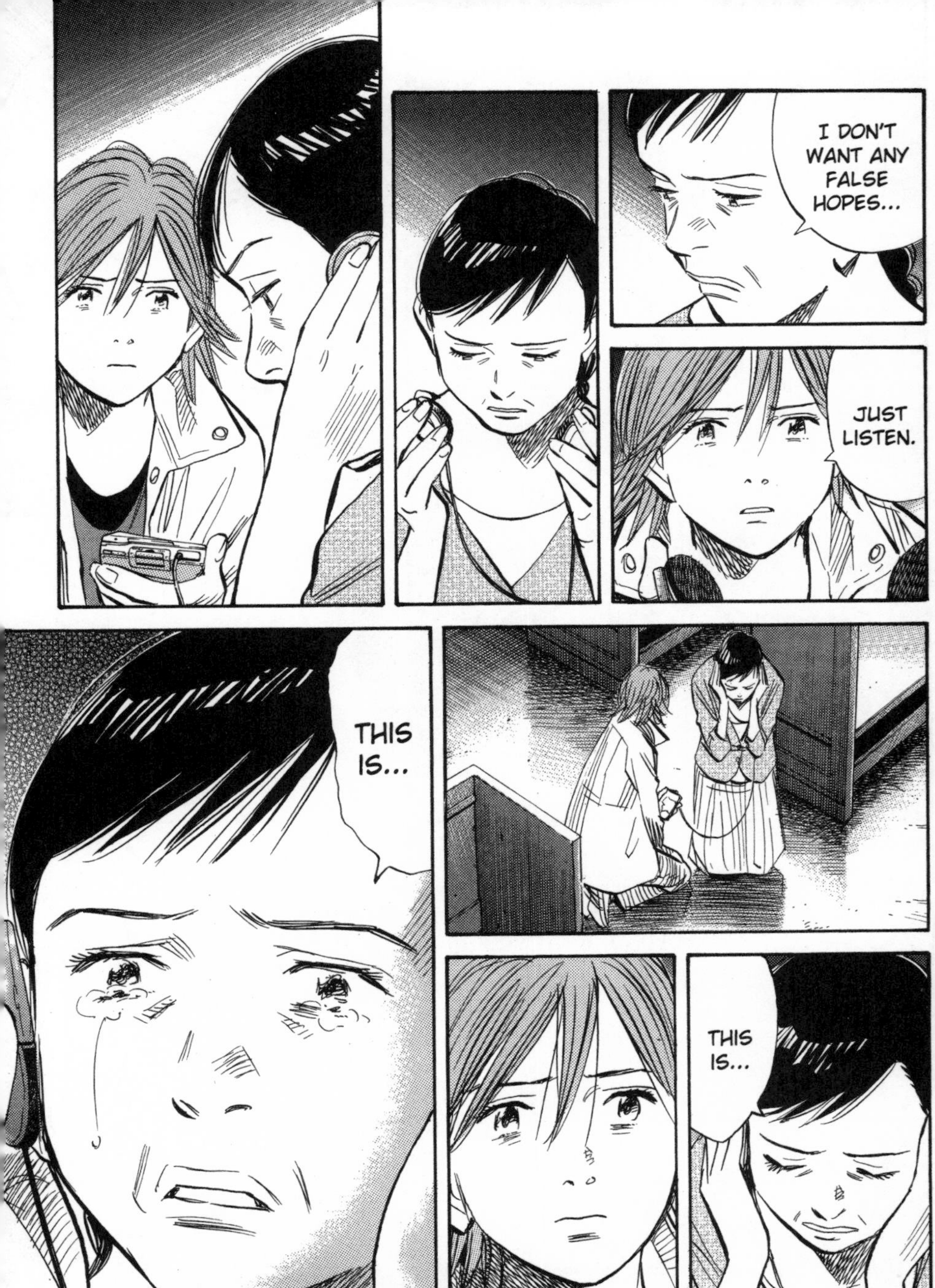
I DON'T WANT ANY FALSE HOPES...
JUST LISTEN.
THIS IS...
THIS IS...

KENJI'S
VOICE...

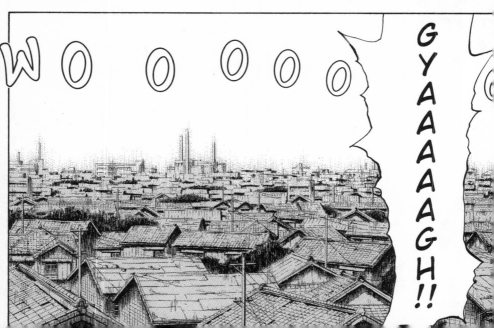

WOOOOO GYAAAAGH!!

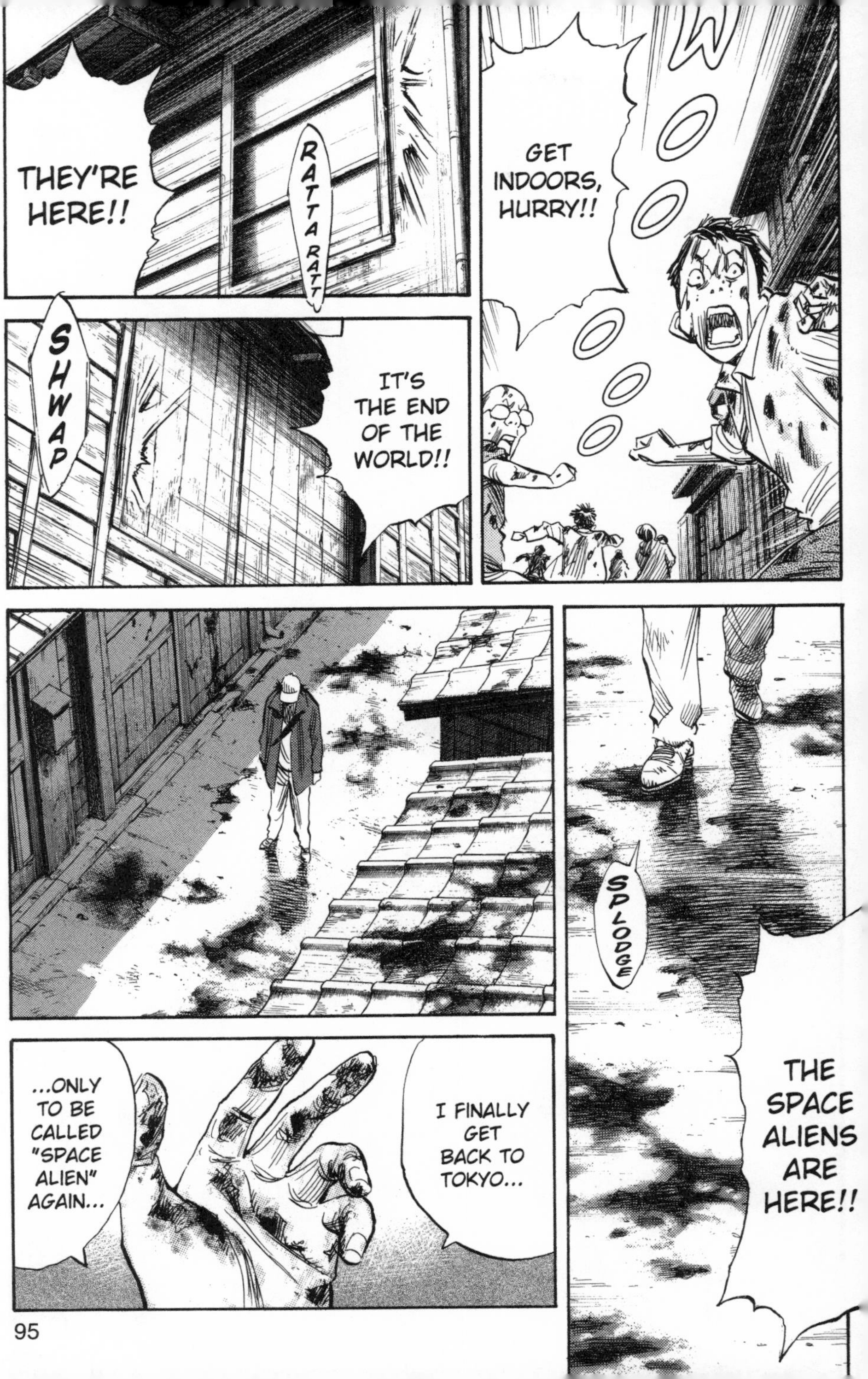
WOOOOOO
GET INDOORS, HURRY!!
THEY'RE HERE!!
RATTA RATT
SHWAP
IT'S THE END OF THE WORLD!!
SPLODGE
THE SPACE ALIENS ARE HERE!!
I FINALLY GET BACK TO TOKYO...
...ONLY TO BE CALLED "SPACE ALIEN" AGAIN...

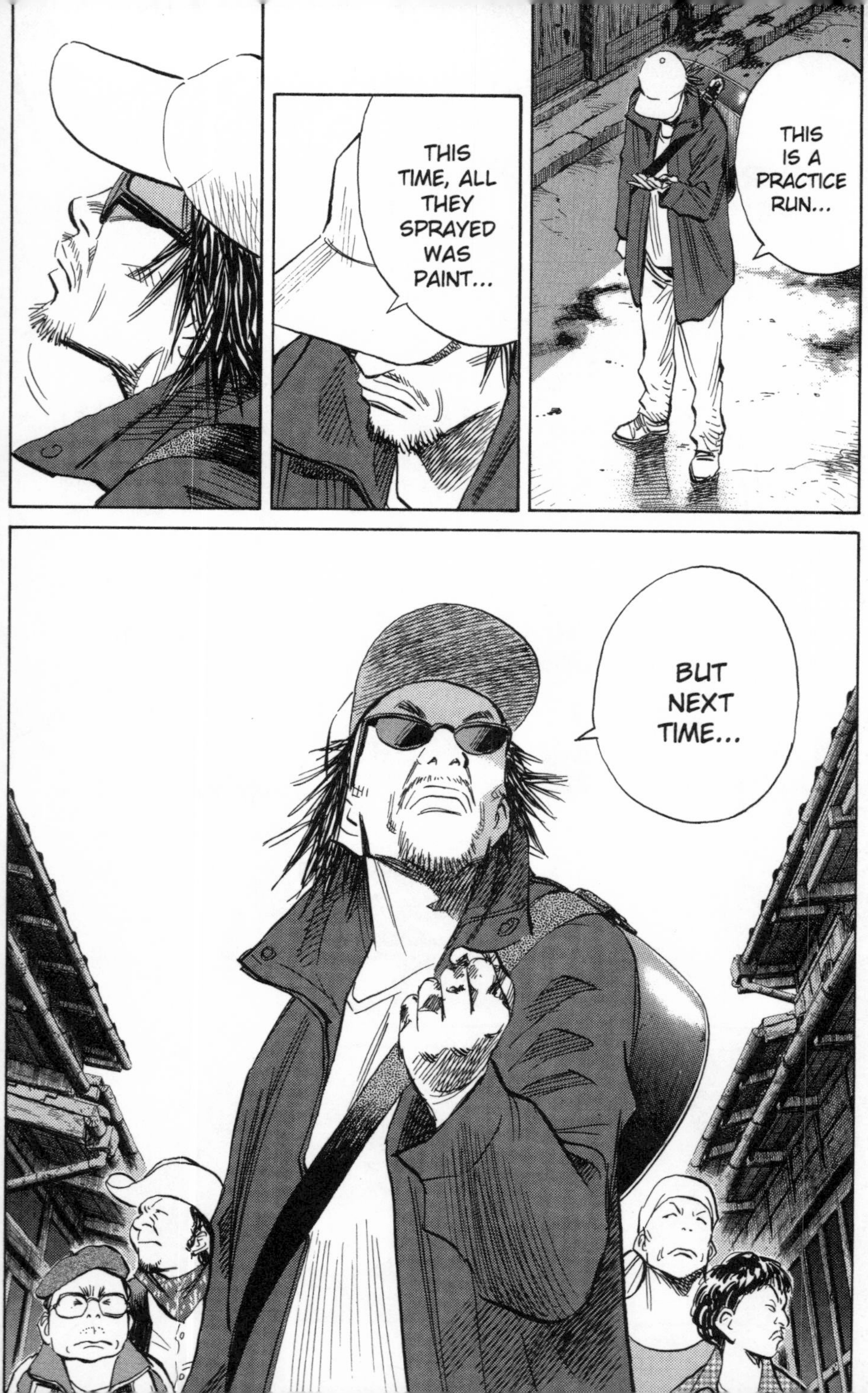
THIS IS A PRACTICE RUN...
THIS TIME, ALL THEY SPRAYED WAS PAINT...
BUT NEXT TIME...

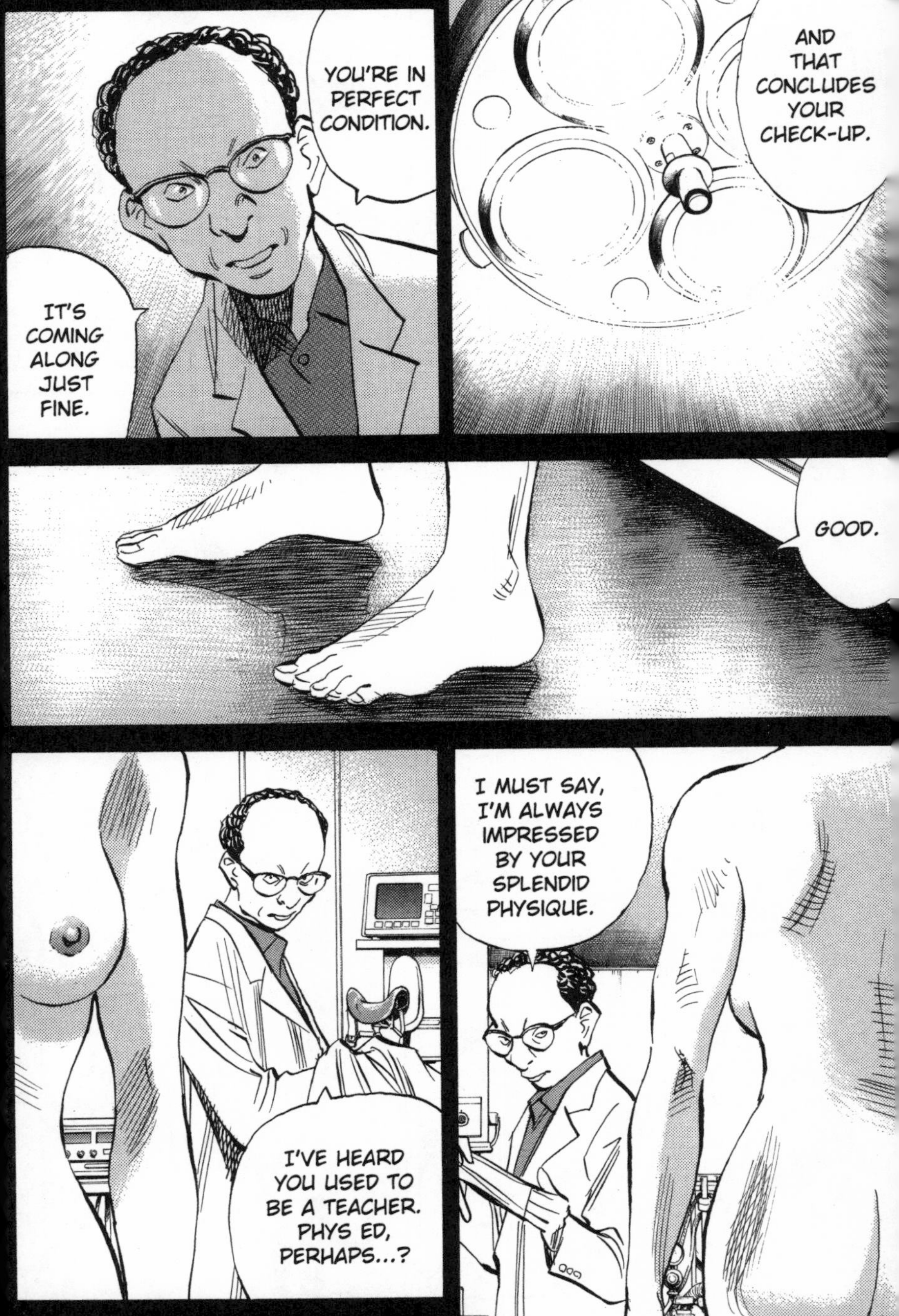
AND THAT CONCLUDES YOUR CHECK-UP.
YOU'RE IN PERFECT CONDITION.
IT'S COMING ALONG JUST FINE.
GOOD.
I MUST SAY, I'M ALWAYS IMPRESSED BY YOUR SPLENDID PHYSIQUE.
I'VE HEARD YOU USED TO BE A TEACHER. PHYS ED, PERHAPS...?

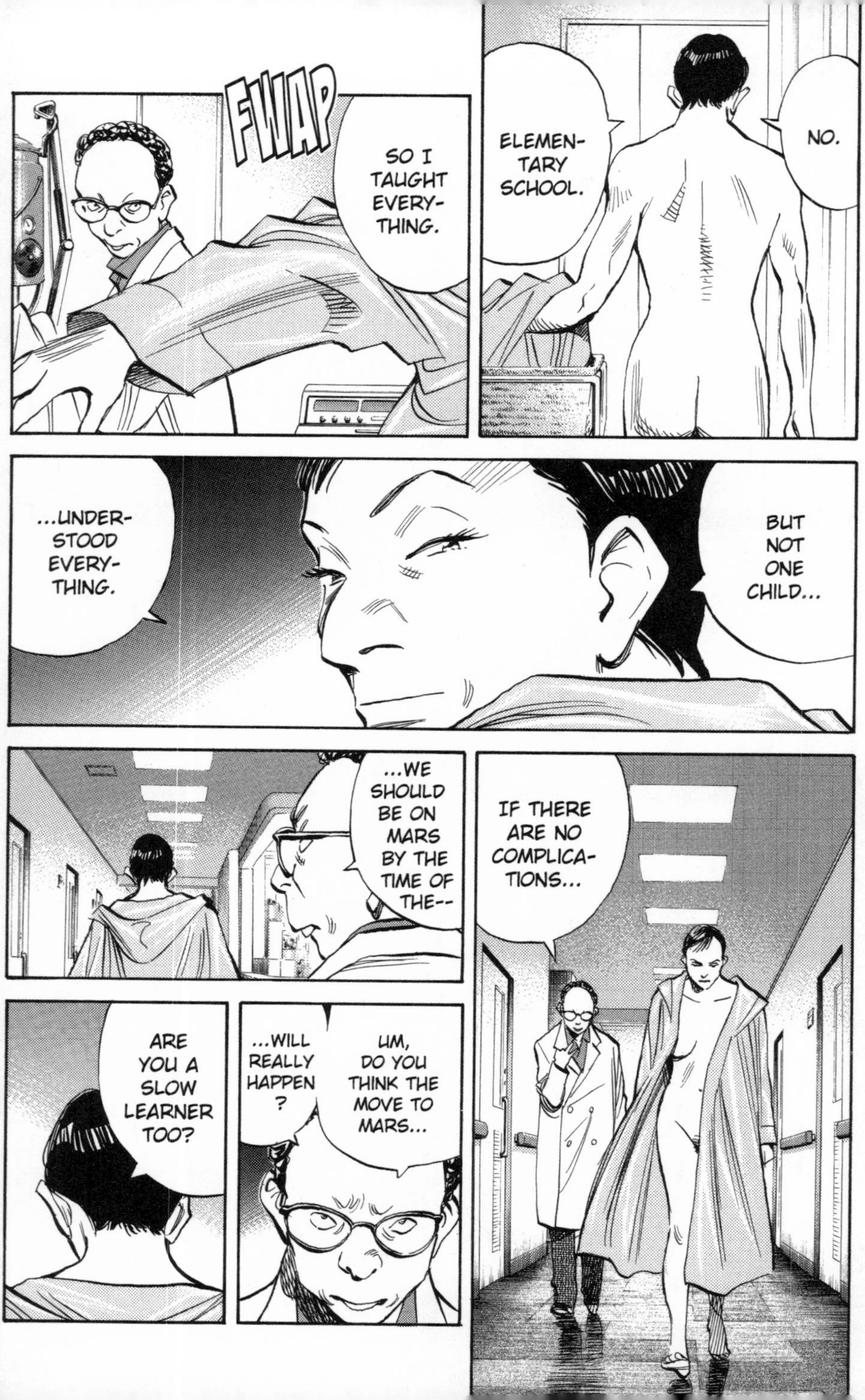
NO.
ELEMENTARY SCHOOL.
FWAP
SO I TAUGHT EVERYTHING.
BUT NOT ONE CHILD...
...UNDERSTOOD EVERYTHING.
IF THERE ARE NO COMPLICATIONS...
...WE SHOULD BE ON MARS BY THE TIME OF THE--
UM, DO YOU THINK THE MOVE TO MARS...
...WILL REALLY HAPPEN?
ARE YOU A SLOW LEARNER TOO?

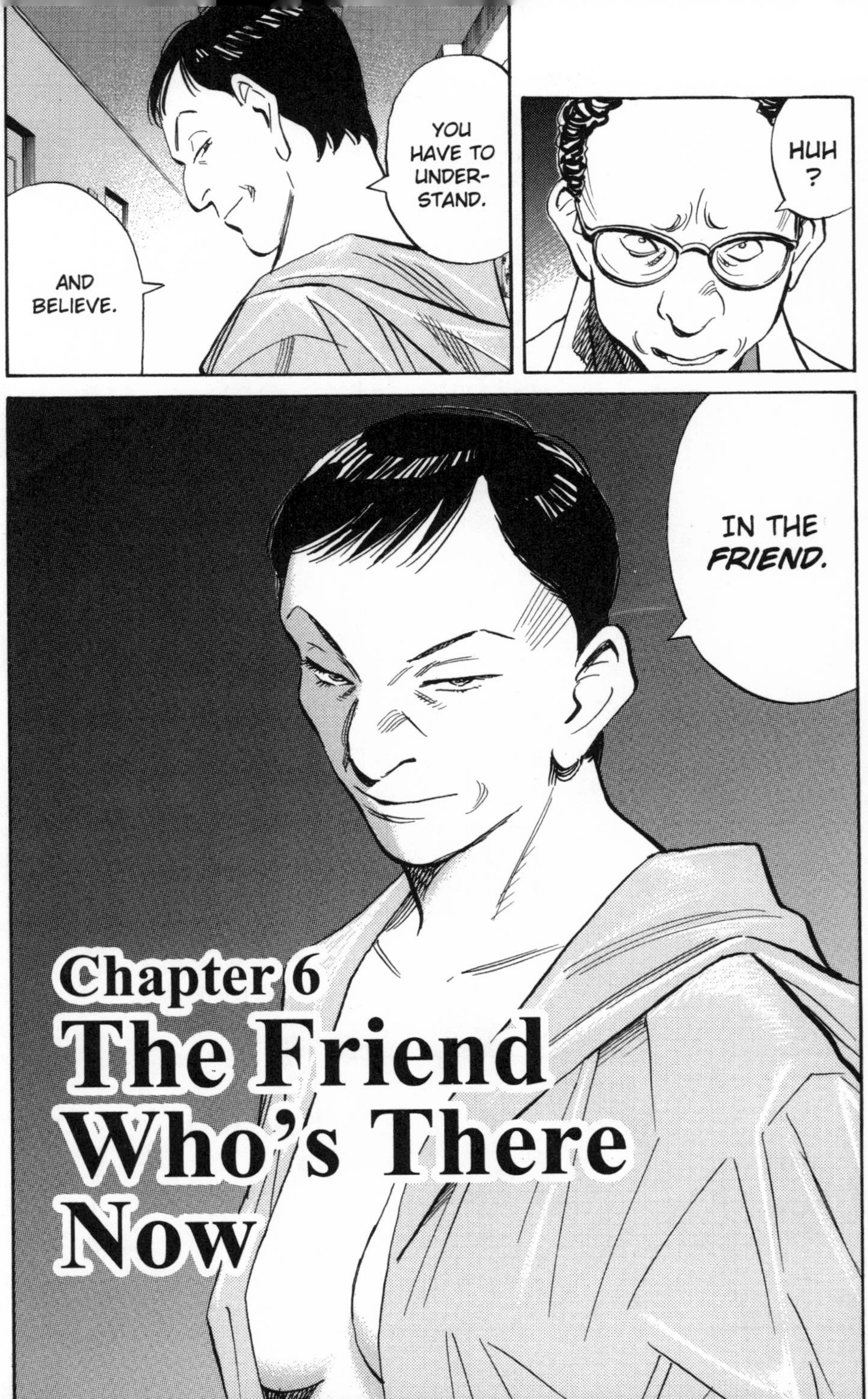
HUH
?
YOU HAVE TO UNDER-STAND.
AND BELIEVE.
IN THE *FRIEND*.

Chapter 6
The Friend Who's There Now

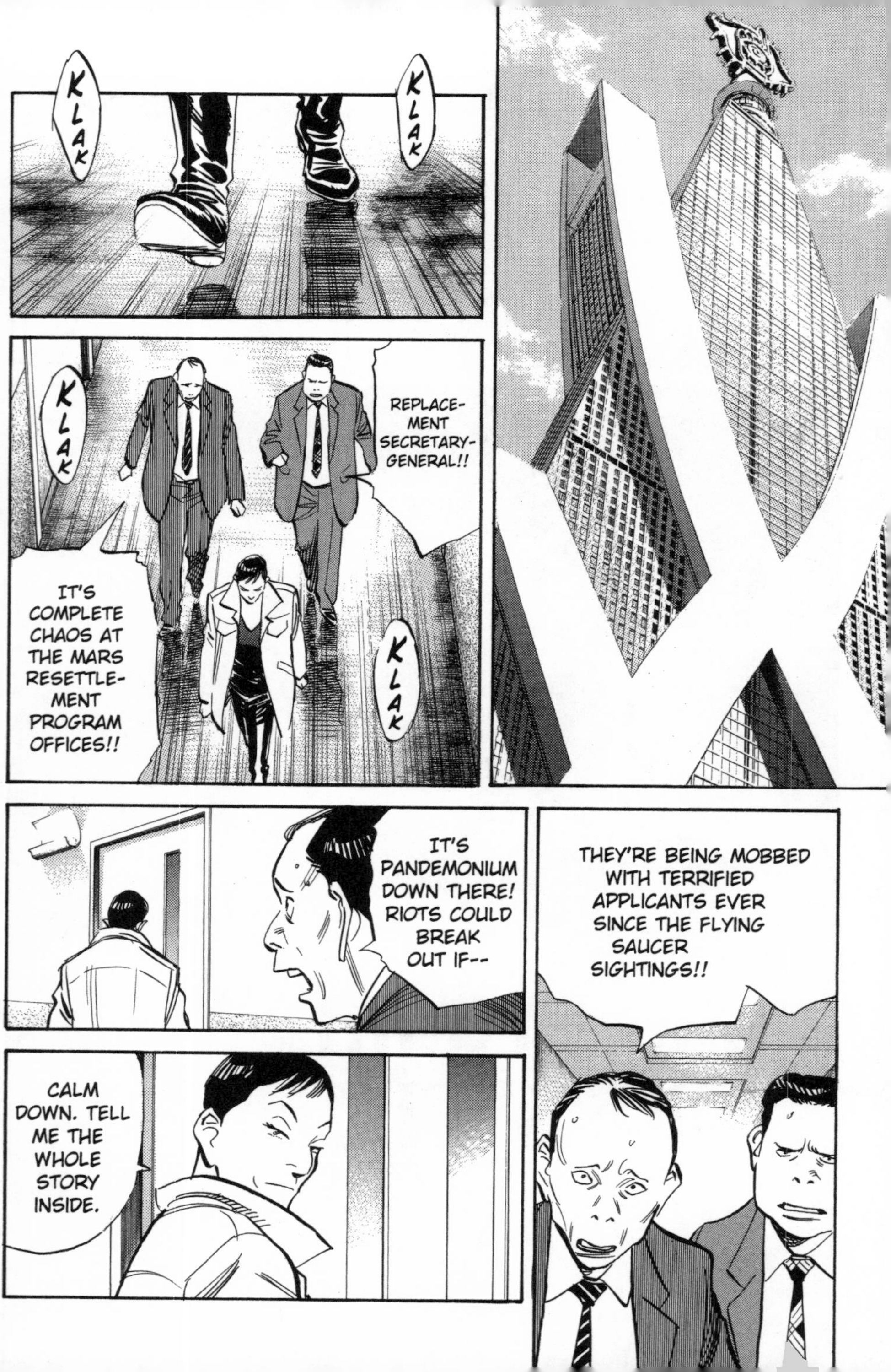
KLAK
KLAK
REPLACEMENT SECRETARY-GENERAL!!
KLAK
IT'S COMPLETE CHAOS AT THE MARS RESETTLEMENT PROGRAM OFFICES!!
KLAK
THEY'RE BEING MOBBED WITH TERRIFIED APPLICANTS EVER SINCE THE FLYING SAUCER SIGHTINGS!!
IT'S PANDEMONIUM DOWN THERE! RIOTS COULD BREAK OUT IF--
CALM DOWN. TELL ME THE WHOLE STORY INSIDE.

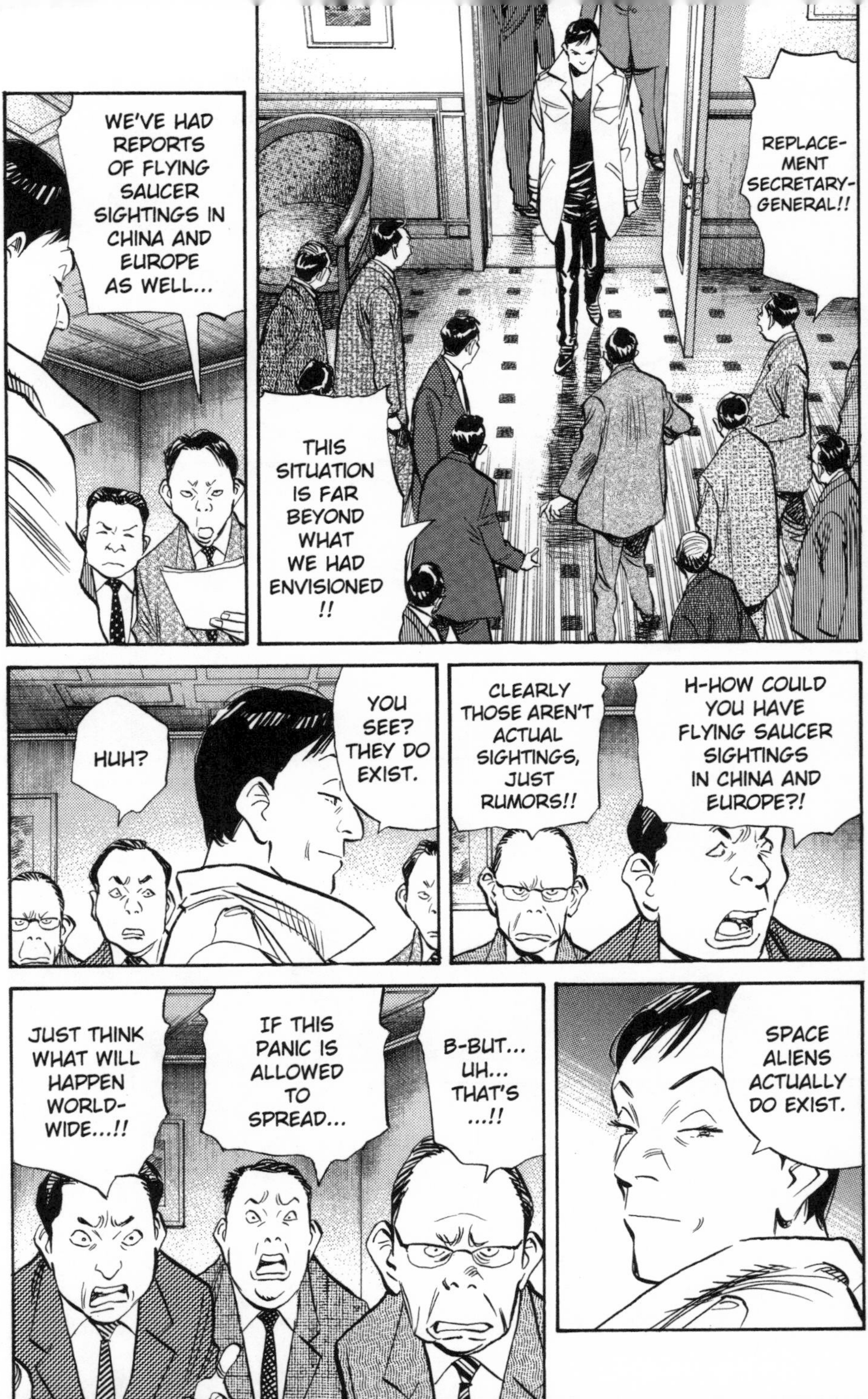
REPLACEMENT SECRETARY-GENERAL!!
THIS SITUATION IS FAR BEYOND WHAT WE HAD ENVISIONED!!
WE'VE HAD REPORTS OF FLYING SAUCER SIGHTINGS IN CHINA AND EUROPE AS WELL...
H-HOW COULD YOU HAVE FLYING SAUCER SIGHTINGS IN CHINA AND EUROPE?!
CLEARLY THOSE AREN'T ACTUAL SIGHTINGS, JUST RUMORS!!
YOU SEE? THEY DO EXIST.
HUH?
SPACE ALIENS ACTUALLY DO EXIST.
B-BUT... UH... THAT'S ...!!
IF THIS PANIC IS ALLOWED TO SPREAD...
JUST THINK WHAT WILL HAPPEN WORLD-WIDE...!!

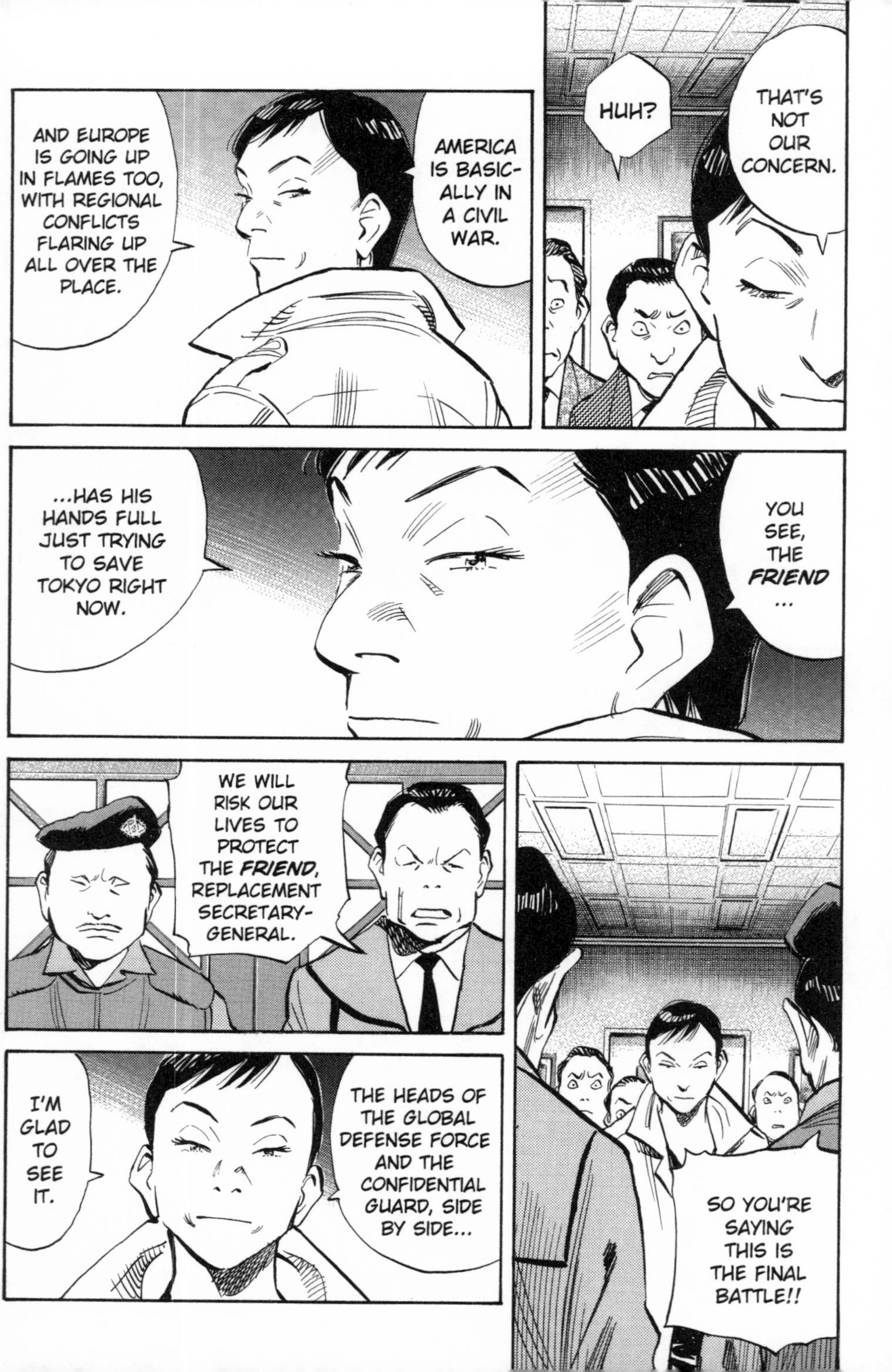
THAT'S NOT OUR CONCERN.
HUH?
AMERICA IS BASIC-ALLY IN A CIVIL WAR.
AND EUROPE IS GOING UP IN FLAMES TOO, WITH REGIONAL CONFLICTS FLARING UP ALL OVER THE PLACE.
YOU SEE, THE *FRIEND*...
...HAS HIS HANDS FULL JUST TRYING TO SAVE TOKYO RIGHT NOW.
SO YOU'RE SAYING THIS IS THE FINAL BATTLE!!
WE WILL RISK OUR LIVES TO PROTECT THE *FRIEND*, REPLACEMENT SECRETARY-GENERAL.
THE HEADS OF THE GLOBAL DEFENSE FORCE AND THE CONFIDENTIAL GUARD, SIDE BY SIDE...
I'M GLAD TO SEE IT.

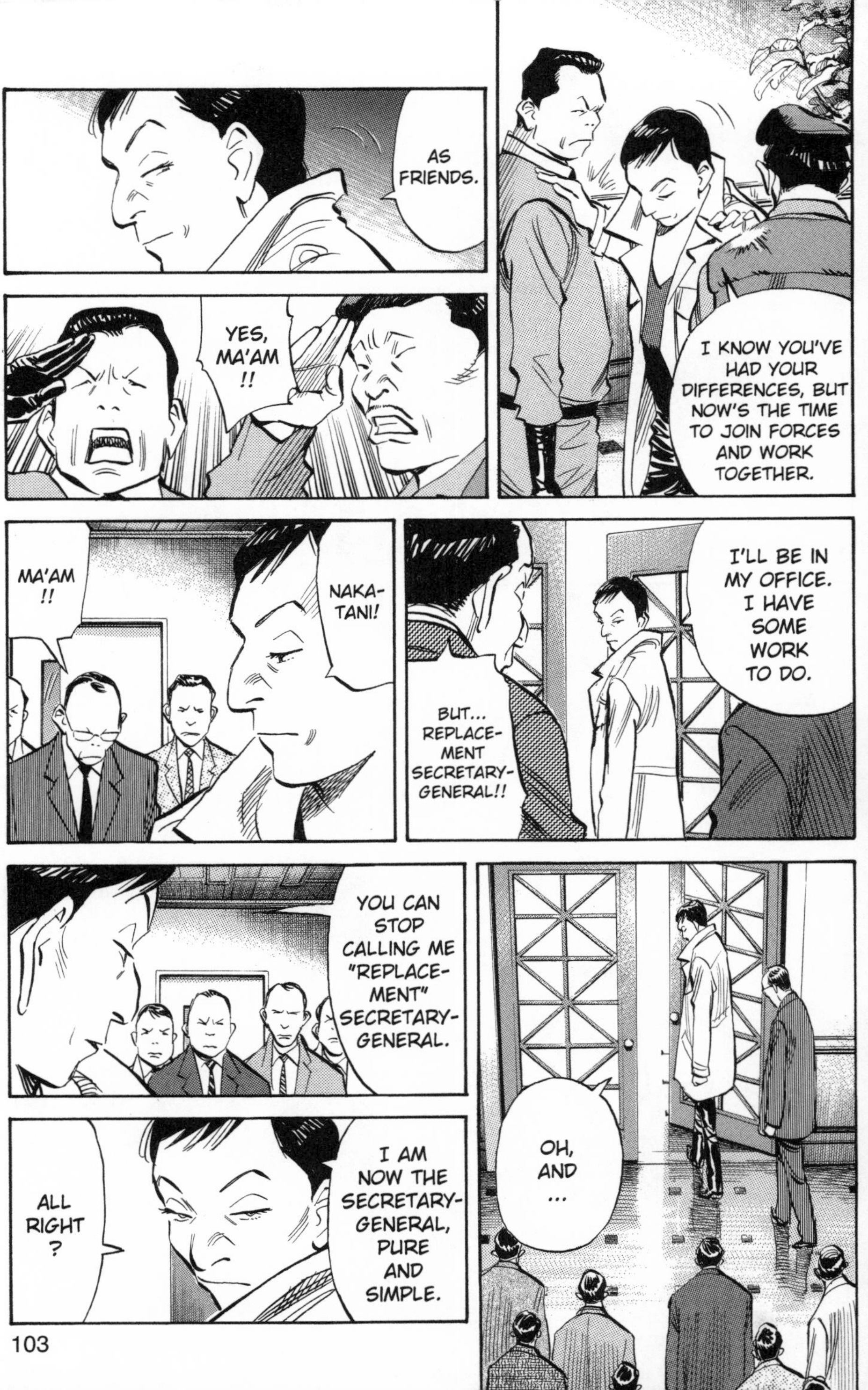
I KNOW YOU'VE HAD YOUR DIFFERENCES, BUT NOW'S THE TIME TO JOIN FORCES AND WORK TOGETHER.
AS FRIENDS.
YES, MA'AM !!
I'LL BE IN MY OFFICE. I HAVE SOME WORK TO DO.
BUT... REPLACE-MENT SECRETARY-GENERAL!!
NAKA-TANI!
MA'AM !!
OH, AND ...
YOU CAN STOP CALLING ME "REPLACE-MENT" SECRETARY-GENERAL.
I AM NOW THE SECRETARY-GENERAL, PURE AND SIMPLE.
ALL RIGHT ?

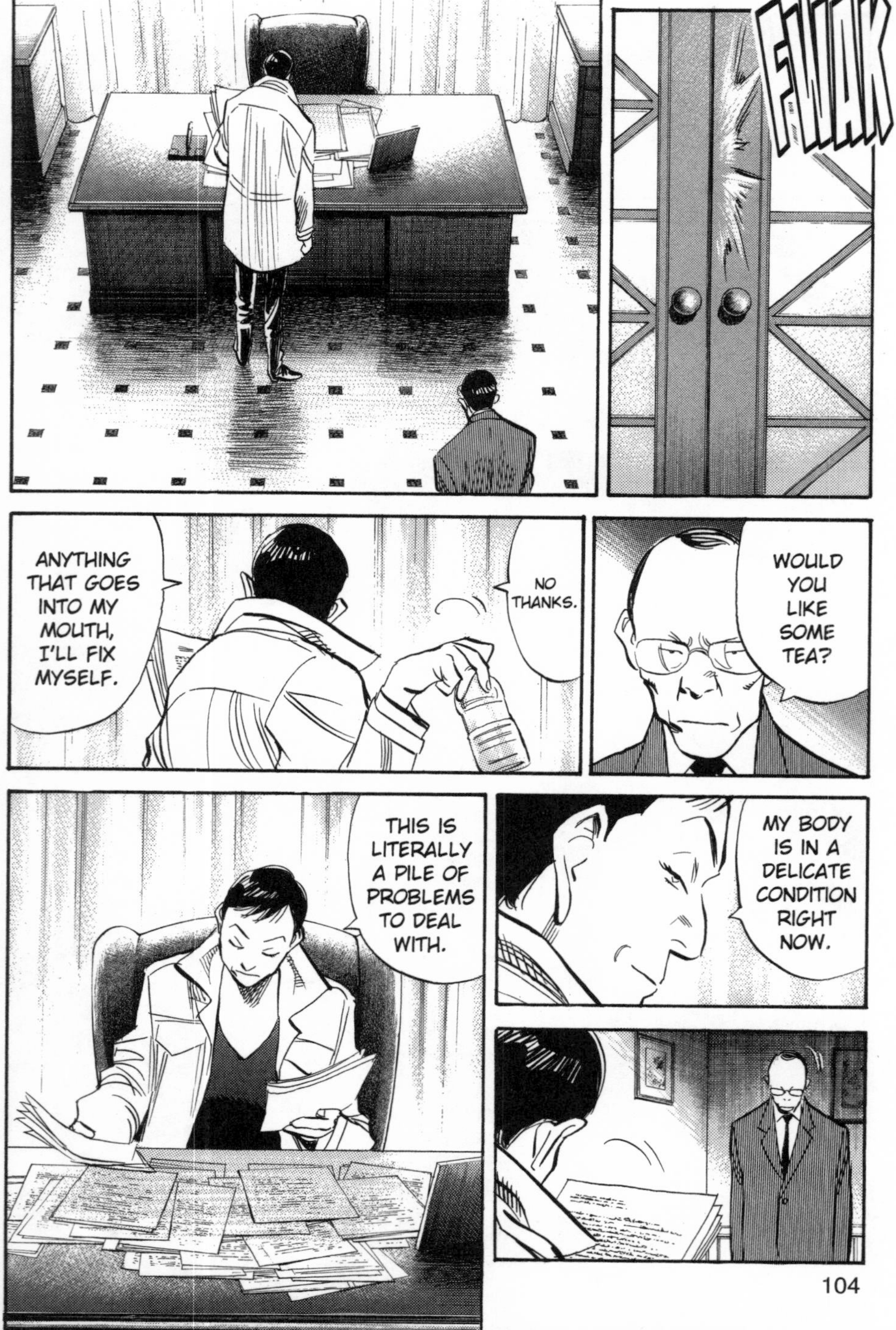
FWAK
WOULD YOU LIKE SOME TEA?
NO THANKS.
ANYTHING THAT GOES INTO MY MOUTH, I'LL FIX MYSELF.
MY BODY IS IN A DELICATE CONDITION RIGHT NOW.
THIS IS LITERALLY A PILE OF PROBLEMS TO DEAL WITH.

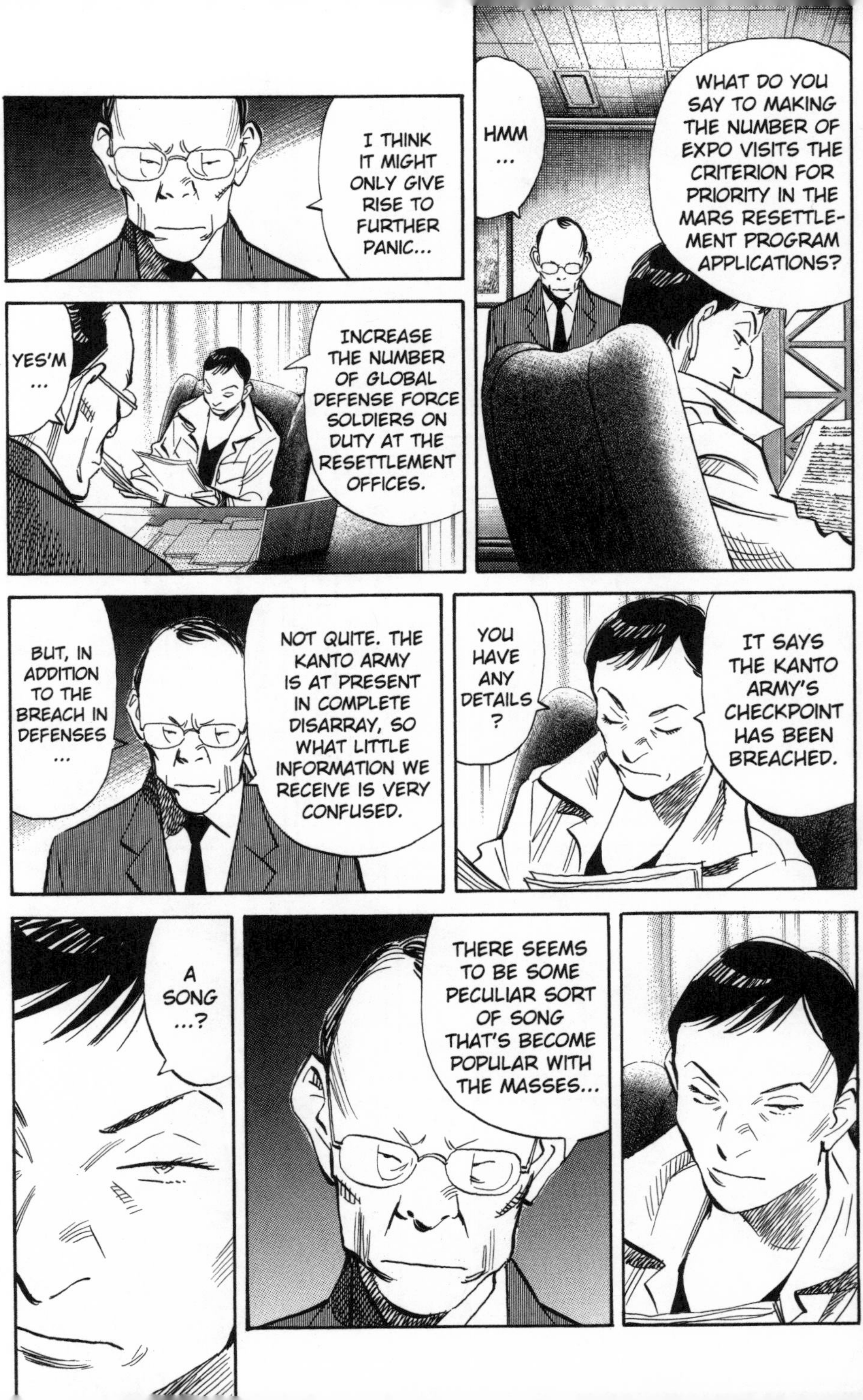

WHAT DO YOU SAY TO MAKING THE NUMBER OF EXPO VISITS THE CRITERION FOR PRIORITY IN THE MARS RESETTLE-MENT PROGRAM APPLICATIONS?
HMM ...
I THINK IT MIGHT ONLY GIVE RISE TO FURTHER PANIC...
INCREASE THE NUMBER OF GLOBAL DEFENSE FORCE SOLDIERS ON DUTY AT THE RESETTLEMENT OFFICES.
YES'M ...
IT SAYS THE KANTO ARMY'S CHECKPOINT HAS BEEN BREACHED.
YOU HAVE ANY DETAILS ?
NOT QUITE. THE KANTO ARMY IS AT PRESENT IN COMPLETE DISARRAY, SO WHAT LITTLE INFORMATION WE RECEIVE IS VERY CONFUSED.
BUT, IN ADDITION TO THE BREACH IN DEFENSES ...
THERE SEEMS TO BE SOME PECULIAR SORT OF SONG THAT'S BECOME POPULAR WITH THE MASSES...
A SONG ...?

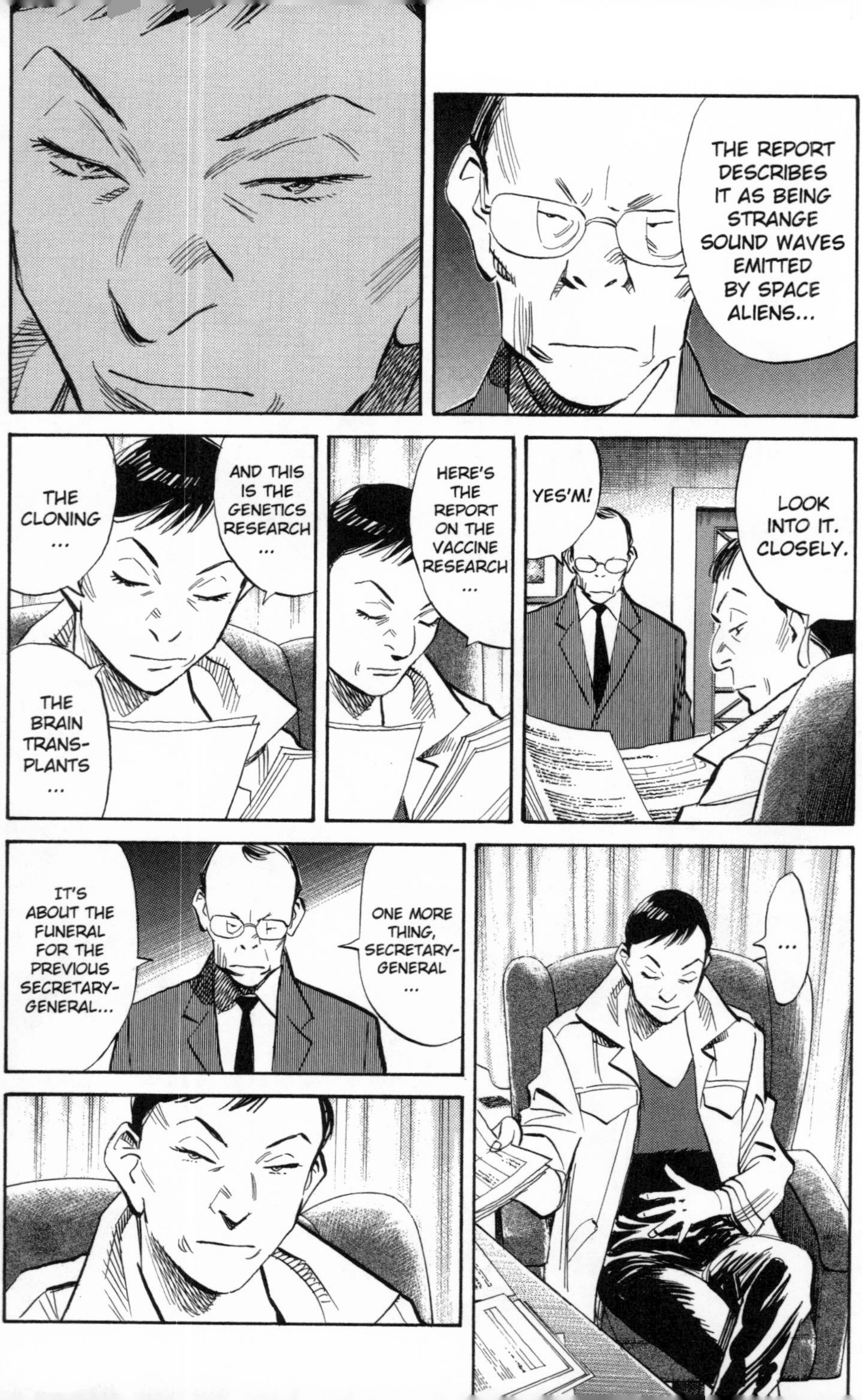
THE REPORT DESCRIBES IT AS BEING STRANGE SOUND WAVES EMITTED BY SPACE ALIENS...
LOOK INTO IT. CLOSELY.
YES'M!
HERE'S THE REPORT ON THE VACCINE RESEARCH...
AND THIS IS THE GENETICS RESEARCH...
THE CLONING...
THE BRAIN TRANS-PLANTS...
...
ONE MORE THING, SECRETARY-GENERAL...
IT'S ABOUT THE FUNERAL FOR THE PREVIOUS SECRETARY-GENERAL...

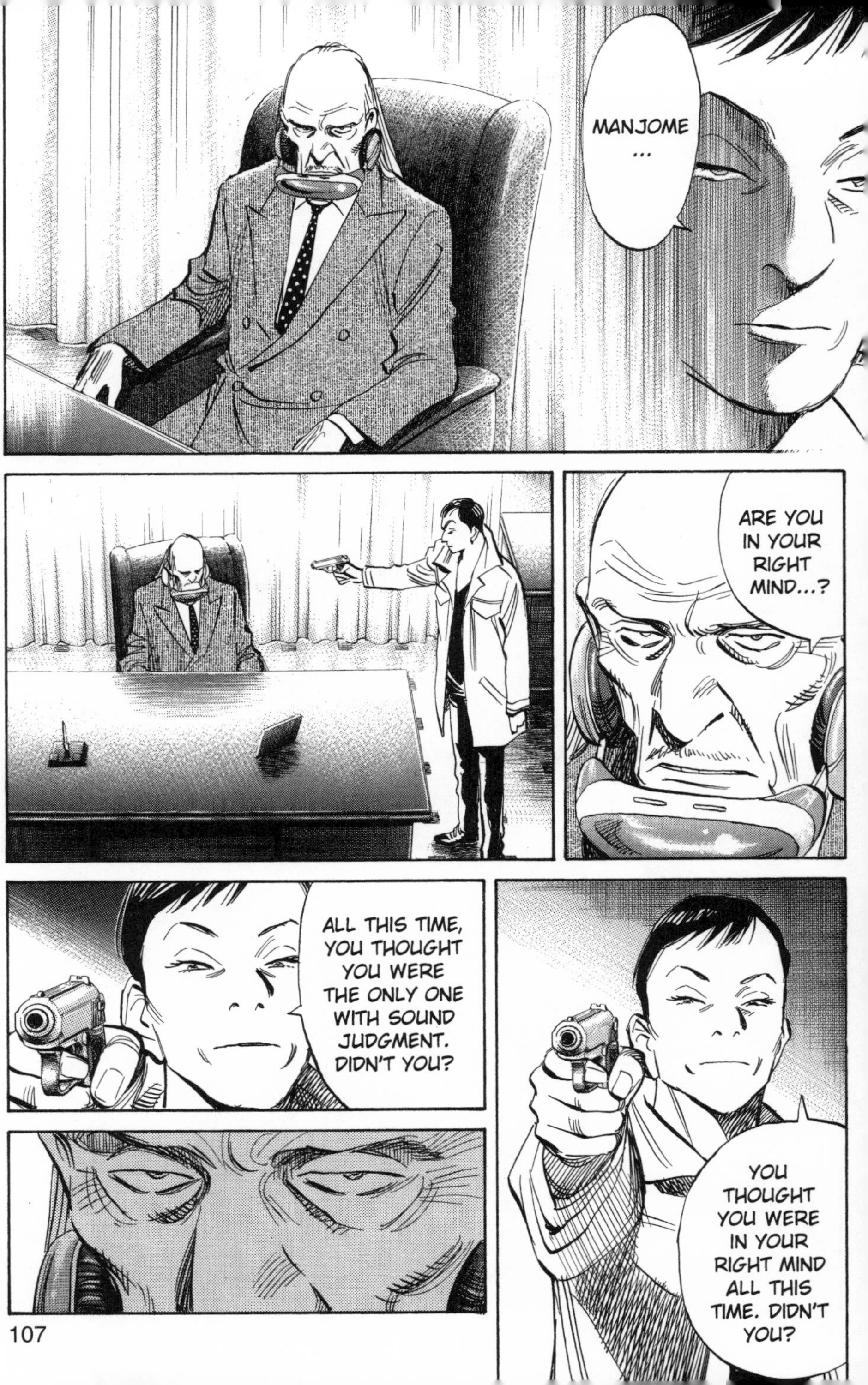
MANJOME ...
ARE YOU IN YOUR RIGHT MIND...?
YOU THOUGHT YOU WERE IN YOUR RIGHT MIND ALL THIS TIME. DIDN'T YOU?
ALL THIS TIME, YOU THOUGHT YOU WERE THE ONLY ONE WITH SOUND JUDGMENT. DIDN'T YOU?

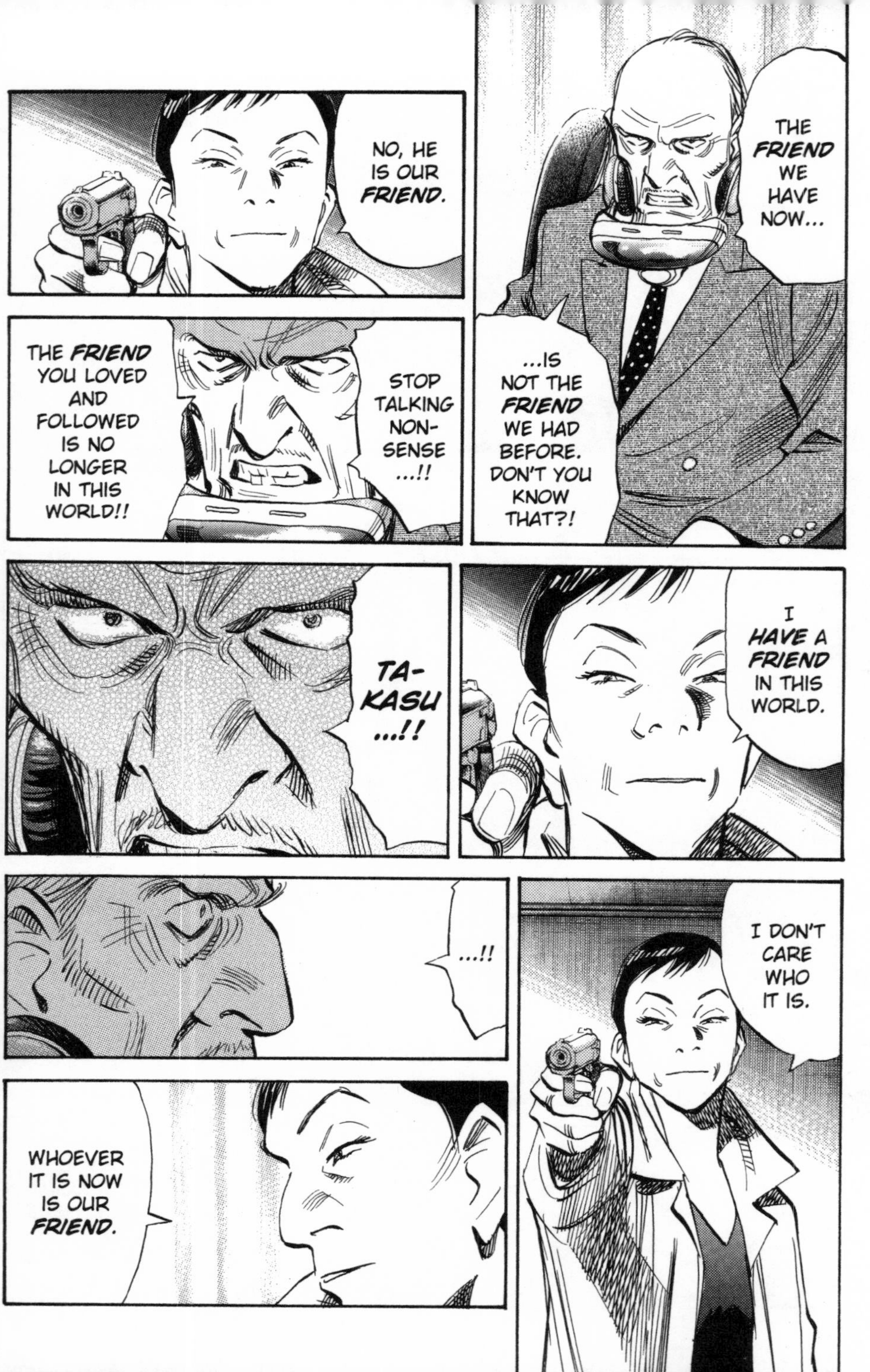
THE FRIEND WE HAVE NOW...
...IS NOT THE FRIEND WE HAD BEFORE. DON'T YOU KNOW THAT?!
NO, HE IS OUR FRIEND.
STOP TALKING NON-SENSE ...!!
THE FRIEND YOU LOVED AND FOLLOWED IS NO LONGER IN THIS WORLD!!
I HAVE A FRIEND IN THIS WORLD.
TA-KASU ...!!
I DON'T CARE WHO IT IS.
...!!
WHOEVER IT IS NOW IS OUR FRIEND.

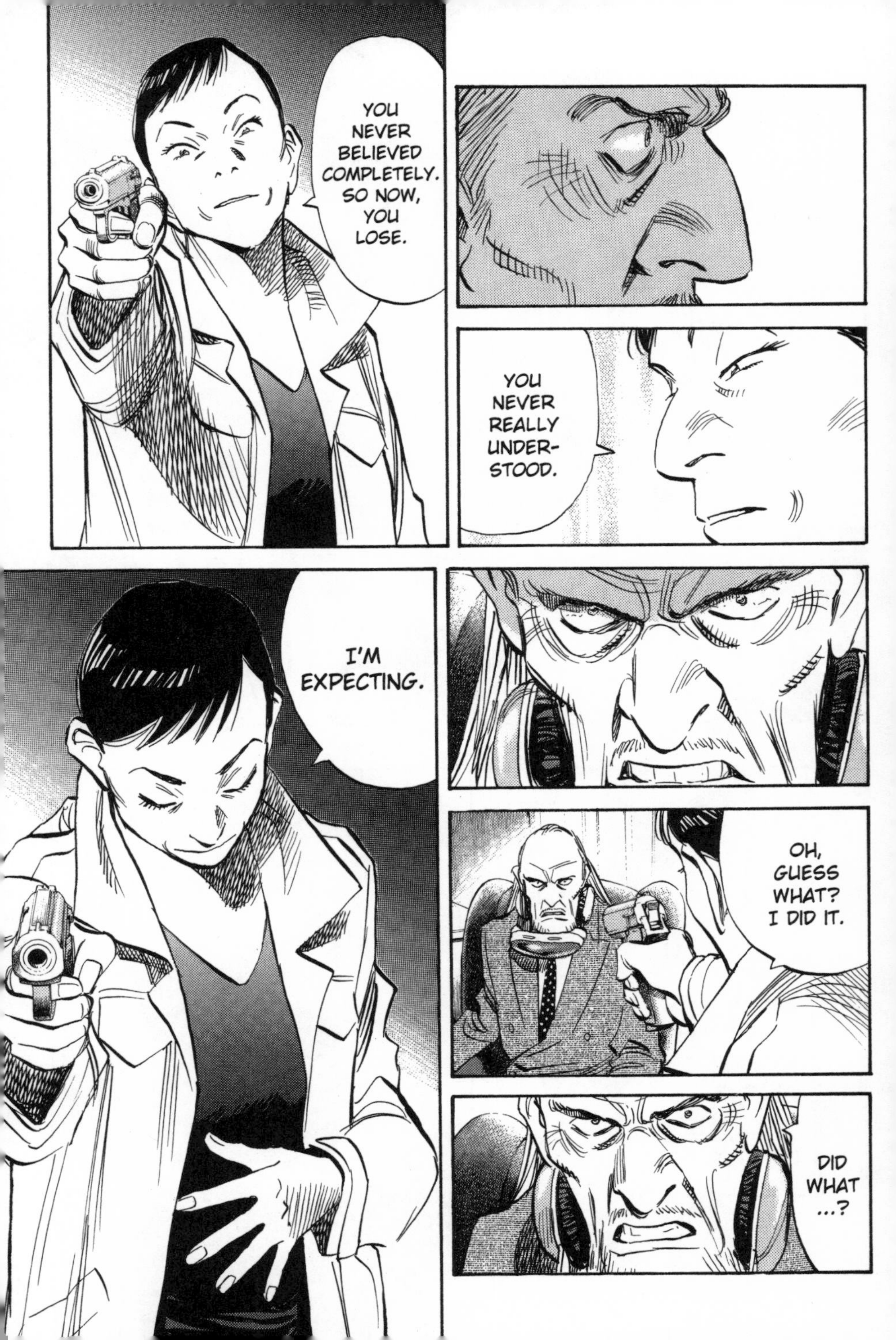
YOU NEVER REALLY UNDER-STOOD.
YOU NEVER BELIEVED COMPLETELY. SO NOW, YOU LOSE.
OH, GUESS WHAT? I DID IT.
DID WHAT ...?
I'M EXPECTING.

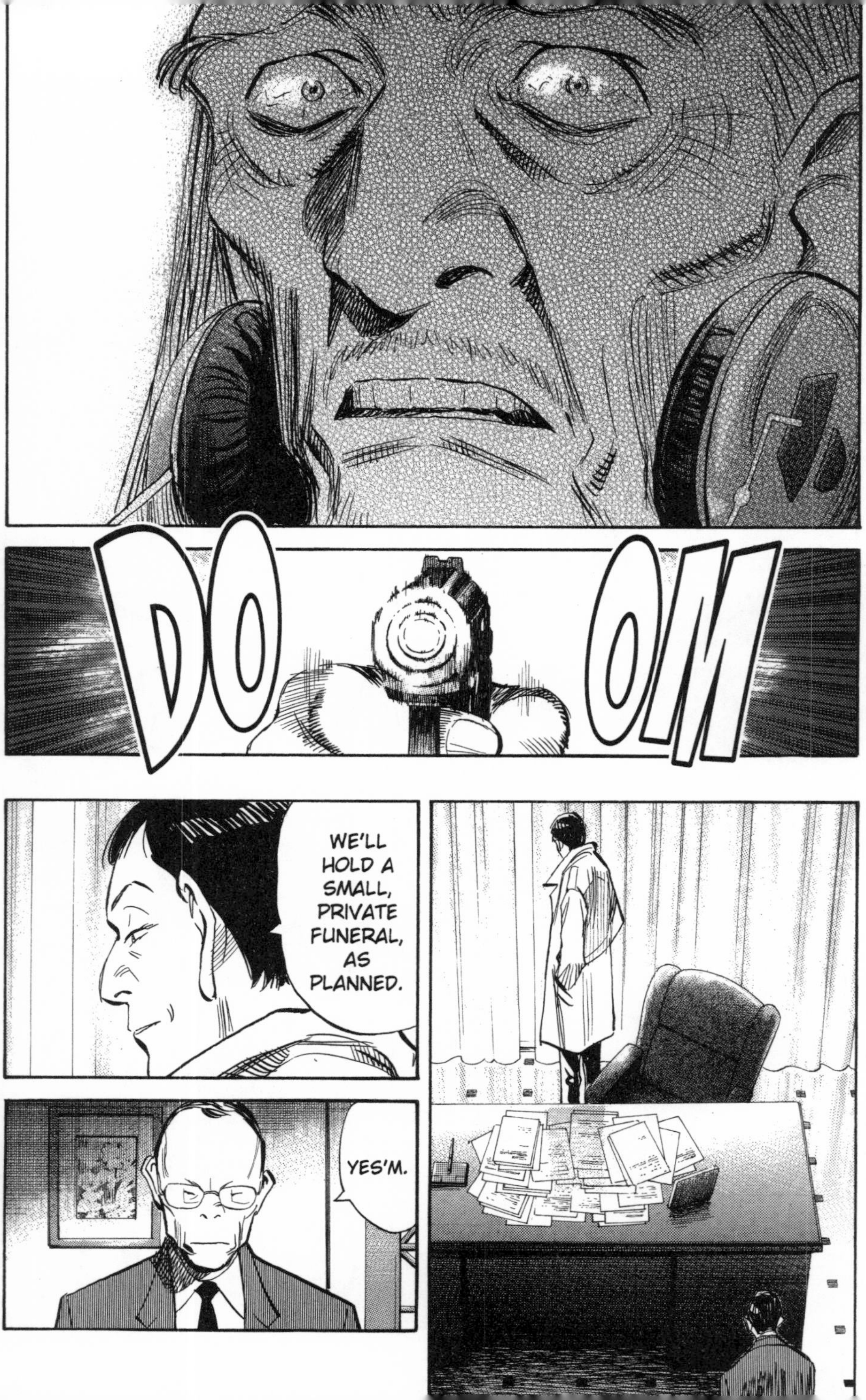
DOOM
WE'LL HOLD A SMALL, PRIVATE FUNERAL, AS PLANNED.
YES'M.

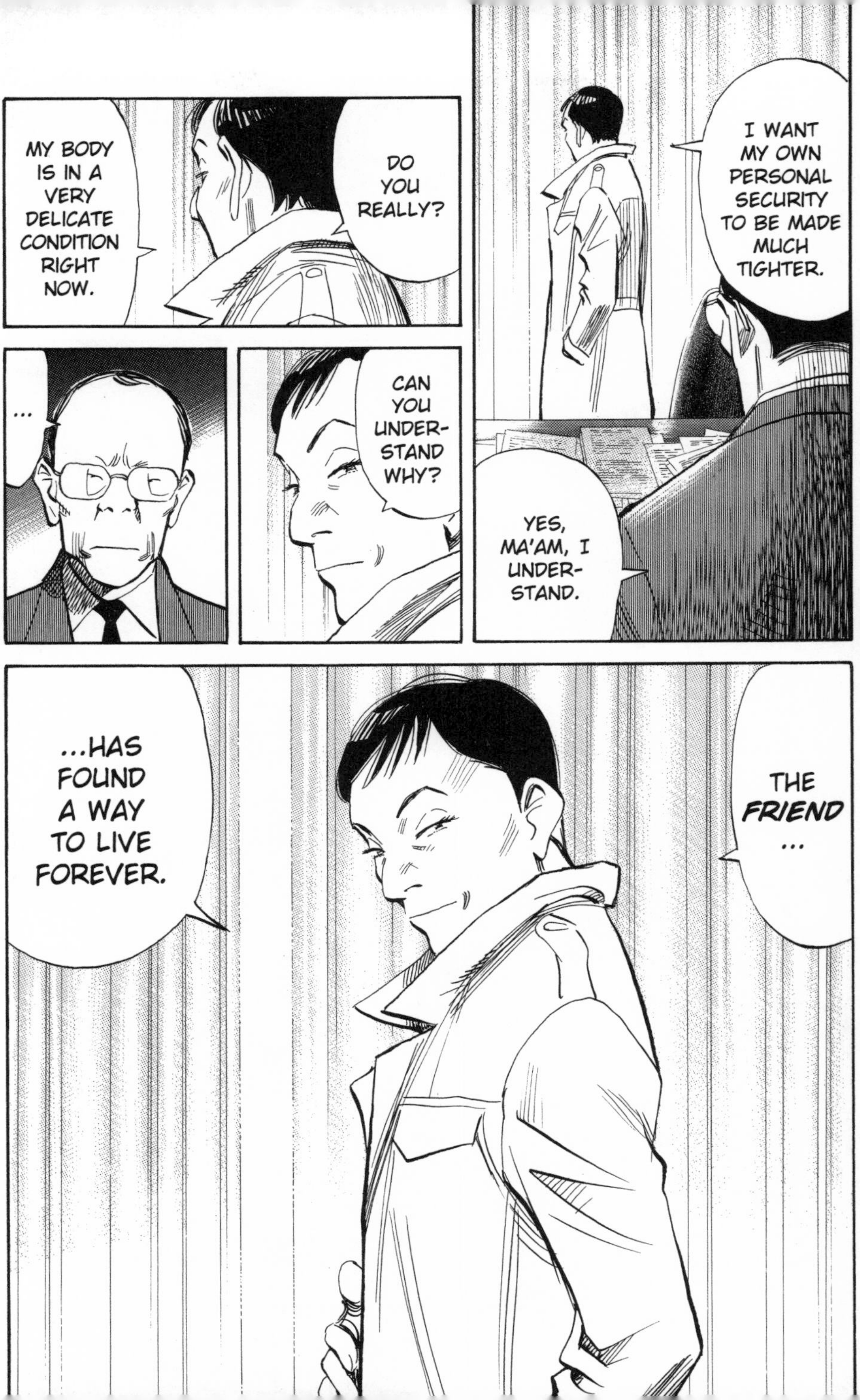
I WANT MY OWN PERSONAL SECURITY TO BE MADE MUCH TIGHTER.
YES, MA'AM, I UNDER-STAND.
DO YOU REALLY?
MY BODY IS IN A VERY DELICATE CONDITION RIGHT NOW.
CAN YOU UNDER-STAND WHY?
...
THE *FRIEND*...
...HAS FOUND A WAY TO LIVE FOREVER.

YOU
BETTER
UNDER-
STAND
WHAT THAT
MEANS.

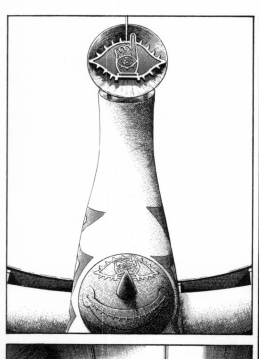

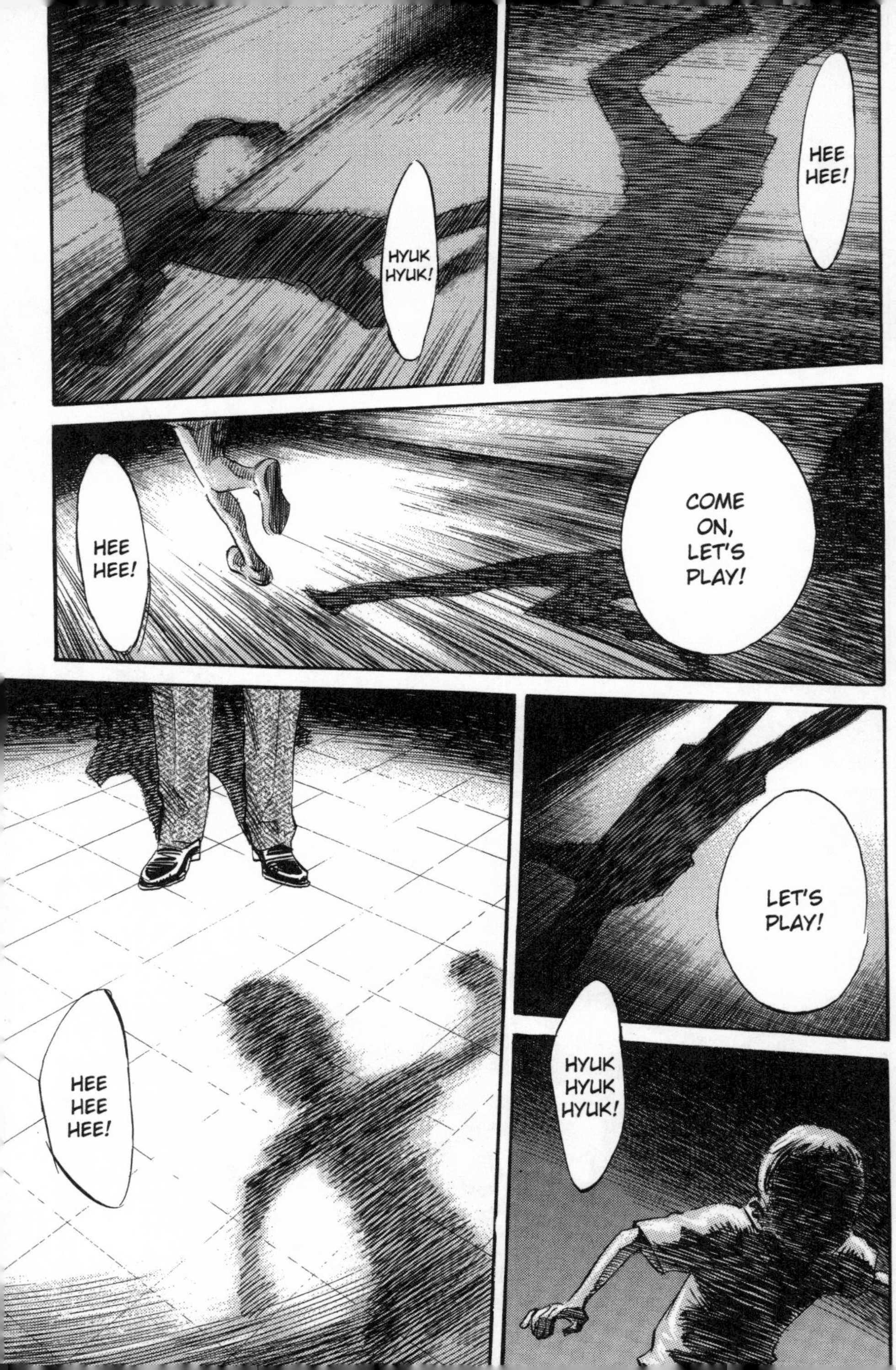
HEE HEE!
HYUK HYUK!
COME ON, LET'S PLAY!
HEE HEE!
LET'S PLAY!
HYUK HYUK HYUK!
HEE HEE HEE!

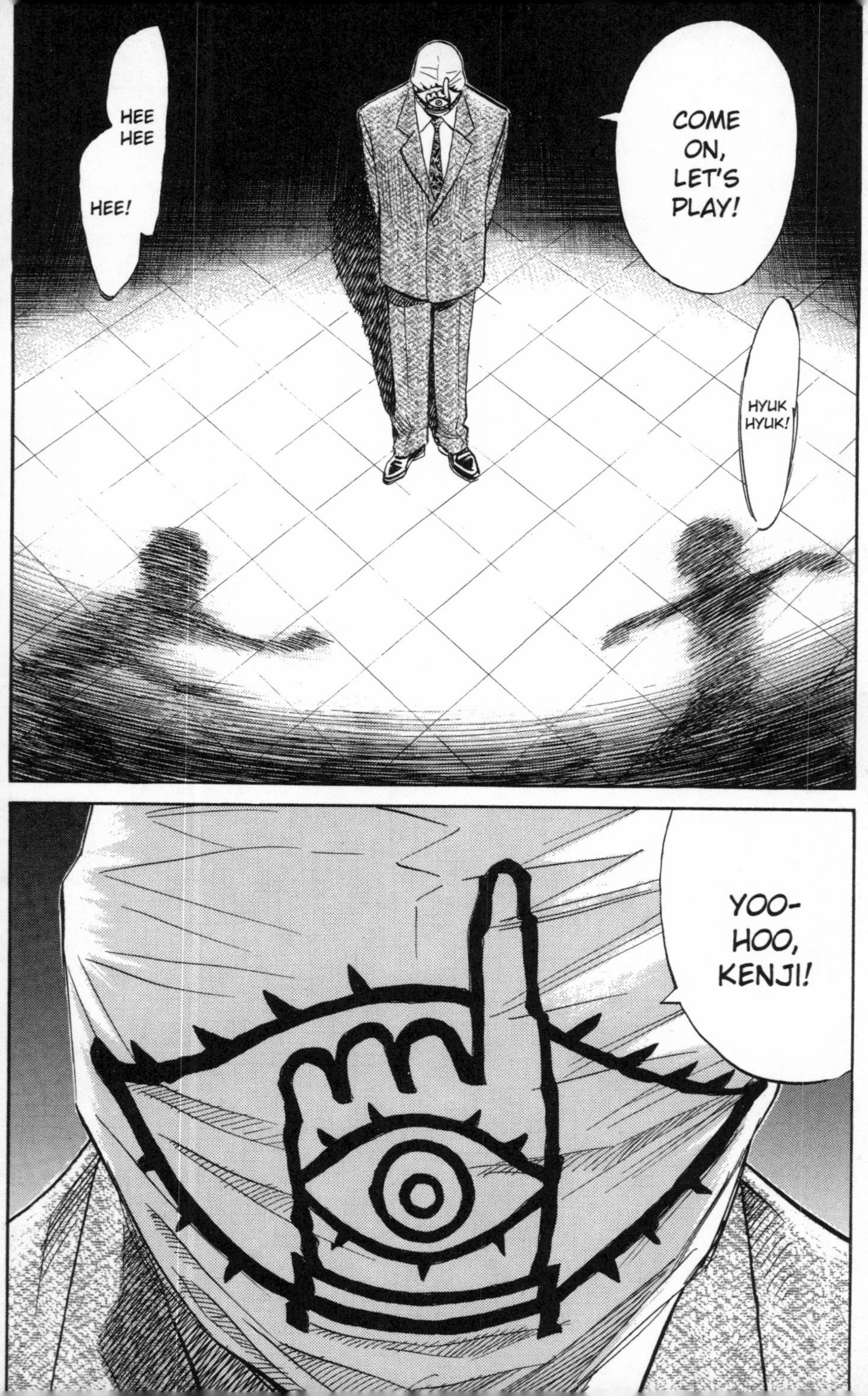
COME ON, LET'S PLAY!
HEE HEE HEE!
HYUK HYUK!
YOO-HOO, KENJI!

EXPO,
HURRAY!
EXPO,
HURRAY!

PROGRESS
AND
HARMONY
FOR
HUMANITY.

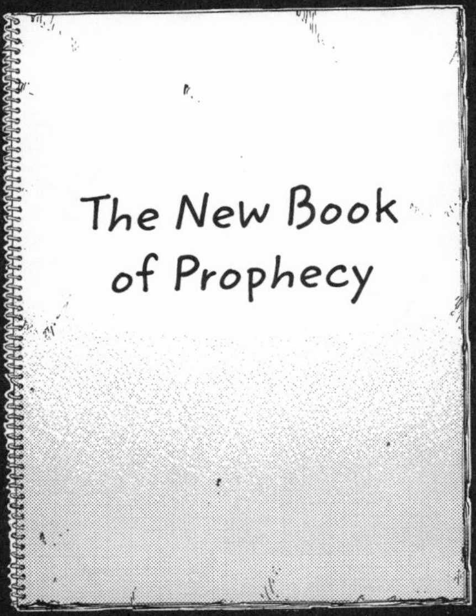
The New Book of Prophecy

Chapter 7

The Book of Prophecy Continued

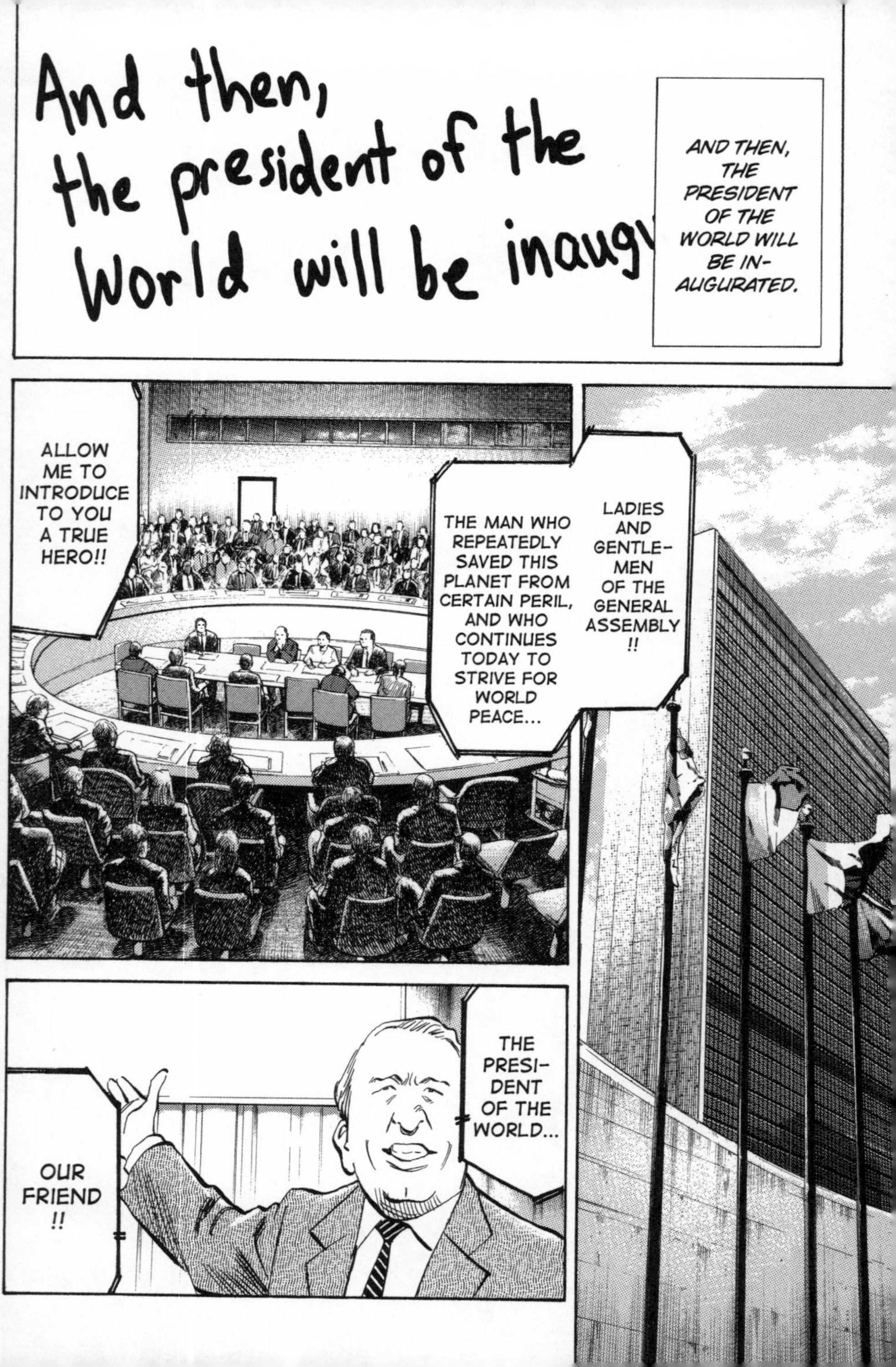
AND THEN, THE PRESIDENT OF THE WORLD WILL BE IN-AUGURATED.
And then, the president of the World will be inaugu
LADIES AND GENTLE-MEN OF THE GENERAL ASSEMBLY !!
THE MAN WHO REPEATEDLY SAVED THIS PLANET FROM CERTAIN PERIL, AND WHO CONTINUES TODAY TO STRIVE FOR WORLD PEACE...
ALLOW ME TO INTRODUCE TO YOU A TRUE HERO!!
THE PRESI-DENT OF THE WORLD...
OUR FRIEND !!

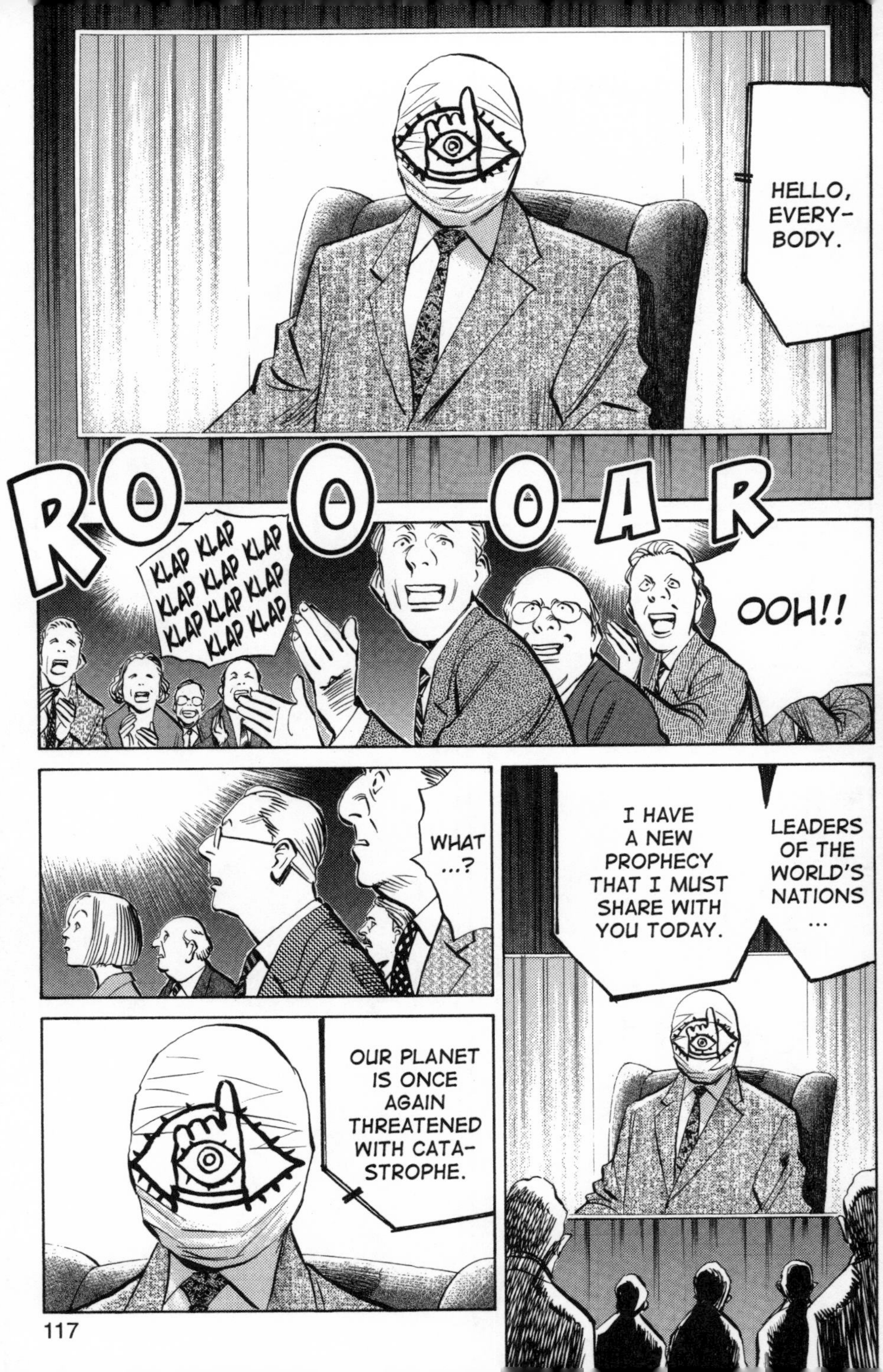
HELLO, EVERY-BODY.
ROOOAR
OOH!!
KLAP KLAP KLAP KLAP KLAP KLAP KLAP KLAP KLAP KLAP KLAP KLAP KLAP
LEADERS OF THE WORLD'S NATIONS ...
I HAVE A NEW PROPHECY THAT I MUST SHARE WITH YOU TODAY.
WHAT ...?
OUR PLANET IS ONCE AGAIN THREATENED WITH CATA-STROPHE.

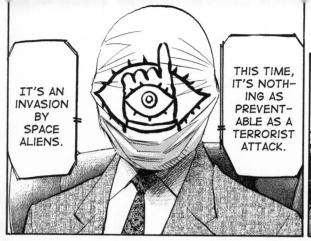

HUB BUB
WH- WHAT ?!
THIS TIME, IT'S NOTH- ING AS PREVENT- ABLE AS A TERRORIST ATTACK.
IT'S AN INVASION BY SPACE ALIENS.
HUB BUB
WHAAAAT ?!
THE SPACE ALIENS WILL SPREAD THE DEADLIEST VIRUS WE HAVE EVER SEEN, ALL OVER EARTH.
HUB BUB
HUB BUB
SPACE ALIENS ...?
COULD THAT BE POSSIBLE ...?!
HUMANITY IS LEFT WITH JUST ONE COURSE FOR SURVIVAL.
AND THAT IS TO MOVE TO MARS.

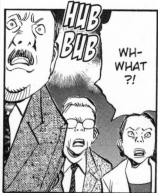

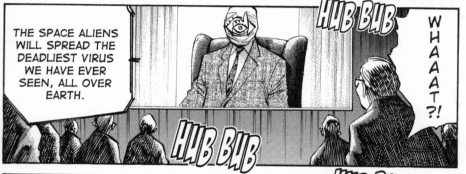

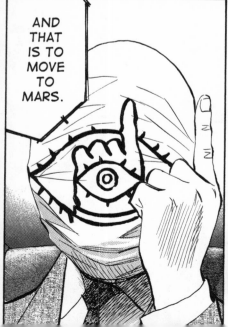

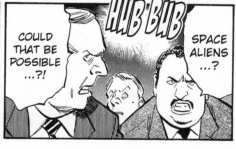

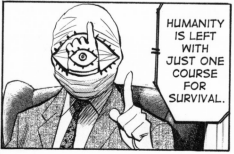

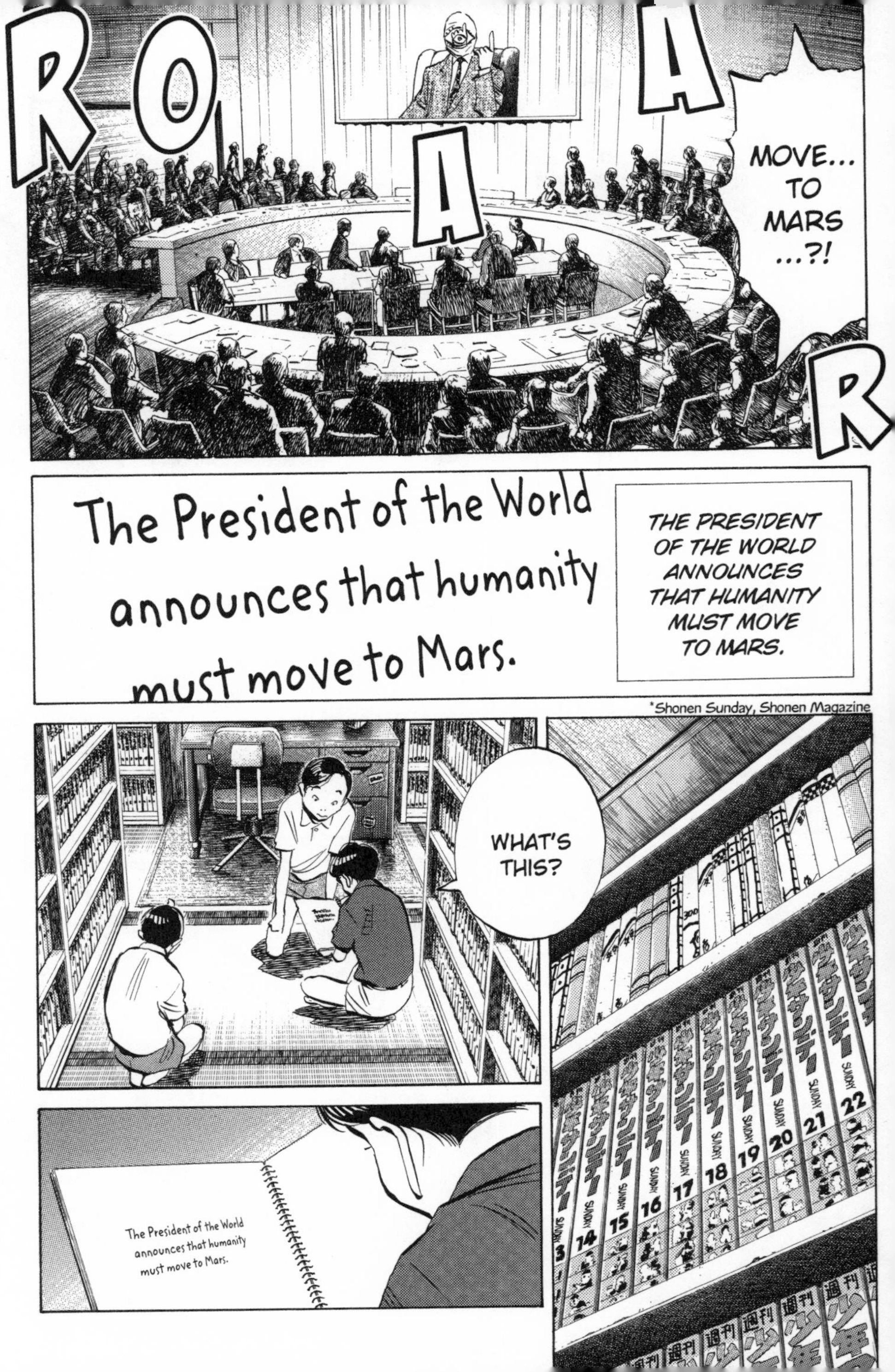
ROAAR
MOVE... TO MARS ...?!
The President of the World announces that humanity must move to Mars.
THE PRESIDENT OF THE WORLD ANNOUNCES THAT HUMANITY MUST MOVE TO MARS.
*Shonen Sunday, Shonen Magazine
SUNDAY 13 14 15 16 17 18 19 20 21 22
WHAT'S THIS?
The President of the World announces that humanity must move to Mars.

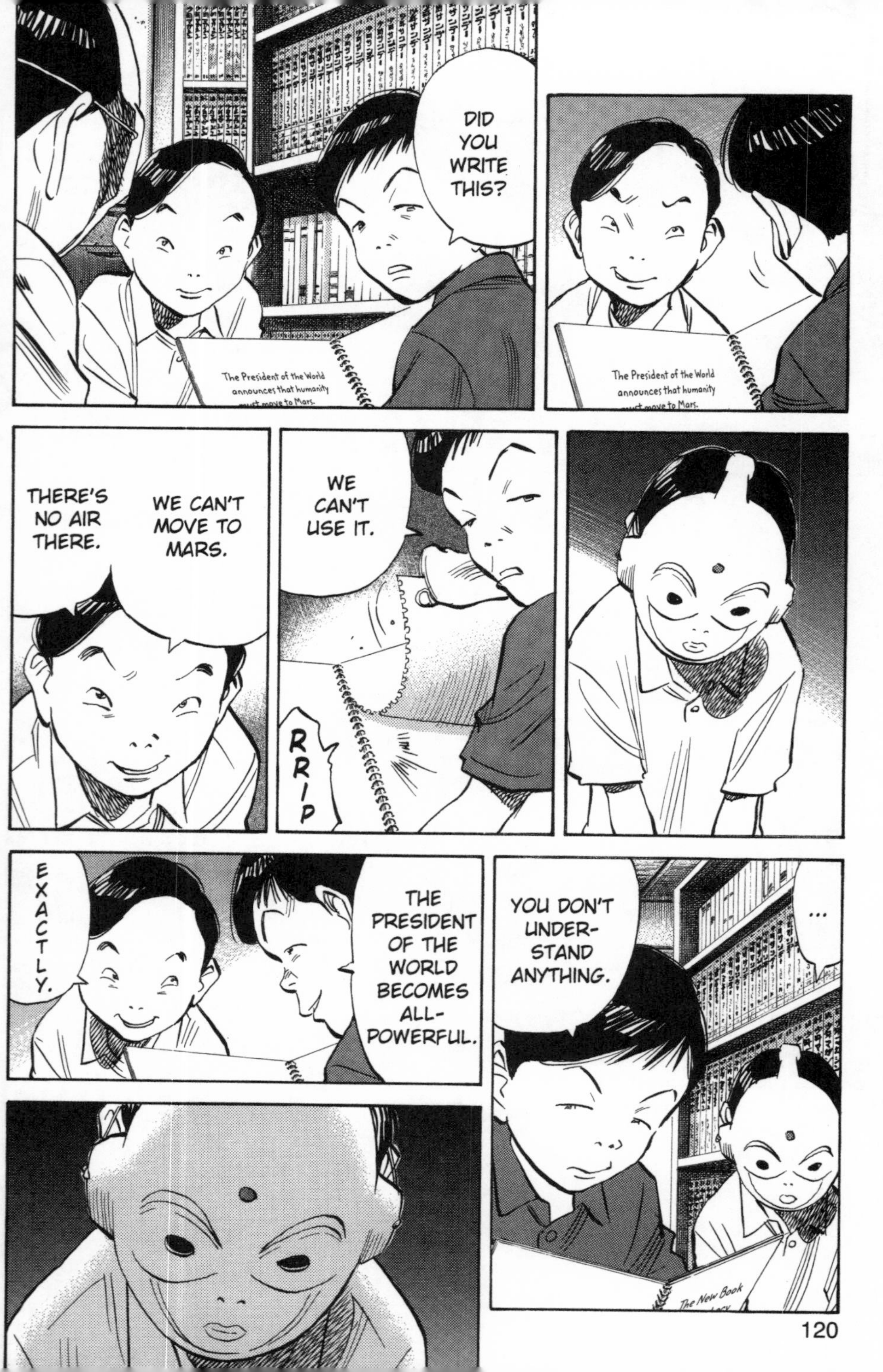
The President of the World announces that humanity must move to Mars.
DID YOU WRITE THIS?
The President of the World announces that humanity must move to Mars.
WE CAN'T USE IT.
RRIP
WE CAN'T MOVE TO MARS.
THERE'S NO AIR THERE.
...
YOU DON'T UNDER-STAND ANYTHING.
The New Book
THE PRESIDENT OF THE WORLD BECOMES ALL-POWERFUL.
EXACTLY.

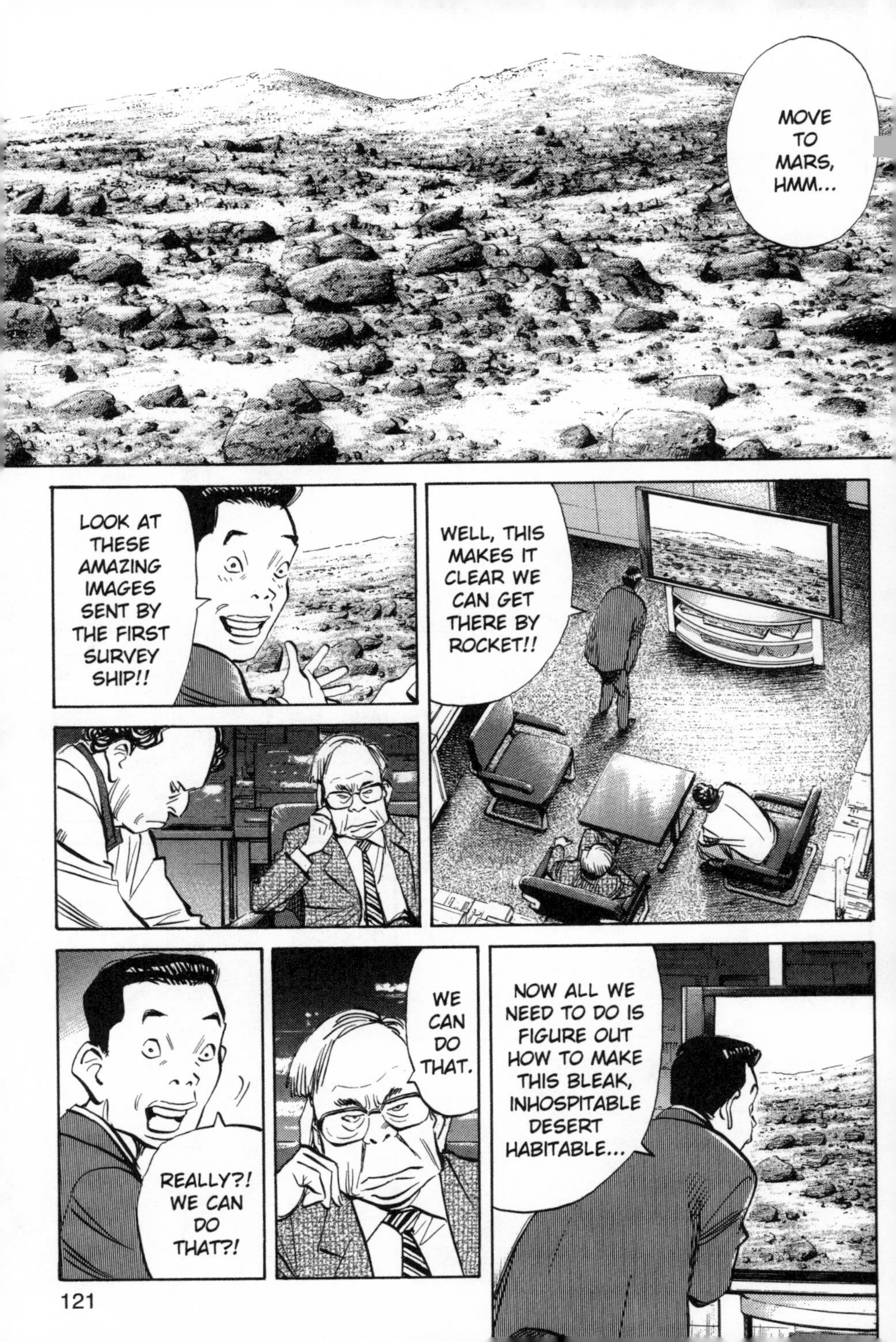
MOVE TO MARS, HMM...
WELL, THIS MAKES IT CLEAR WE CAN GET THERE BY ROCKET!!
LOOK AT THESE AMAZING IMAGES SENT BY THE FIRST SURVEY SHIP!!
NOW ALL WE NEED TO DO IS FIGURE OUT HOW TO MAKE THIS BLEAK, INHOSPITABLE DESERT HABITABLE...
WE CAN DO THAT.
REALLY?! WE CAN DO THAT?!

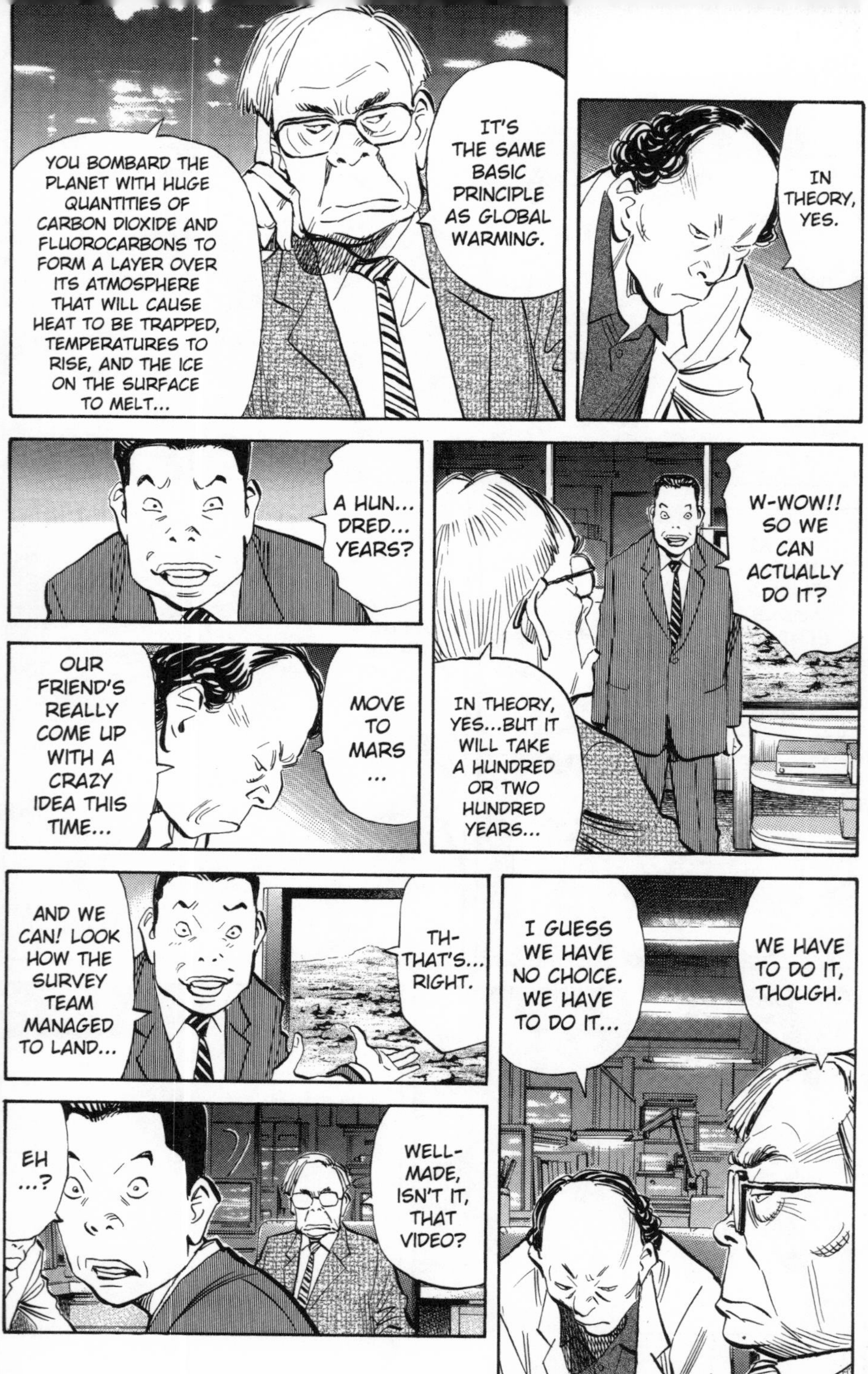
IN THEORY, YES.
IT'S THE SAME BASIC PRINCIPLE AS GLOBAL WARMING.
YOU BOMBARD THE PLANET WITH HUGE QUANTITIES OF CARBON DIOXIDE AND FLUOROCARBONS TO FORM A LAYER OVER ITS ATMOSPHERE THAT WILL CAUSE HEAT TO BE TRAPPED, TEMPERATURES TO RISE, AND THE ICE ON THE SURFACE TO MELT...
W-WOW!! SO WE CAN ACTUALLY DO IT?
IN THEORY, YES...BUT IT WILL TAKE A HUNDRED OR TWO HUNDRED YEARS...
A HUN... DRED... YEARS?
MOVE TO MARS...
OUR FRIEND'S REALLY COME UP WITH A CRAZY IDEA THIS TIME...
WE HAVE TO DO IT, THOUGH.
I GUESS WE HAVE NO CHOICE. WE HAVE TO DO IT...
TH-THAT'S... RIGHT.
AND WE CAN! LOOK HOW THE SURVEY TEAM MANAGED TO LAND...
WELL-MADE, ISN'T IT, THAT VIDEO?
EH ...?

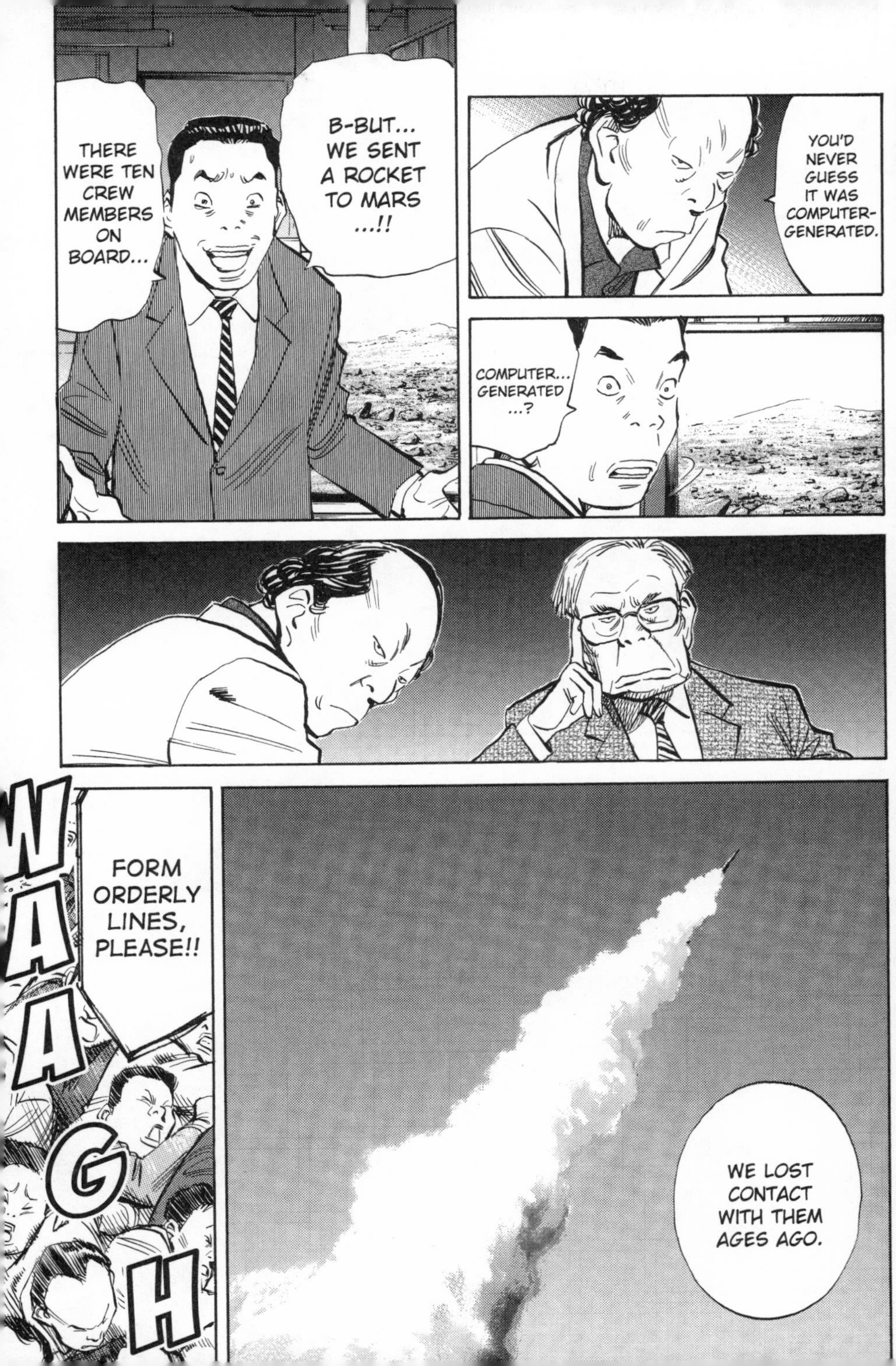

YOU'D NEVER GUESS IT WAS COMPUTER-GENERATED.
COMPUTER... GENERATED ...?
B-BUT... WE SENT A ROCKET TO MARS ...!!
THERE WERE TEN CREW MEMBERS ON BOARD...
WE LOST CONTACT WITH THEM AGES AGO.
FORM ORDERLY LINES, PLEASE!!
WAAGH

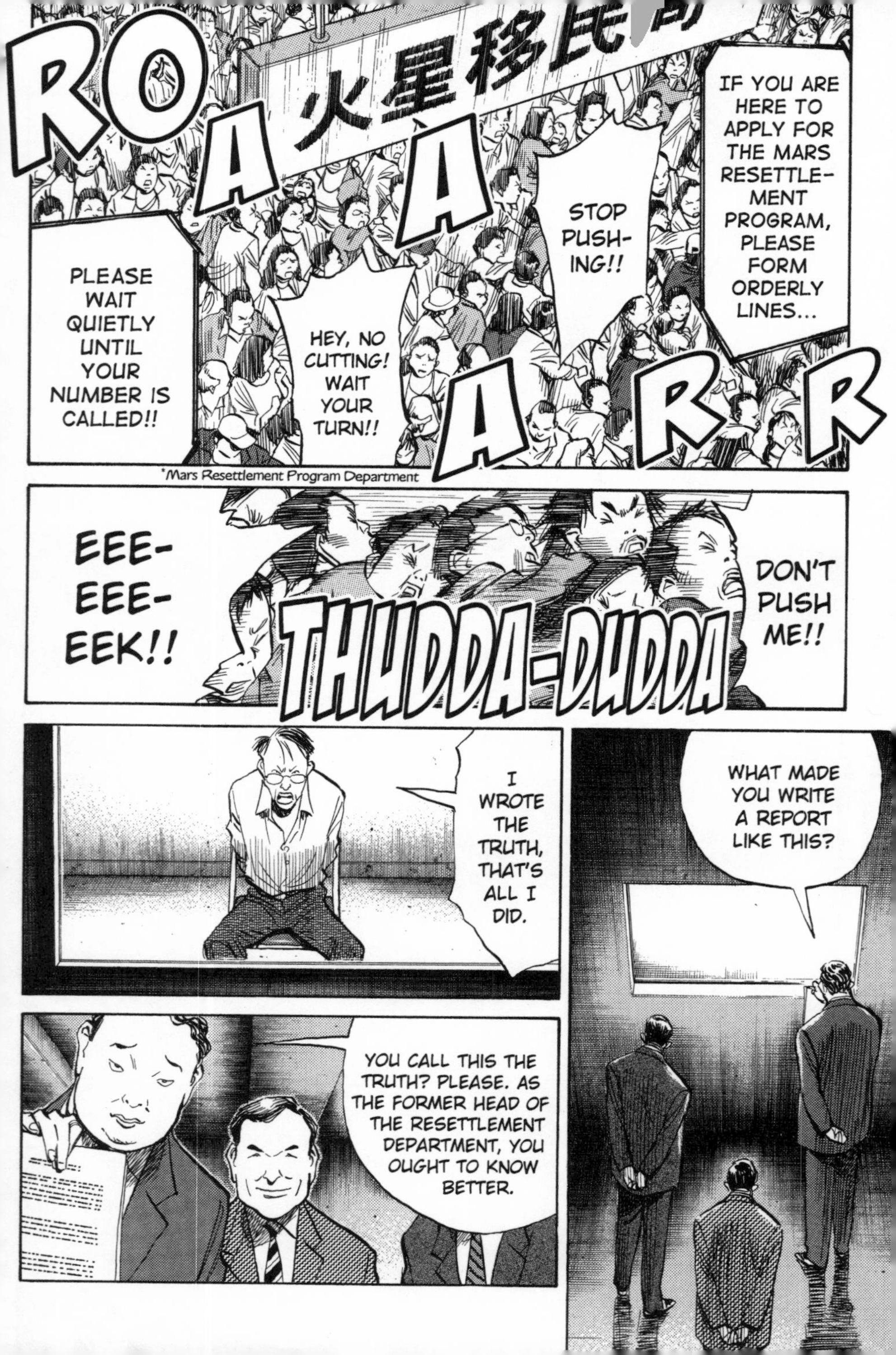
火星移民
IF YOU ARE HERE TO APPLY FOR THE MARS RESETTLEMENT PROGRAM, PLEASE FORM ORDERLY LINES...
STOP PUSHING!!
HEY, NO CUTTING! WAIT YOUR TURN!!
PLEASE WAIT QUIETLY UNTIL YOUR NUMBER IS CALLED!!
ROAAAARR
DON'T PUSH ME!!
THUDDA-DUDDA
EEE-EEE-EEK!!
WHAT MADE YOU WRITE A REPORT LIKE THIS?
I WROTE THE TRUTH, THAT'S ALL I DID.
YOU CALL THIS THE TRUTH? PLEASE. AS THE FORMER HEAD OF THE RESETTLEMENT DEPARTMENT, YOU OUGHT TO KNOW BETTER.
*Mars Resettlement Program Department

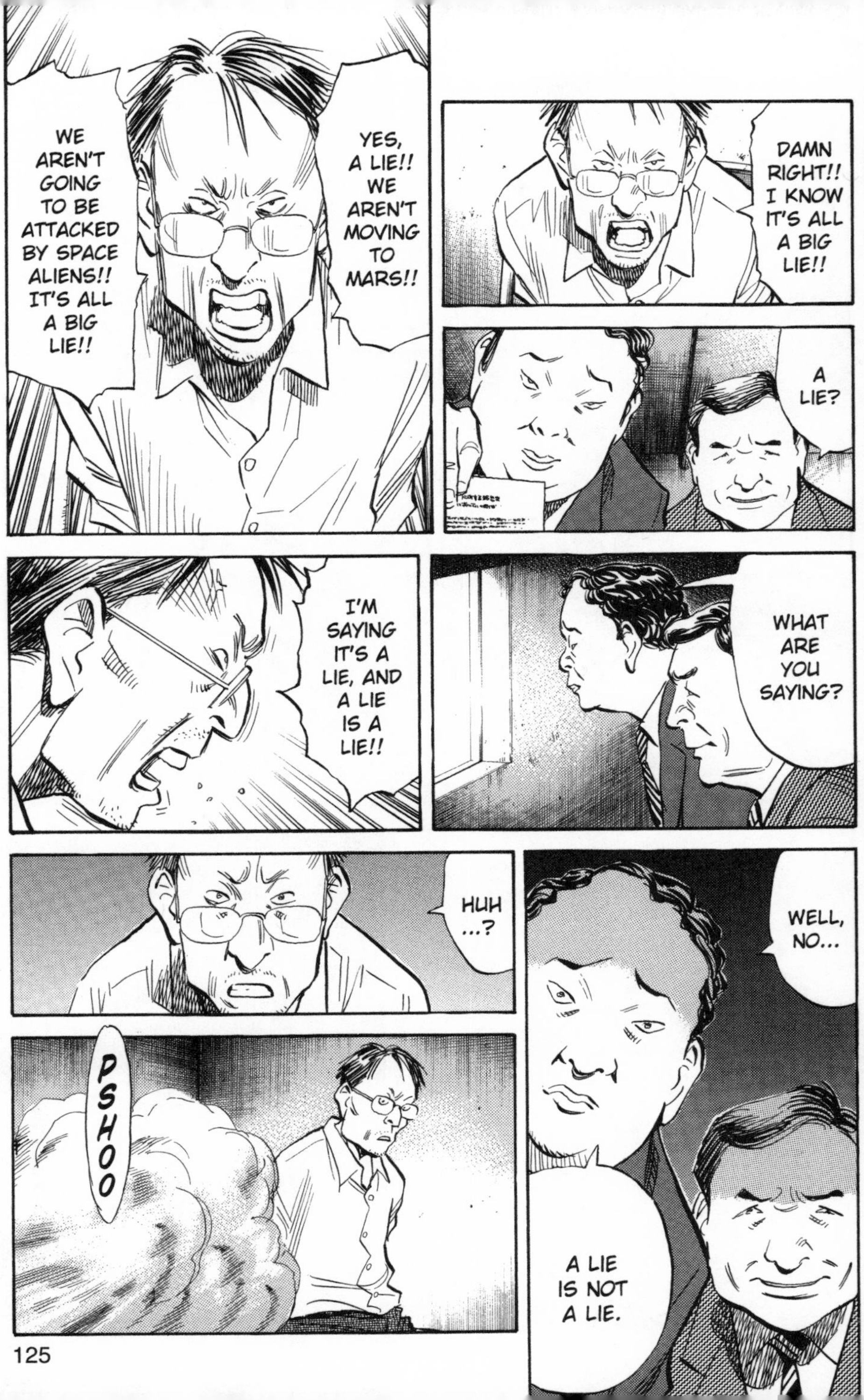
DAMN RIGHT!! I KNOW IT'S ALL A BIG LIE!!
A LIE?
YES, A LIE!! WE AREN'T MOVING TO MARS!!
WE AREN'T GOING TO BE ATTACKED BY SPACE ALIENS!! IT'S ALL A BIG LIE!!
WHAT ARE YOU SAYING?
I'M SAYING IT'S A LIE, AND A LIE IS A LIE!!
WELL, NO...
A LIE IS NOT A LIE.
HUH ...?
PSHOO

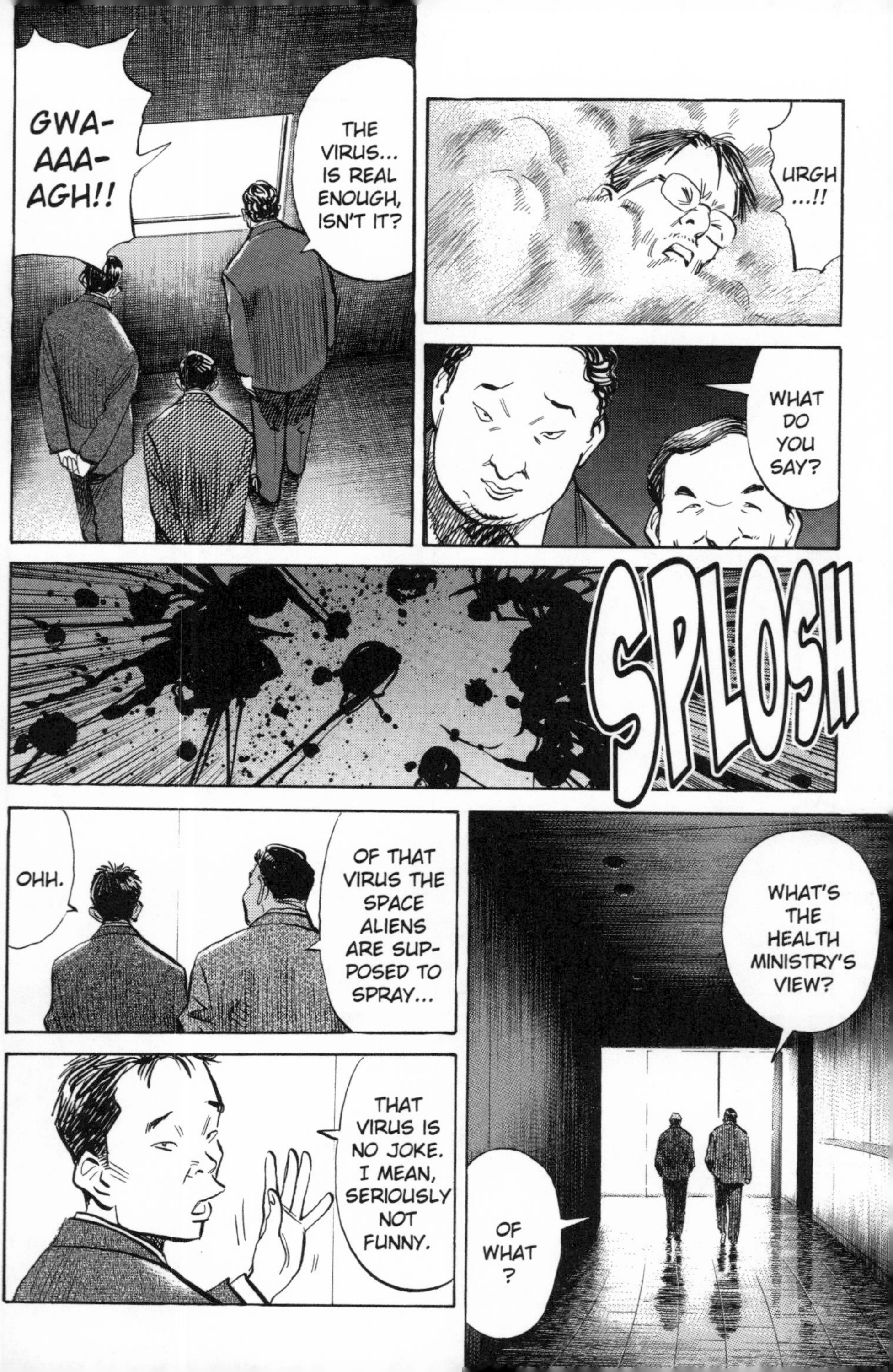
URGH ...!!
WHAT DO YOU SAY?
THE VIRUS... IS REAL ENOUGH, ISN'T IT?
GWA-AAA-AGH!!
SPLOSH
WHAT'S THE HEALTH MINISTRY'S VIEW?
OF WHAT?
OF THAT VIRUS THE SPACE ALIENS ARE SUP-POSED TO SPRAY...
OHH.
THAT VIRUS IS NO JOKE. I MEAN, SERIOUSLY NOT FUNNY.

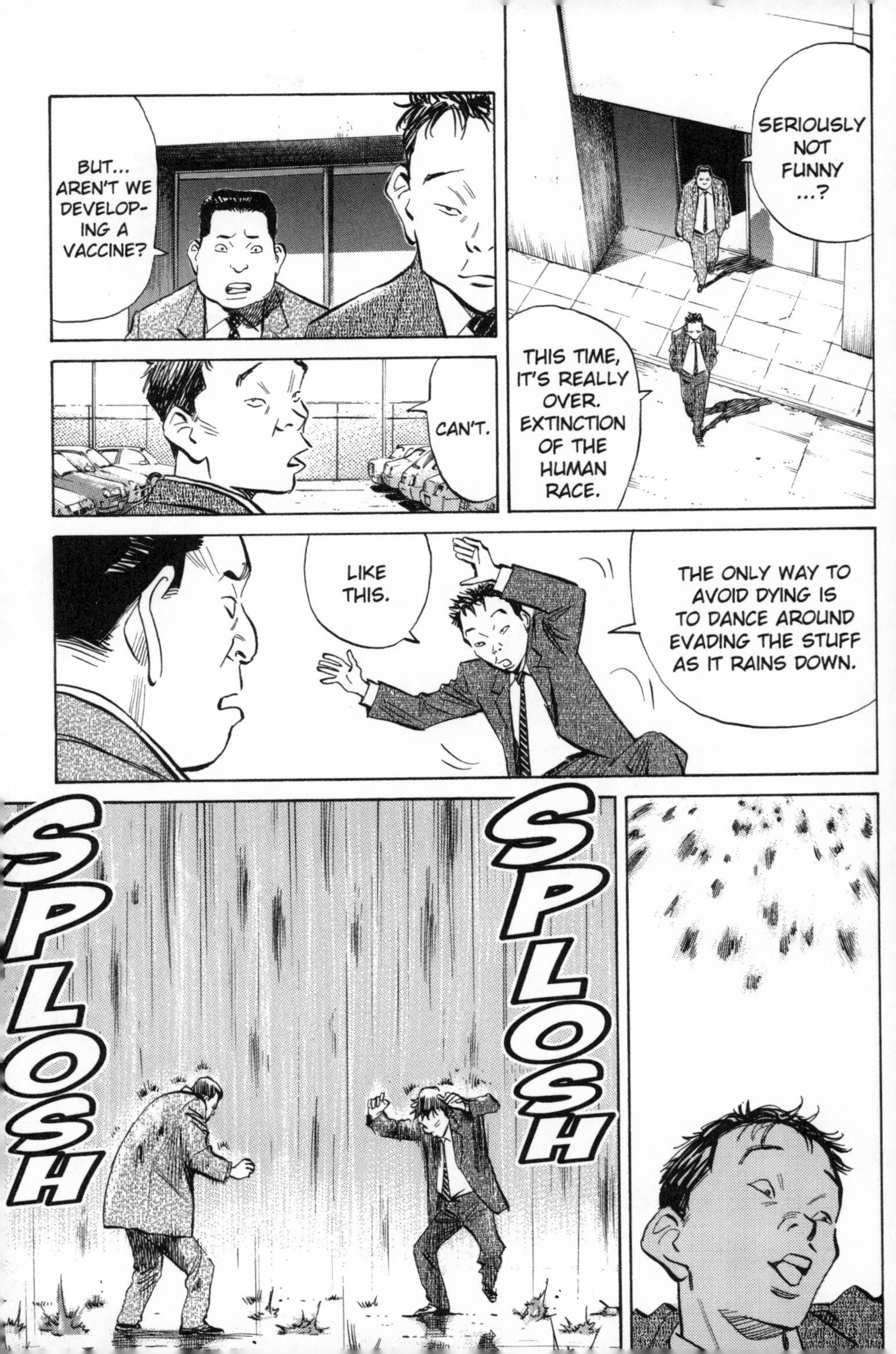
SERIOUSLY NOT FUNNY ...?
THIS TIME, IT'S REALLY OVER. EXTINCTION OF THE HUMAN RACE.
BUT... AREN'T WE DEVELOP-ING A VACCINE?
CAN'T.
THE ONLY WAY TO AVOID DYING IS TO DANCE AROUND EVADING THE STUFF AS IT RAINS DOWN.
LIKE THIS.
SPLOSH
SPLOSH

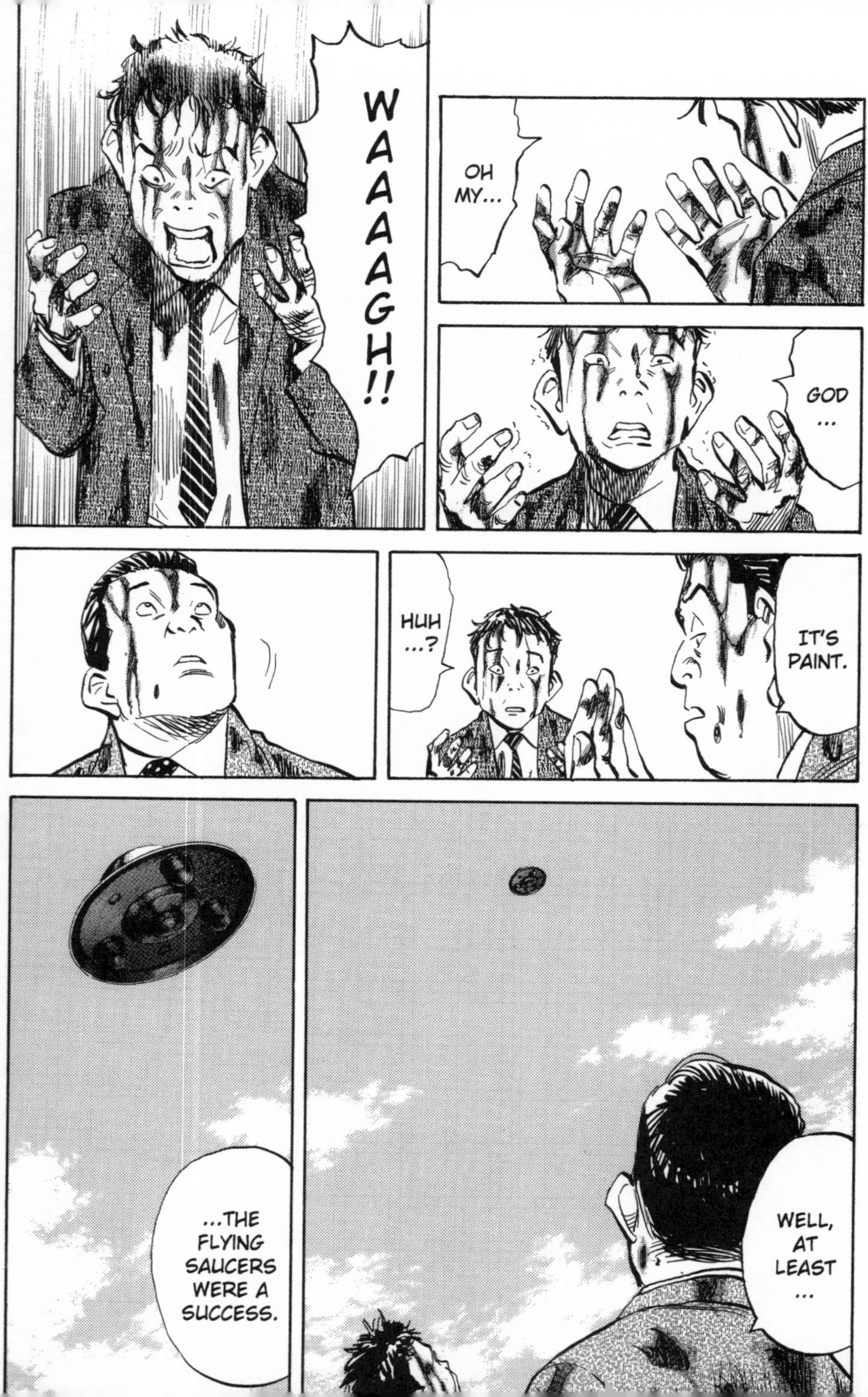
OH MY...
GOD...
WAAAAAGH!!
IT'S PAINT.
HUH...?
WELL, AT LEAST...
...THE FLYING SAUCERS WERE A SUCCESS.

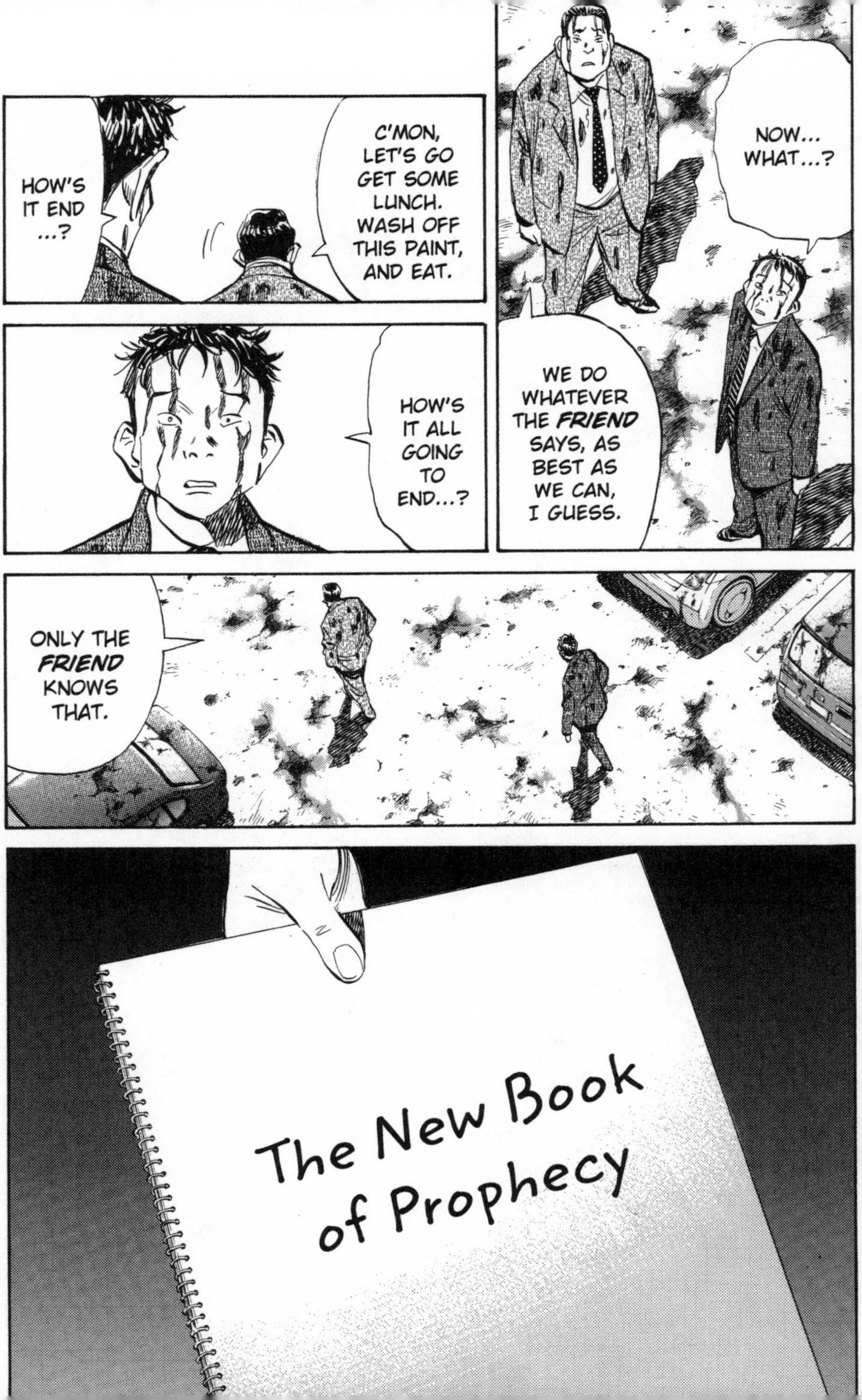
NOW... WHAT...?
WE DO WHATEVER THE FRIEND SAYS, AS BEST AS WE CAN, I GUESS.
C'MON, LET'S GO GET SOME LUNCH. WASH OFF THIS PAINT, AND EAT.
HOW'S IT END ...?
HOW'S IT ALL GOING TO END...?
ONLY THE FRIEND KNOWS THAT.
The New Book of Prophecy

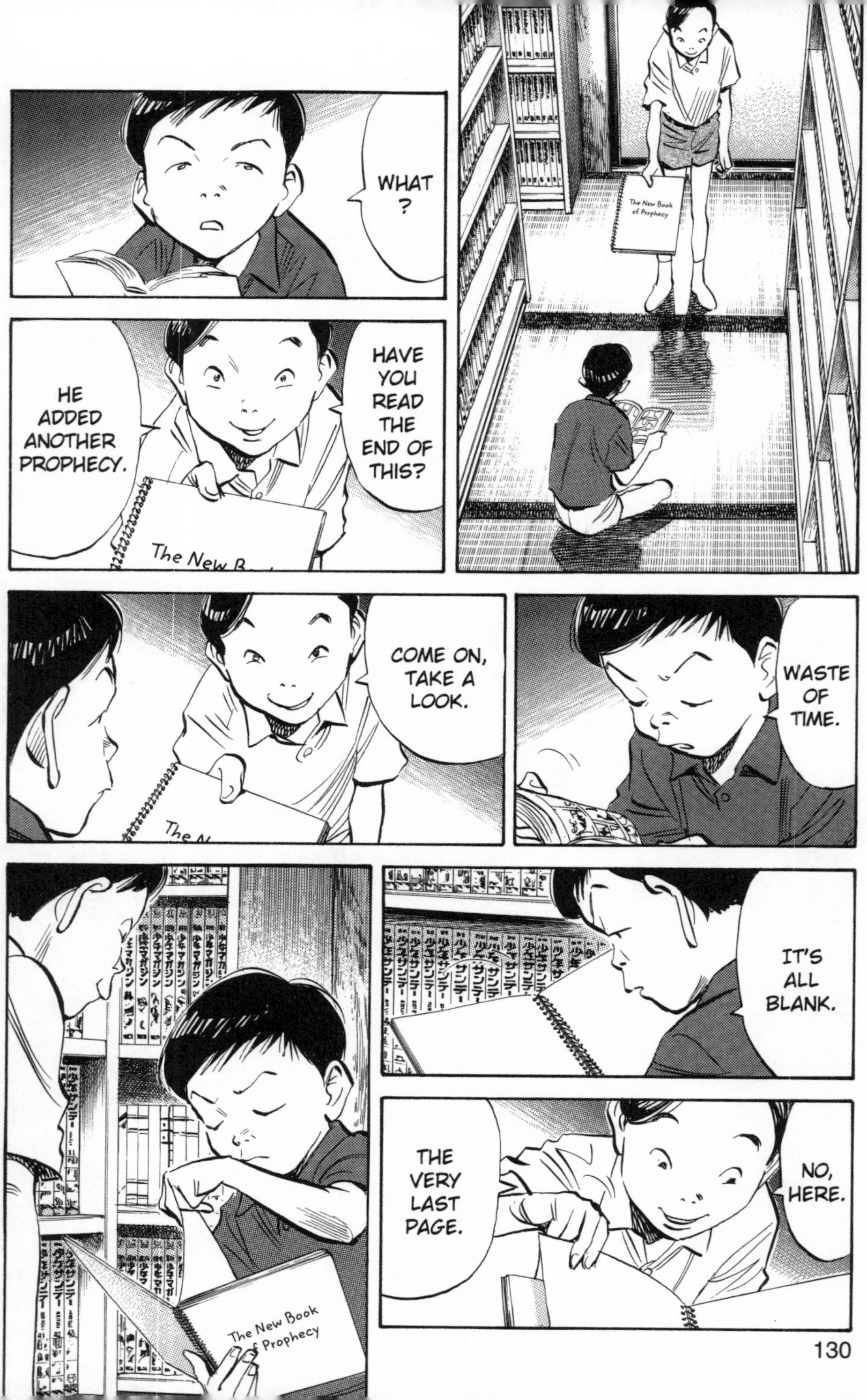
The New Book of Prophecy
WHAT?
HAVE YOU READ THE END OF THIS?
HE ADDED ANOTHER PROPHECY.
WASTE OF TIME.
COME ON, TAKE A LOOK.
IT'S ALL BLANK.
NO, HERE.
THE VERY LAST PAGE.
The New Book of Prophecy

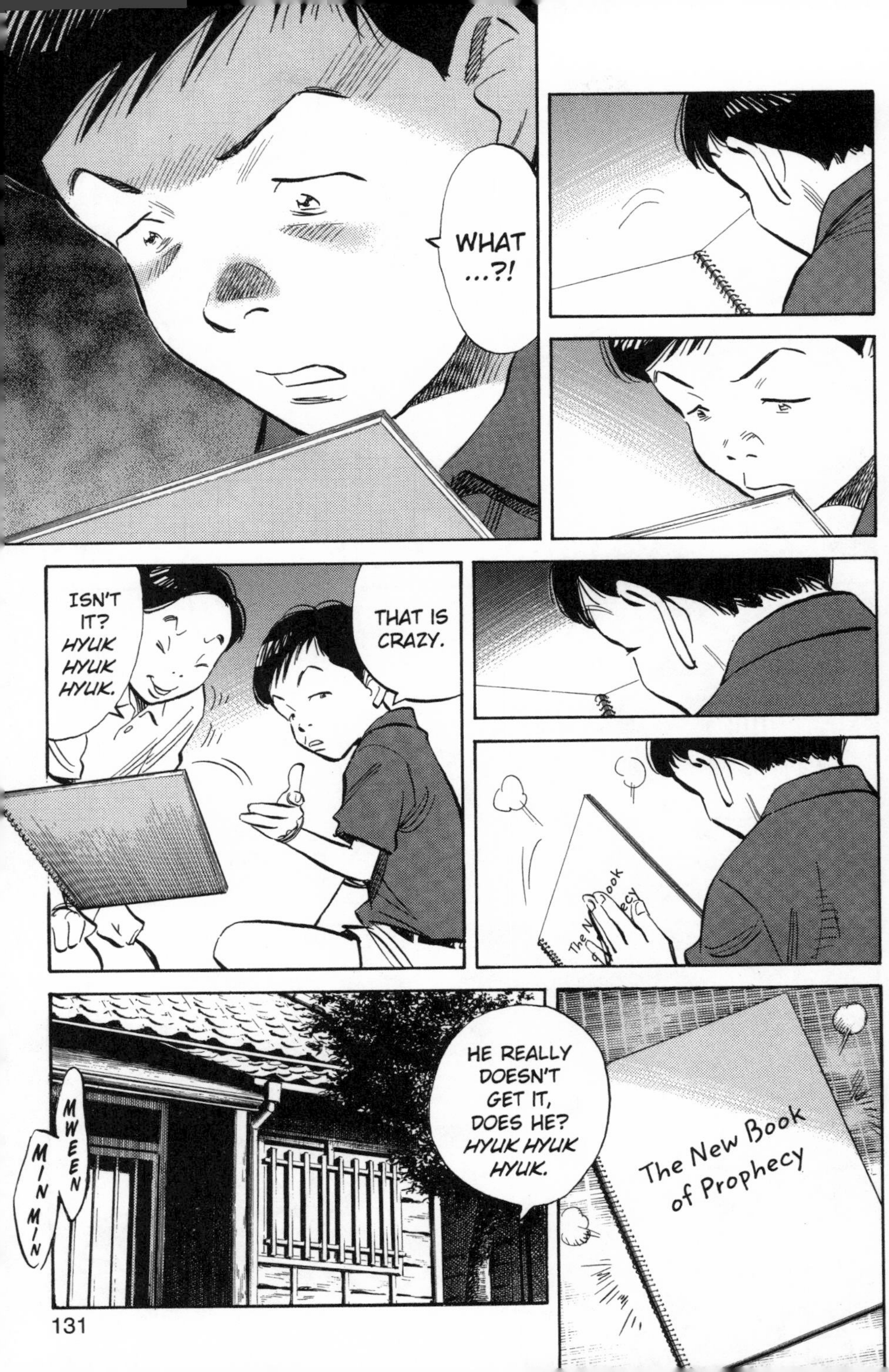
WHAT ...?!
THAT IS CRAZY.
ISN'T IT? HYUK HYUK HYUK.
The New Book of Prophecy
HE REALLY DOESN'T GET IT, DOES HE? HYUK HYUK HYUK.
MWEEN
MIN MIN

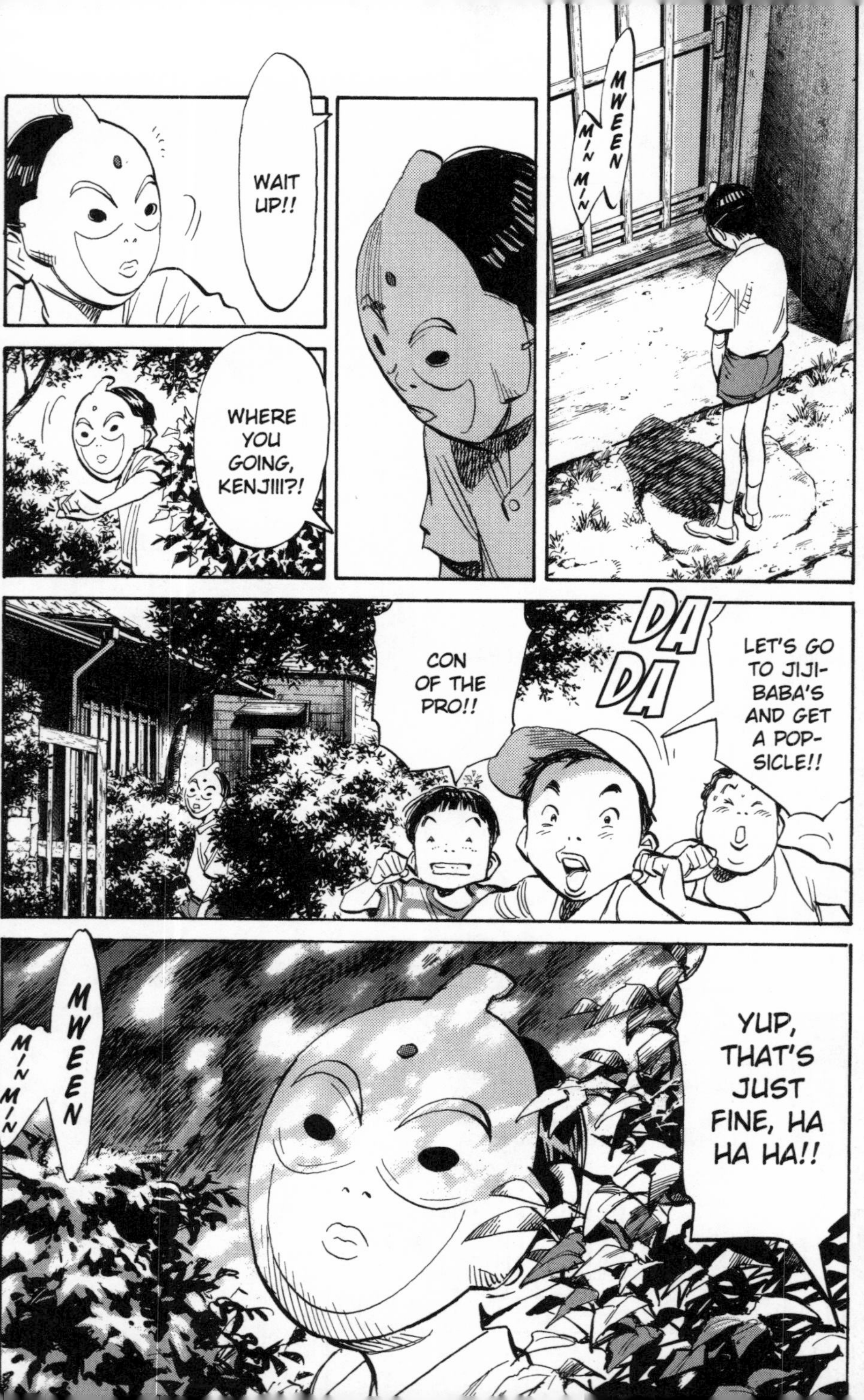
MWEEN
MIN MIN
WAIT UP!!
WHERE YOU GOING, KENJIII?!
DA DA
LET'S GO TO JIJI-BABA'S AND GET A POP-SICLE!!
CON OF THE PRO!!
YUP, THAT'S JUST FINE, HA HA HA!!
MWEEN
MIN MIN

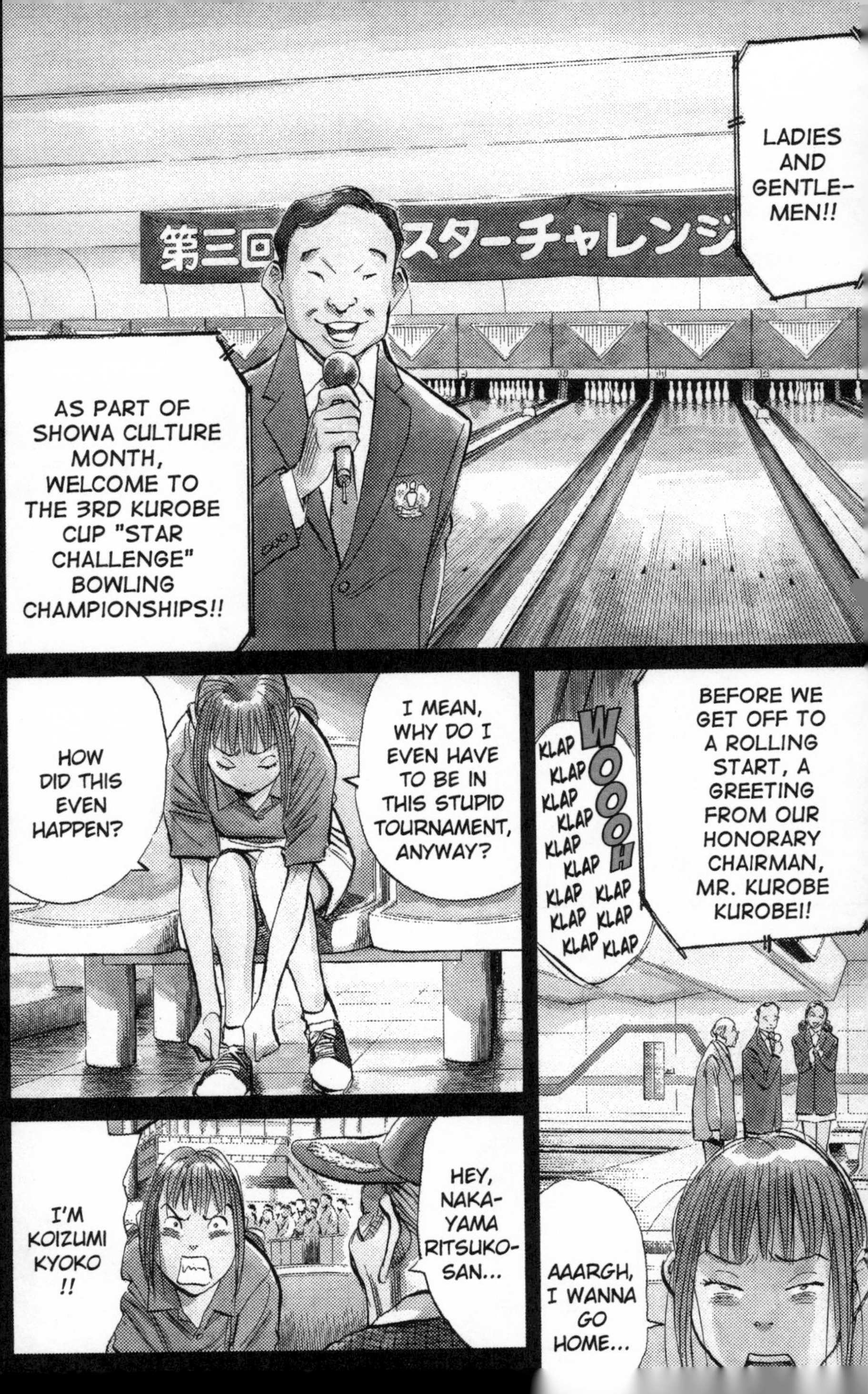
LADIES AND GENTLEMEN!!
第三回
スターチャレンジ
AS PART OF SHOWA CULTURE MONTH, WELCOME TO THE 3RD KUROBE CUP "STAR CHALLENGE" BOWLING CHAMPIONSHIPS!!
BEFORE WE GET OFF TO A ROLLING START, A GREETING FROM OUR HONORARY CHAIRMAN, MR. KUROBE KUROBE!!
WOOOH
KLAP KLAP KLAP KLAP KLAP KLAP KLAP KLAP KLAP KLAP KLAP KLAP
AAARGH, I WANNA GO HOME...
I MEAN, WHY DO I EVEN HAVE TO BE IN THIS STUPID TOURNAMENT, ANYWAY?
HOW DID THIS EVEN HAPPEN?
HEY, NAKAYAMA RITSUKO-SAN...
I'M KOIZUMI KYOKO!!

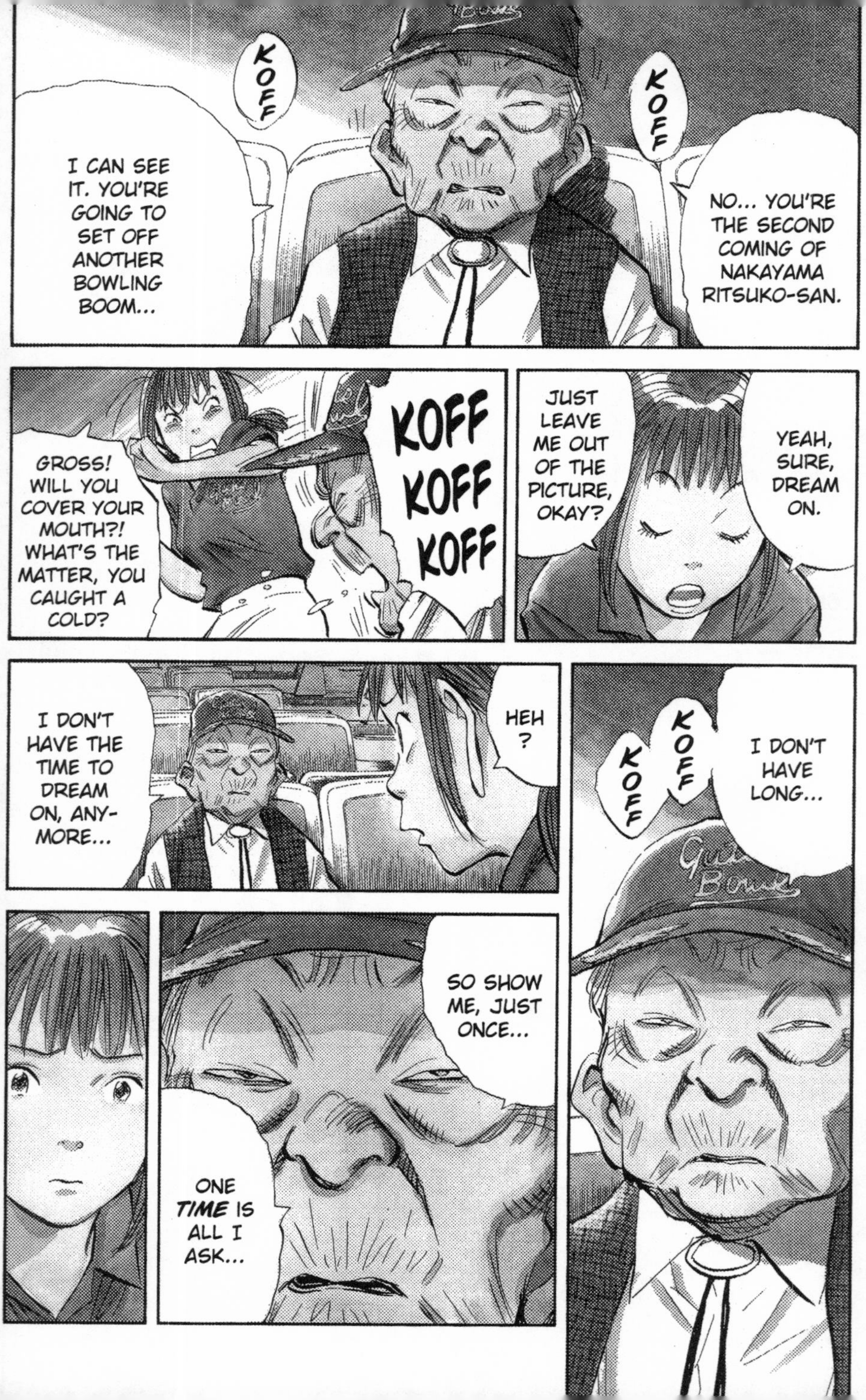
KOFF
NO... YOU'RE THE SECOND COMING OF NAKAYAMA RITSUKO-SAN.
KOFF
I CAN SEE IT. YOU'RE GOING TO SET OFF ANOTHER BOWLING BOOM...
YEAH, SURE, DREAM ON.
JUST LEAVE ME OUT OF THE PICTURE, OKAY?
KOFF KOFF KOFF
GROSS! WILL YOU COVER YOUR MOUTH?! WHAT'S THE MATTER, YOU CAUGHT A COLD?
KOFF
KOFF
I DON'T HAVE LONG...
HEH?
I DON'T HAVE THE TIME TO DREAM ON, ANY-MORE...
SO SHOW ME, JUST ONCE...
ONE *TIME* IS ALL I ASK...

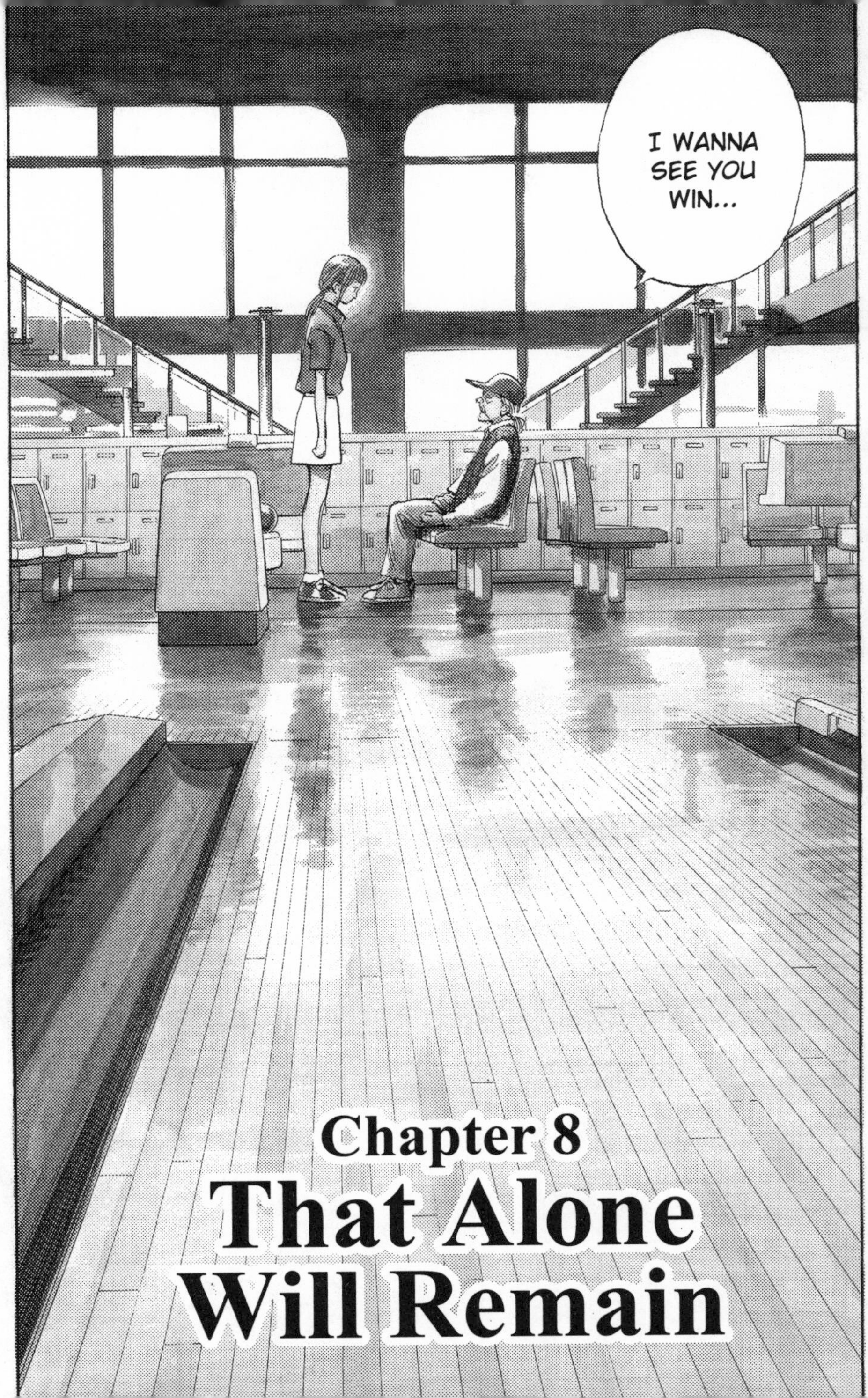
I WANNA SEE YOU WIN...

Chapter 8
That Alone Will Remain

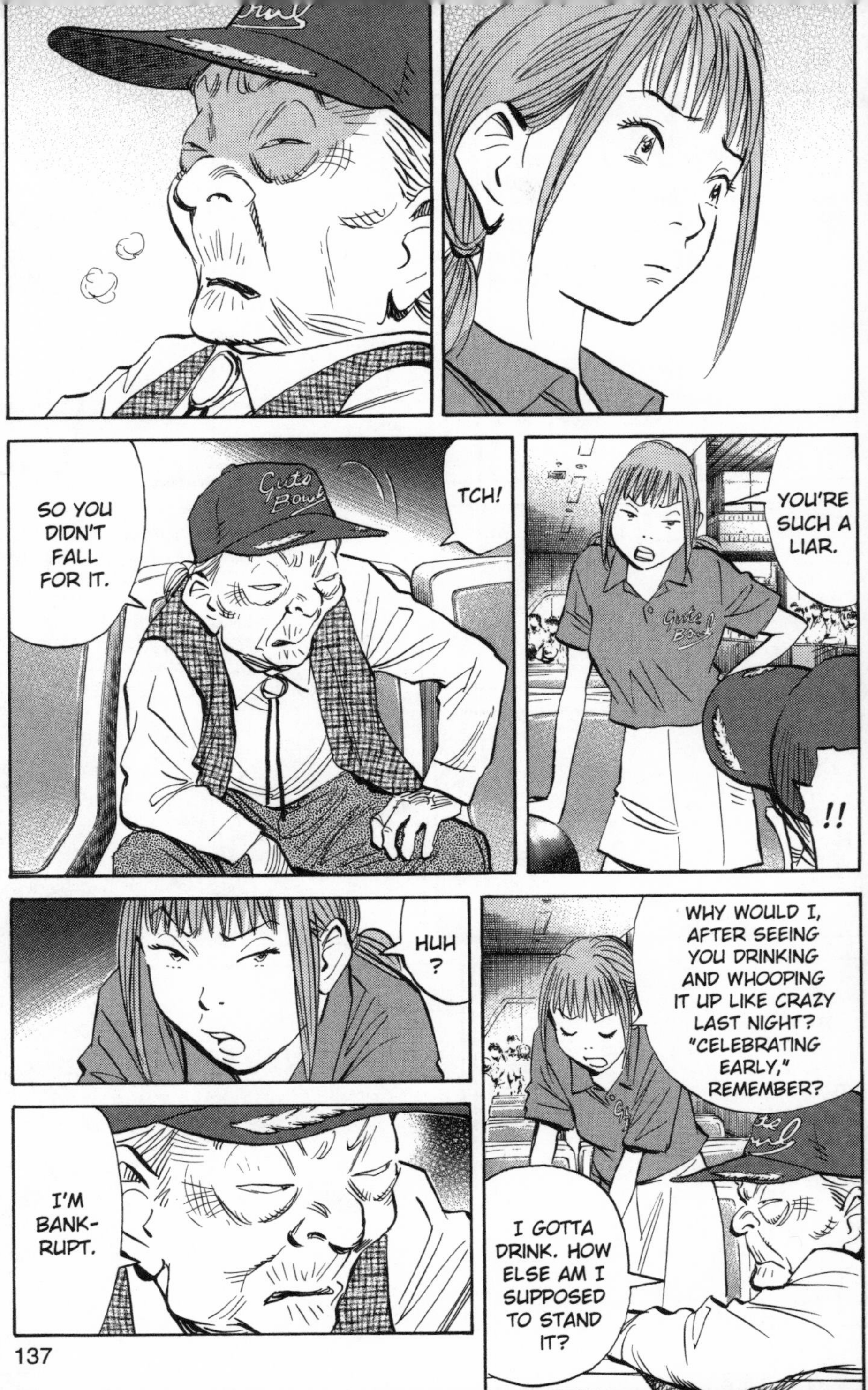
YOU'RE SUCH A LIAR.
!!
TCH!
SO YOU DIDN'T FALL FOR IT.
WHY WOULD I, AFTER SEEING YOU DRINKING AND WHOOPING IT UP LIKE CRAZY LAST NIGHT? "CELEBRATING EARLY," REMEMBER?
I GOTTA DRINK. HOW ELSE AM I SUPPOSED TO STAND IT?
HUH?
I'M BANK-RUPT.

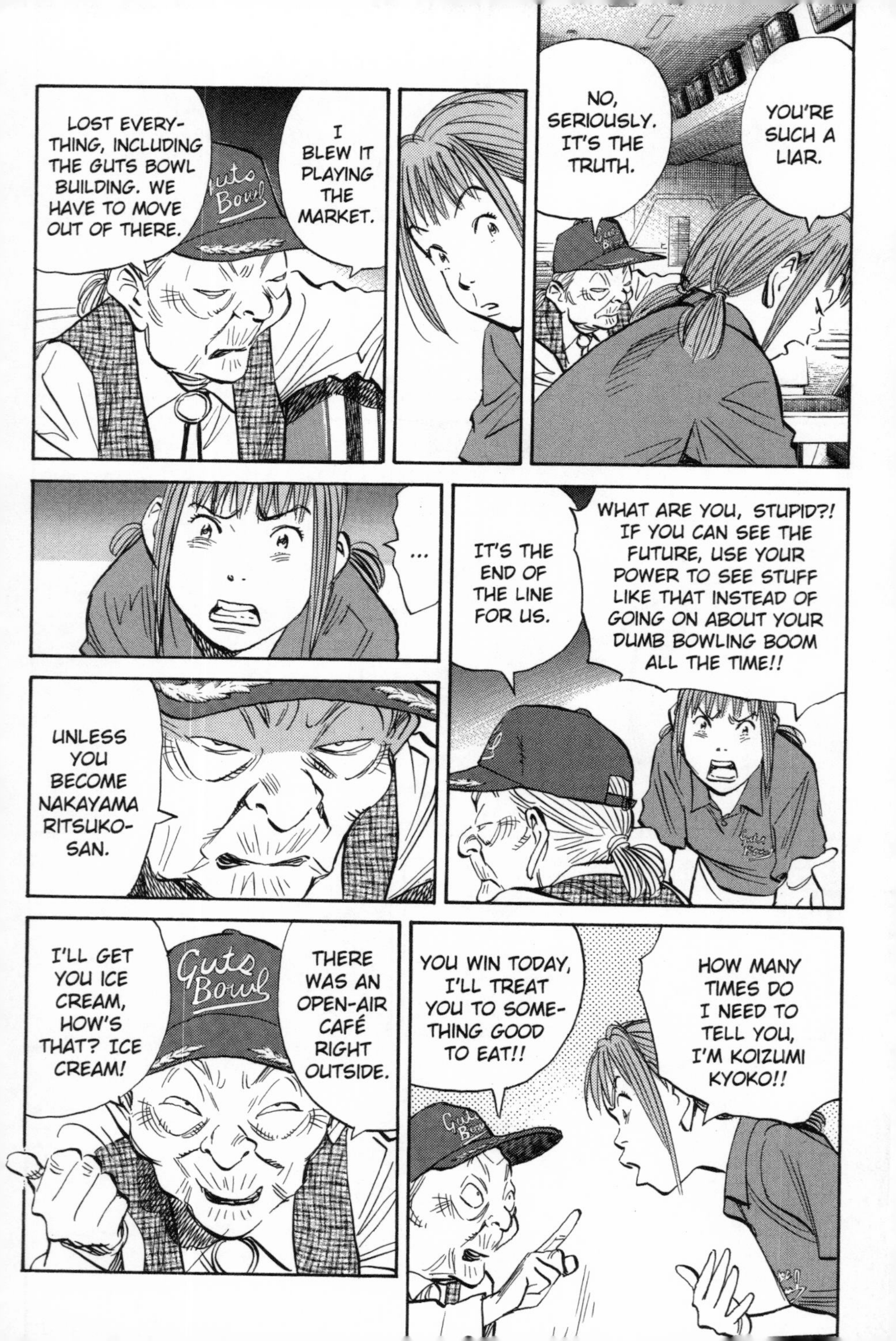
YOU'RE SUCH A LIAR.
NO, SERIOUSLY. IT'S THE TRUTH.
I BLEW IT PLAYING THE MARKET.
LOST EVERY-THING, INCLUDING THE GUTS BOWL BUILDING. WE HAVE TO MOVE OUT OF THERE.
WHAT ARE YOU, STUPID?! IF YOU CAN SEE THE FUTURE, USE YOUR POWER TO SEE STUFF LIKE THAT INSTEAD OF GOING ON ABOUT YOUR DUMB BOWLING BOOM ALL THE TIME!!
IT'S THE END OF THE LINE FOR US.
...
UNLESS YOU BECOME NAKAYAMA RITSUKO-SAN.
HOW MANY TIMES DO I NEED TO TELL YOU, I'M KOIZUMI KYOKO!!
YOU WIN TODAY, I'LL TREAT YOU TO SOME-THING GOOD TO EAT!!
THERE WAS AN OPEN-AIR CAFÉ RIGHT OUTSIDE.
I'LL GET YOU ICE CREAM, HOW'S THAT? ICE CREAM!

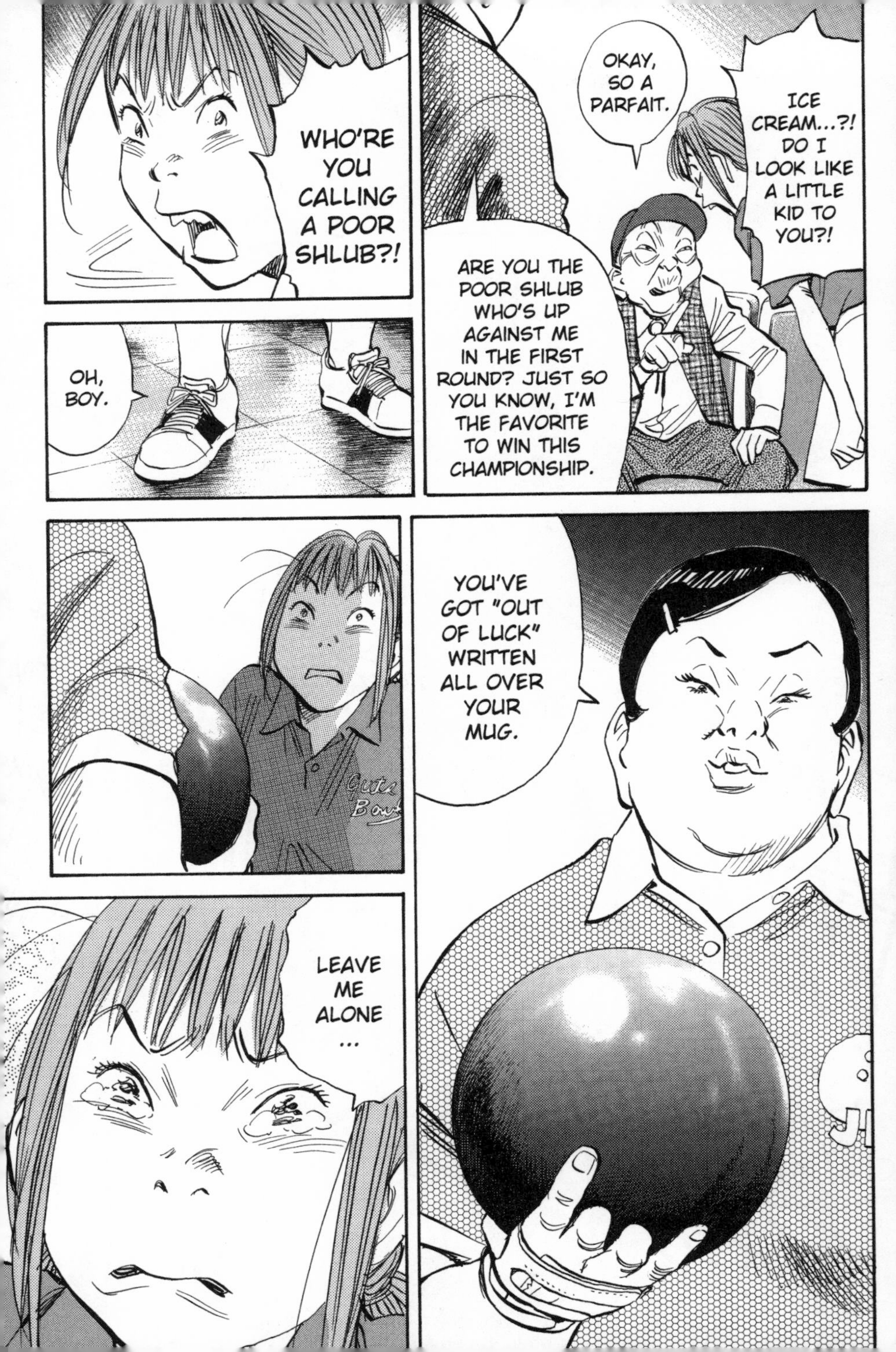
ICE CREAM...?! DO I LOOK LIKE A LITTLE KID TO YOU?!
OKAY, SO A PARFAIT.
ARE YOU THE POOR SHLUB WHO'S UP AGAINST ME IN THE FIRST ROUND? JUST SO YOU KNOW, I'M THE FAVORITE TO WIN THIS CHAMPIONSHIP.
WHO'RE YOU CALLING A POOR SHLUB?!
OH, BOY.
YOU'VE GOT "OUT OF LUCK" WRITTEN ALL OVER YOUR MUG.
LEAVE ME ALONE ...

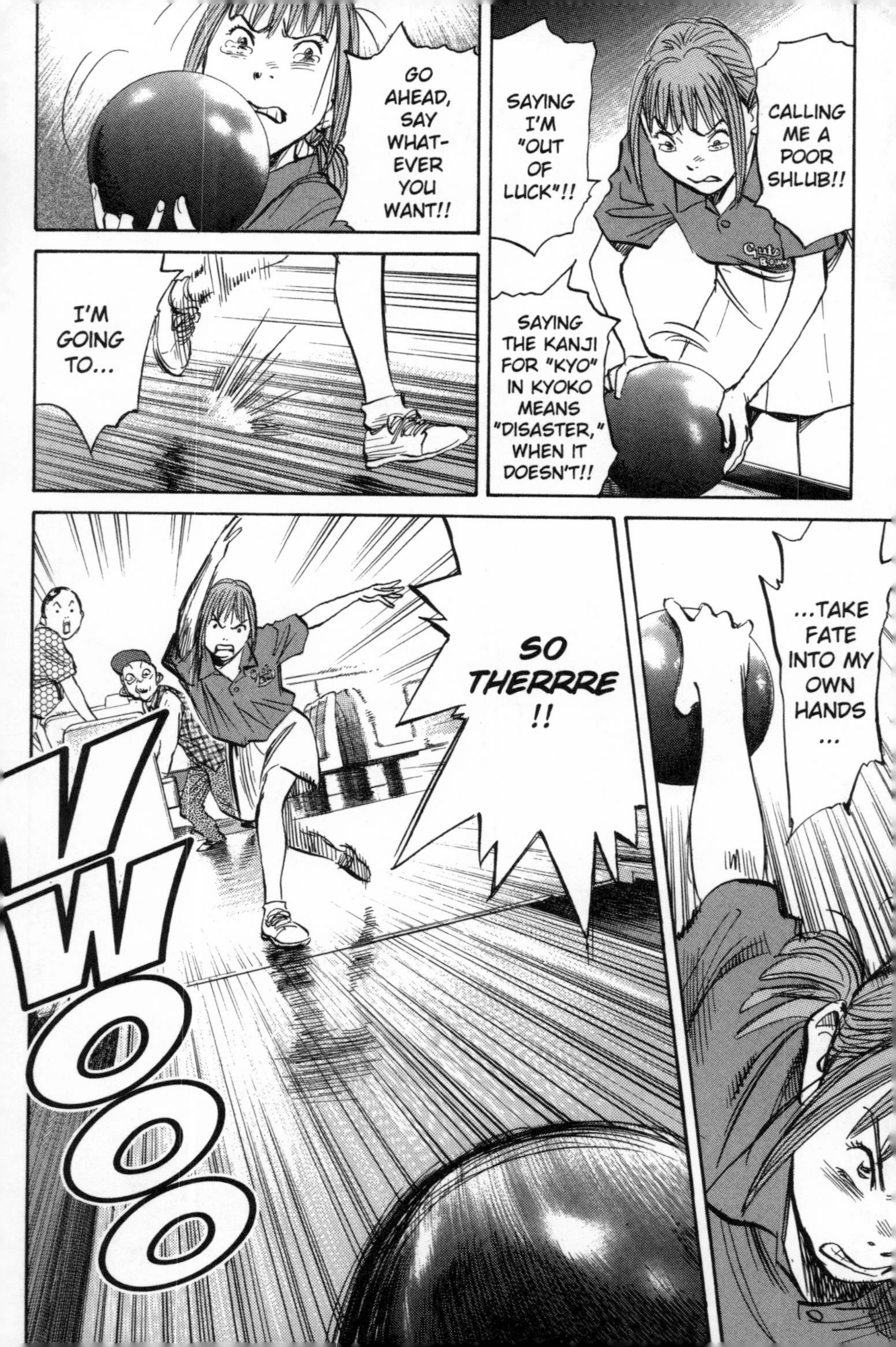
CALLING ME A POOR SHLUB!!
SAYING I'M "OUT OF LUCK"!!
SAYING THE KANJI FOR "KYO" IN KYOKO MEANS "DISASTER," WHEN IT DOESN'T!!
GO AHEAD, SAY WHAT-EVER YOU WANT!!
I'M GOING TO...
...TAKE FATE INTO MY OWN HANDS...
SO THERRRE!!
VWOOOO

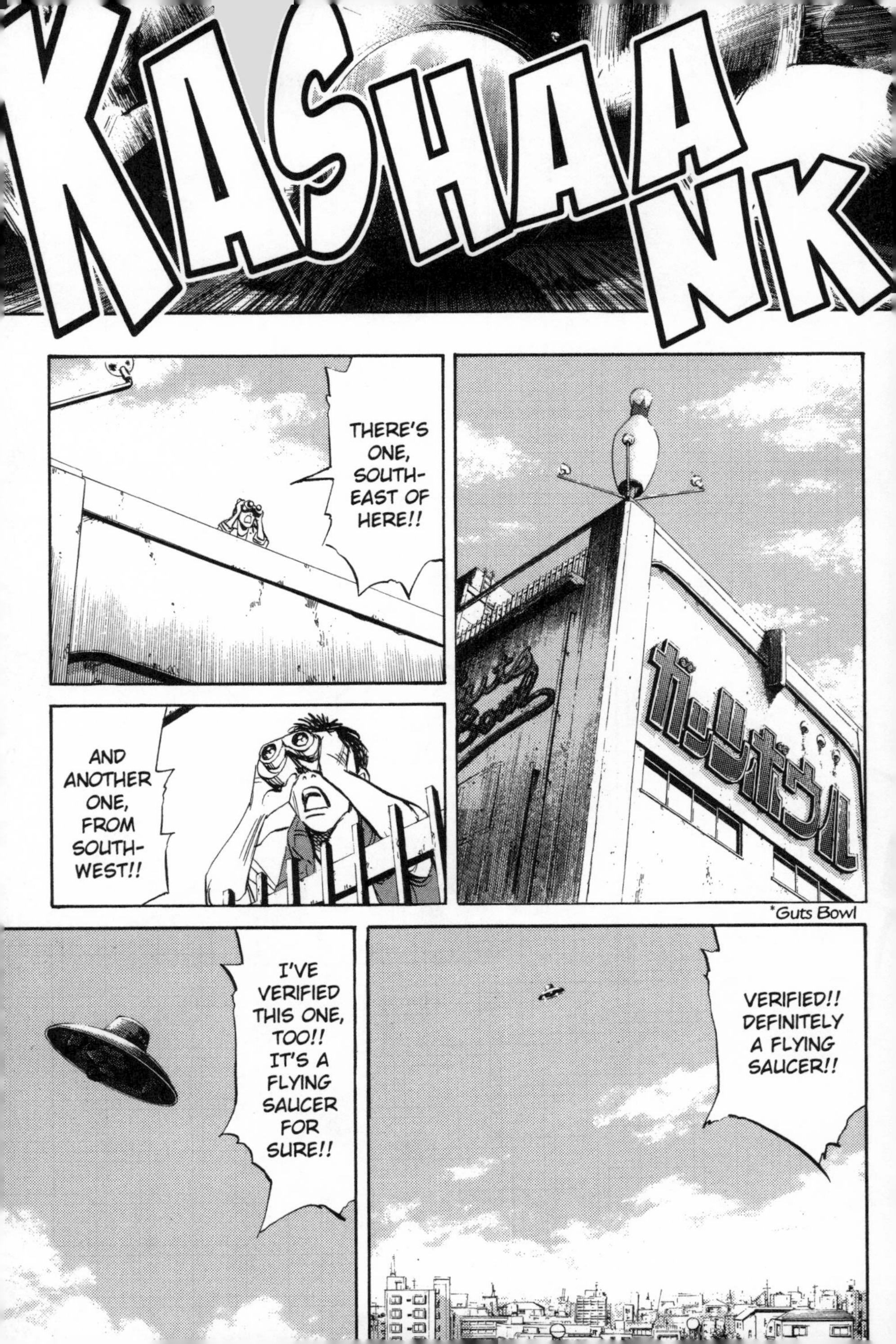
KASHAAANK
*Guts Bowl
THERE'S ONE, SOUTH-EAST OF HERE!!
AND ANOTHER ONE, FROM SOUTH-WEST!!
VERIFIED!! DEFINITELY A FLYING SAUCER!!
I'VE VERIFIED THIS ONE, TOO!! IT'S A FLYING SAUCER FOR SURE!!

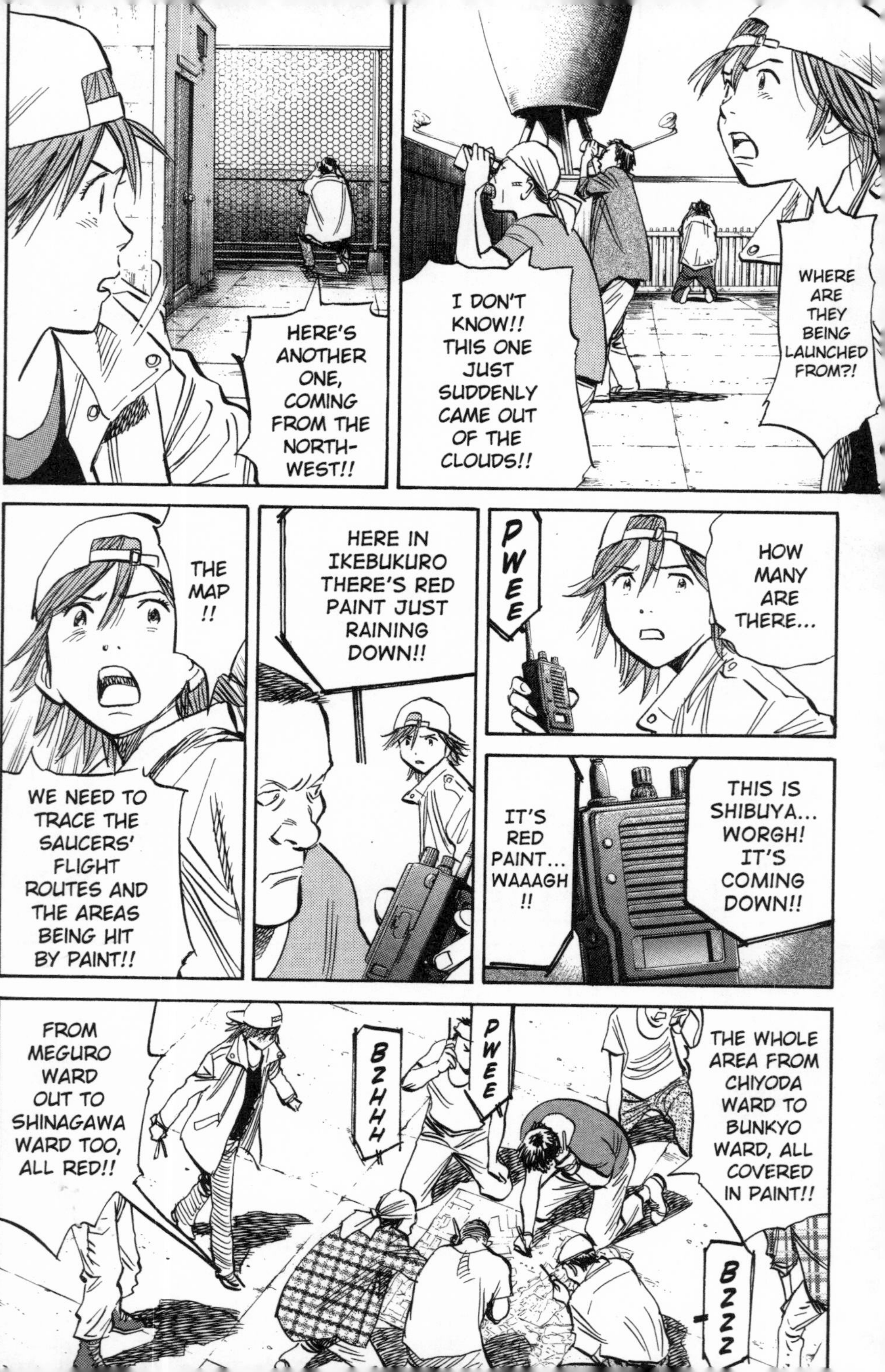
WHERE ARE THEY BEING LAUNCHED FROM?!
I DON'T KNOW!! THIS ONE JUST SUDDENLY CAME OUT OF THE CLOUDS!!
HERE'S ANOTHER ONE, COMING FROM THE NORTH-WEST!!
HOW MANY ARE THERE...
PWEE
THIS IS SHIBUYA... WORGH! IT'S COMING DOWN!!
IT'S RED PAINT... WAAAGH!!
HERE IN IKEBUKURO THERE'S RED PAINT JUST RAINING DOWN!!
THE MAP!!
WE NEED TO TRACE THE SAUCERS' FLIGHT ROUTES AND THE AREAS BEING HIT BY PAINT!!
THE WHOLE AREA FROM CHIYODA WARD TO BUNKYO WARD, ALL COVERED IN PAINT!!
BZZZ
PWEE
BZHHH
FROM MEGURO WARD OUT TO SHINAGAWA WARD TOO, ALL RED!!

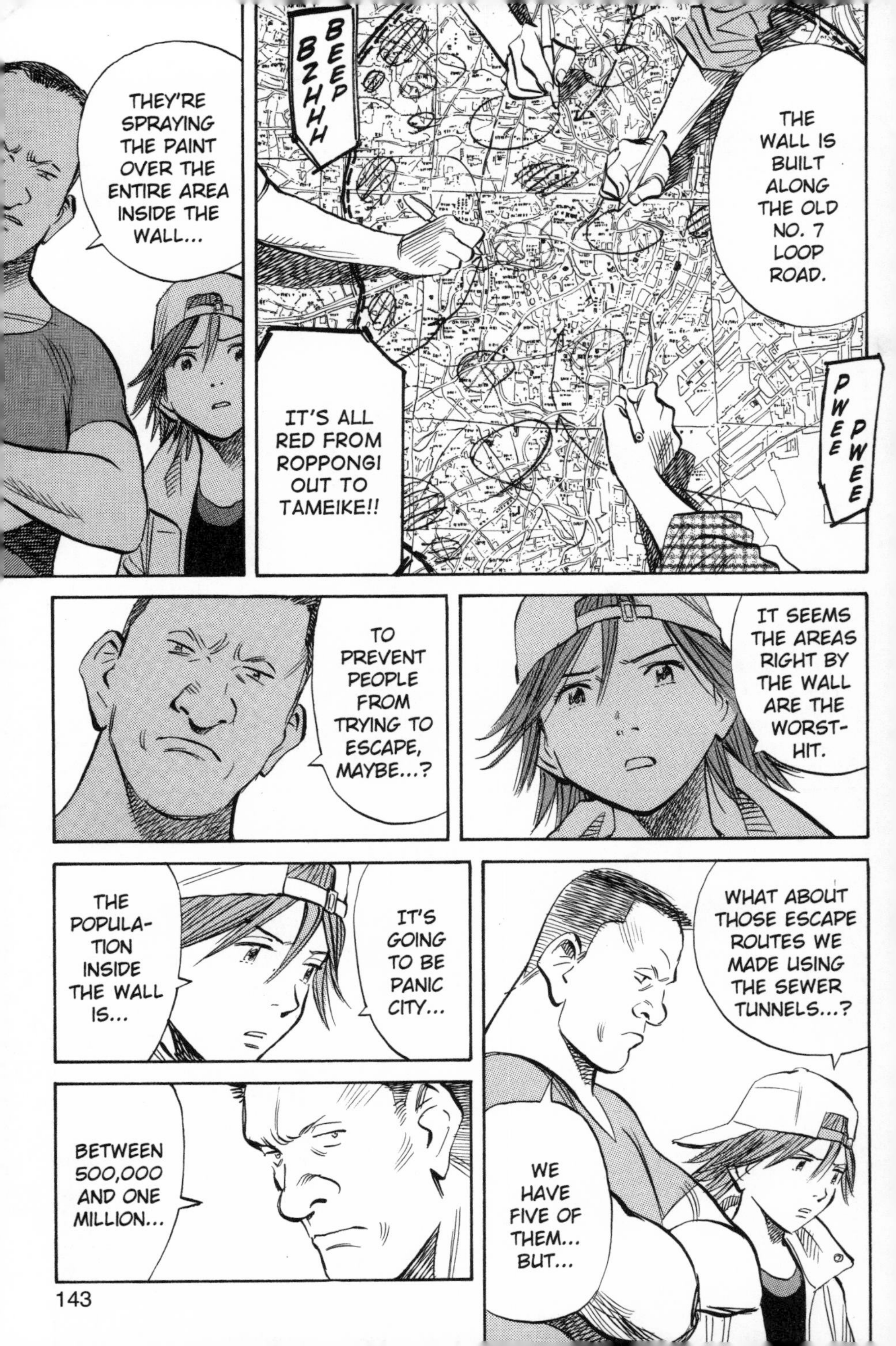
THE WALL IS BUILT ALONG THE OLD NO. 7 LOOP ROAD.
BEEP BZHHH
PWEE PWEE
IT'S ALL RED FROM ROPPONGI OUT TO TAMEIKE!!
THEY'RE SPRAYING THE PAINT OVER THE ENTIRE AREA INSIDE THE WALL...
IT SEEMS THE AREAS RIGHT BY THE WALL ARE THE WORST-HIT.
TO PREVENT PEOPLE FROM TRYING TO ESCAPE, MAYBE...?
WHAT ABOUT THOSE ESCAPE ROUTES WE MADE USING THE SEWER TUNNELS...?
WE HAVE FIVE OF THEM... BUT...
IT'S GOING TO BE PANIC CITY...
THE POPULATION INSIDE THE WALL IS...
BETWEEN 500,000 AND ONE MILLION...

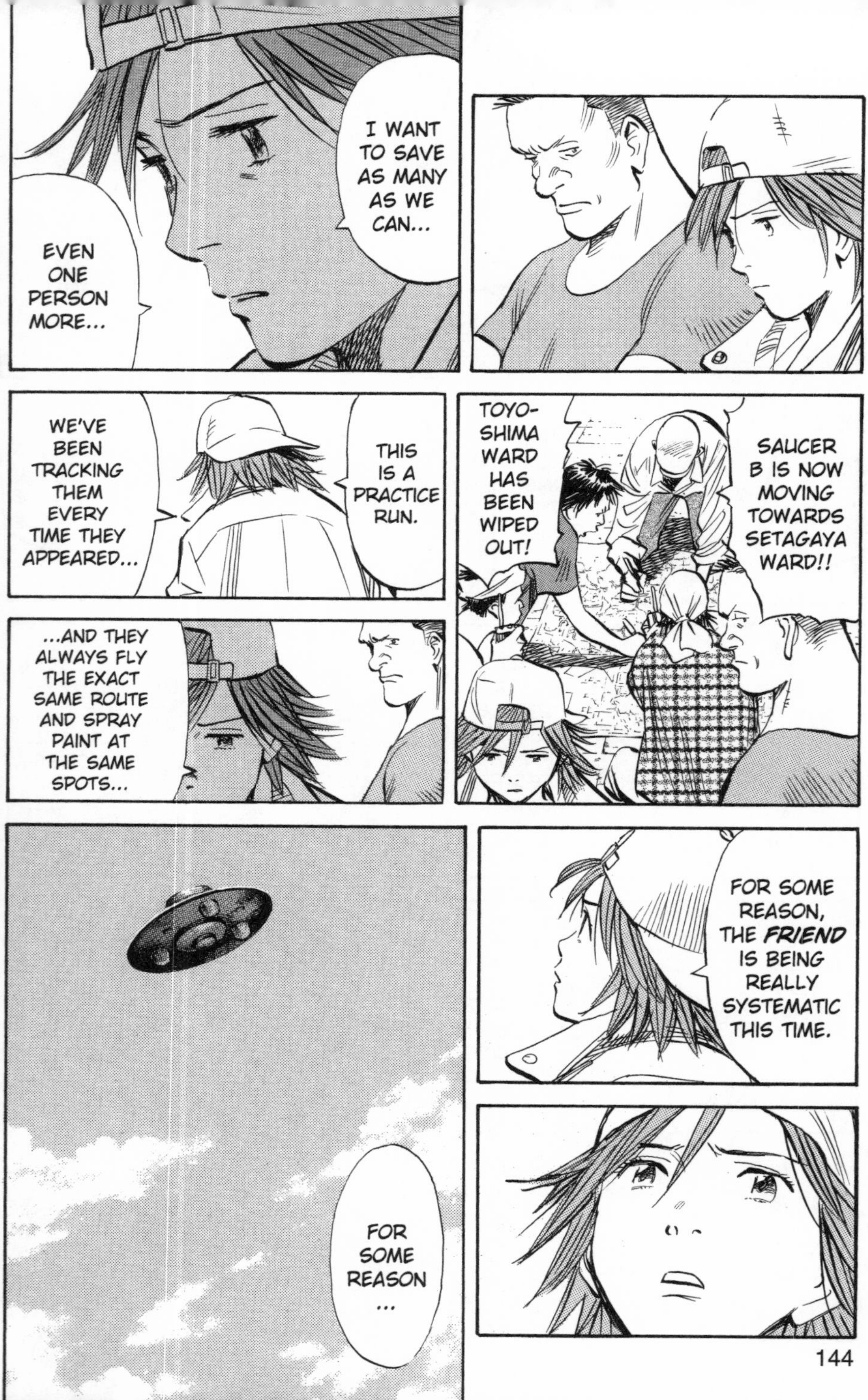
I WANT TO SAVE AS MANY AS WE CAN...
EVEN ONE PERSON MORE...
SAUCER B IS NOW MOVING TOWARDS SETAGAYA WARD!!
TOYO-SHIMA WARD HAS BEEN WIPED OUT!
THIS IS A PRACTICE RUN.
WE'VE BEEN TRACKING THEM EVERY TIME THEY APPEARED...
...AND THEY ALWAYS FLY THE EXACT SAME ROUTE AND SPRAY PAINT AT THE SAME SPOTS...
FOR SOME REASON, THE ***FRIEND*** IS BEING REALLY SYSTEMATIC THIS TIME.
FOR SOME REASON...

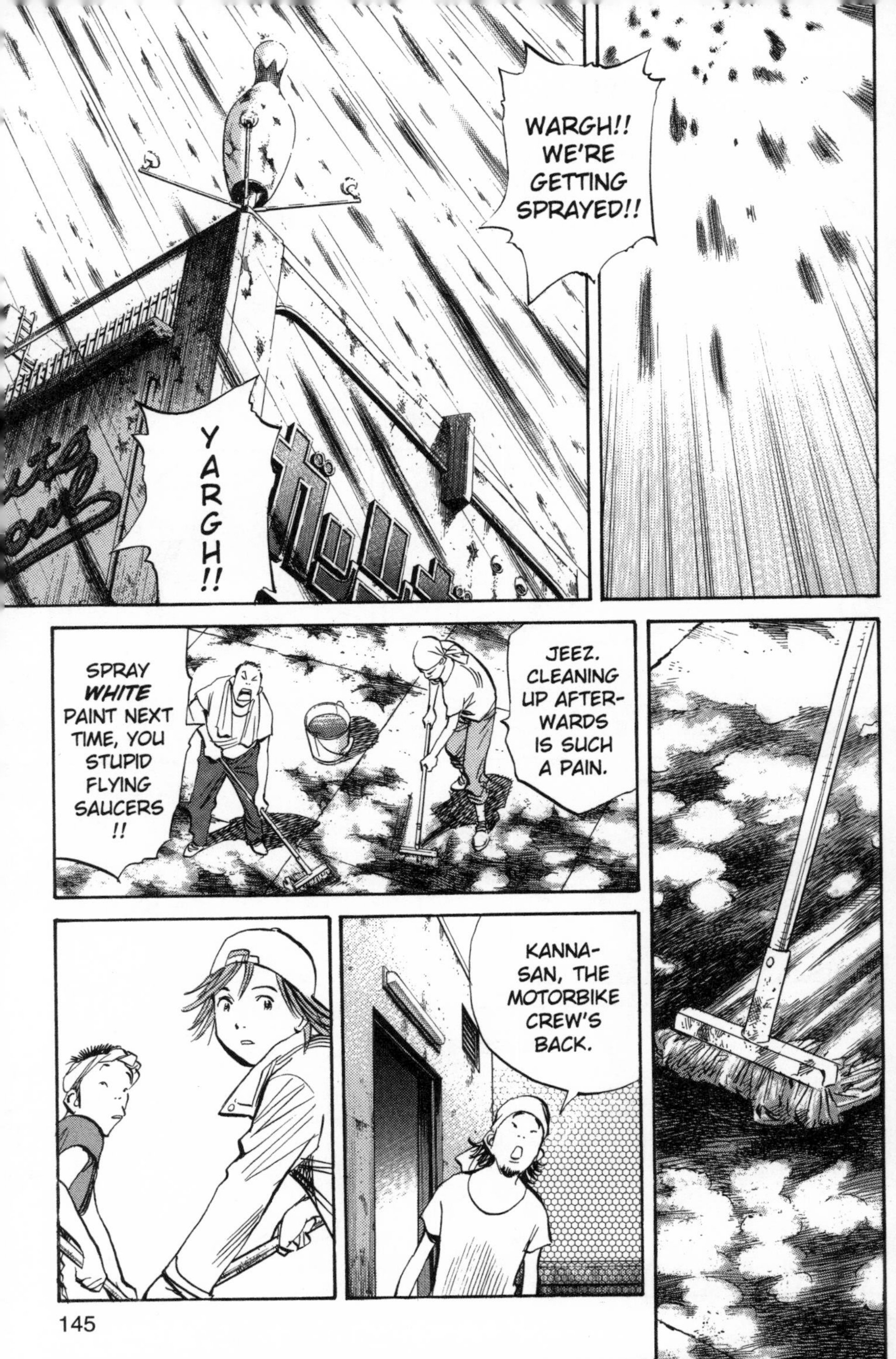
WARGH!! WE'RE GETTING SPRAYED!!
YARGH!!
JEEZ. CLEANING UP AFTER- WARDS IS SUCH A PAIN.
SPRAY *WHITE* PAINT NEXT TIME, YOU STUPID FLYING SAUCERS !!
KANNA- SAN, THE MOTORBIKE CREW'S BACK.

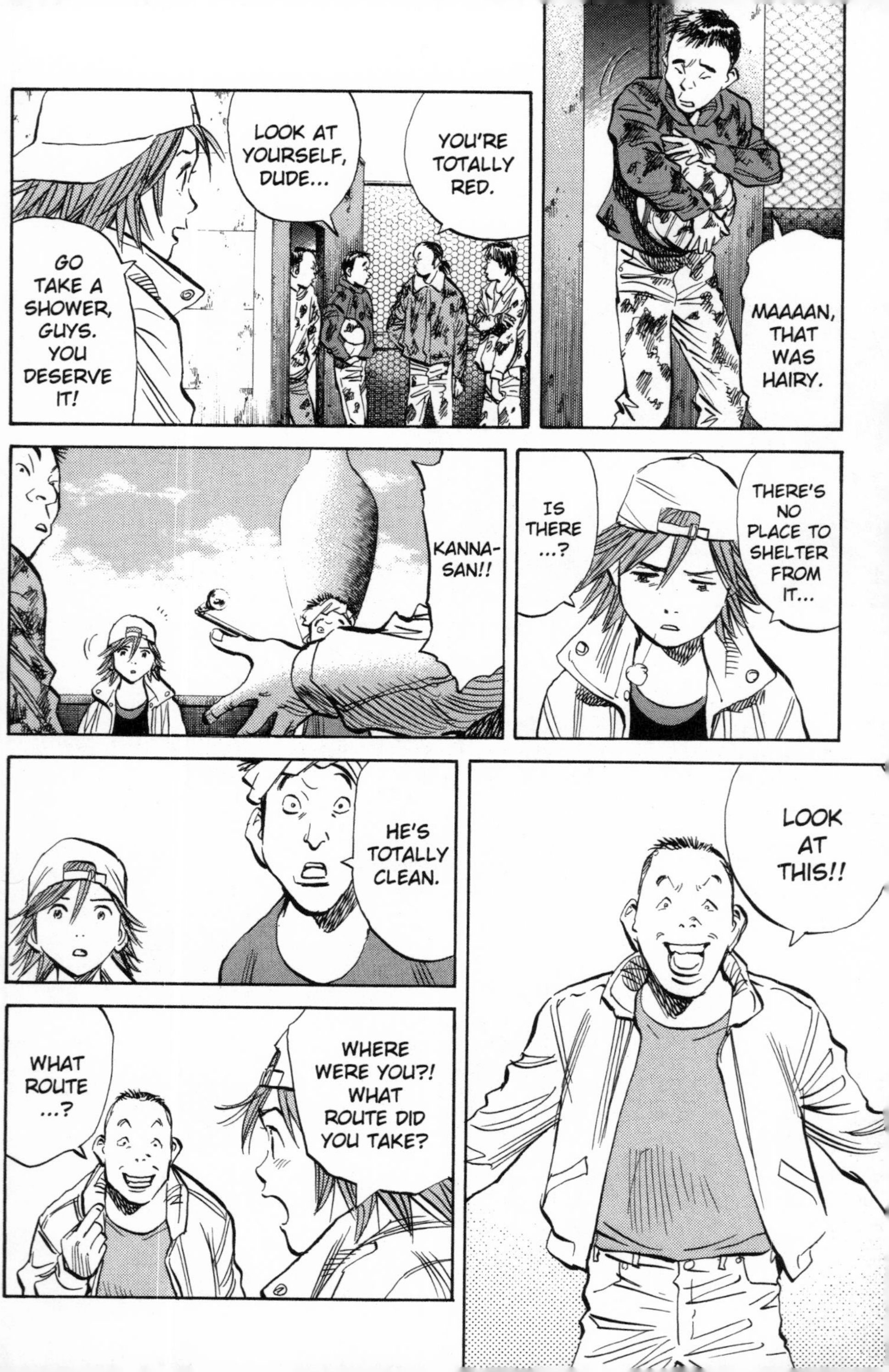
MAAAAN, THAT WAS HAIRY.
YOU'RE TOTALLY RED.
LOOK AT YOURSELF, DUDE...
GO TAKE A SHOWER, GUYS. YOU DESERVE IT!
THERE'S NO PLACE TO SHELTER FROM IT...
IS THERE ...?
KANNA-SAN!!
LOOK AT THIS!!
HE'S TOTALLY CLEAN.
WHERE WERE YOU?! WHAT ROUTE DID YOU TAKE?
WHAT ROUTE ...?

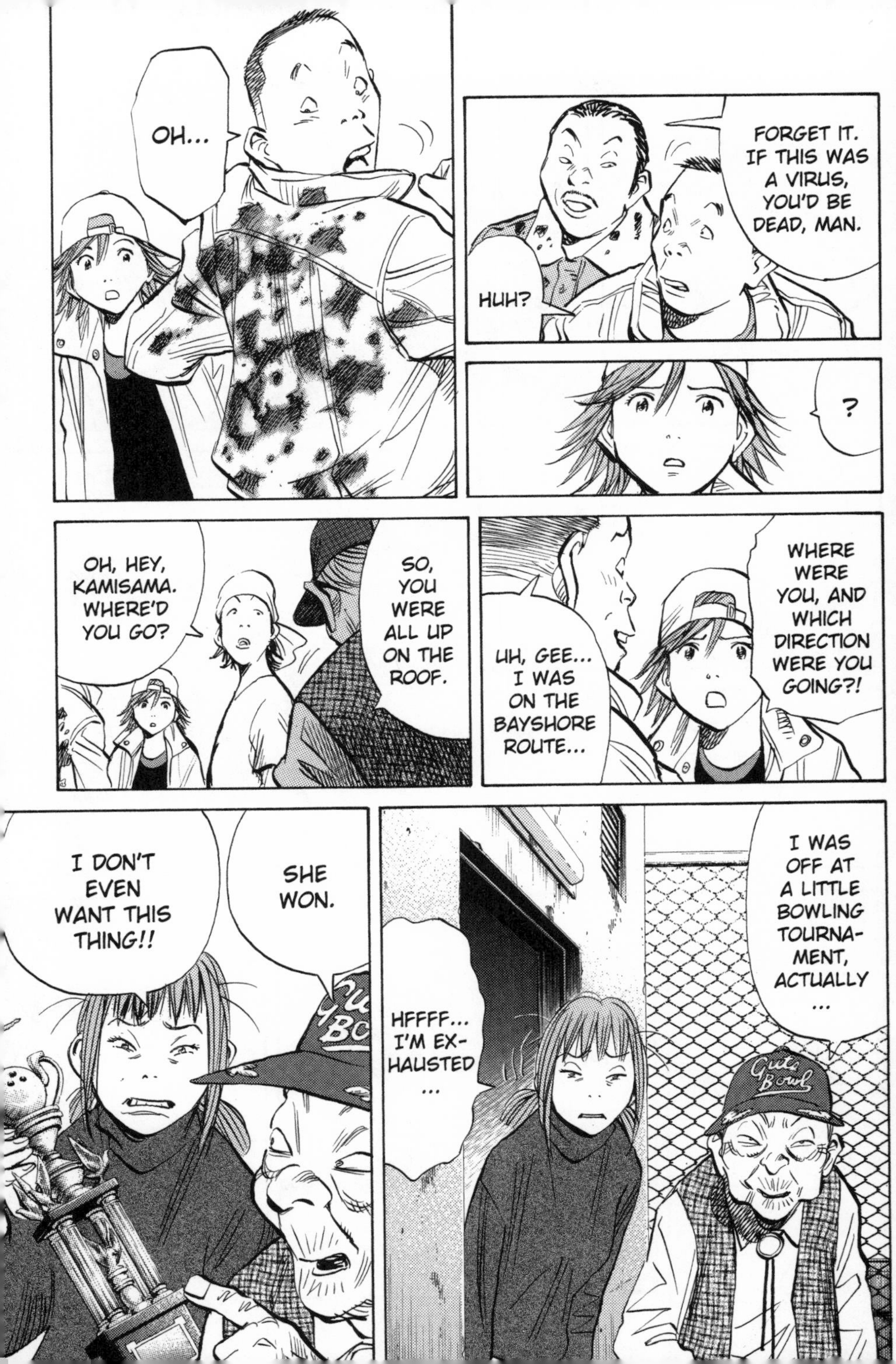
FORGET IT. IF THIS WAS A VIRUS, YOU'D BE DEAD, MAN.
HUH?
?
OH...
WHERE WERE YOU, AND WHICH DIRECTION WERE YOU GOING?!
UH, GEE... I WAS ON THE BAYSHORE ROUTE...
SO, YOU WERE ALL UP ON THE ROOF.
OH, HEY, KAMISAMA. WHERE'D YOU GO?
I WAS OFF AT A LITTLE BOWLING TOURNAMENT, ACTUALLY...
HFFFF... I'M EXHAUSTED...
SHE WON.
I DON'T EVEN WANT THIS THING!!

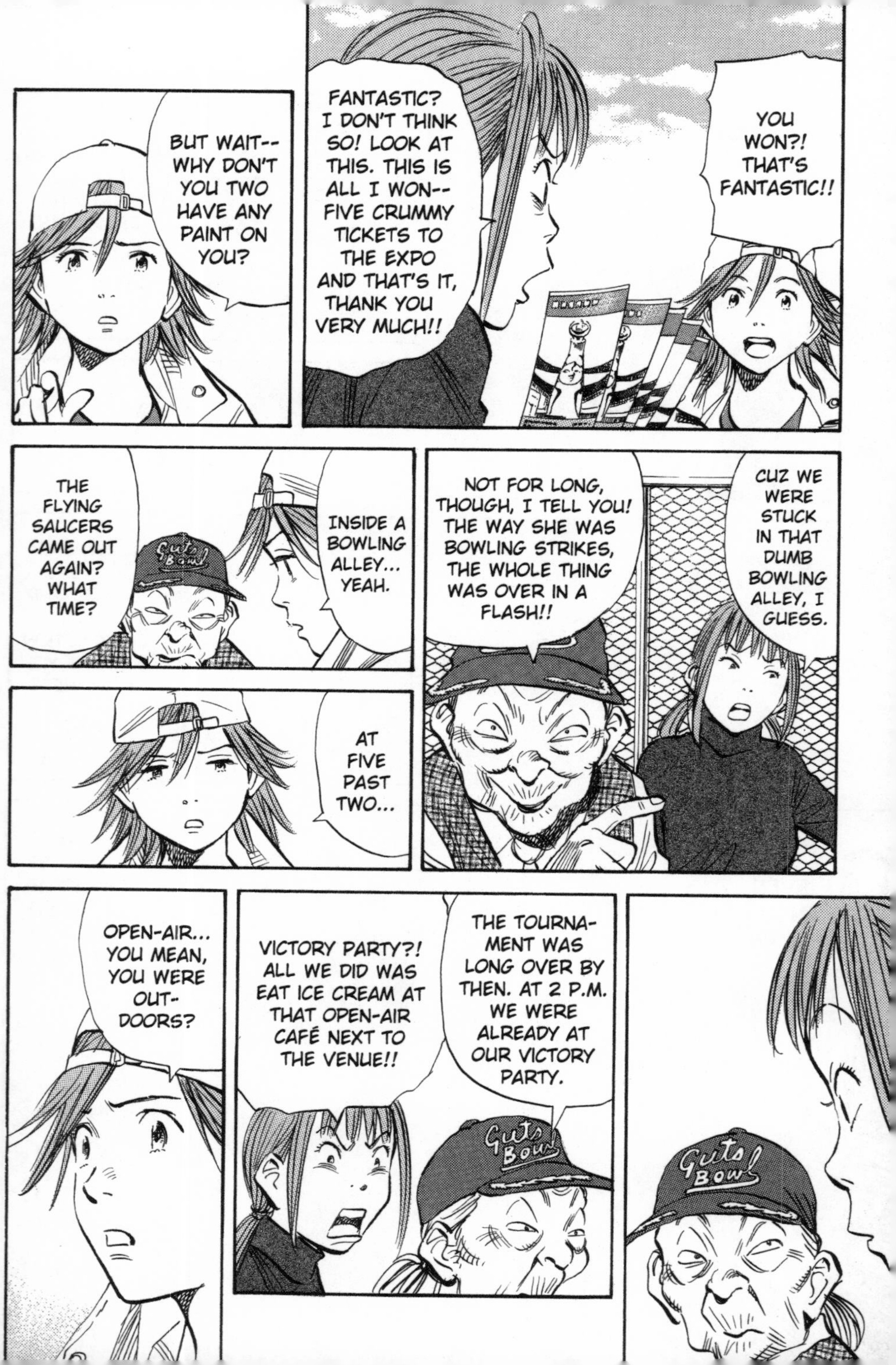
YOU WON?! THAT'S FANTASTIC!!
FANTASTIC? I DON'T THINK SO! LOOK AT THIS. THIS IS ALL I WON--FIVE CRUMMY TICKETS TO THE EXPO AND THAT'S IT, THANK YOU VERY MUCH!!
BUT WAIT--WHY DON'T YOU TWO HAVE ANY PAINT ON YOU?
CUZ WE WERE STUCK IN THAT DUMB BOWLING ALLEY, I GUESS.
NOT FOR LONG, THOUGH, I TELL YOU! THE WAY SHE WAS BOWLING STRIKES, THE WHOLE THING WAS OVER IN A FLASH!!
INSIDE A BOWLING ALLEY... YEAH.
THE FLYING SAUCERS CAME OUT AGAIN? WHAT TIME?
AT FIVE PAST TWO...
Guts Bowl
THE TOURNAMENT WAS LONG OVER BY THEN. AT 2 P.M. WE WERE ALREADY AT OUR VICTORY PARTY.
VICTORY PARTY?! ALL WE DID WAS EAT ICE CREAM AT THAT OPEN-AIR CAFÉ NEXT TO THE VENUE!!
OPEN-AIR... YOU MEAN, YOU WERE OUTDOORS?

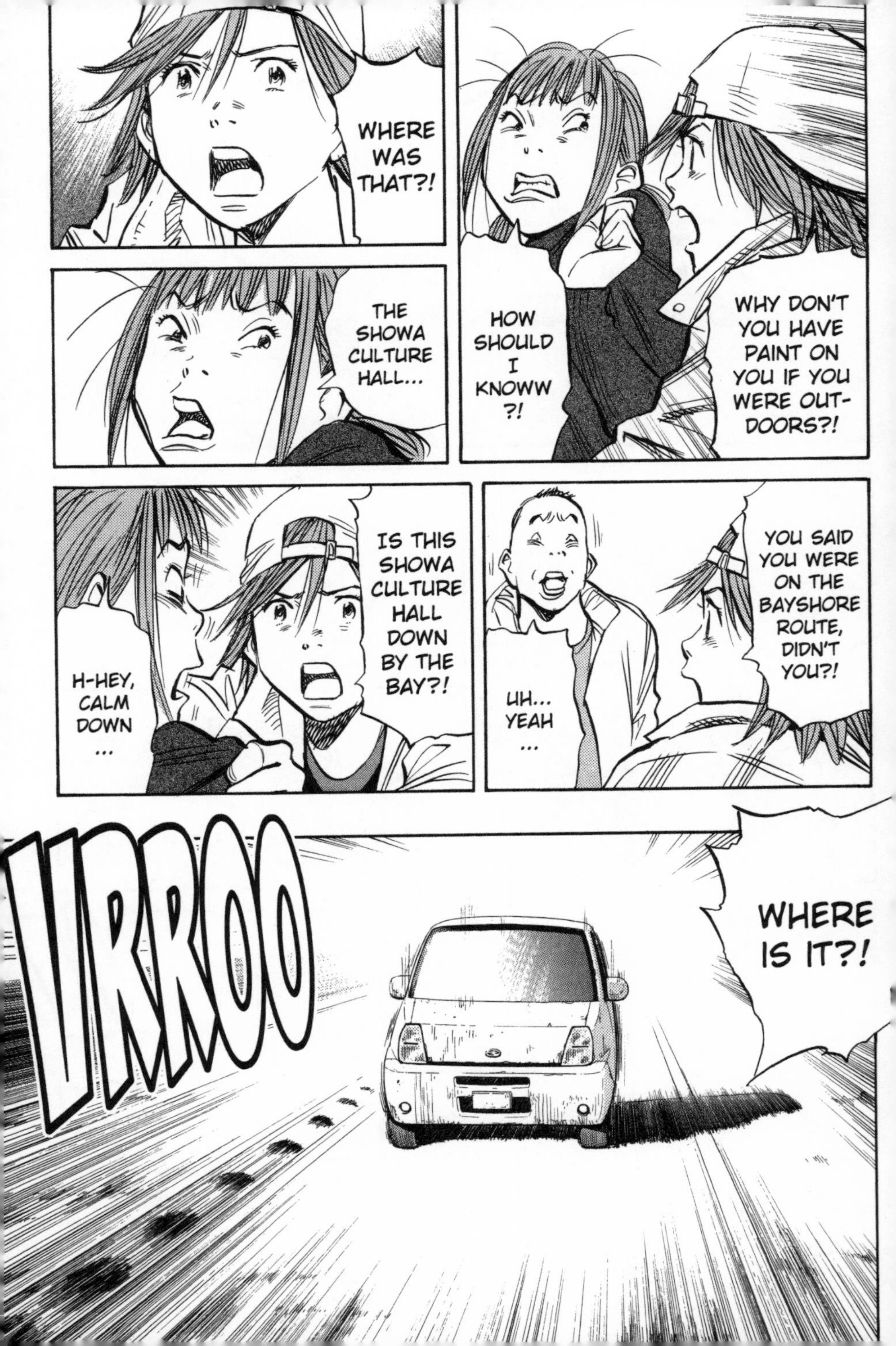
WHY DON'T YOU HAVE PAINT ON YOU IF YOU WERE OUT-DOORS?!
HOW SHOULD I KNOWW?!
WHERE WAS THAT?!
THE SHOWA CULTURE HALL...
YOU SAID YOU WERE ON THE BAYSHORE ROUTE, DIDN'T YOU?!
UH... YEAH...
IS THIS SHOWA CULTURE HALL DOWN BY THE BAY?!
H-HEY, CALM DOWN...
WHERE IS IT?!
URROO

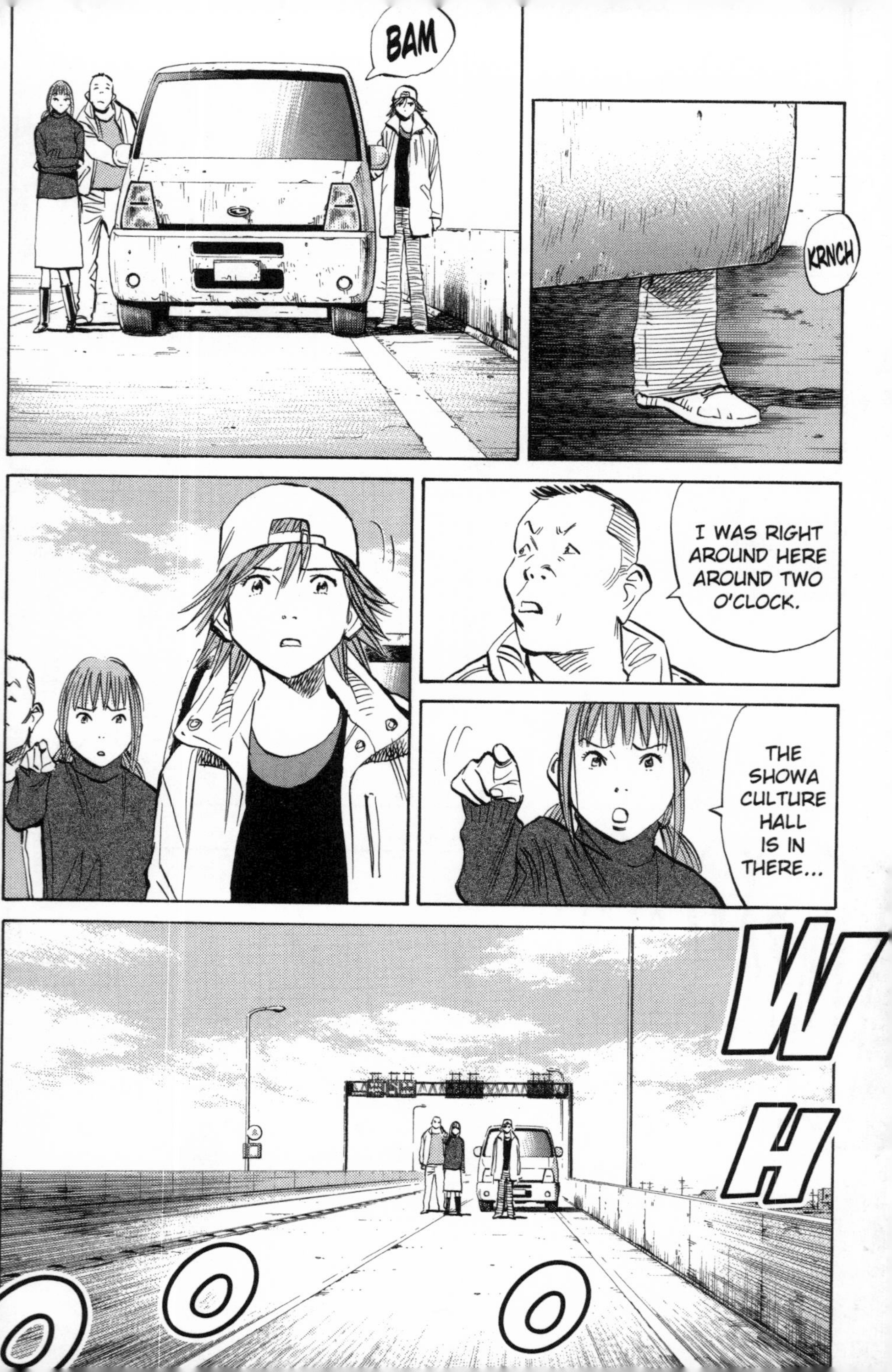
KRNCH
BAM
I WAS RIGHT AROUND HERE AROUND TWO O'CLOCK.
THE SHOWA CULTURE HALL IS IN THERE...
WHOOO

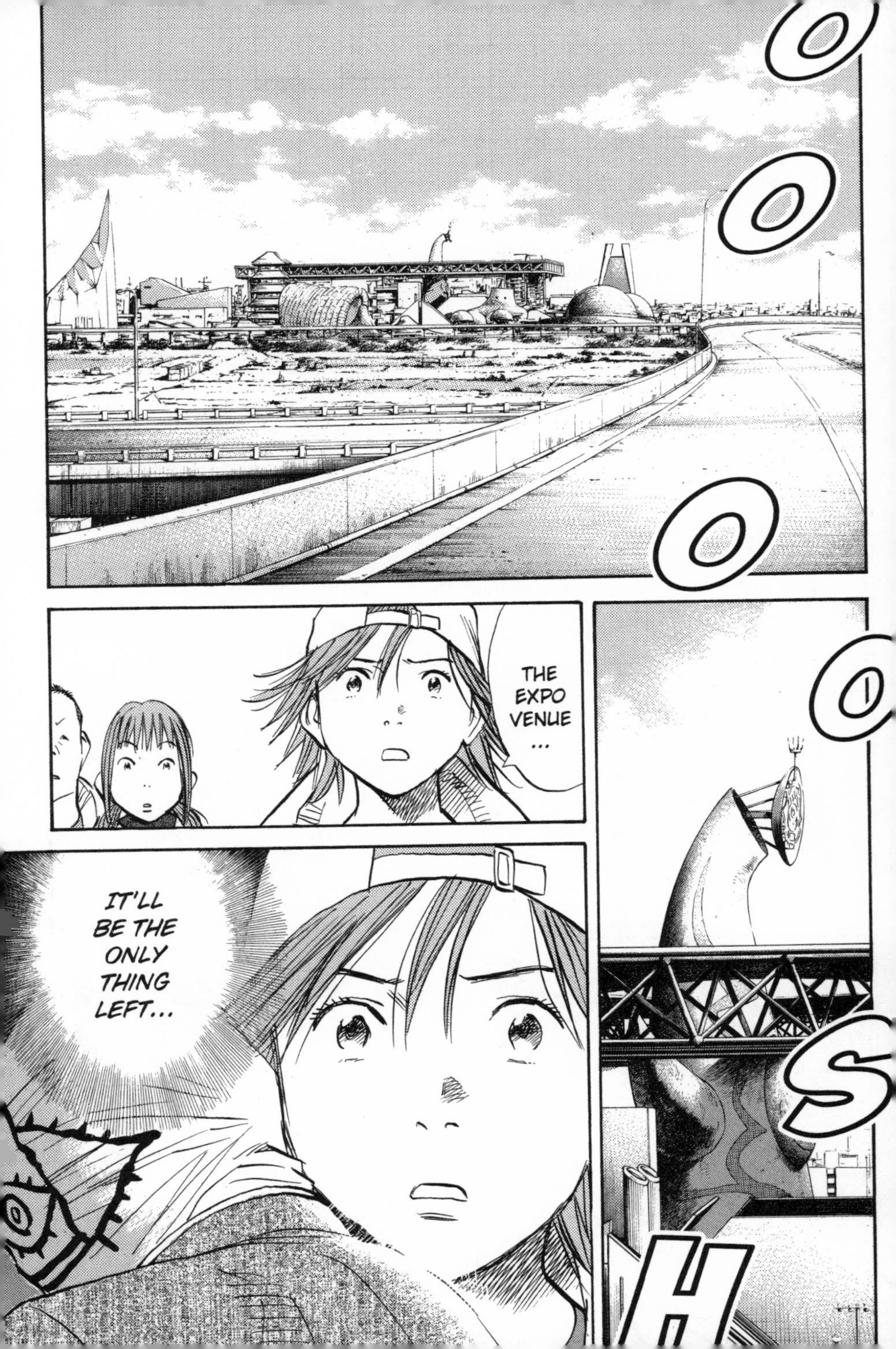

OOOOSH
THE EXPO VENUE...
IT'LL BE THE ONLY THING LEFT...

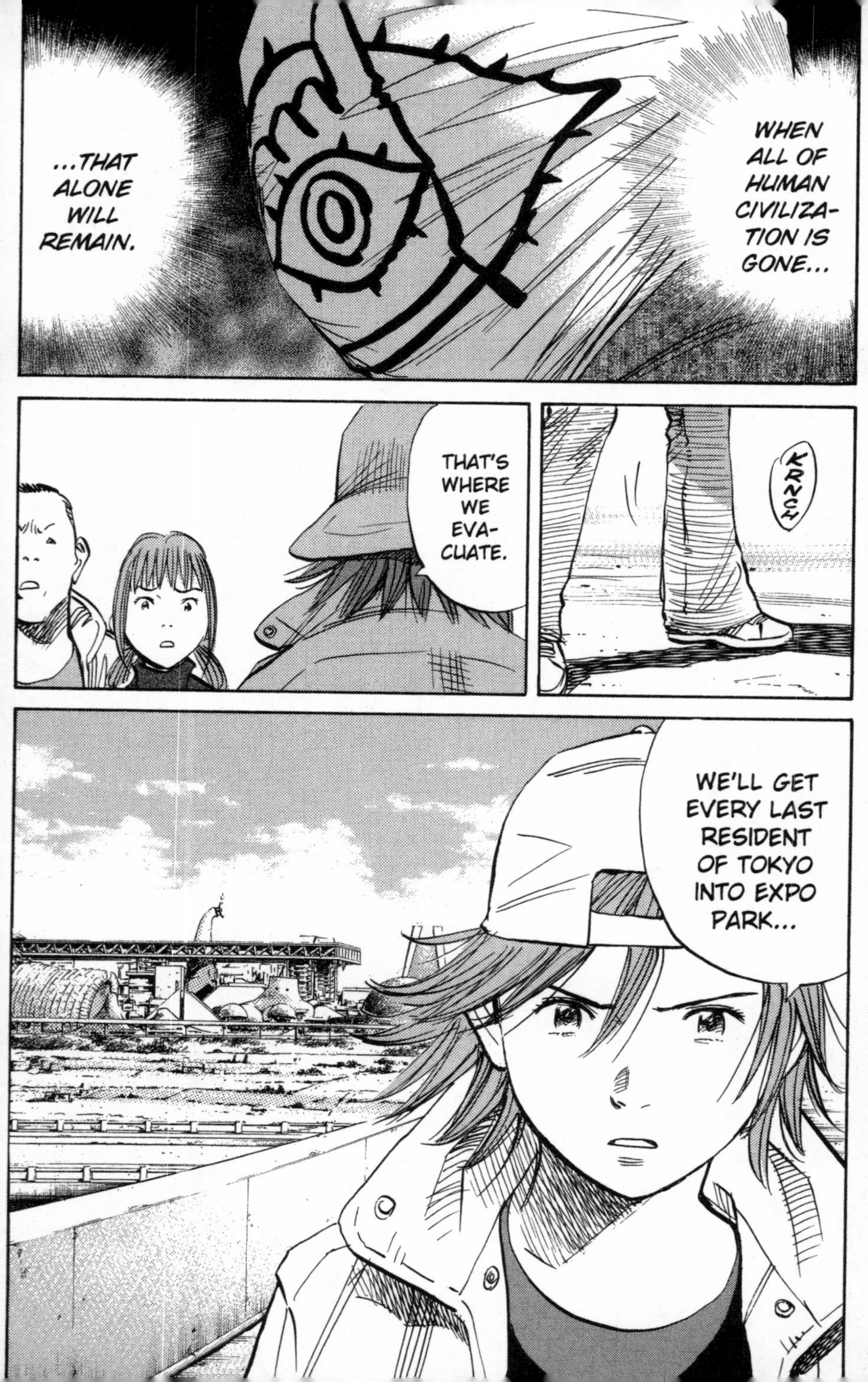
WHEN ALL OF HUMAN CIVILIZA-TION IS GONE...
...THAT ALONE WILL REMAIN.
KRNCH
THAT'S WHERE WE EVA-CUATE.
WE'LL GET EVERY LAST RESIDENT OF TOKYO INTO EXPO PARK...

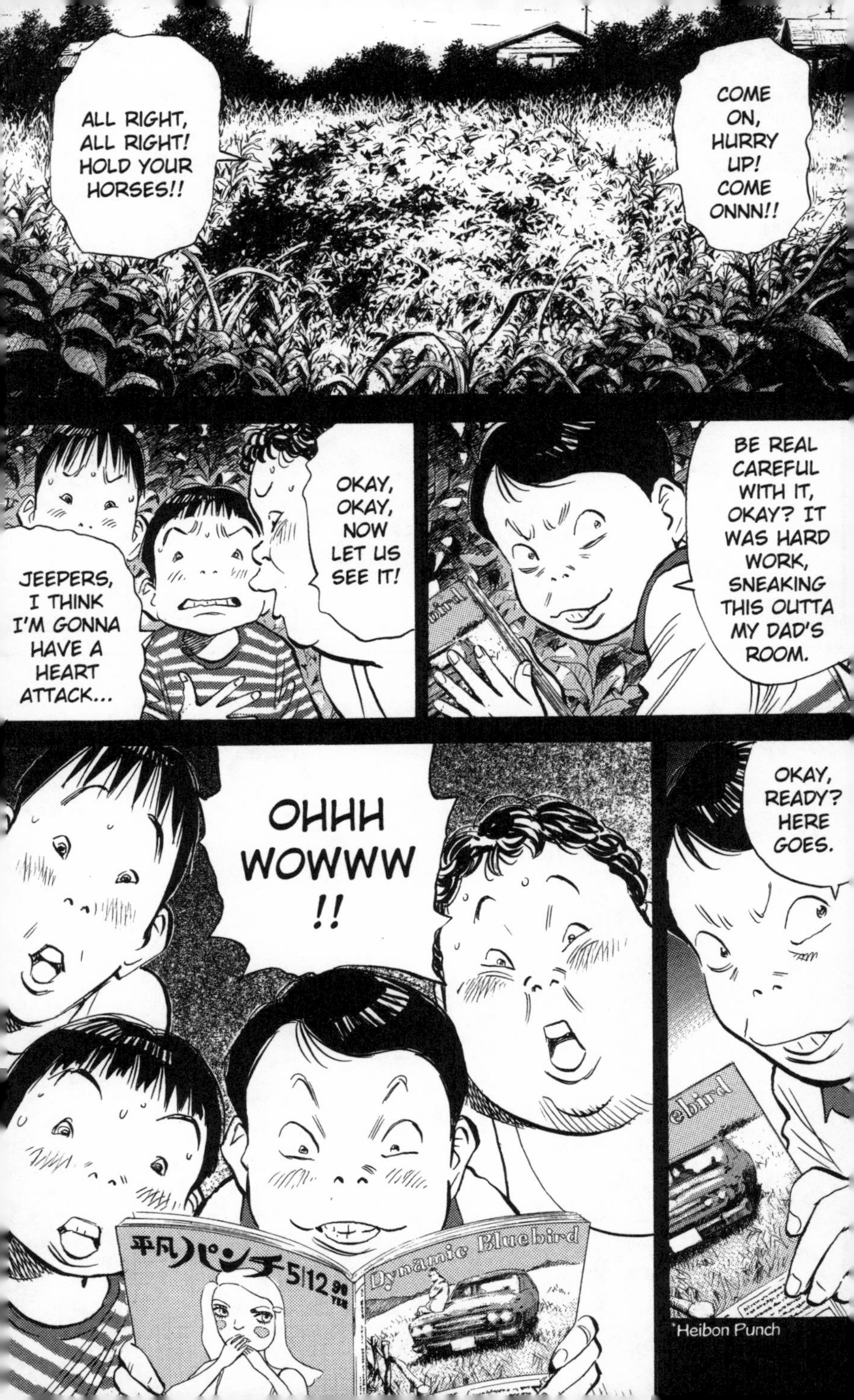
COME ON, HURRY UP! COME ONNN!!
ALL RIGHT, ALL RIGHT! HOLD YOUR HORSES!!
BE REAL CAREFUL WITH IT, OKAY? IT WAS HARD WORK, SNEAKING THIS OUTTA MY DAD'S ROOM.
OKAY, OKAY, NOW LET US SEE IT!
JEEPERS, I THINK I'M GONNA HAVE A HEART ATTACK...
OKAY, READY? HERE GOES.
*Heibon Punch
OHHH WOWWW !!
平凡パンチ 5/12
Dynamic Bluebird

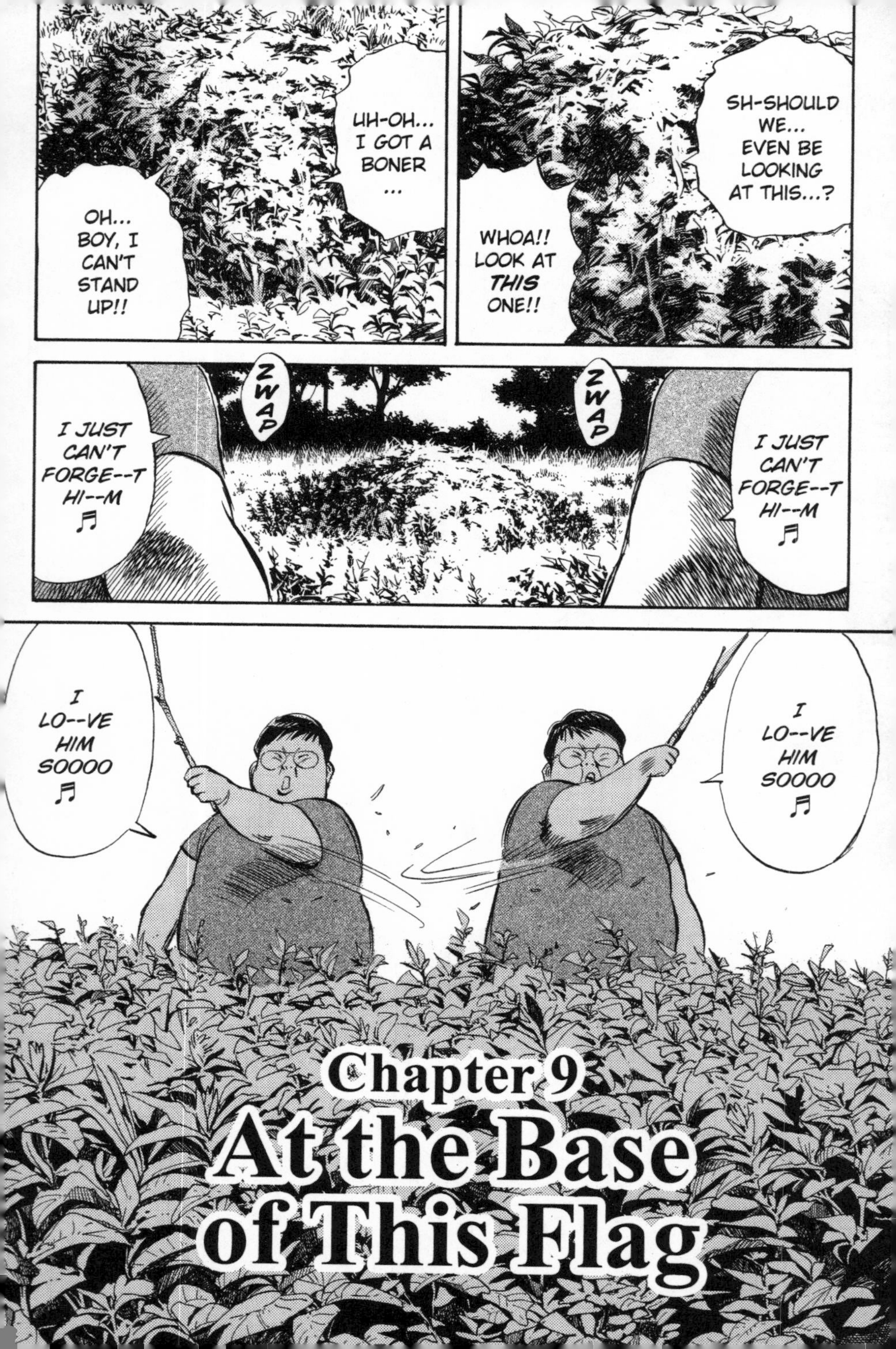
SH-SHOULD WE... EVEN BE LOOKING AT THIS...?
WHOA!! LOOK AT *THIS* ONE!!
UH-OH... I GOT A BONER ...
OH... BOY, I CAN'T STAND UP!!
I JUST CAN'T FORGE--T HI--M ♬
ZWAP
ZWAP
I JUST CAN'T FORGE--T HI--M ♬
I LO--VE HIM SOOOO ♬
I LO--VE HIM SOOOO ♬

Chapter 9
At the Base of This Flag

YOU SURE YOU WANT ME TO TAKE THIS DOWN?

DAAAD !!

YEAR 3 OF THE FRIENDSHIP ERA

*Frogdoom

YEAH.

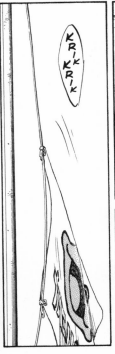

KRIK KRIK

KRIK KRIK

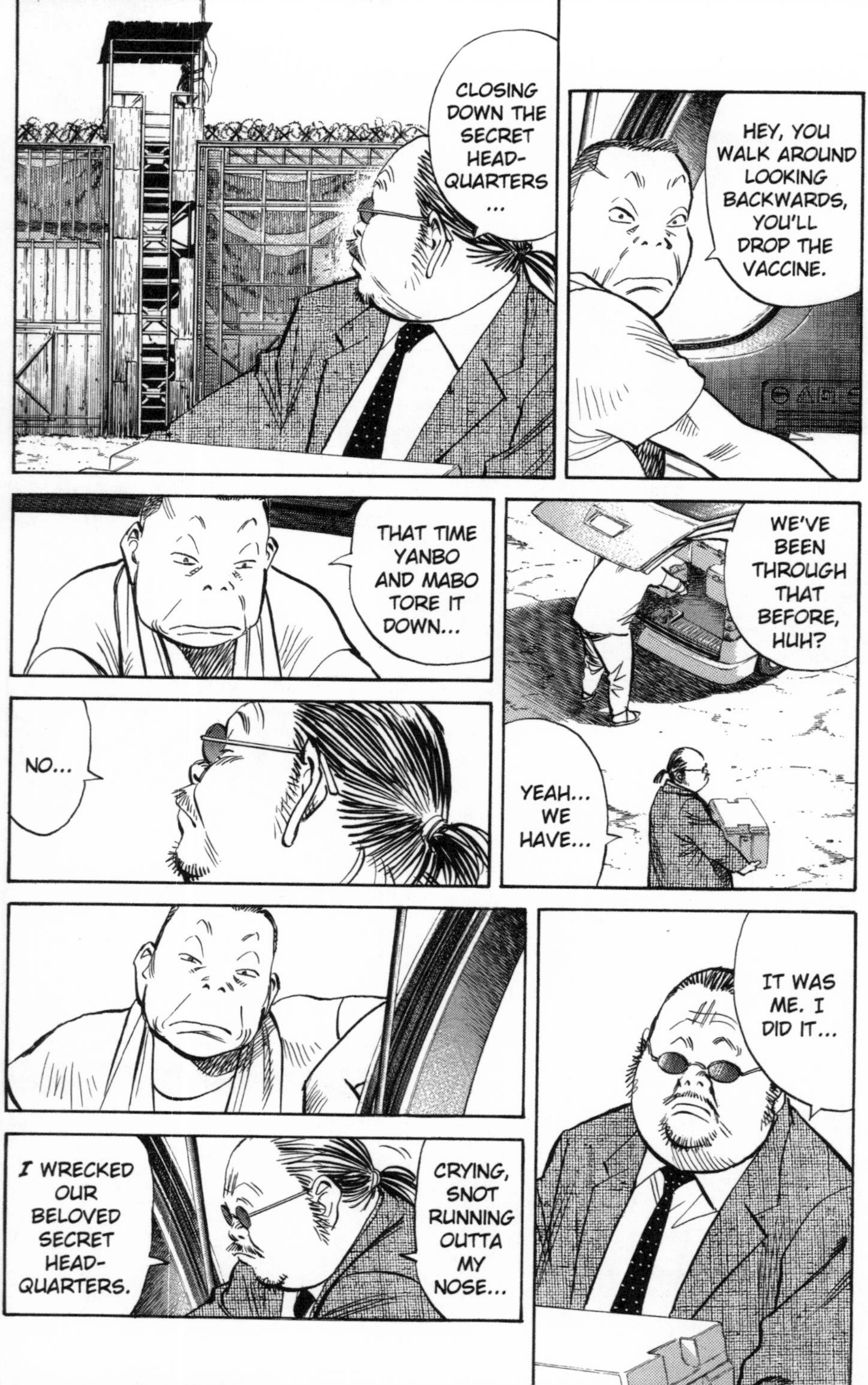
HEY, YOU WALK AROUND LOOKING BACKWARDS, YOU'LL DROP THE VACCINE.
CLOSING DOWN THE SECRET HEAD-QUARTERS ...
WE'VE BEEN THROUGH THAT BEFORE, HUH?
YEAH... WE HAVE...
THAT TIME YANBO AND MABO TORE IT DOWN...
NO...
IT WAS ME. I DID IT...
CRYING, SNOT RUNNING OUTTA MY NOSE...
I WRECKED OUR BELOVED SECRET HEAD-QUARTERS.

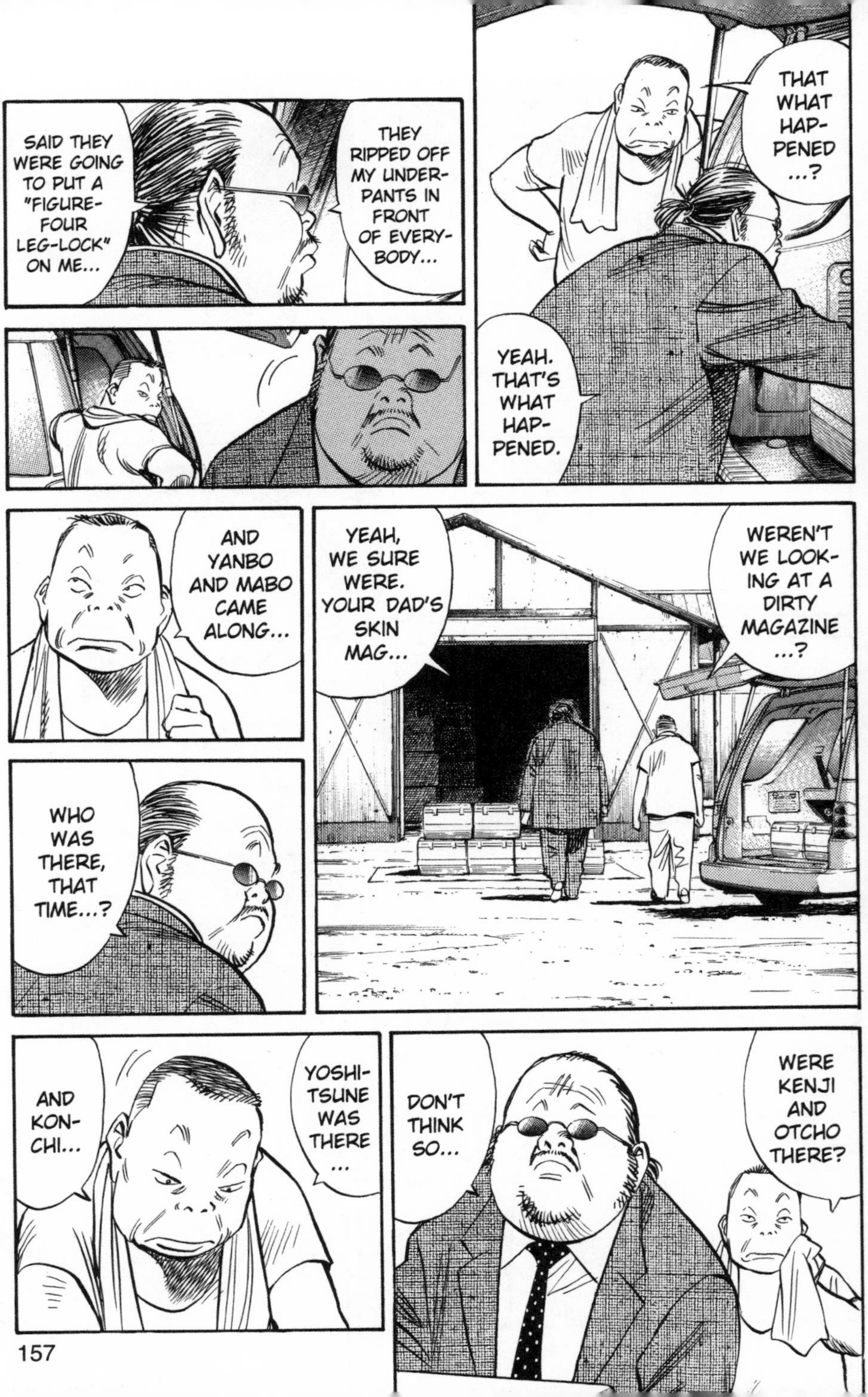
THAT WHAT HAP-PENED ...?
YEAH. THAT'S WHAT HAP-PENED.
THEY RIPPED OFF MY UNDER-PANTS IN FRONT OF EVERY-BODY...
SAID THEY WERE GOING TO PUT A "FIGURE-FOUR LEG-LOCK" ON ME...
WEREN'T WE LOOK-ING AT A DIRTY MAGAZINE ...?
YEAH, WE SURE WERE. YOUR DAD'S SKIN MAG...
AND YANBO AND MABO CAME ALONG...
WHO WAS THERE, THAT TIME...?
WERE KENJI AND OTCHO THERE?
DON'T THINK SO...
YOSHI-TSUNE WAS THERE ...
AND KON-CHI...

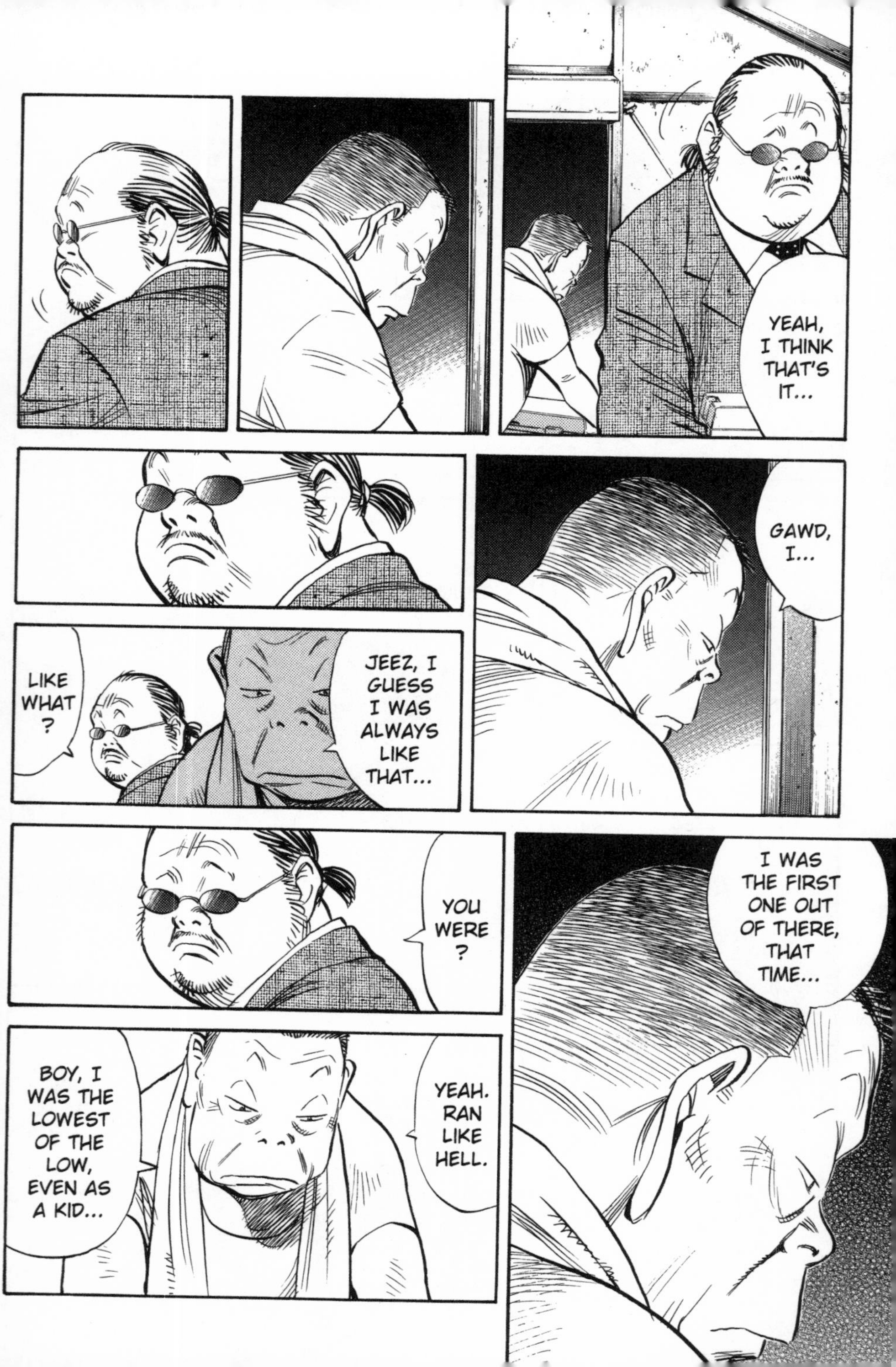
YEAH, I THINK THAT'S IT...
GAWD, I...
JEEZ, I GUESS I WAS ALWAYS LIKE THAT...
LIKE WHAT?
I WAS THE FIRST ONE OUT OF THERE, THAT TIME...
YOU WERE?
YEAH. RAN LIKE HELL.
BOY, I WAS THE LOWEST OF THE LOW, EVEN AS A KID...

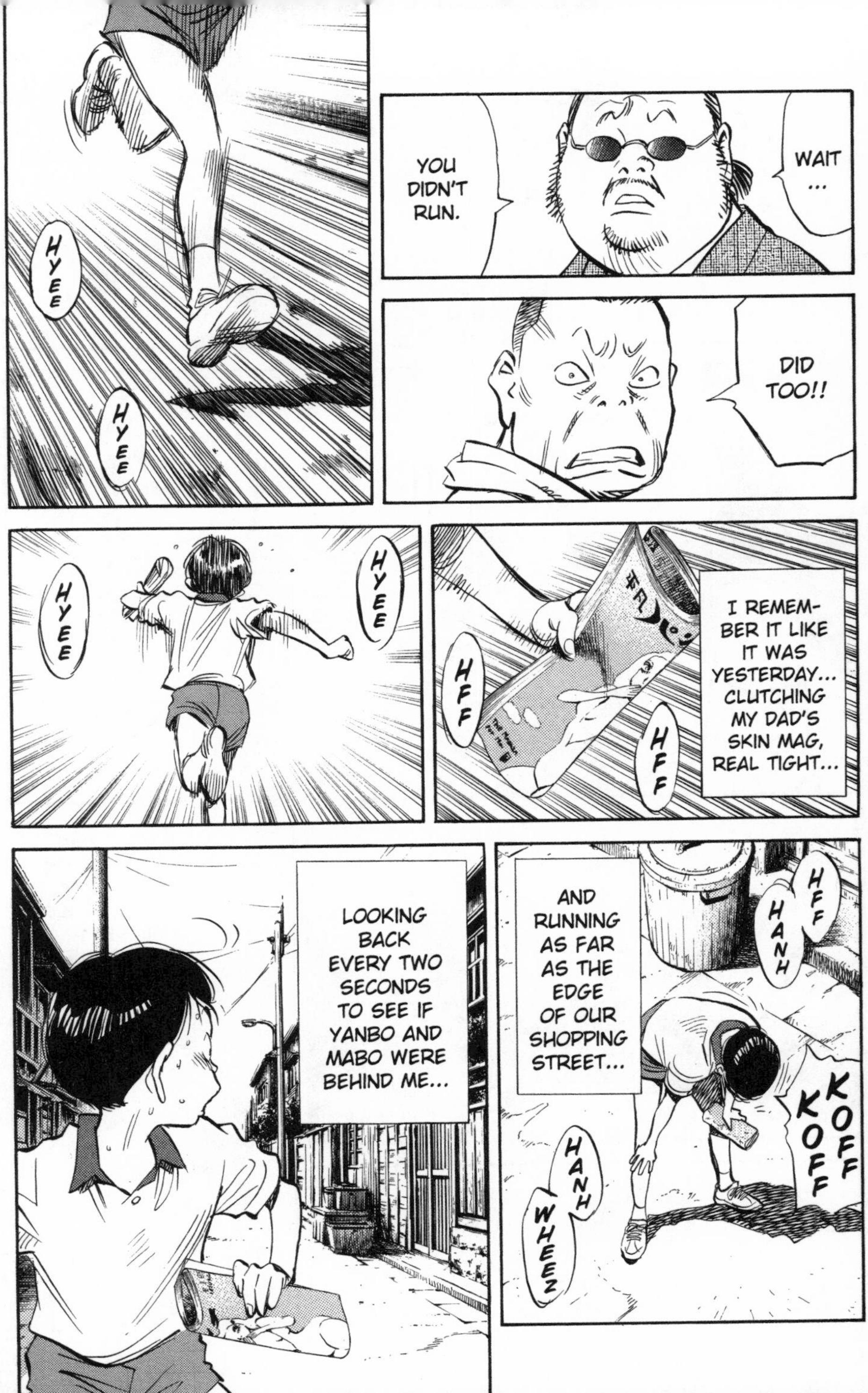
WAIT ...
YOU DIDN'T RUN.
DID TOO!!
HYEE
HYEE
I REMEMBER IT LIKE IT WAS YESTERDAY... CLUTCHING MY DAD'S SKIN MAG, REAL TIGHT...
HFF
HFF
HYEE
HYEE
HFF
HANH
AND RUNNING AS FAR AS THE EDGE OF OUR SHOPPING STREET...
KOFF
KOFF
HANH
WHEEZ
LOOKING BACK EVERY TWO SECONDS TO SEE IF YANBO AND MABO WERE BEHIND ME...

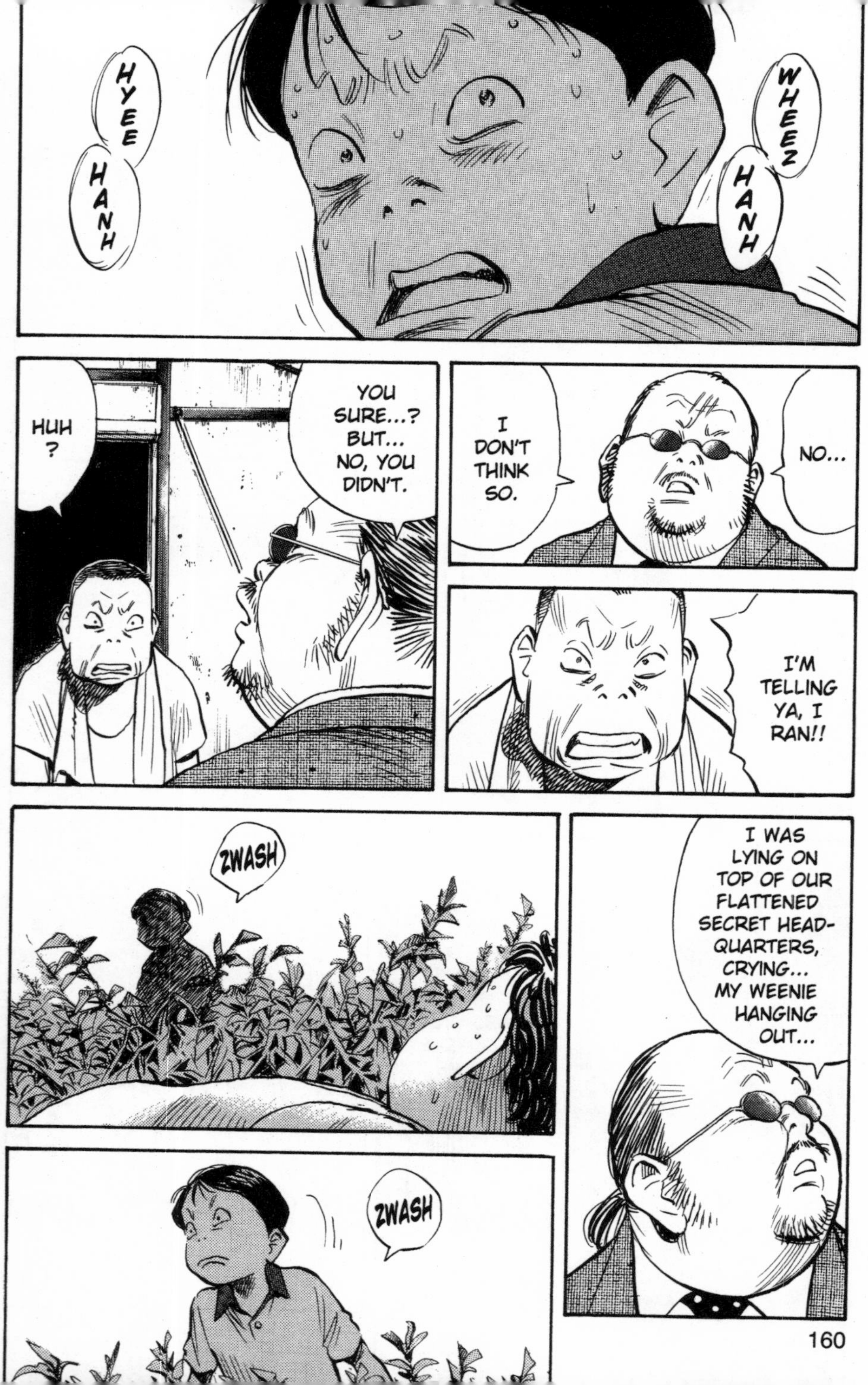
WHEEZ HANH
HYEE HANH
NO...
I DON'T THINK SO.
I'M TELLING YA, I RAN!!
YOU SURE...? BUT... NO, YOU DIDN'T.
HUH?
I WAS LYING ON TOP OF OUR FLATTENED SECRET HEAD-QUARTERS, CRYING... MY WEENIE HANGING OUT...
ZWASH
ZWASH

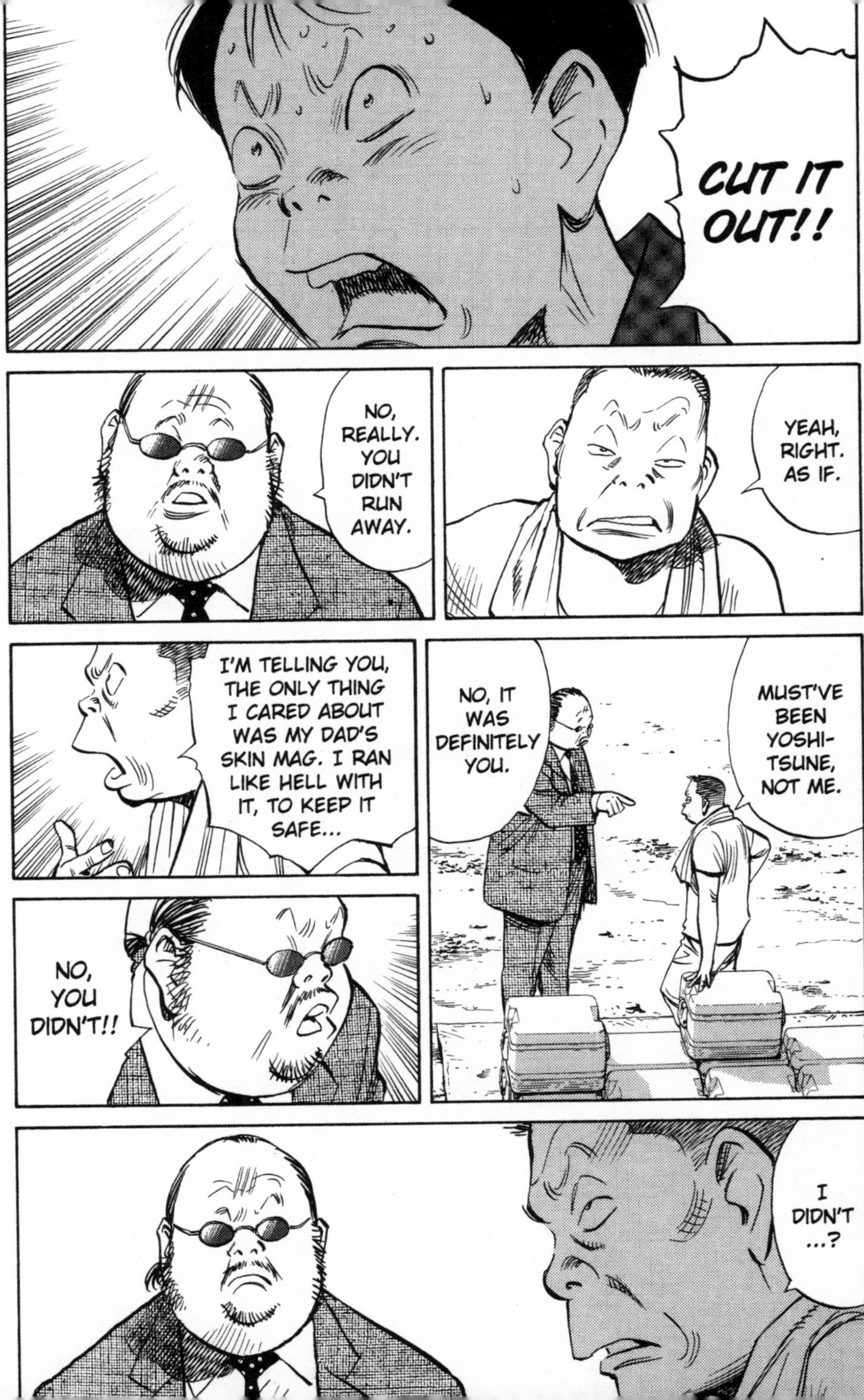
CUT IT OUT!!
YEAH, RIGHT. AS IF.
NO, REALLY. YOU DIDN'T RUN AWAY.
MUST'VE BEEN YOSHI-TSUNE, NOT ME.
NO, IT WAS DEFINITELY YOU.
I'M TELLING YOU, THE ONLY THING I CARED ABOUT WAS MY DAD'S SKIN MAG. I RAN LIKE HELL WITH IT, TO KEEP IT SAFE...
NO, YOU DIDN'T!!
I DIDN'T ...?

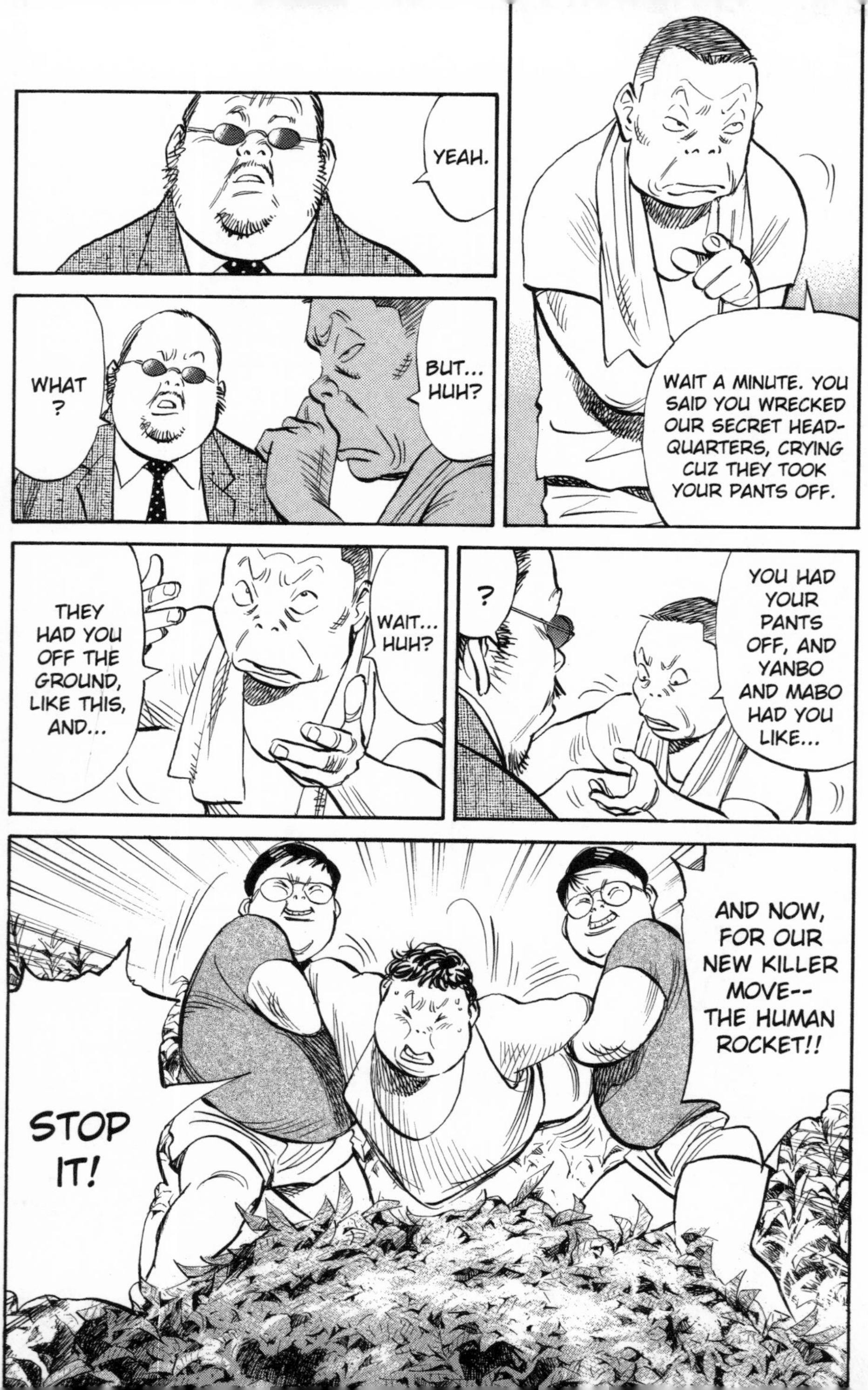

WAIT A MINUTE. YOU SAID YOU WRECKED OUR SECRET HEAD-QUARTERS, CRYING CUZ THEY TOOK YOUR PANTS OFF.
YEAH.
BUT... HUH?
WHAT ?
YOU HAD YOUR PANTS OFF, AND YANBO AND MABO HAD YOU LIKE...
?
WAIT... HUH?
THEY HAD YOU OFF THE GROUND, LIKE THIS, AND...
AND NOW, FOR OUR NEW KILLER MOVE-- THE HUMAN ROCKET!!
STOP IT!

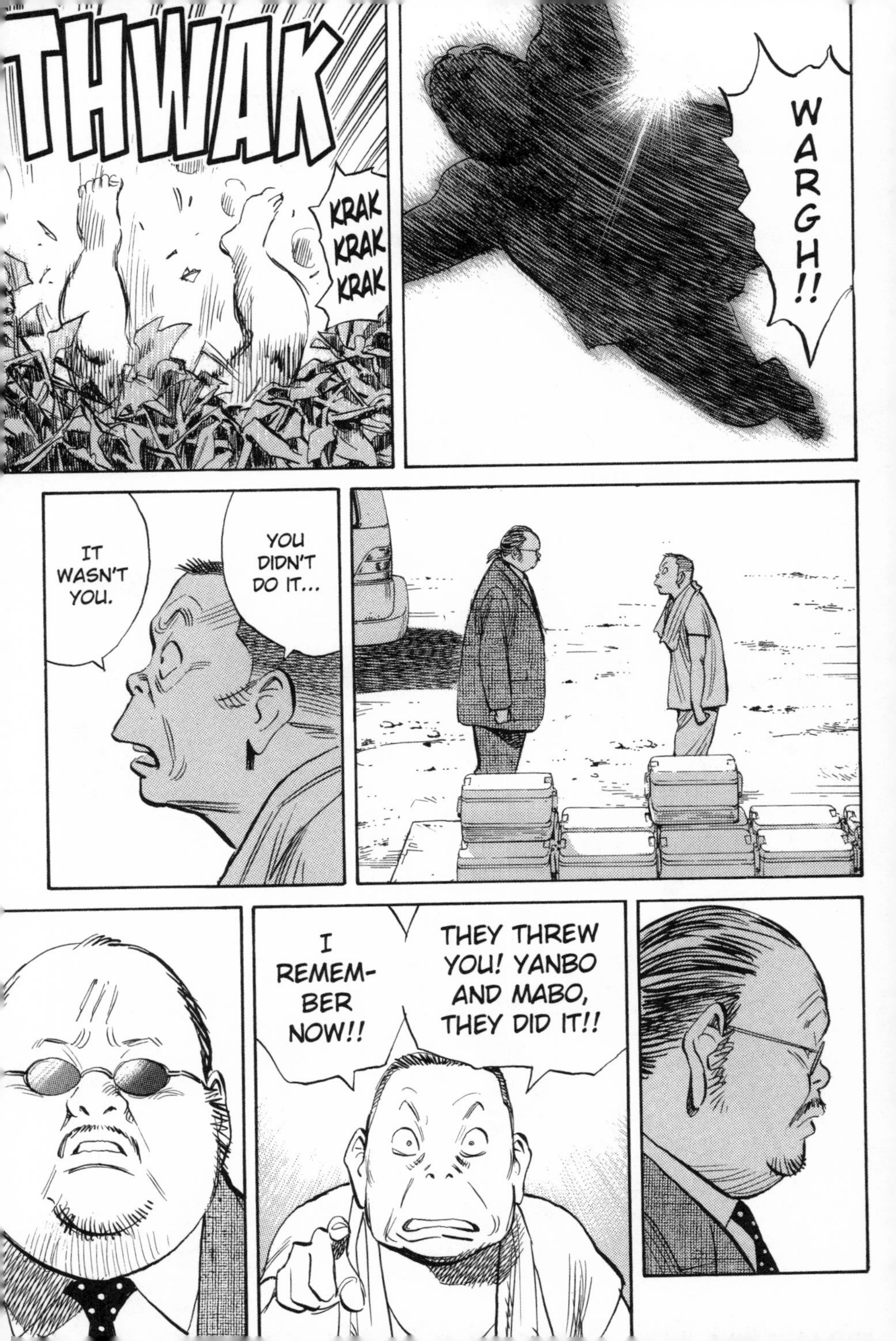
WARGH!!
THWAK
KRAK KRAK KRAK
YOU DIDN'T DO IT...
IT WASN'T YOU.
THEY THREW YOU! YANBO AND MABO, THEY DID IT!!
I REMEM-BER NOW!!

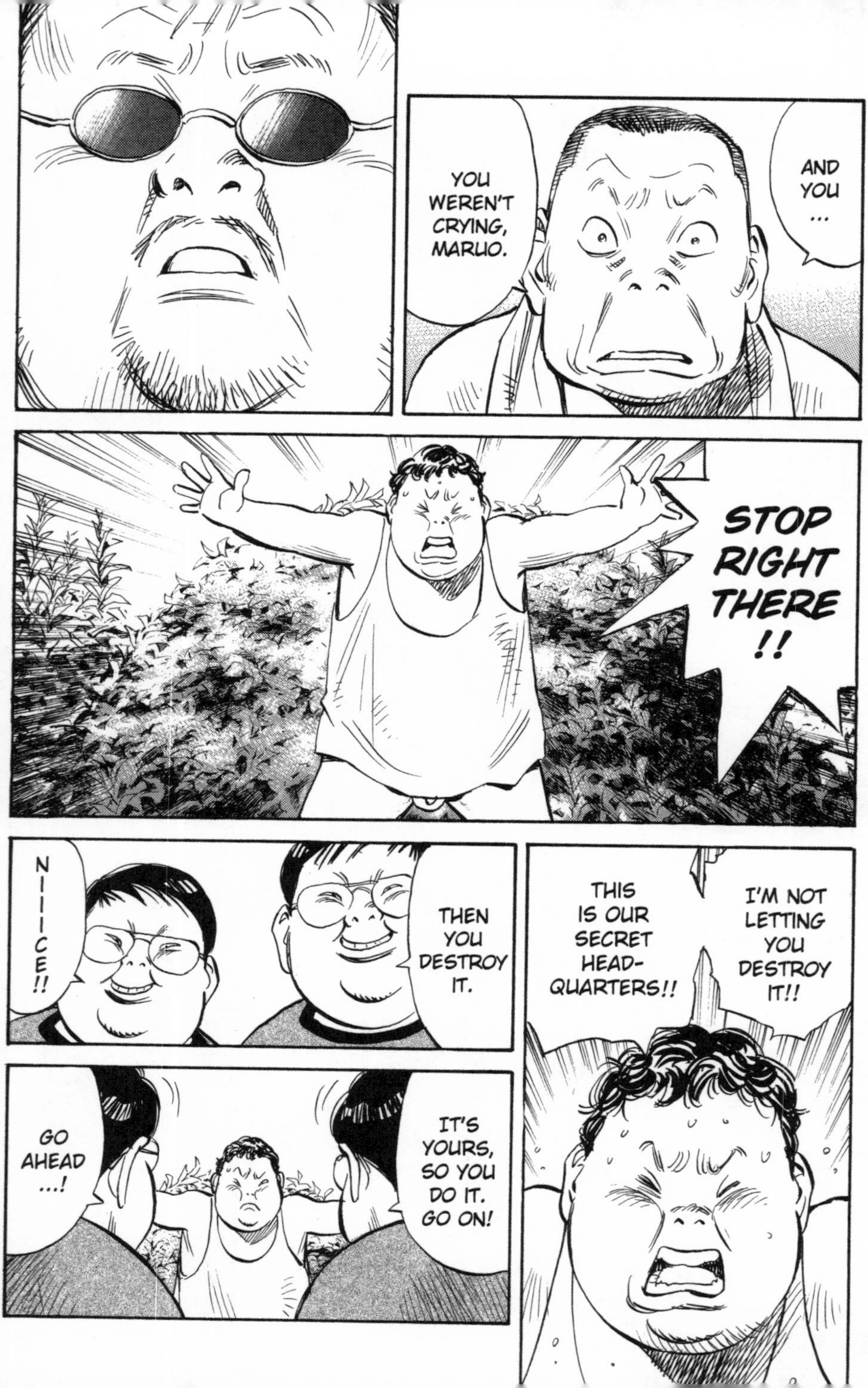
AND YOU ...
YOU WEREN'T CRYING, MARUO.
STOP RIGHT THERE!!
I'M NOT LETTING YOU DESTROY IT!!
THIS IS OUR SECRET HEAD-QUARTERS!!
THEN YOU DESTROY IT.
NIIICE!!
IT'S YOURS, SO YOU DO IT. GO ON!
GO AHEAD ...!

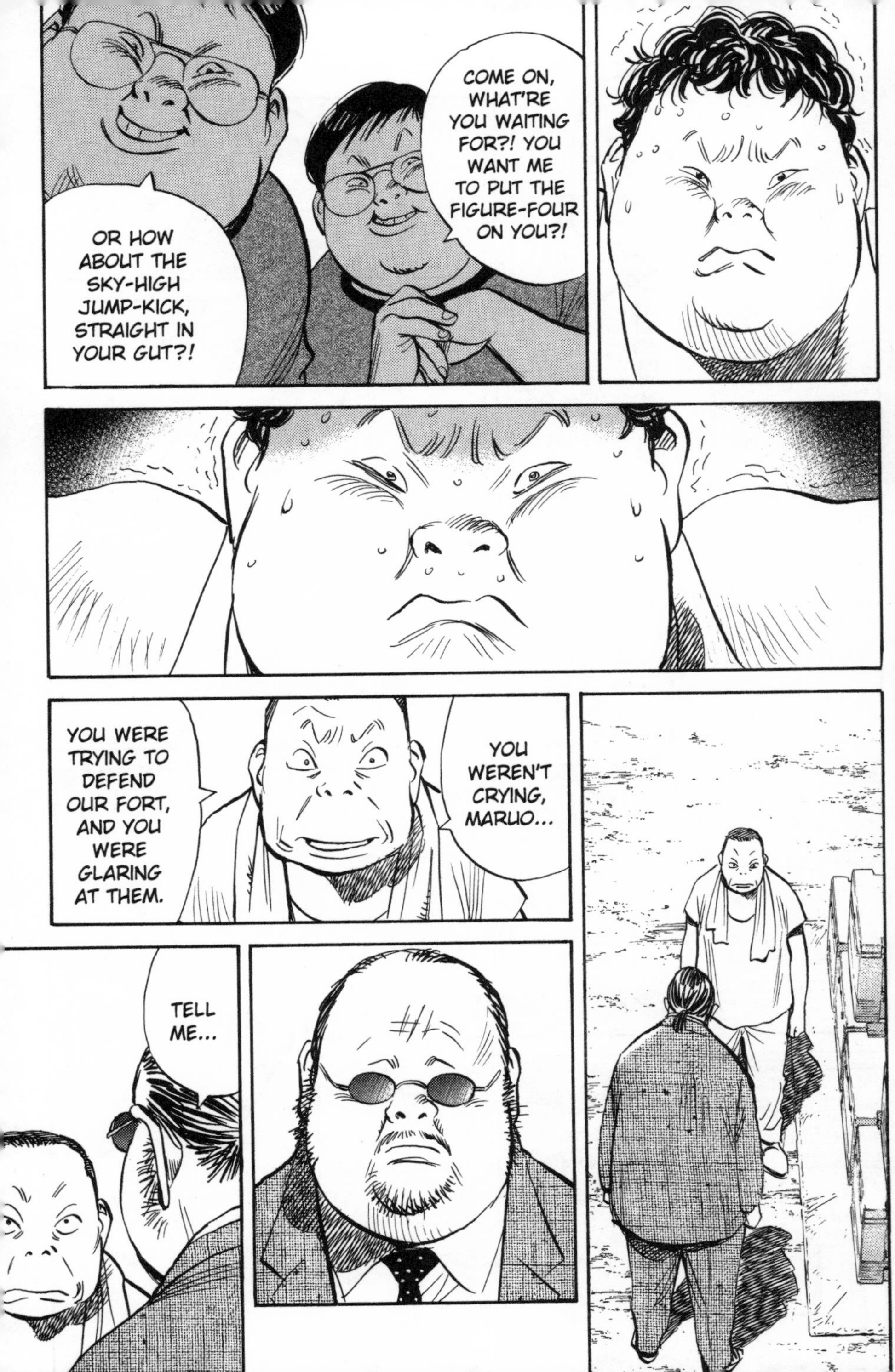
COME ON, WHAT'RE YOU WAITING FOR?! YOU WANT ME TO PUT THE FIGURE-FOUR ON YOU?!
OR HOW ABOUT THE SKY-HIGH JUMP-KICK, STRAIGHT IN YOUR GUT?!
YOU WEREN'T CRYING, MARUO...
YOU WERE TRYING TO DEFEND OUR FORT, AND YOU WERE GLARING AT THEM.
TELL ME...

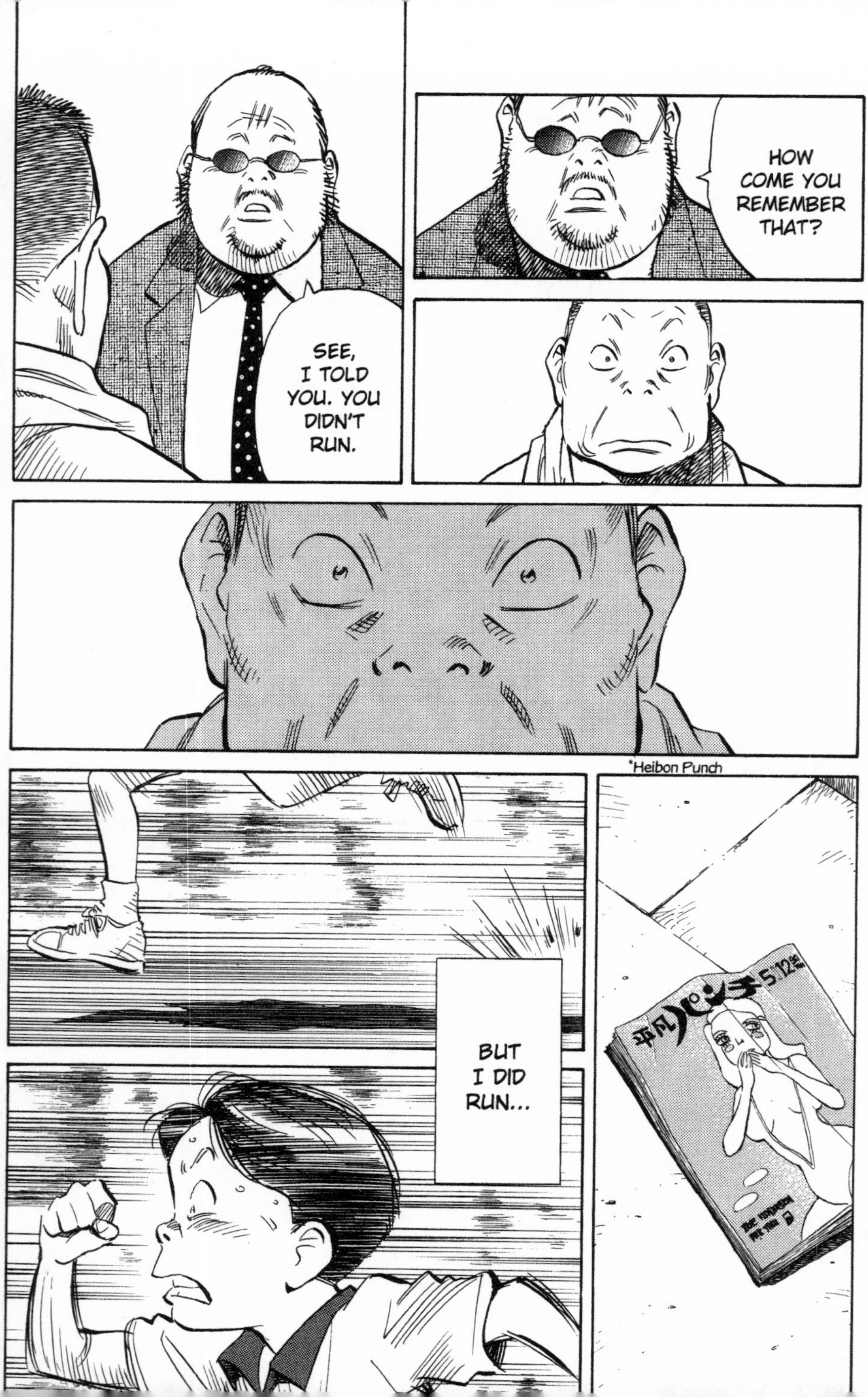
HOW COME YOU REMEMBER THAT?
SEE, I TOLD YOU. YOU DIDN'T RUN.
*Heibon Punch
BUT I DID RUN...

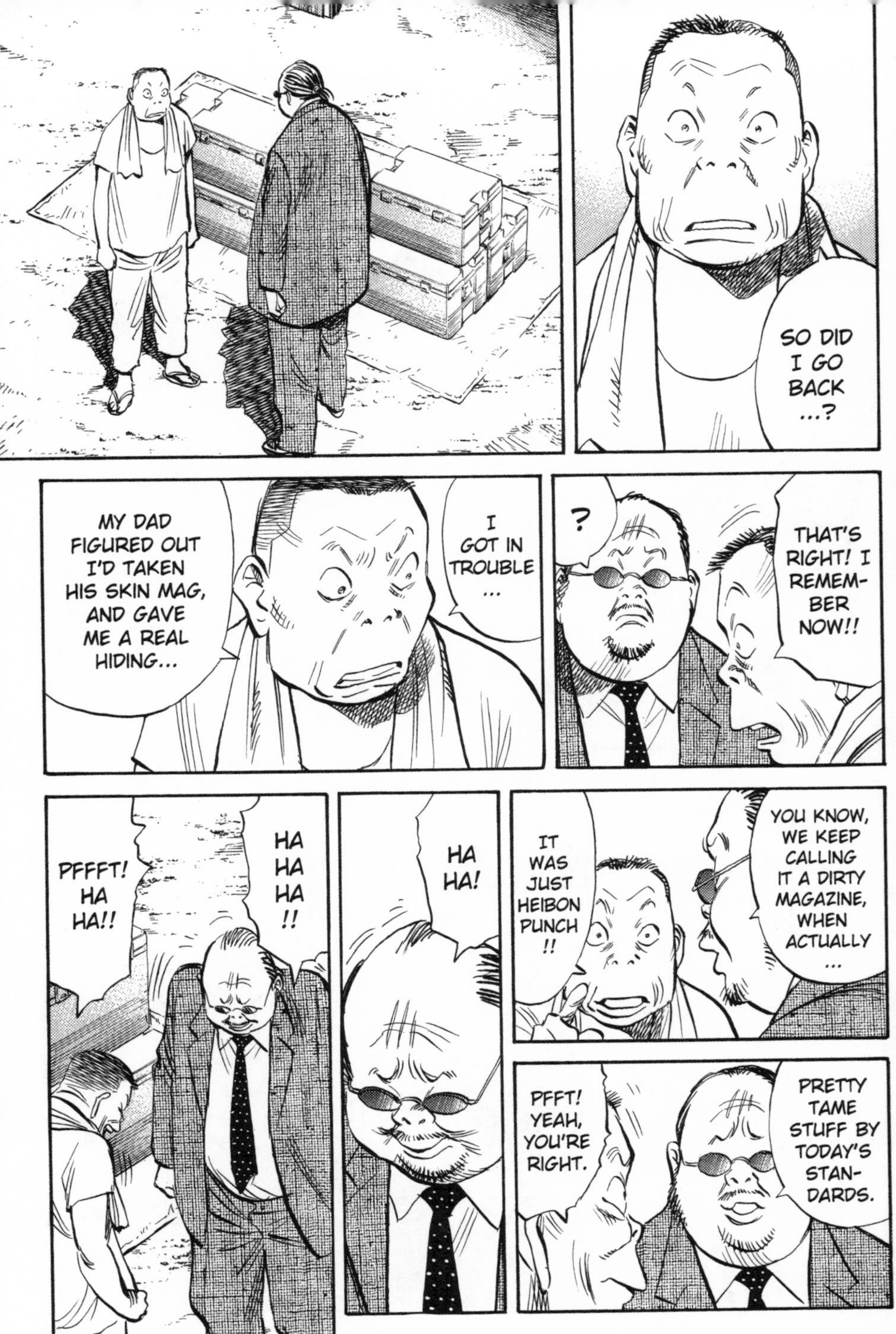

SO DID I GO BACK ...?
THAT'S RIGHT! I REMEMBER NOW!!
?
I GOT IN TROUBLE ...
MY DAD FIGURED OUT I'D TAKEN HIS SKIN MAG, AND GAVE ME A REAL HIDING...
YOU KNOW, WE KEEP CALLING IT A DIRTY MAGAZINE, WHEN ACTUALLY ...
IT WAS JUST HEIBON PUNCH!!
PRETTY TAME STUFF BY TODAY'S STANDARDS.
PFFT! YEAH, YOU'RE RIGHT.
HA HA!
HA HA HA!!
PFFFT! HA HA!!

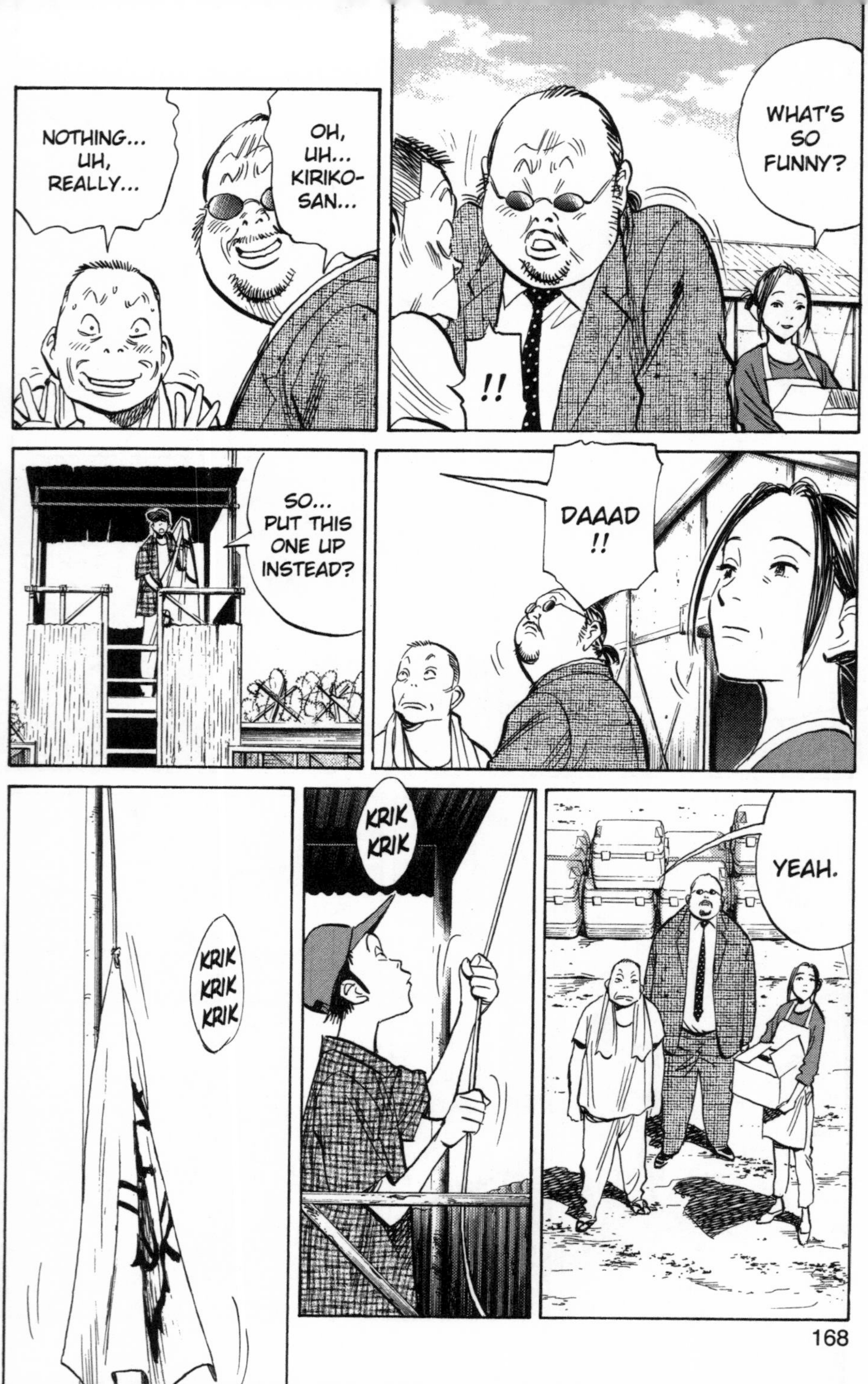
WHAT'S SO FUNNY?
!!
OH, UH... KIRIKO-SAN...
NOTHING... UH, REALLY...
DAAAD !!
SO... PUT THIS ONE UP INSTEAD?
YEAH.
KRIK KRIK
KRIK KRIK KRIK

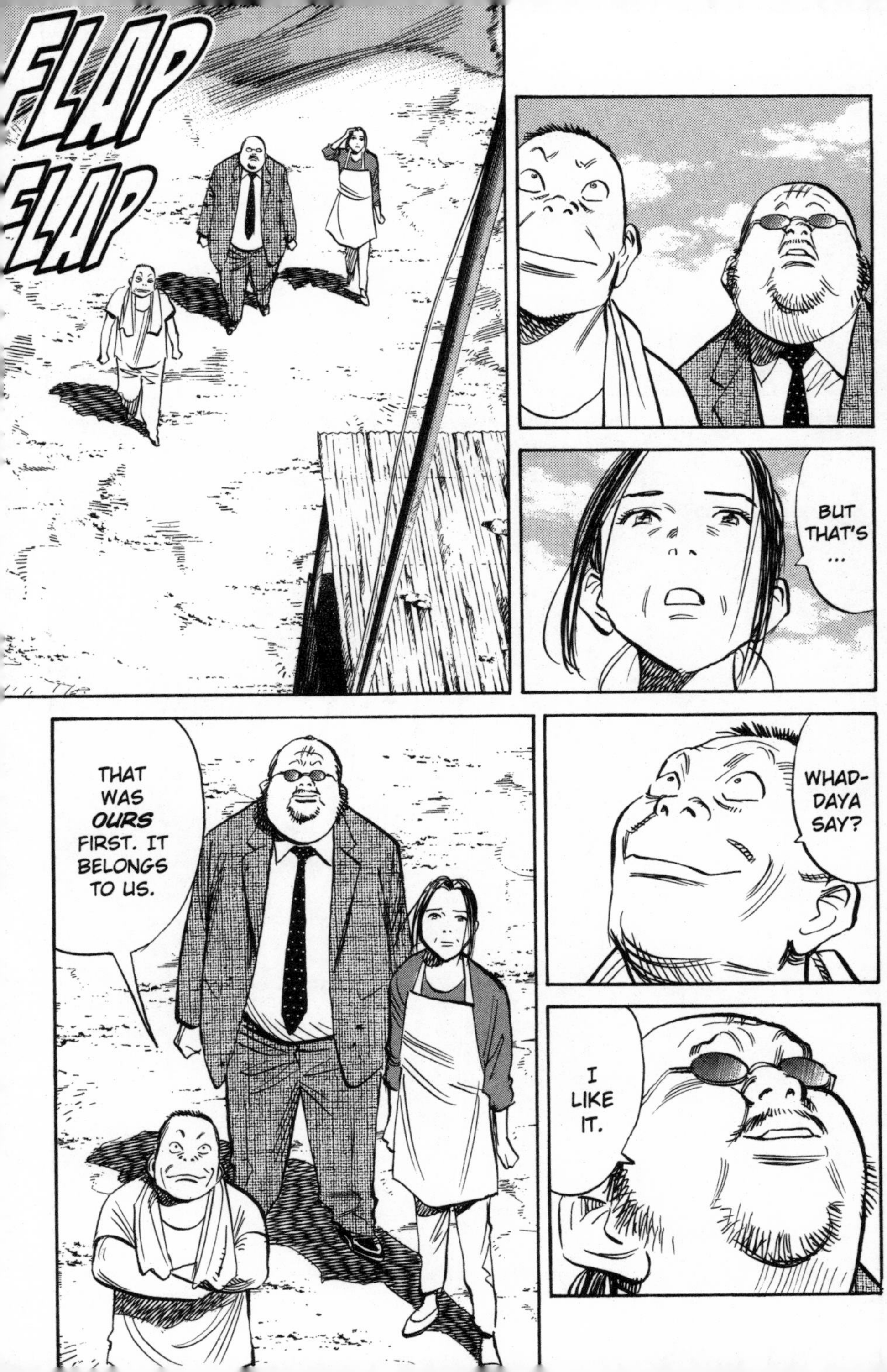
BUT THAT'S ...
FLAP FLAP
WHAD-DAYA SAY?
I LIKE IT.
THAT WAS *OURS* FIRST. IT BELONGS TO US.

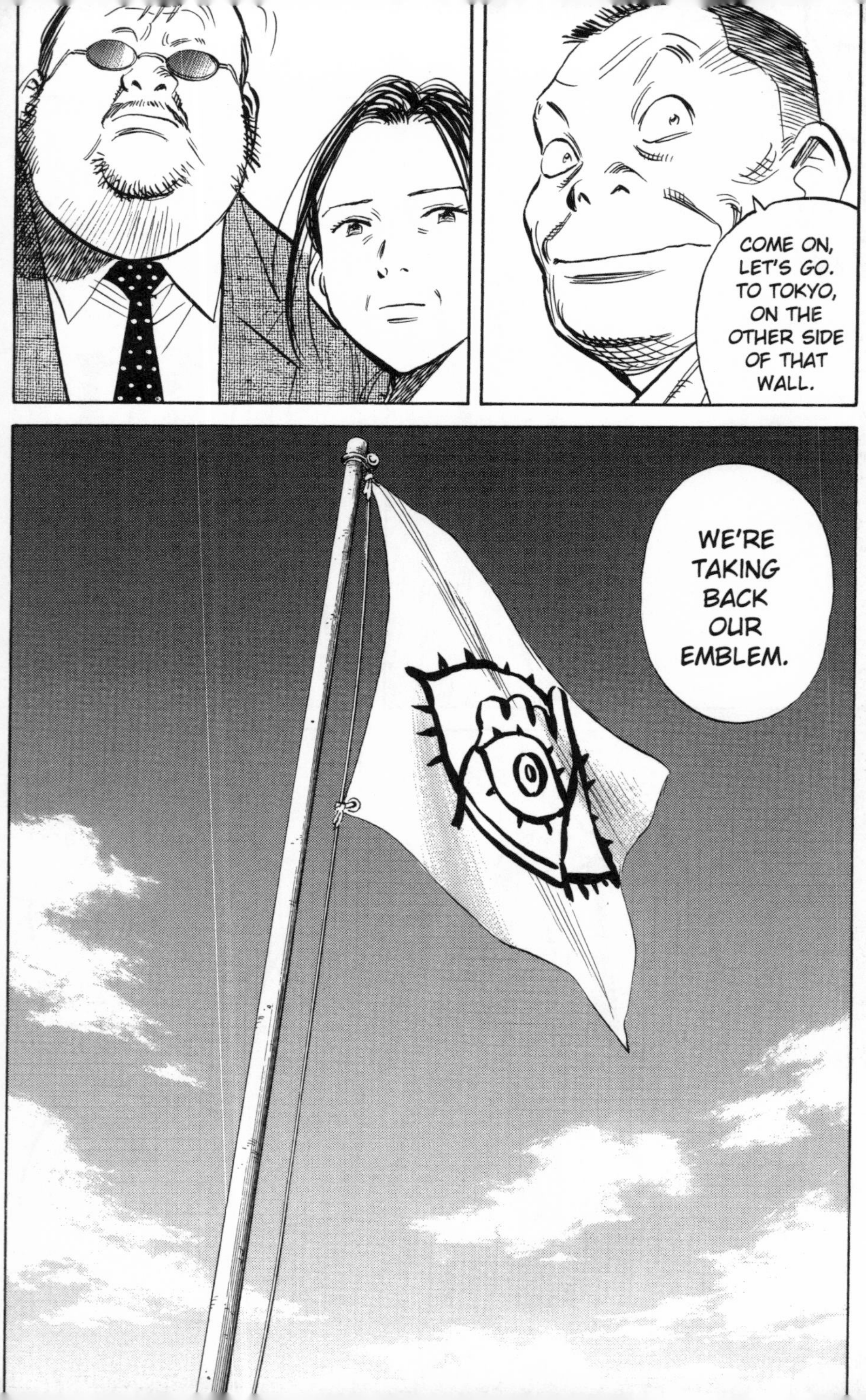
COME ON, LET'S GO. TO TOKYO, ON THE OTHER SIDE OF THAT WALL.
WE'RE TAKING BACK OUR EMBLEM.

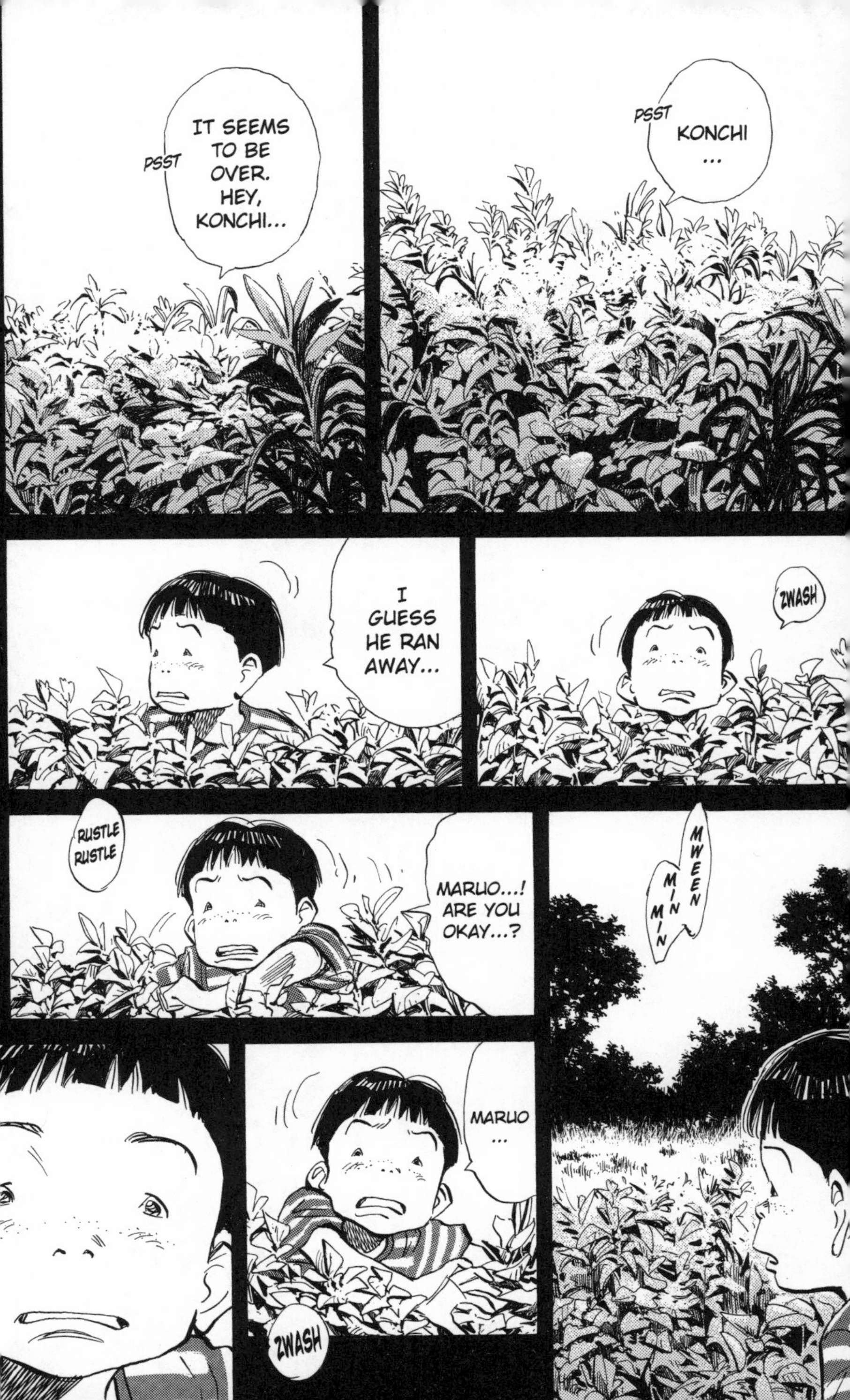
PSST
KONCHI ...
PSST
IT SEEMS TO BE OVER. HEY, KONCHI...
ZWASH
I GUESS HE RAN AWAY...
MWEEN
MIN MIN
MARUO...! ARE YOU OKAY...?
RUSTLE RUSTLE
MARUO ...
ZWASH

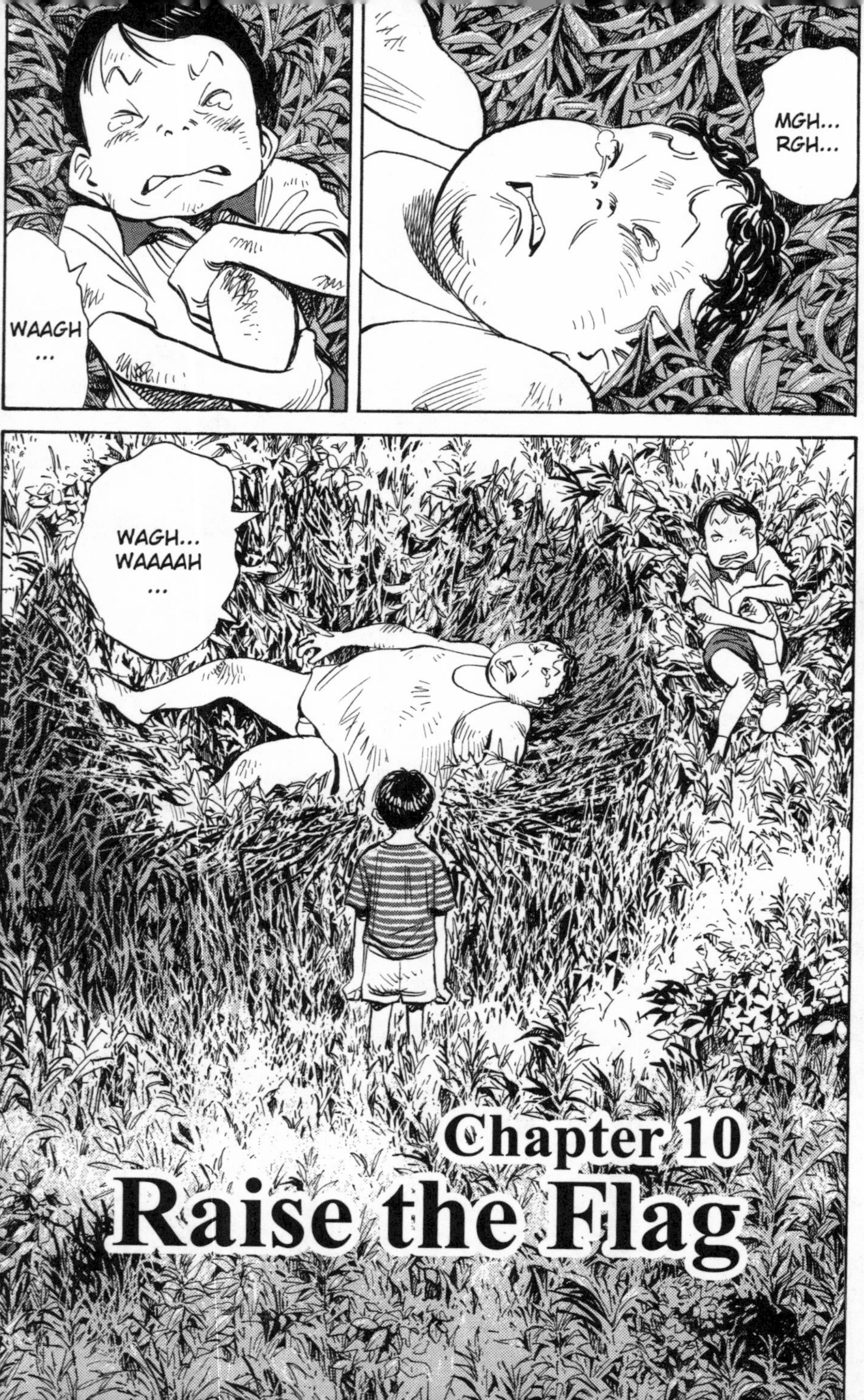
MGH... RGH...
WAAGH ...
WAGH... WAAAAH ...
Chapter 10
Raise the Flag

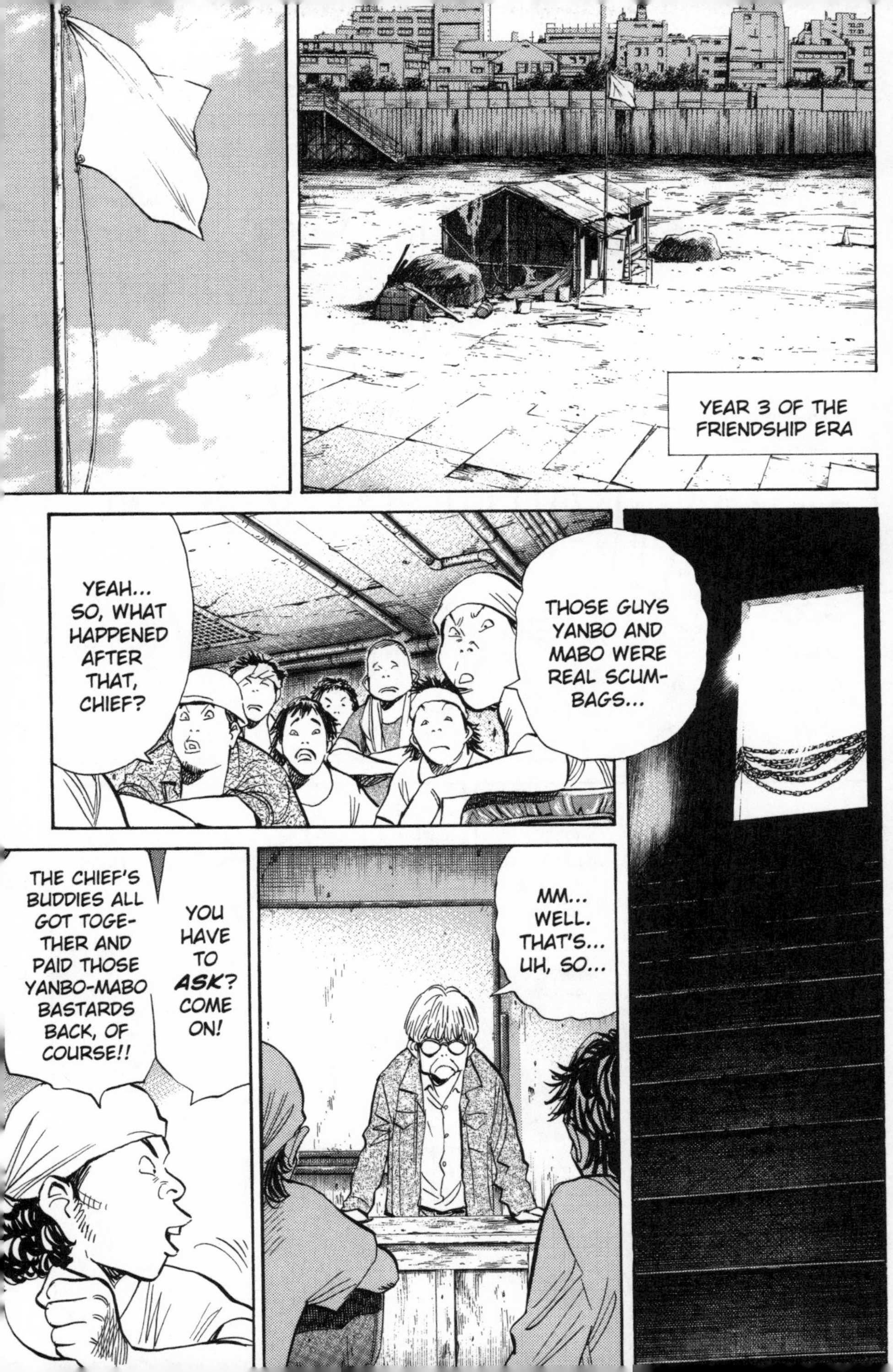
YEAR 3 OF THE FRIENDSHIP ERA
THOSE GUYS YANBO AND MABO WERE REAL SCUM-BAGS...
YEAH... SO, WHAT HAPPENED AFTER THAT, CHIEF?
MM... WELL. THAT'S... UH, SO...
YOU HAVE TO ***ASK***? COME ON!
THE CHIEF'S BUDDIES ALL GOT TOGE-THER AND PAID THOSE YANBO-MABO BASTARDS BACK, OF COURSE!!

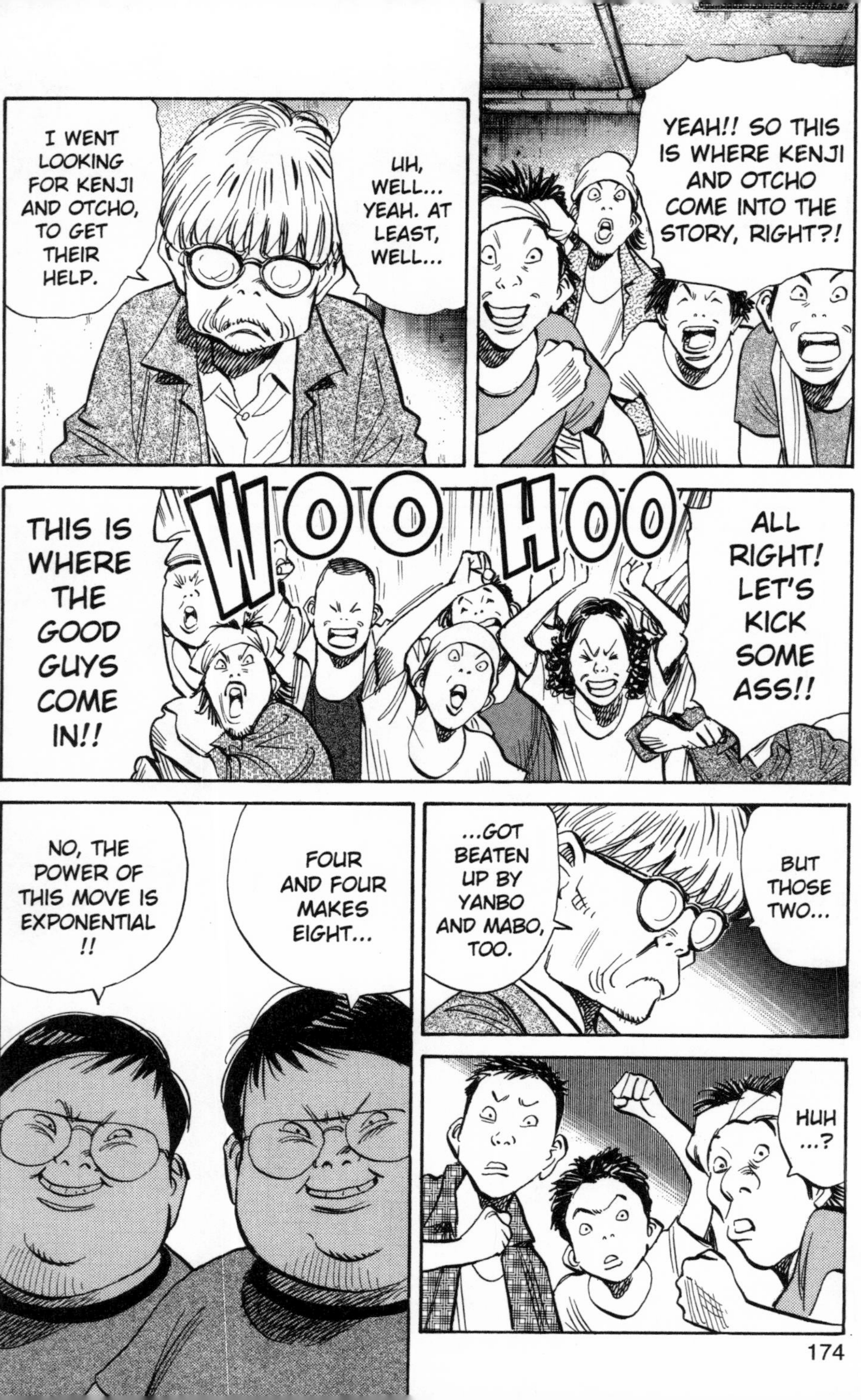
YEAH!! SO THIS IS WHERE KENJI AND OTCHO COME INTO THE STORY, RIGHT?!
UH, WELL... YEAH. AT LEAST, WELL...
I WENT LOOKING FOR KENJI AND OTCHO, TO GET THEIR HELP.
ALL RIGHT! LET'S KICK SOME ASS!!
WOO HOO
THIS IS WHERE THE GOOD GUYS COME IN!!
BUT THOSE TWO...
...GOT BEATEN UP BY YANBO AND MABO, TOO.
HUH ...?
FOUR AND FOUR MAKES EIGHT...
NO, THE POWER OF THIS MOVE IS EXPONENTIAL !!

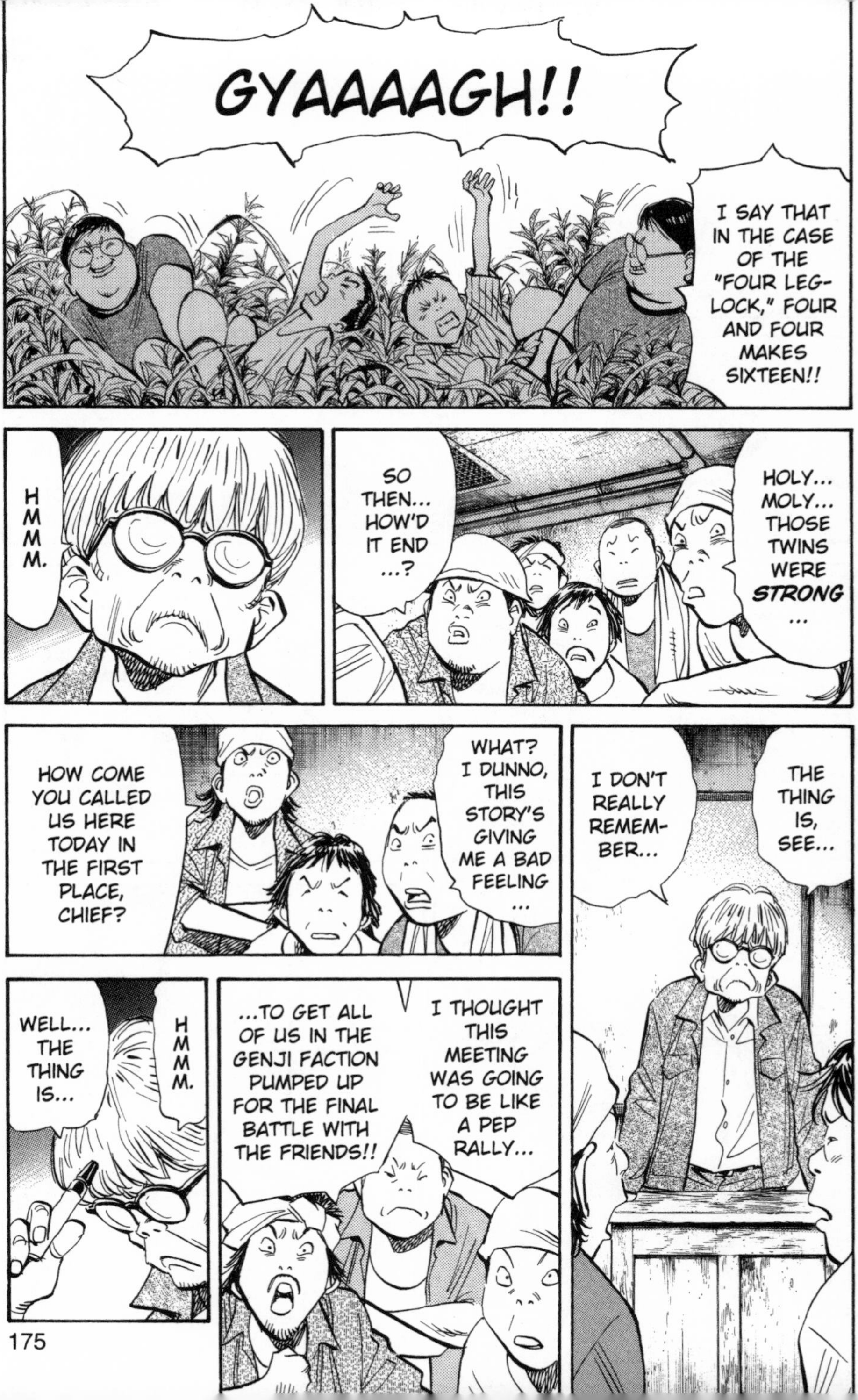
GYAAAAGH!!
I SAY THAT IN THE CASE OF THE "FOUR LEG-LOCK," FOUR AND FOUR MAKES SIXTEEN!!
HOLY... MOLY... THOSE TWINS WERE STRONG...
SO THEN... HOW'D IT END ...?
HMMM.
THE THING IS, SEE...
I DON'T REALLY REMEMBER...
WHAT? I DUNNO, THIS STORY'S GIVING ME A BAD FEELING...
HOW COME YOU CALLED US HERE TODAY IN THE FIRST PLACE, CHIEF?
I THOUGHT THIS MEETING WAS GOING TO BE LIKE A PEP RALLY...
...TO GET ALL OF US IN THE GENJI FACTION PUMPED UP FOR THE FINAL BATTLE WITH THE FRIENDS!!
HMMM.
WELL... THE THING IS...

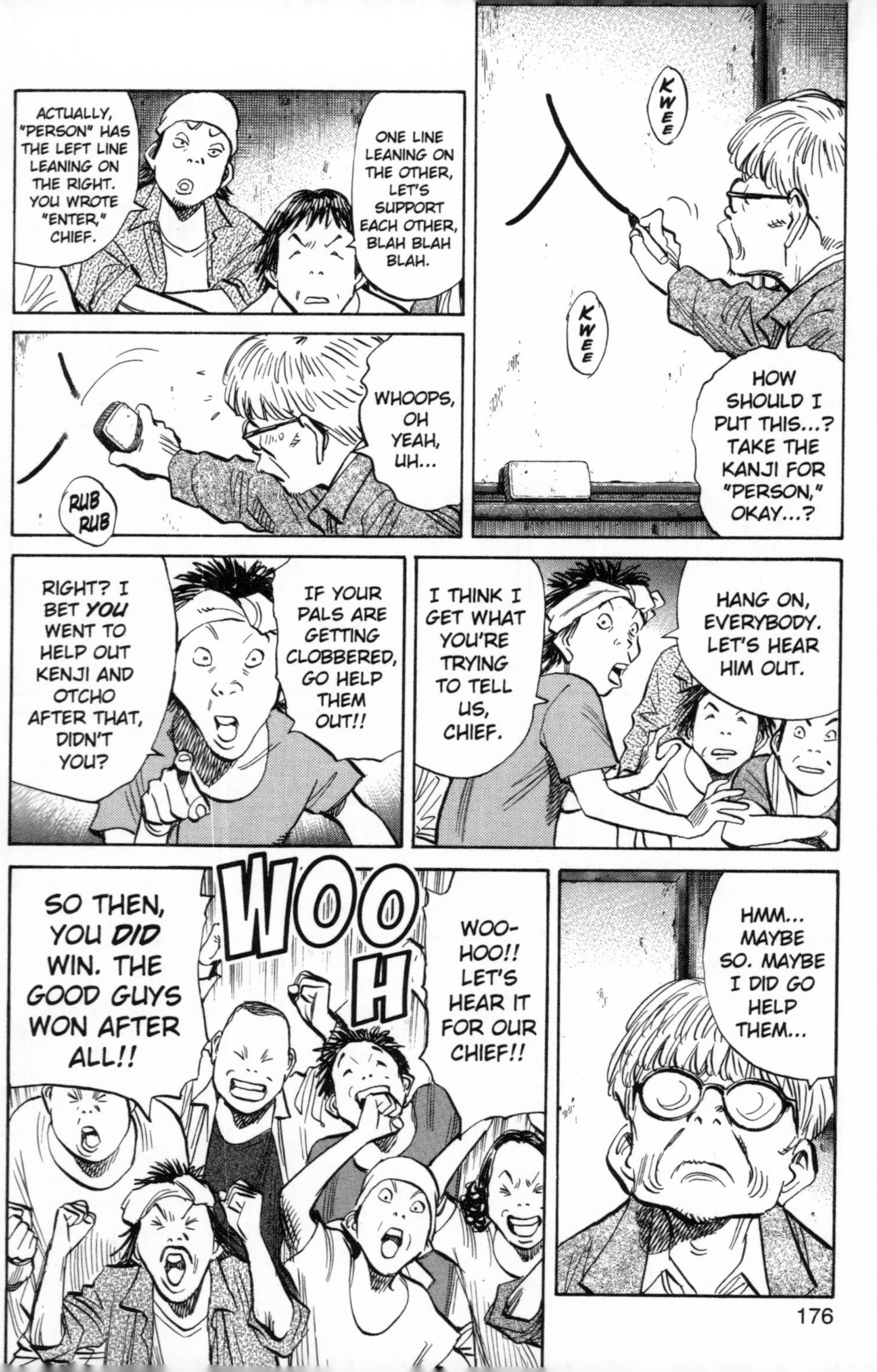
KWEE
KWEE
HOW SHOULD I PUT THIS...? TAKE THE KANJI FOR "PERSON," OKAY...?
ONE LINE LEANING ON THE OTHER, LET'S SUPPORT EACH OTHER, BLAH BLAH BLAH.
ACTUALLY, "PERSON" HAS THE LEFT LINE LEANING ON THE RIGHT. YOU WROTE "ENTER," CHIEF.
WHOOPS, OH YEAH, UH...
RUB RUB
HANG ON, EVERYBODY. LET'S HEAR HIM OUT.
I THINK I GET WHAT YOU'RE TRYING TO TELL US, CHIEF.
IF YOUR PALS ARE GETTING CLOBBERED, GO HELP THEM OUT!!
RIGHT? I BET *YOU* WENT TO HELP OUT KENJI AND OTCHO AFTER THAT, DIDN'T YOU?
HMM... MAYBE SO. MAYBE I DID GO HELP THEM...
WOO-HOO!! LET'S HEAR IT FOR OUR CHIEF!!
WOOOH
SO THEN, YOU *DID* WIN. THE GOOD GUYS WON AFTER ALL!!

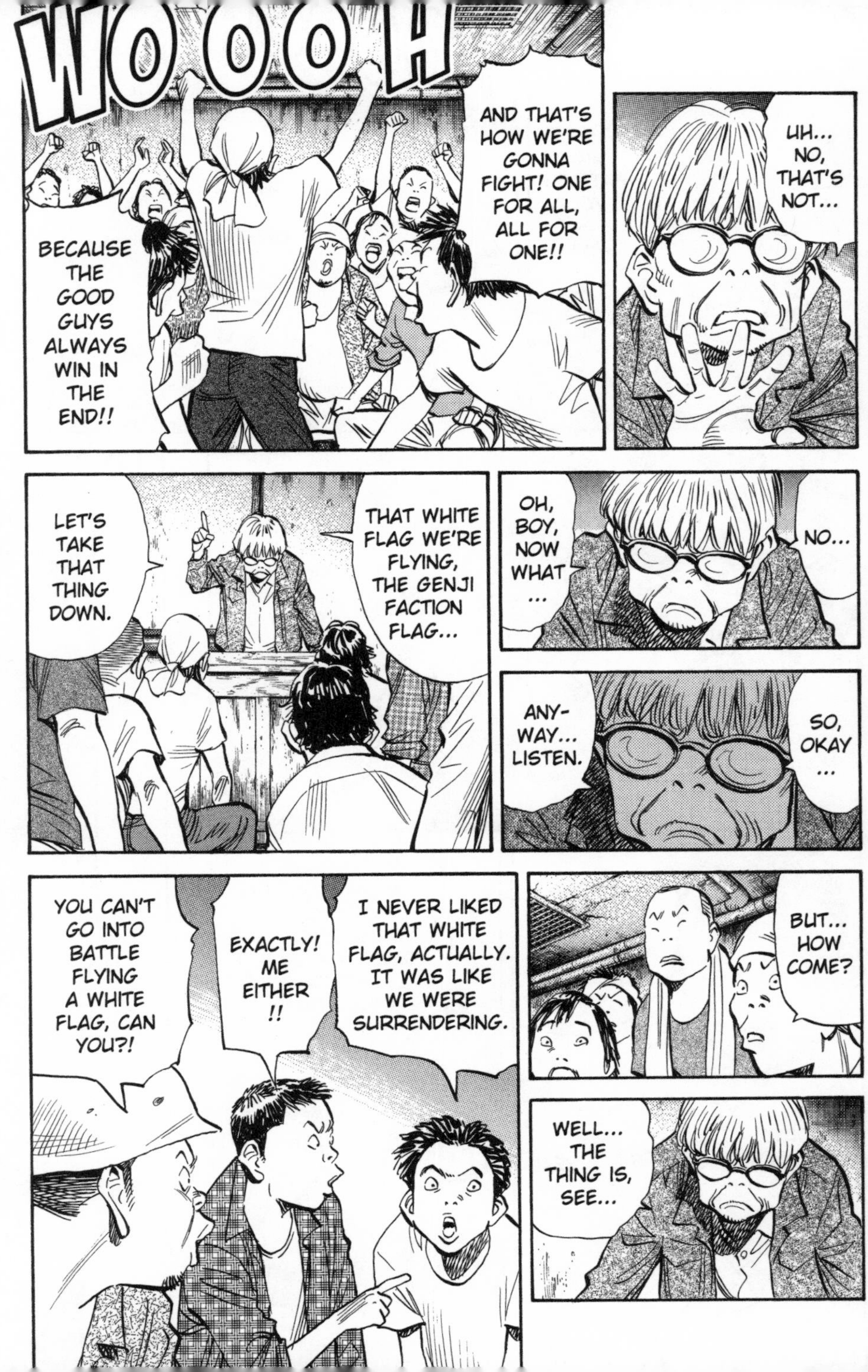
UH... NO, THAT'S NOT...
AND THAT'S HOW WE'RE GONNA FIGHT! ONE FOR ALL, ALL FOR ONE!!
WOOOH
BECAUSE THE GOOD GUYS ALWAYS WIN IN THE END!!
NO...
OH, BOY, NOW WHAT...
SO, OKAY...
ANY-WAY... LISTEN.
THAT WHITE FLAG WE'RE FLYING, THE GENJI FACTION FLAG...
LET'S TAKE THAT THING DOWN.
BUT... HOW COME?
WELL... THE THING IS, SEE...
I NEVER LIKED THAT WHITE FLAG, ACTUALLY. IT WAS LIKE WE WERE SURRENDERING.
EXACTLY! ME EITHER!!
YOU CAN'T GO INTO BATTLE FLYING A WHITE FLAG, CAN YOU?!

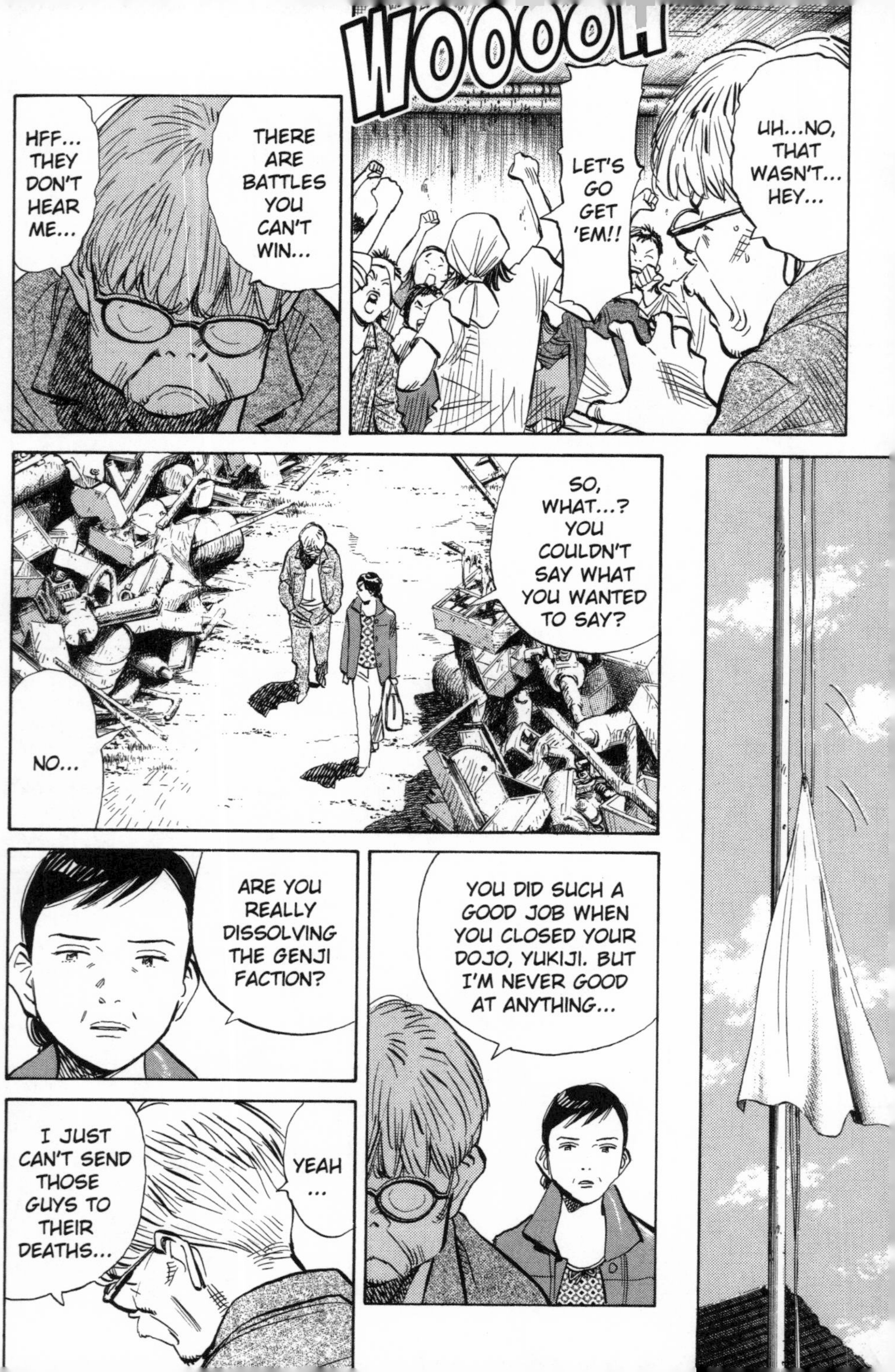
WOOOOH
UH...NO, THAT WASN'T... HEY...
LET'S GO GET 'EM!!
THERE ARE BATTLES YOU CAN'T WIN...
HFF... THEY DON'T HEAR ME...
SO, WHAT...? YOU COULDN'T SAY WHAT YOU WANTED TO SAY?
NO...
YOU DID SUCH A GOOD JOB WHEN YOU CLOSED YOUR DOJO, YUKIJI. BUT I'M NEVER GOOD AT ANYTHING...
ARE YOU REALLY DISSOLVING THE GENJI FACTION?
YEAH ...
I JUST CAN'T SEND THOSE GUYS TO THEIR DEATHS...

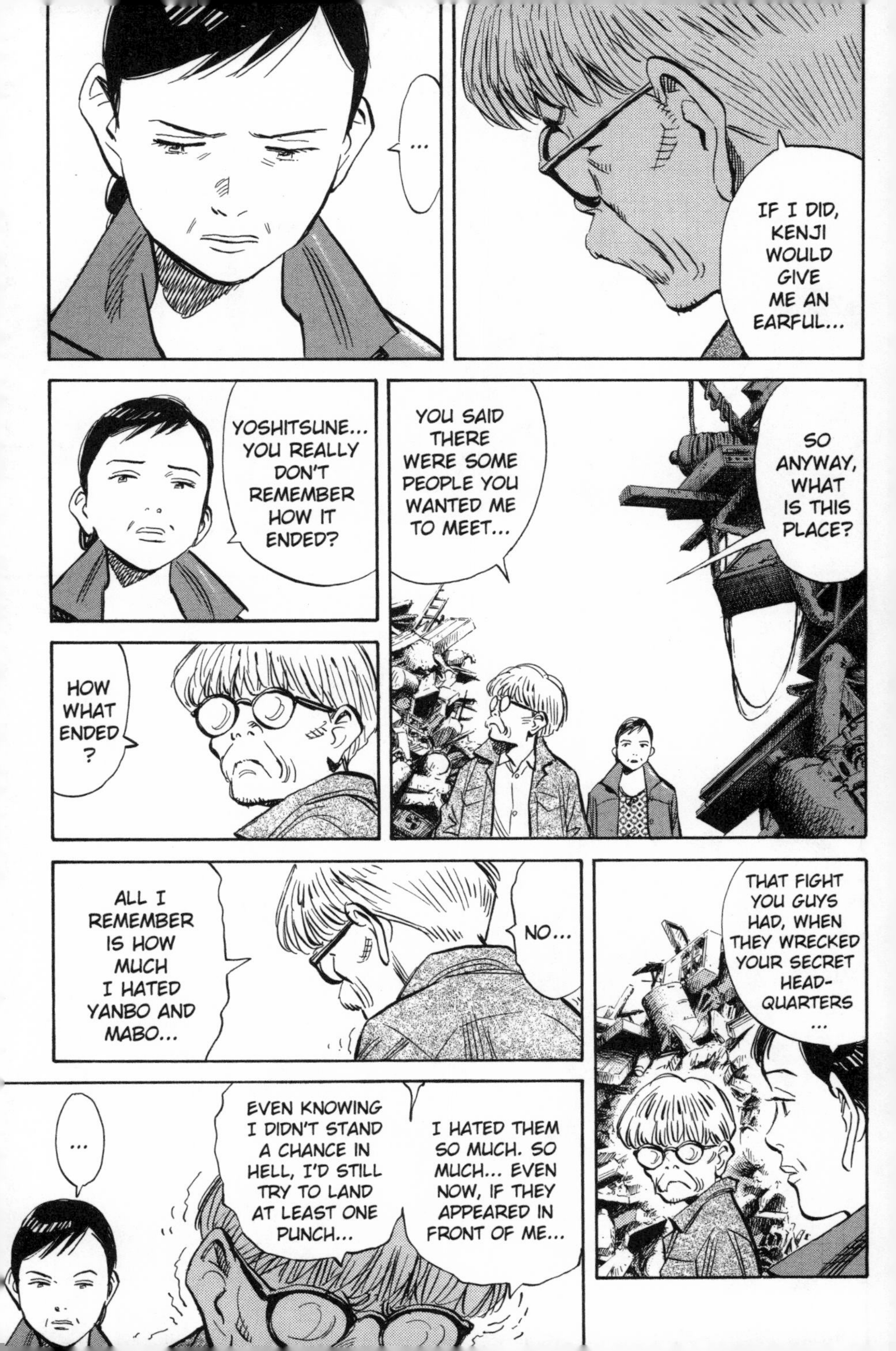
IF I DID, KENJI WOULD GIVE ME AN EARFUL...
...
SO ANYWAY, WHAT IS THIS PLACE?
YOU SAID THERE WERE SOME PEOPLE YOU WANTED ME TO MEET...
YOSHITSUNE... YOU REALLY DON'T REMEMBER HOW IT ENDED?
HOW WHAT ENDED?
THAT FIGHT YOU GUYS HAD, WHEN THEY WRECKED YOUR SECRET HEAD-QUARTERS...
NO...
ALL I REMEMBER IS HOW MUCH I HATED YANBO AND MABO...
I HATED THEM SO MUCH. SO MUCH... EVEN NOW, IF THEY APPEARED IN FRONT OF ME...
EVEN KNOWING I DIDN'T STAND A CHANCE IN HELL, I'D STILL TRY TO LAND AT LEAST ONE PUNCH...
...

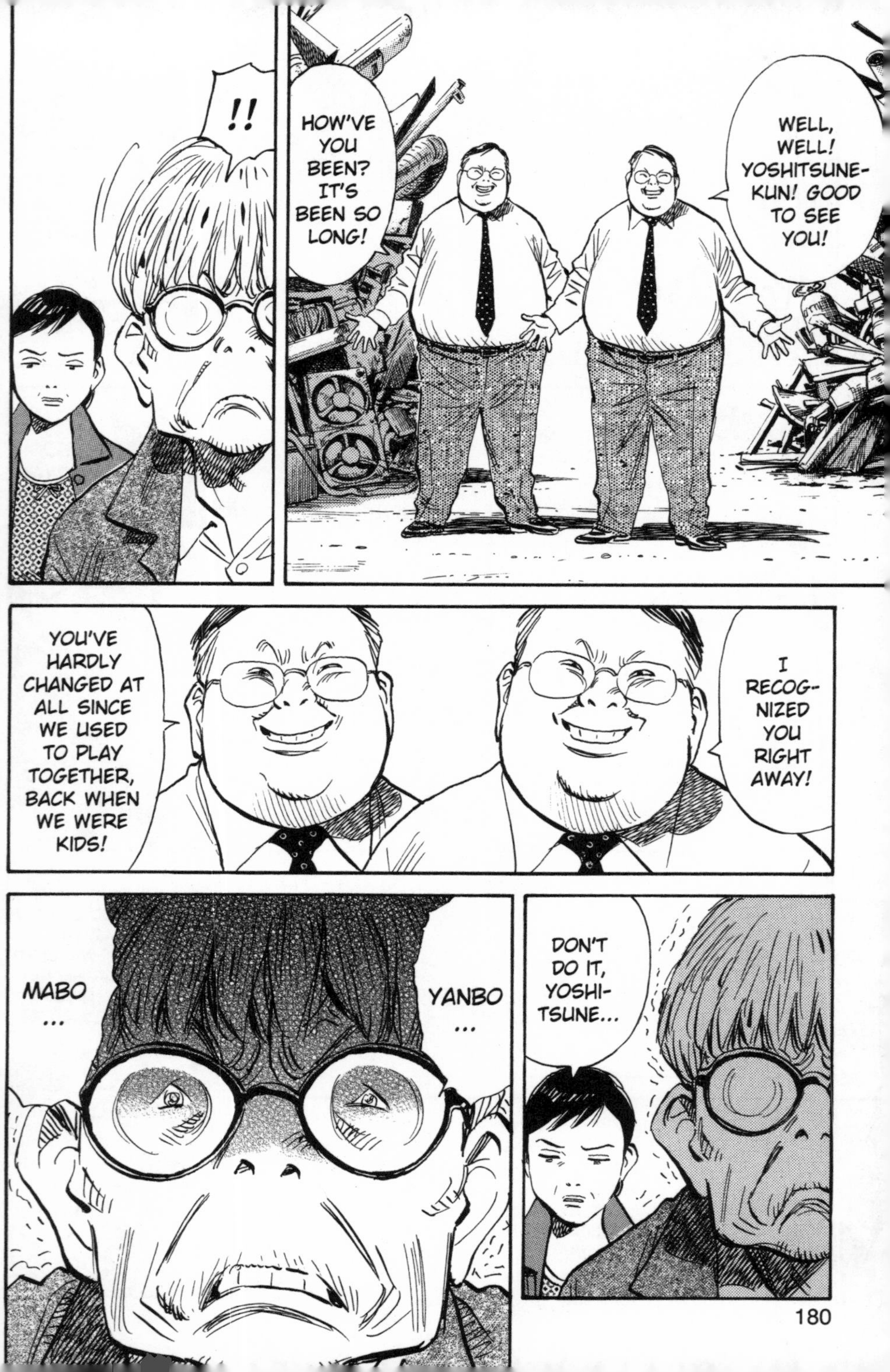
WELL, WELL! YOSHITSUNE-KUN! GOOD TO SEE YOU!
HOW'VE YOU BEEN? IT'S BEEN SO LONG!
!!
I RECOGNIZED YOU RIGHT AWAY!
YOU'VE HARDLY CHANGED AT ALL SINCE WE USED TO PLAY TOGETHER, BACK WHEN WE WERE KIDS!
DON'T DO IT, YOSHITSUNE...
YANBO ...
MABO ...

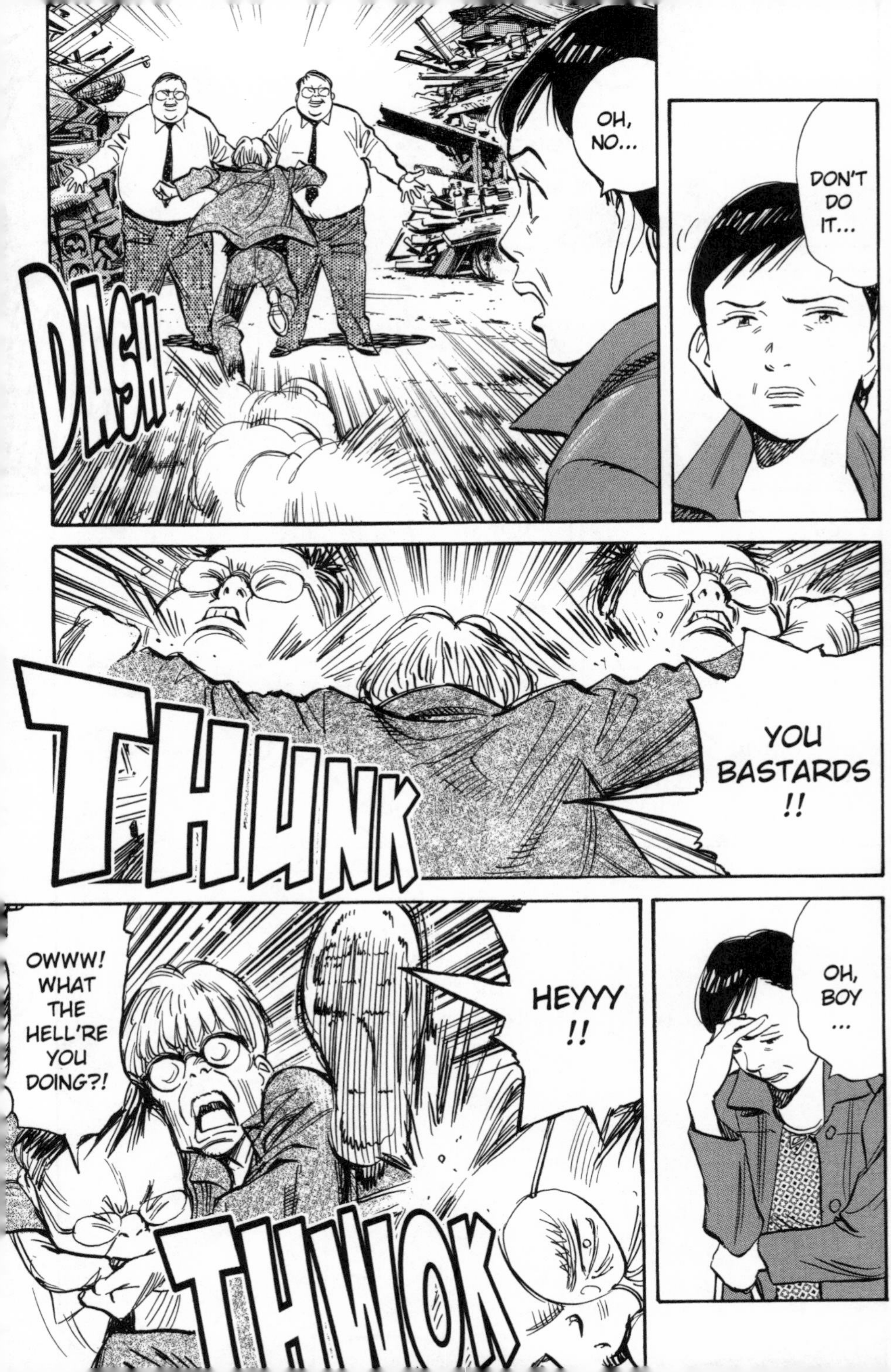
DON'T DO IT...
OH, NO...
DASH
YOU BASTARDS !!
THUNK
OH, BOY ...
HEYYY !!
OWWW! WHAT THE HELL'RE YOU DOING?!
THWOK

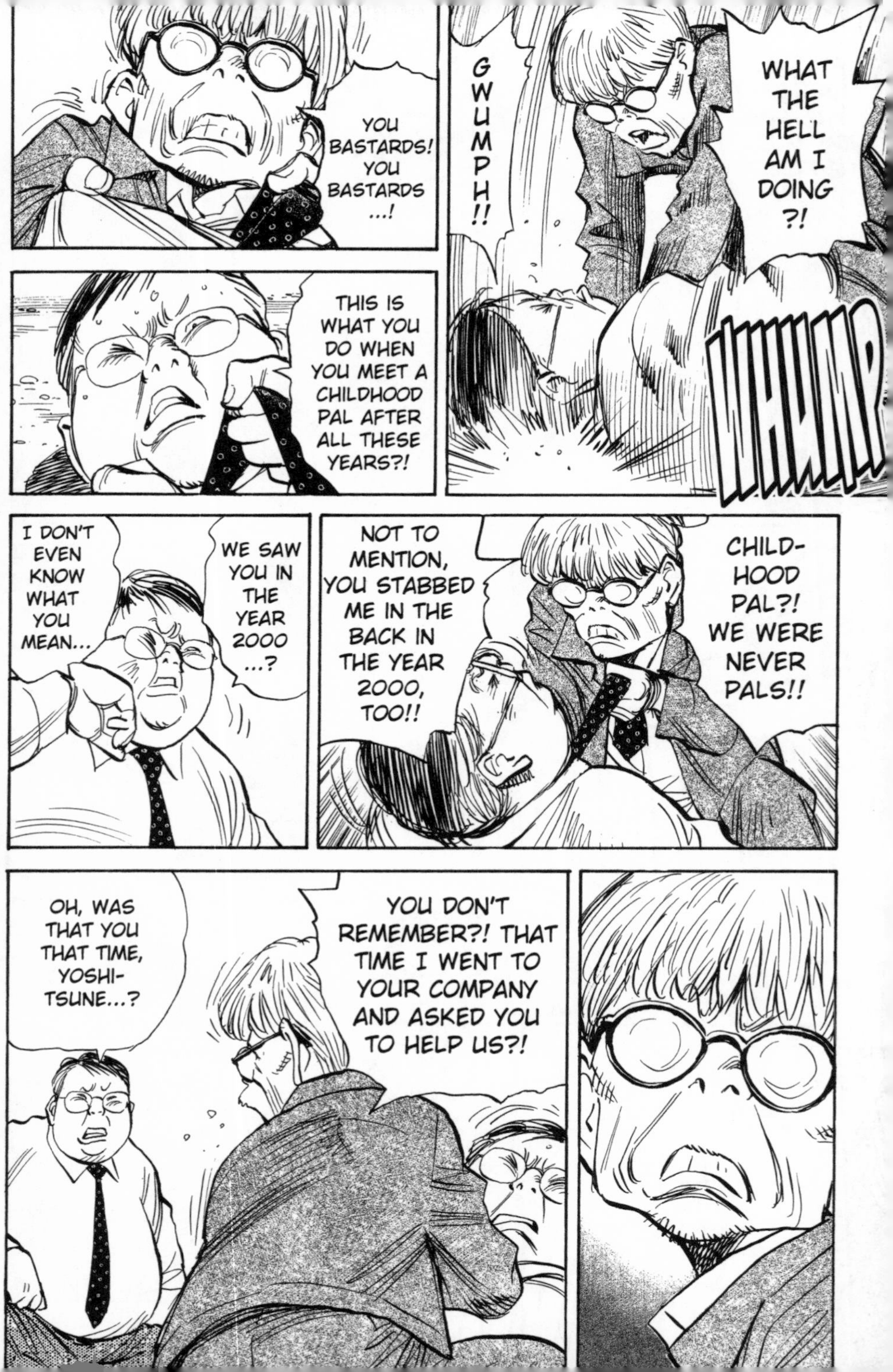
WHAT THE HELL AM I DOING?!
GWUMPH!!
WHUMP
YOU BASTARDS! YOU BASTARDS ...!
THIS IS WHAT YOU DO WHEN YOU MEET A CHILDHOOD PAL AFTER ALL THESE YEARS?!
CHILD-HOOD PAL?! WE WERE NEVER PALS!!
NOT TO MENTION, YOU STABBED ME IN THE BACK IN THE YEAR 2000, TOO!!
WE SAW YOU IN THE YEAR 2000 ...?
I DON'T EVEN KNOW WHAT YOU MEAN...
YOU DON'T REMEMBER?! THAT TIME I WENT TO YOUR COMPANY AND ASKED YOU TO HELP US?!
OH, WAS THAT YOU THAT TIME, YOSHI-TSUNE...?

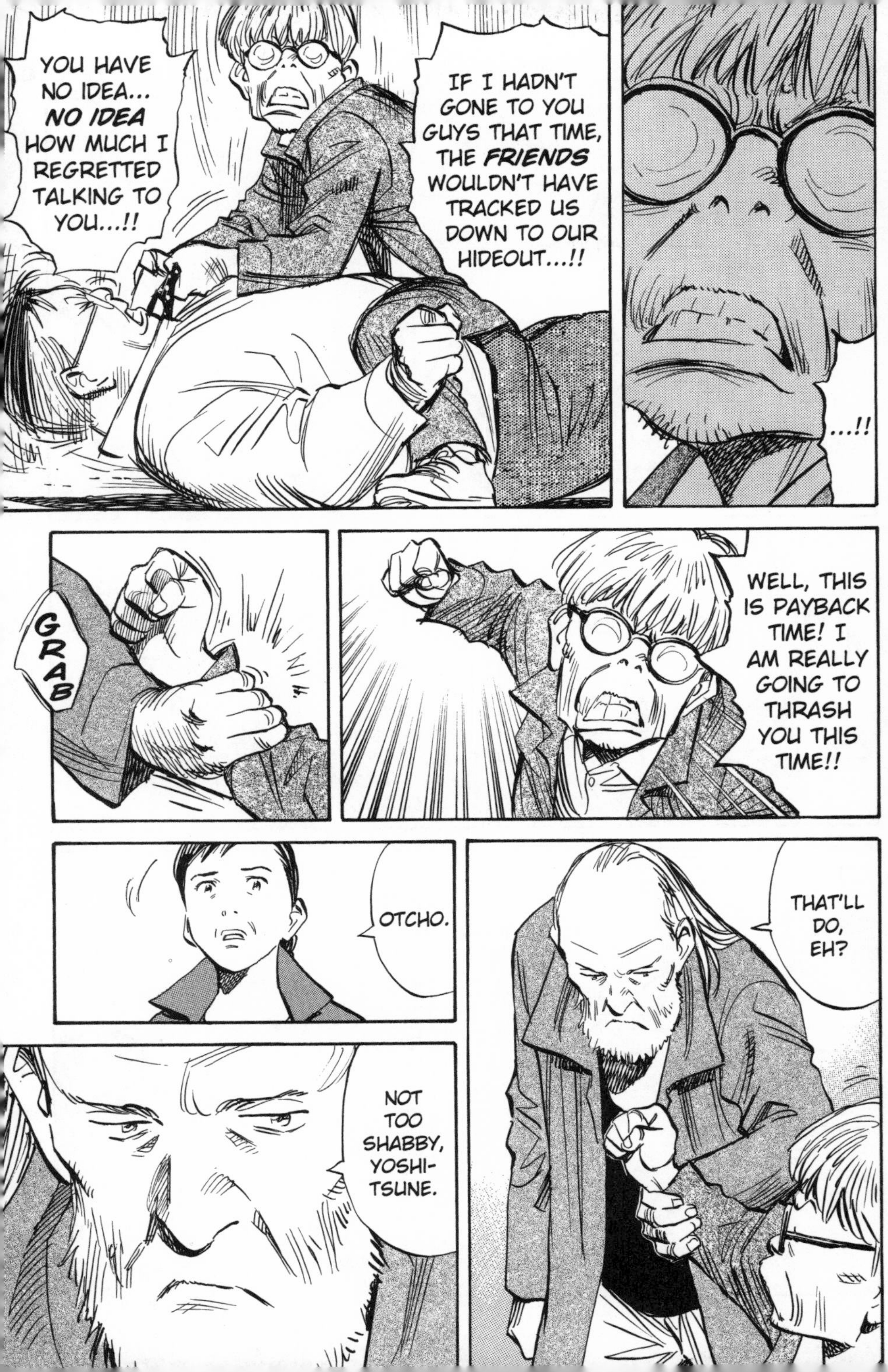
...!!
IF I HADN'T GONE TO YOU GUYS THAT TIME, THE ***FRIENDS*** WOULDN'T HAVE TRACKED US DOWN TO OUR HIDEOUT...!!
YOU HAVE NO IDEA... ***NO IDEA*** HOW MUCH I REGRETTED TALKING TO YOU...!!
WELL, THIS IS PAYBACK TIME! I AM REALLY GOING TO THRASH YOU THIS TIME!!
GRAB
THAT'LL DO, EH?
OTCHO.
NOT TOO SHABBY, YOSHI-TSUNE.

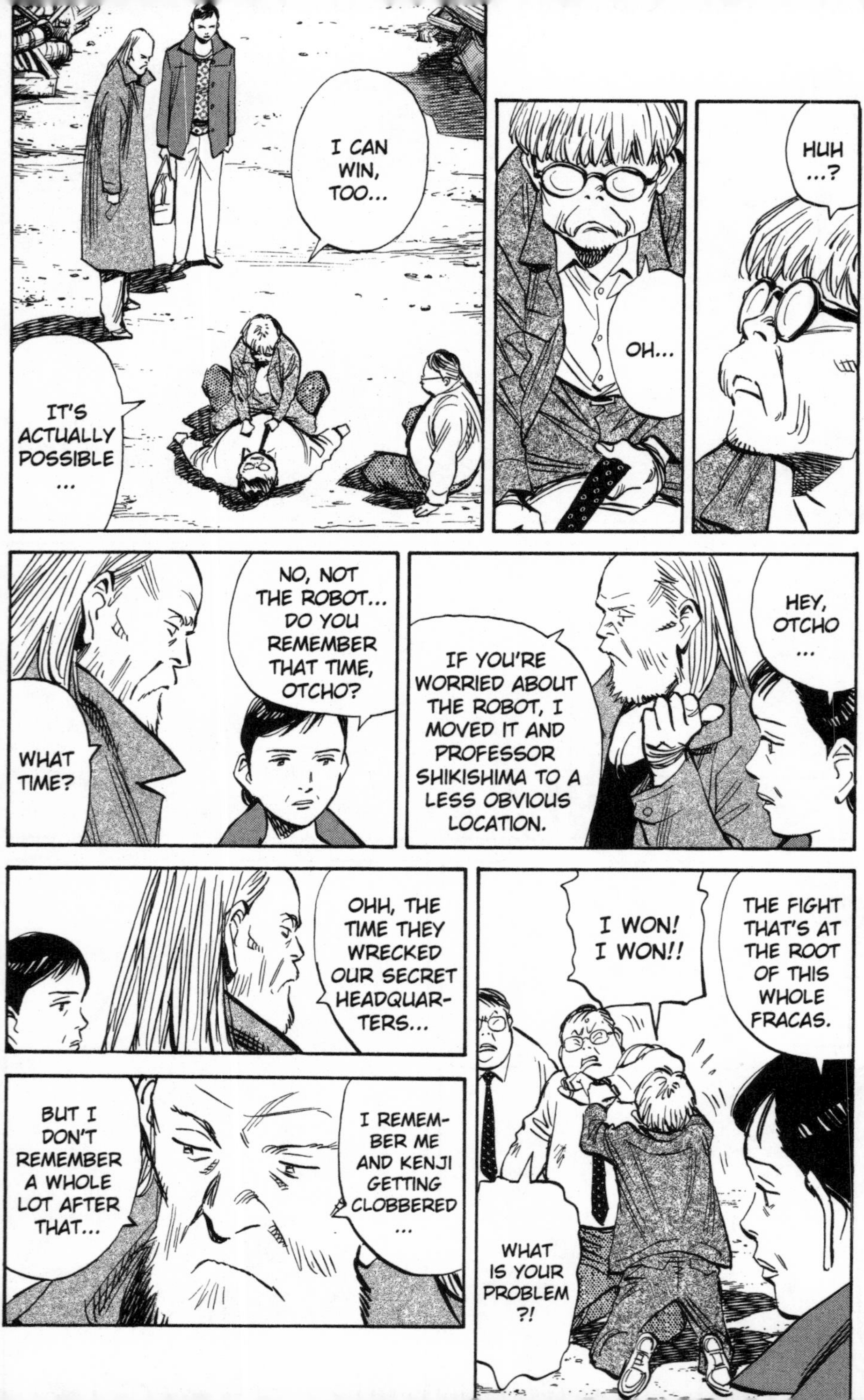
HUH ...?
OH...
I CAN WIN, TOO...
IT'S ACTUALLY POSSIBLE ...
HEY, OTCHO ...
IF YOU'RE WORRIED ABOUT THE ROBOT, I MOVED IT AND PROFESSOR SHIKISHIMA TO A LESS OBVIOUS LOCATION.
NO, NOT THE ROBOT... DO YOU REMEMBER THAT TIME, OTCHO?
WHAT TIME?
THE FIGHT THAT'S AT THE ROOT OF THIS WHOLE FRACAS.
I WON! I WON!!
WHAT IS YOUR PROBLEM ?!
OHH, THE TIME THEY WRECKED OUR SECRET HEADQUAR-TERS...
I REMEM-BER ME AND KENJI GETTING CLOBBERED ...
BUT I DON'T REMEMBER A WHOLE LOT AFTER THAT...

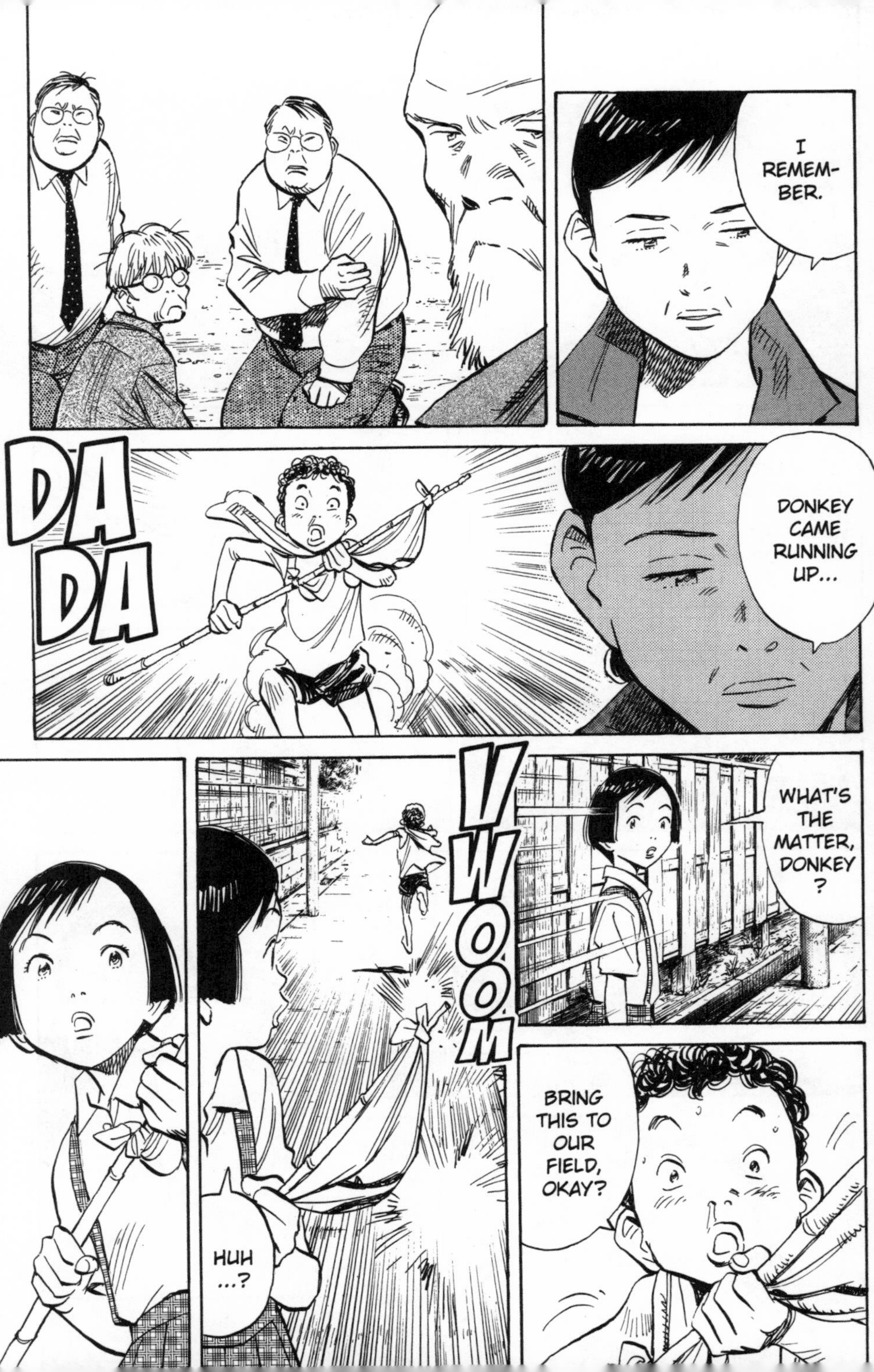
I REMEM-BER.
DONKEY CAME RUNNING UP...
DA DA
WHAT'S THE MATTER, DONKEY?
BRING THIS TO OUR FIELD, OKAY?
VWOOM
HUH ...?

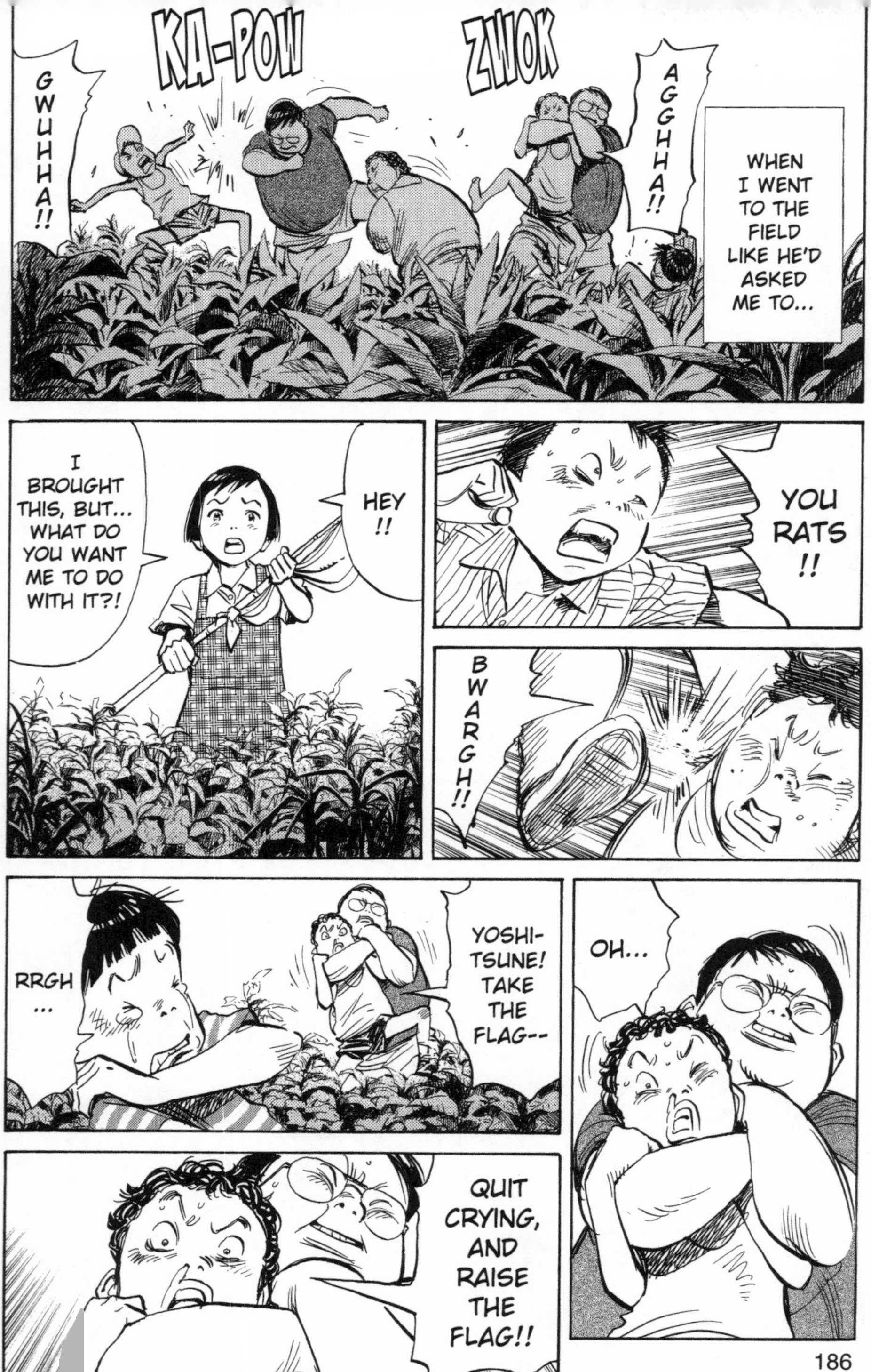
WHEN I WENT TO THE FIELD LIKE HE'D ASKED ME TO...
AGGHHA!!
ZWOK
KA-POW
GWUHHA!!
YOU RATS!!
BWARGH!!
HEY!!
I BROUGHT THIS, BUT... WHAT DO YOU WANT ME TO DO WITH IT?!
OH...
YOSHI-TSUNE! TAKE THE FLAG--
RRGH...
QUIT CRYING, AND RAISE THE FLAG!!

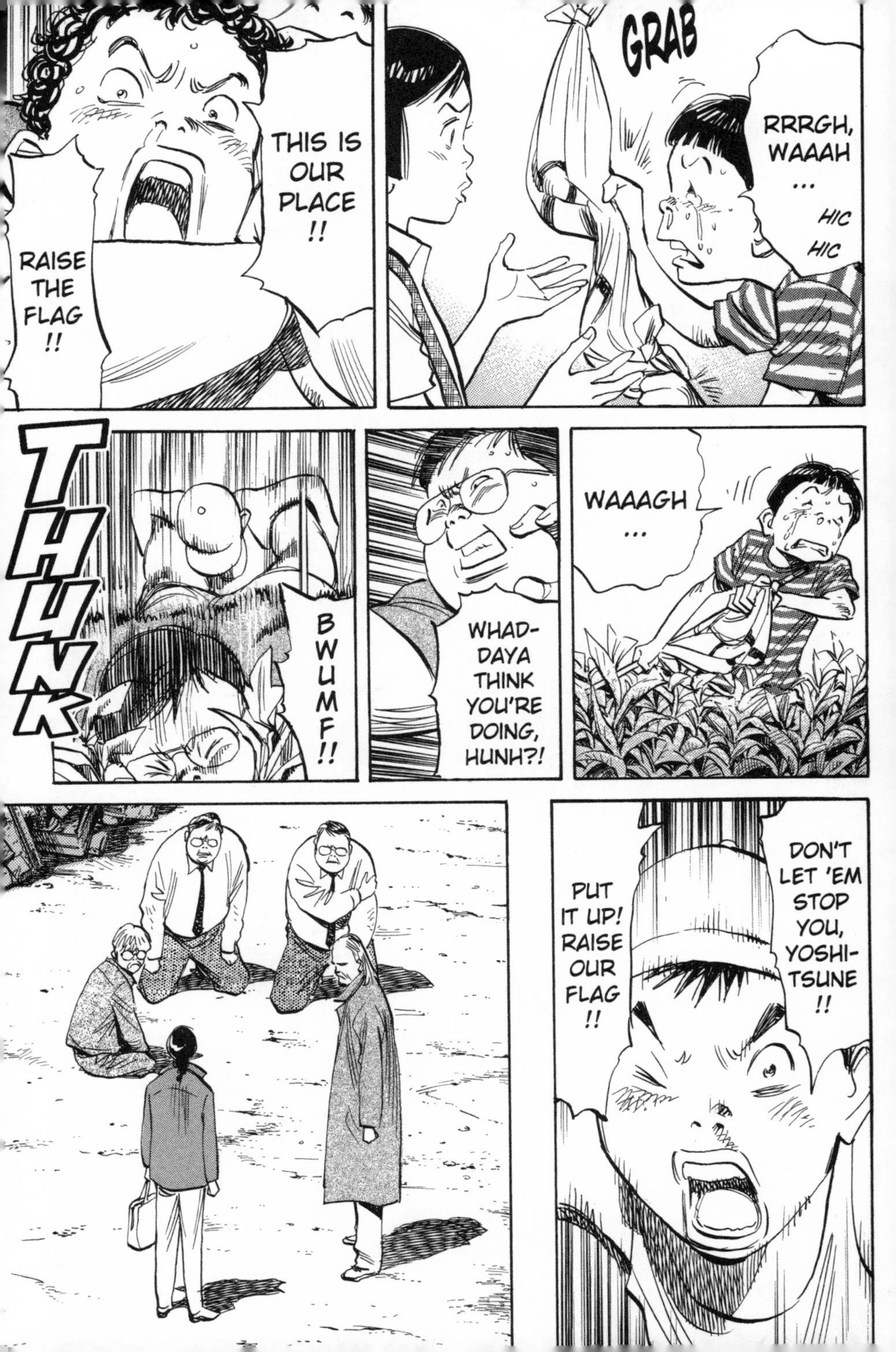
GRAB
RRRGH, WAAAH ...
HIC HIC
THIS IS OUR PLACE !!
RAISE THE FLAG !!
WAAAGH ...
WHAD-DAYA THINK YOU'RE DOING, HUNH?!
THUNK
BWUMF!!
DON'T LET 'EM STOP YOU, YOSHI-TSUNE !!
PUT IT UP! RAISE OUR FLAG !!

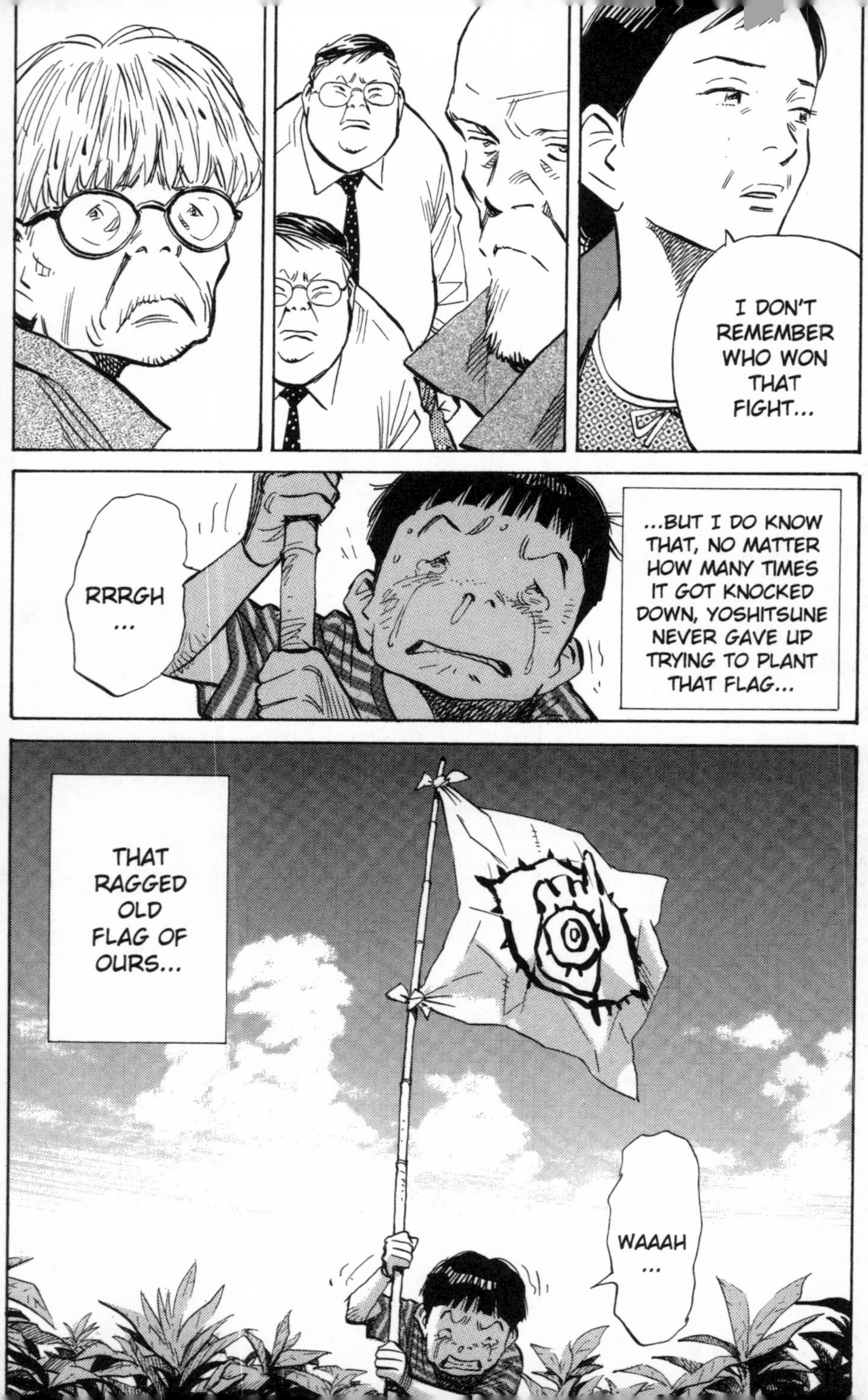
I DON'T REMEMBER WHO WON THAT FIGHT...
...BUT I DO KNOW THAT, NO MATTER HOW MANY TIMES IT GOT KNOCKED DOWN, YOSHITSUNE NEVER GAVE UP TRYING TO PLANT THAT FLAG...
RRRGH ...
THAT RAGGED OLD FLAG OF OURS...
WAAAH ...

Chapter 11 Confession of the Mask

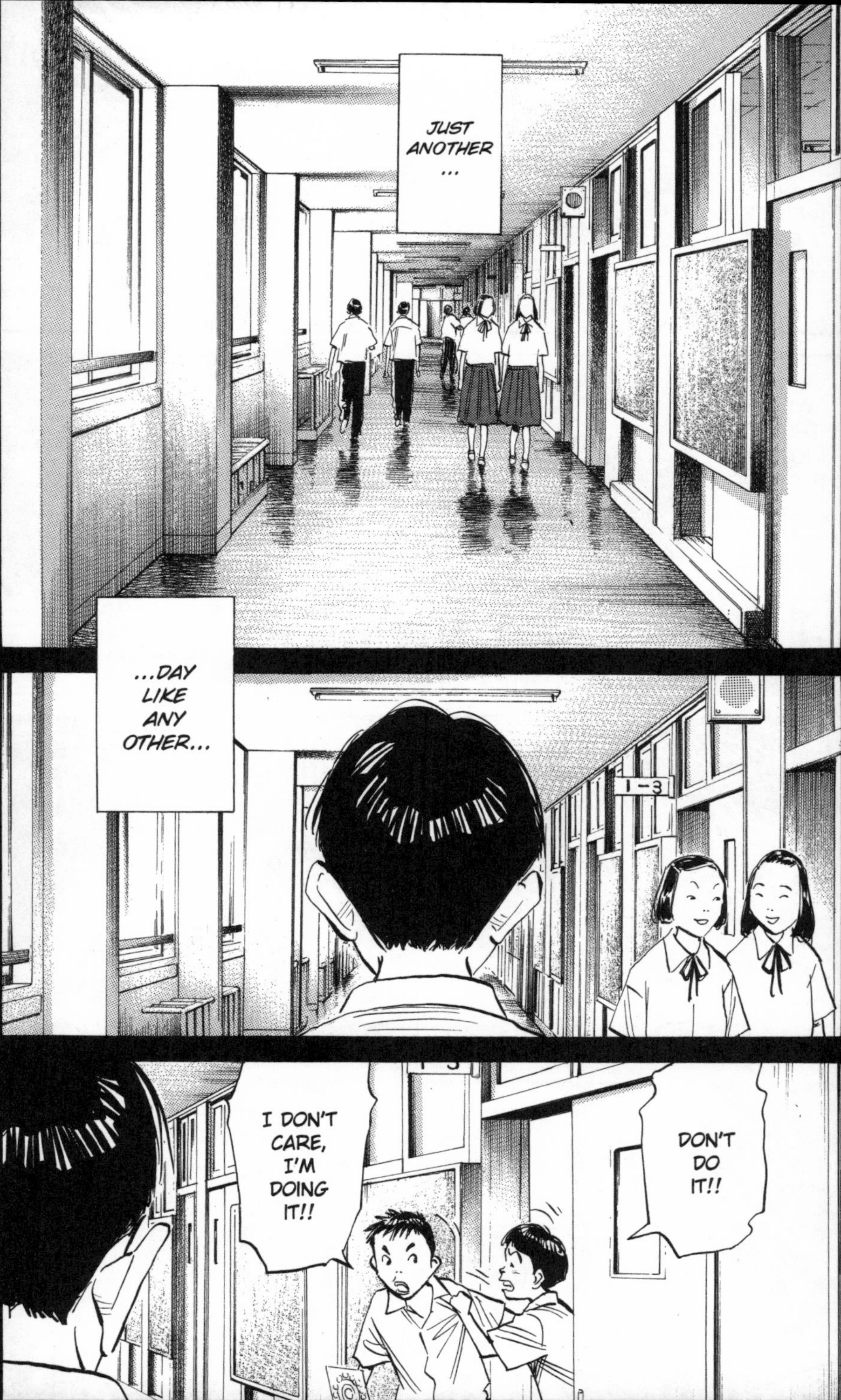
JUST ANOTHER ...
...DAY LIKE ANY OTHER...
1-3
DON'T DO IT!!
I DON'T CARE, I'M DOING IT!!

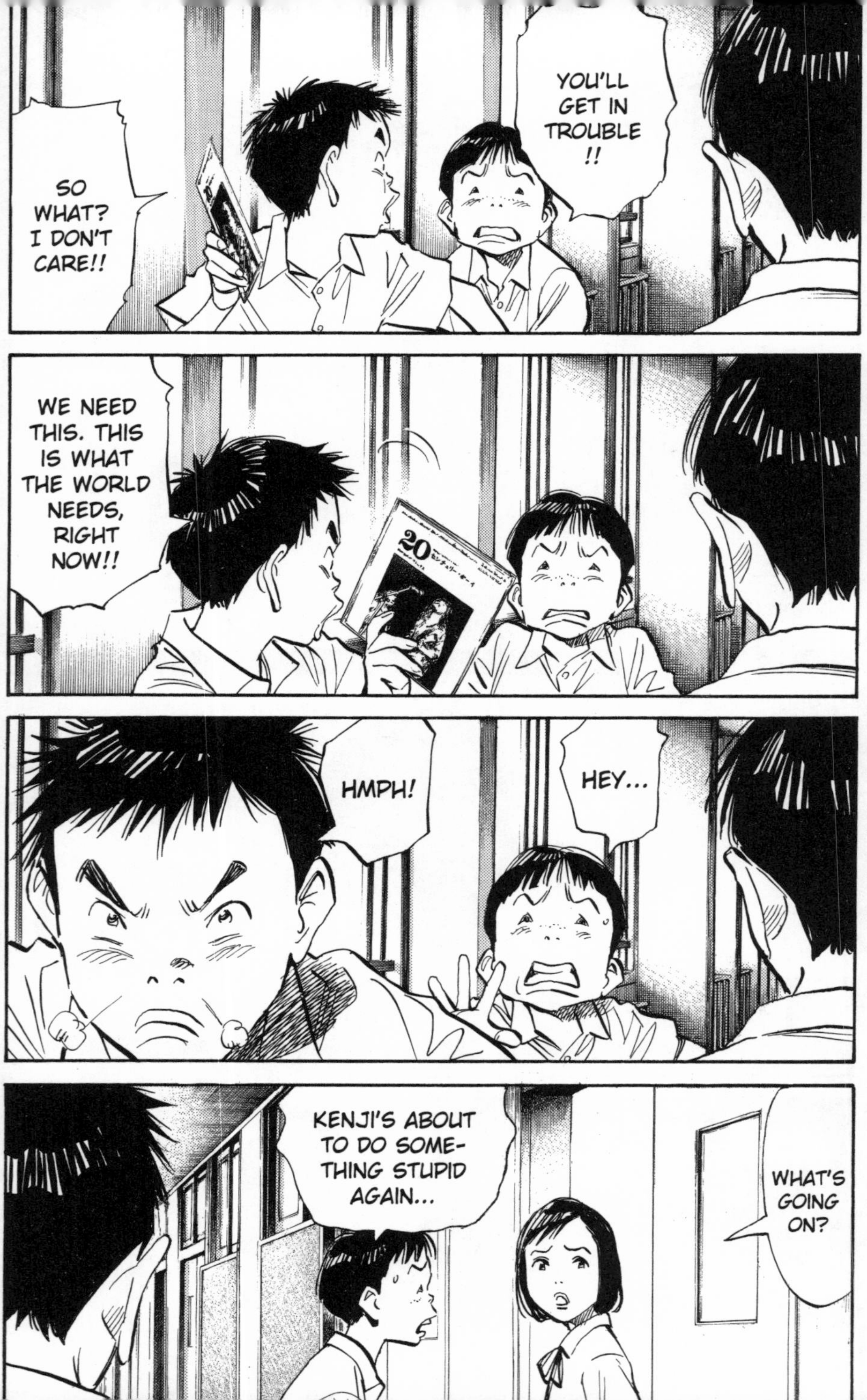
YOU'LL GET IN TROUBLE!!
SO WHAT? I DON'T CARE!!
WE NEED THIS. THIS IS WHAT THE WORLD NEEDS, RIGHT NOW!!
20
HEY...
HMPH!
WHAT'S GOING ON?
KENJI'S ABOUT TO DO SOME-THING STUPID AGAIN...

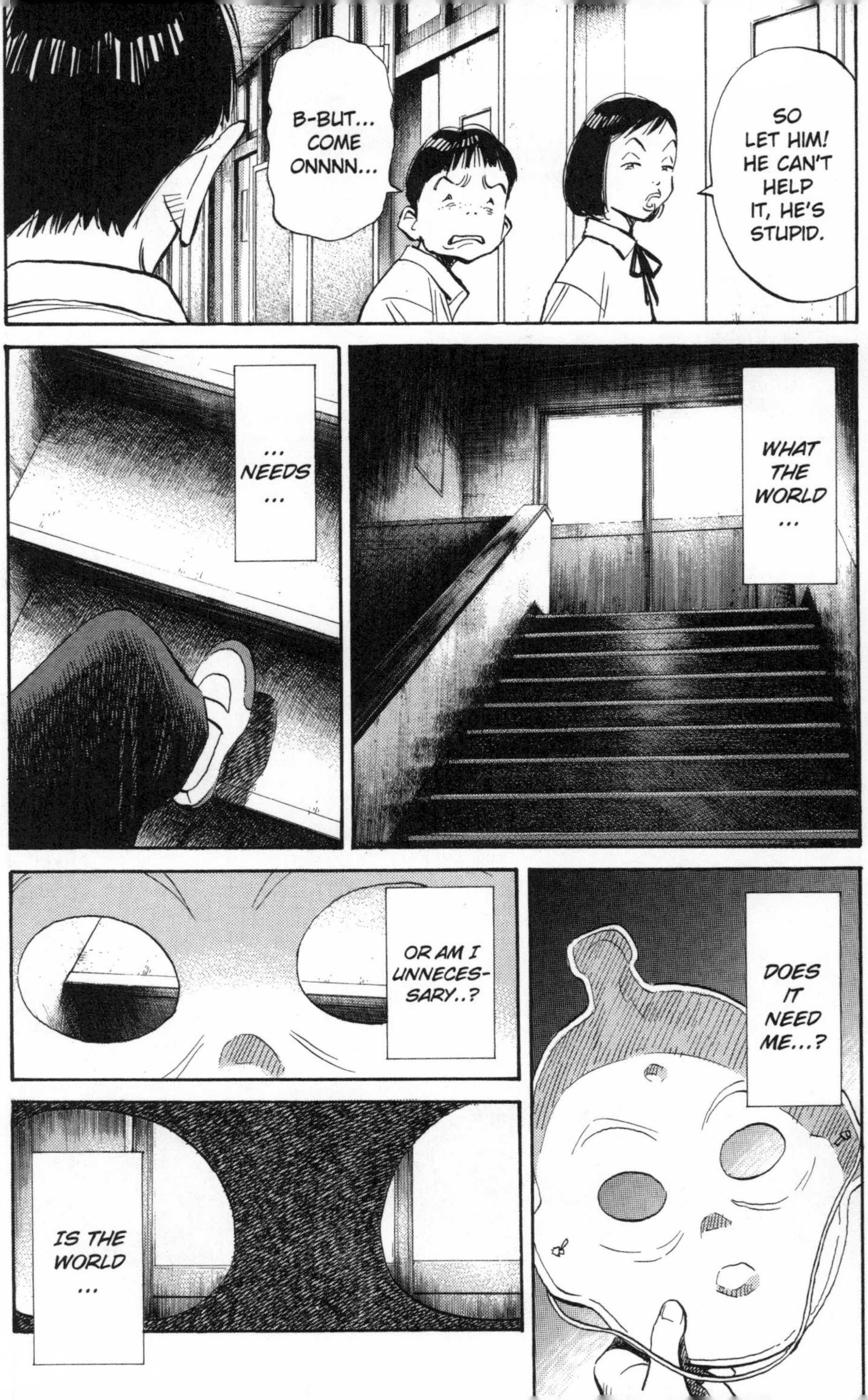
SO LET HIM! HE CAN'T HELP IT, HE'S STUPID.
B-BUT... COME ONNNN...
WHAT THE WORLD ...
... NEEDS ...
DOES IT NEED ME...?
OR AM I UNNECES-SARY..?
IS THE WORLD ...

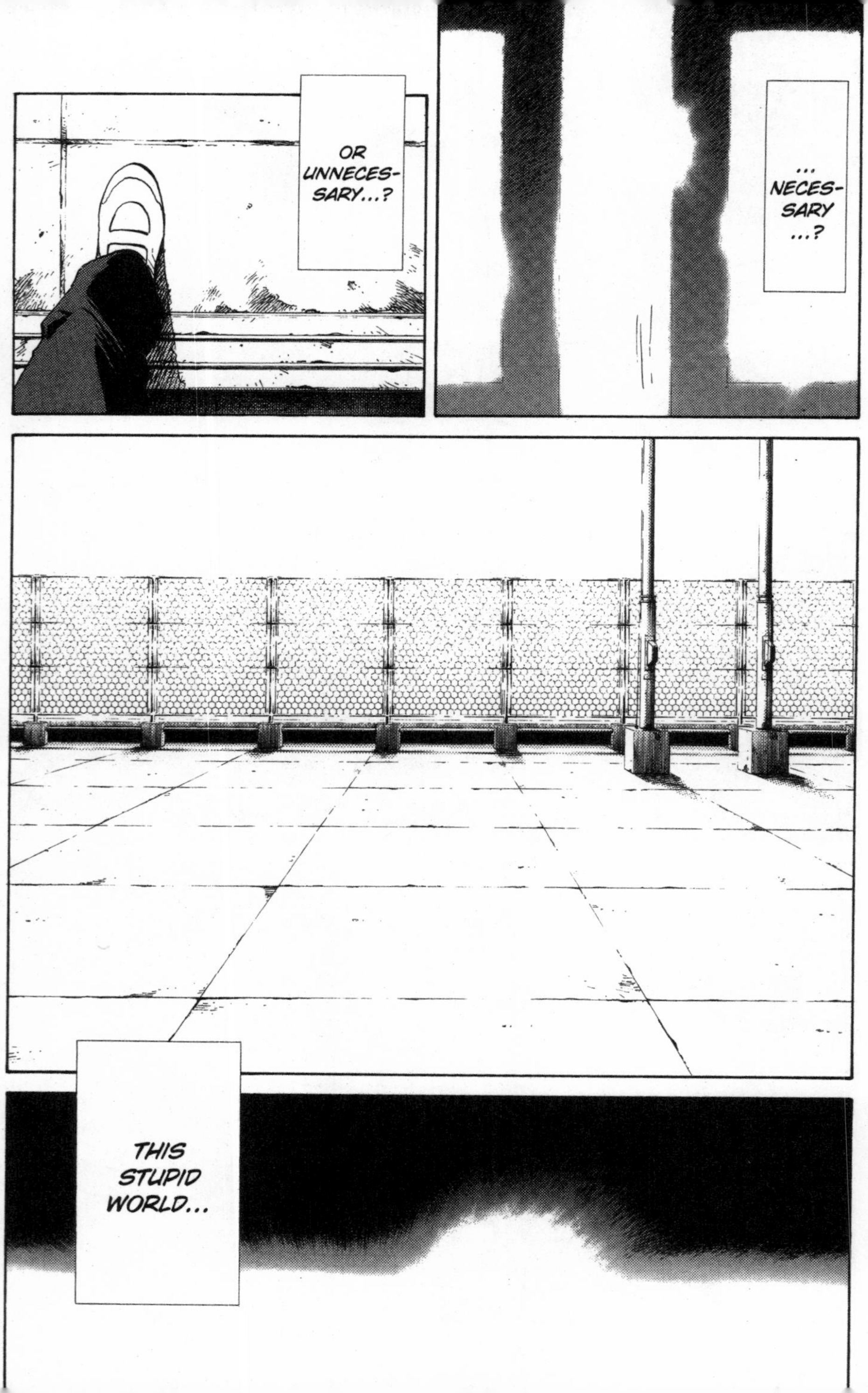
...NECES-SARY...?
OR UNNECES-SARY...?
THIS STUPID WORLD...

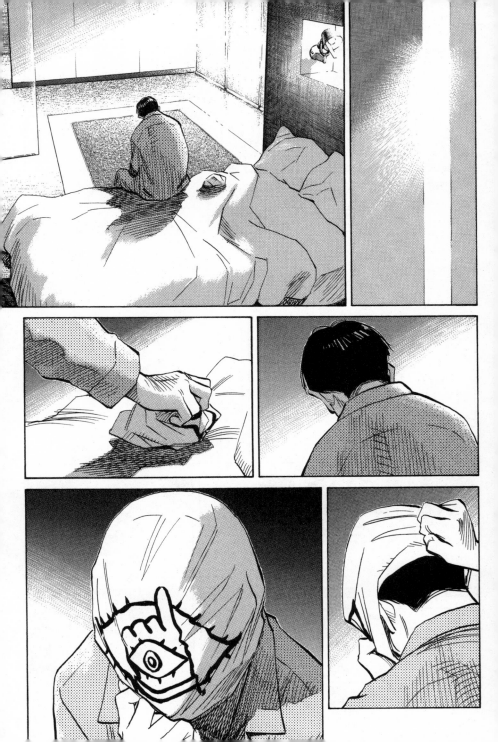

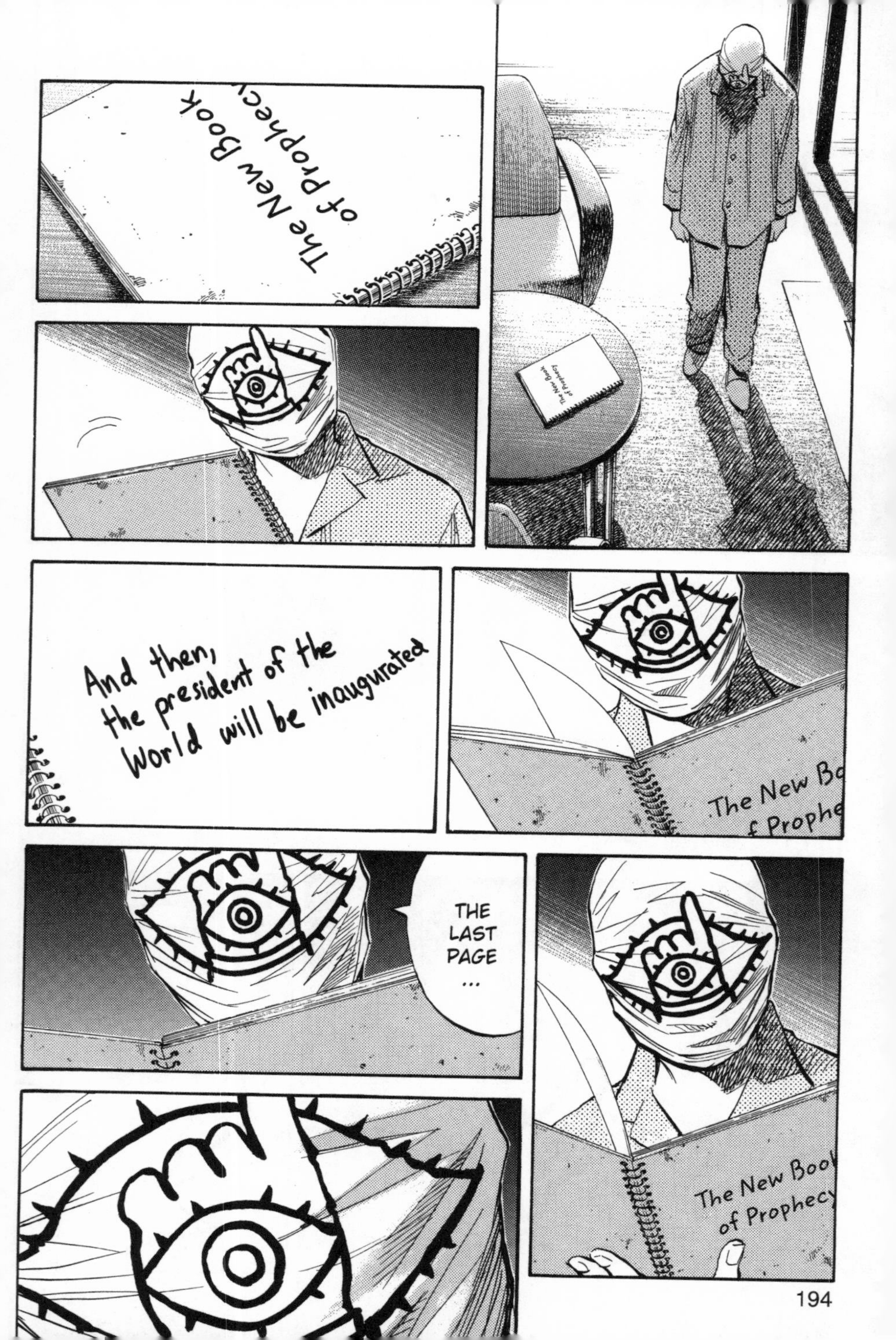
The New Book of Prophecy
The New Bo
f Prophe
And then, the president of the World will be inaugurated
The New Book of Prophecy
THE LAST PAGE ...

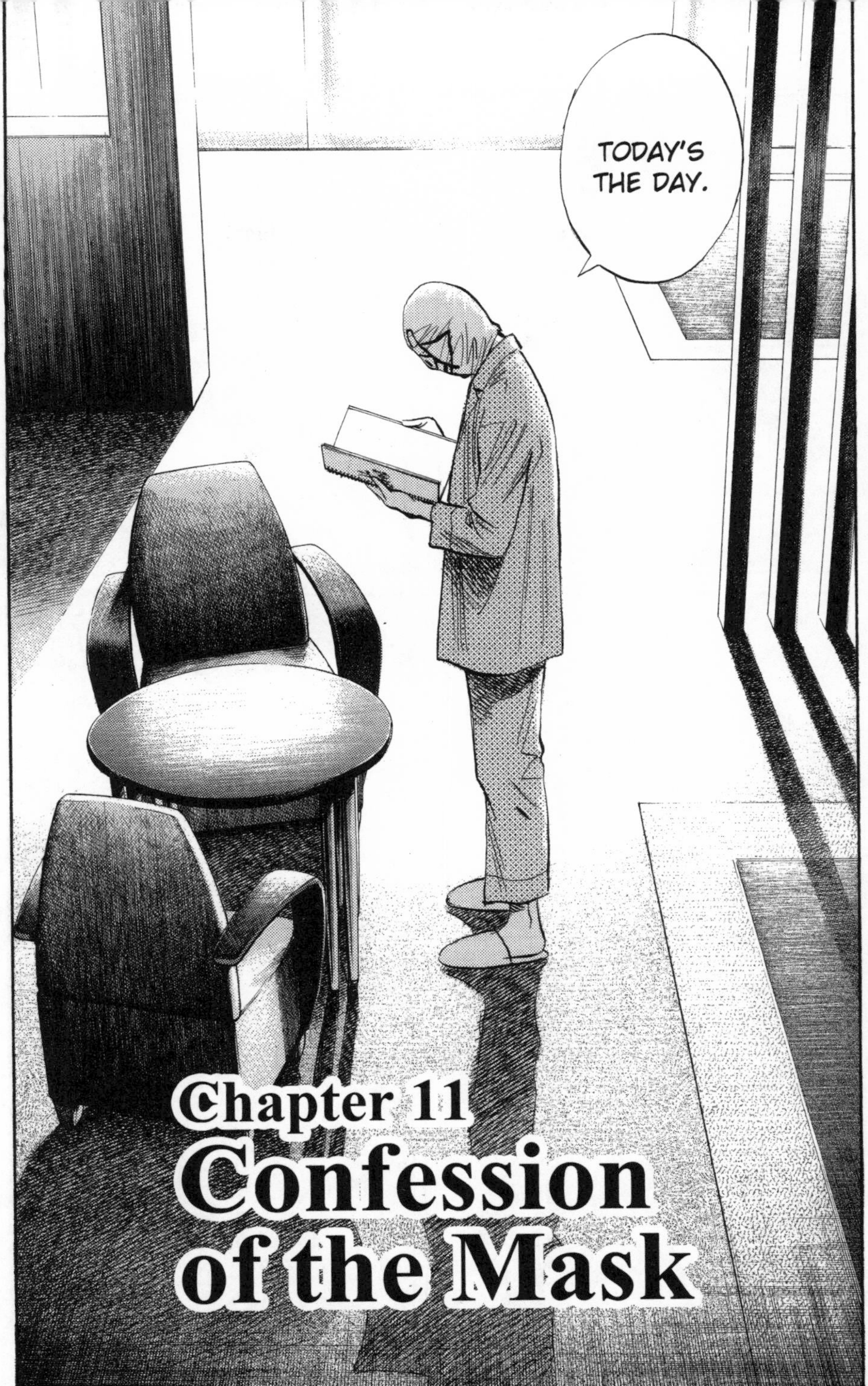
TODAY'S THE DAY.
Chapter 11
Confession of the Mask

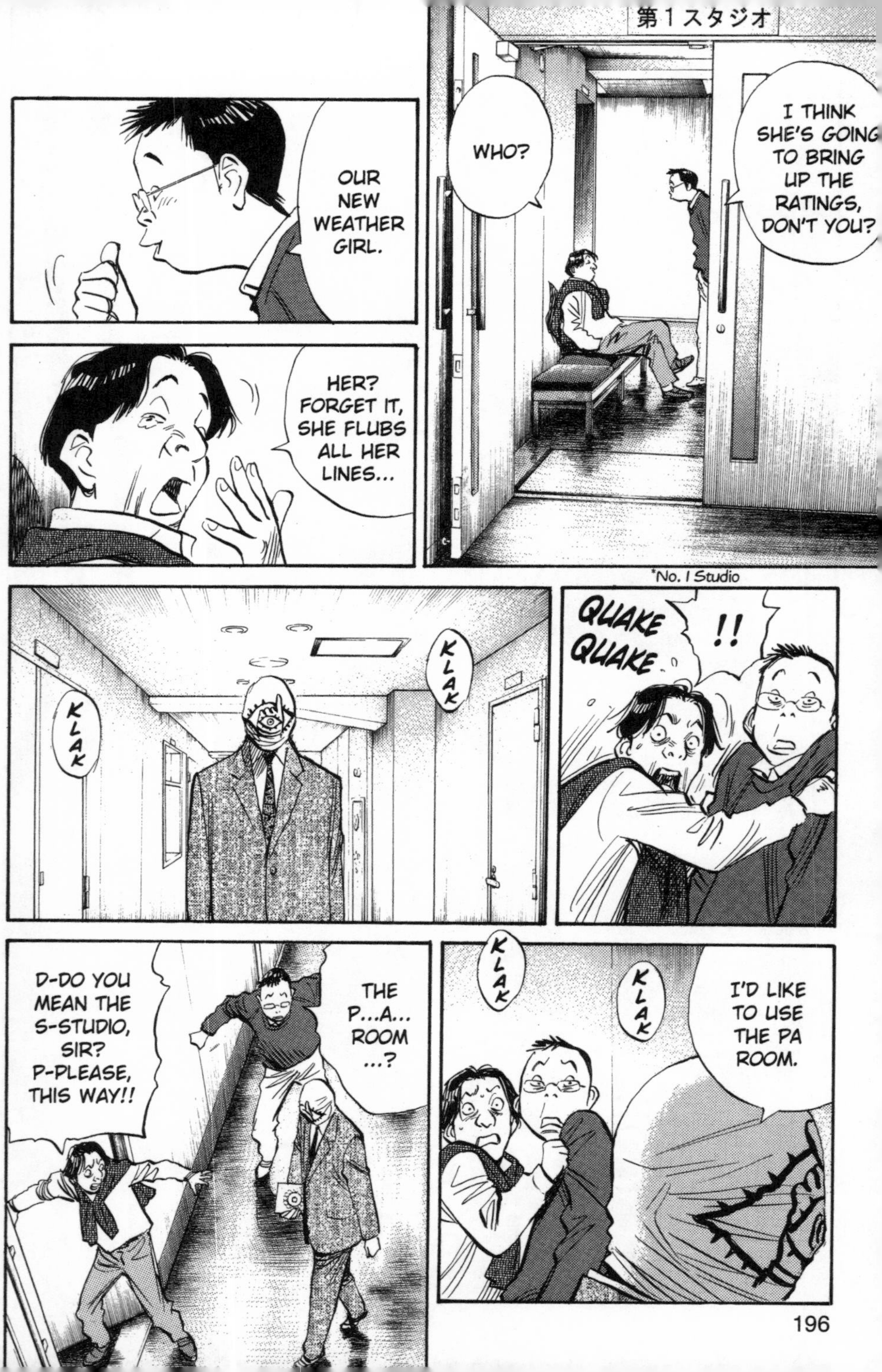
第1スタジオ
I THINK SHE'S GOING TO BRING UP THE RATINGS, DON'T YOU?
WHO?
OUR NEW WEATHER GIRL.
HER? FORGET IT, SHE FLUBS ALL HER LINES...
QUAKE QUAKE
!!
KLAK
KLAK
KLAK
KLAK
I'D LIKE TO USE THE PA ROOM.
THE P...A... ROOM ...?
D-DO YOU MEAN THE S-STUDIO, SIR? P-PLEASE, THIS WAY!!

*No. 1 Studio

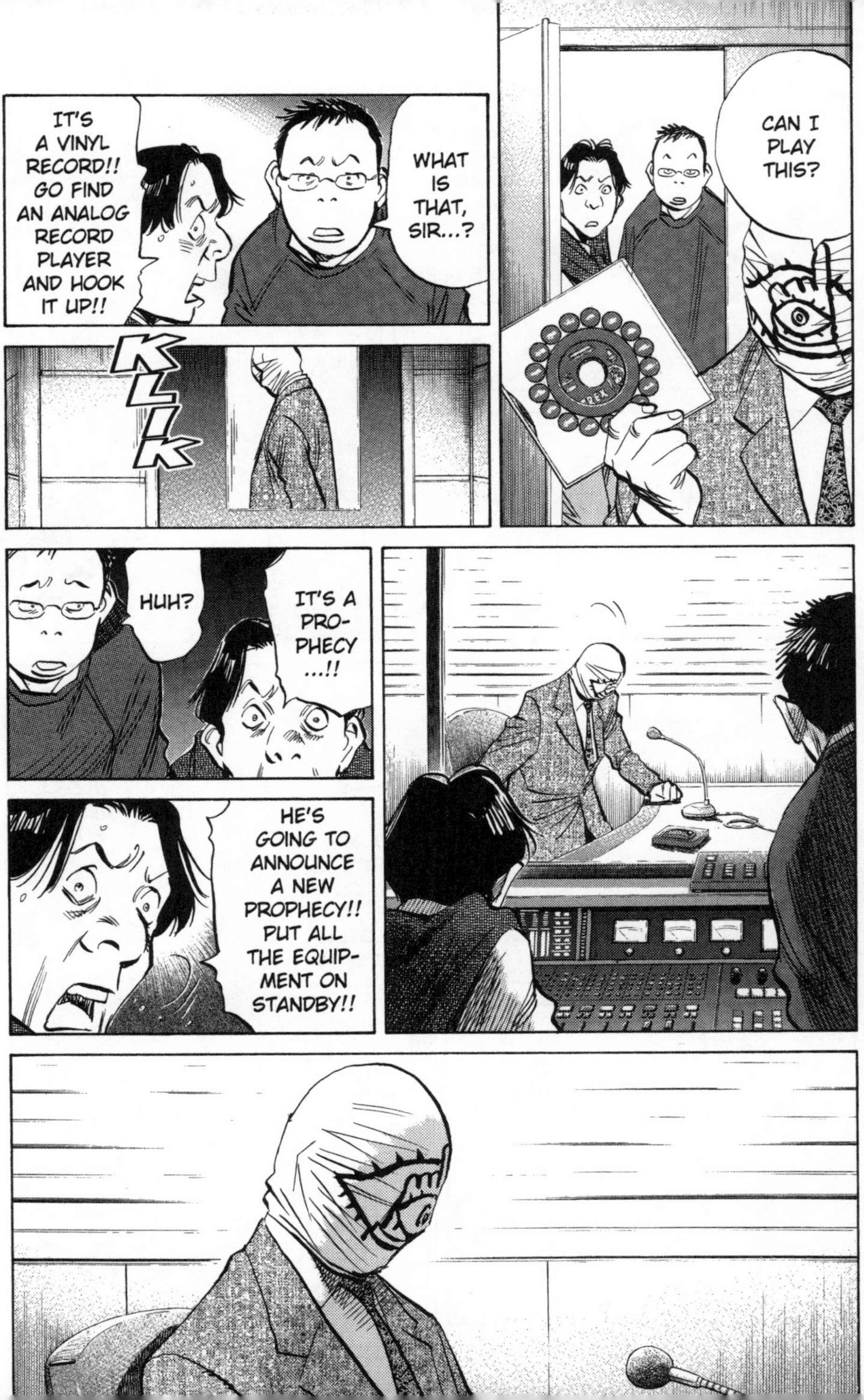
CAN I PLAY THIS?
WHAT IS THAT, SIR...?
IT'S A VINYL RECORD!! GO FIND AN ANALOG RECORD PLAYER AND HOOK IT UP!!
KLIK
IT'S A PROPHECY...!!
HUH?
HE'S GOING TO ANNOUNCE A NEW PROPHECY!! PUT ALL THE EQUIPMENT ON STANDBY!!

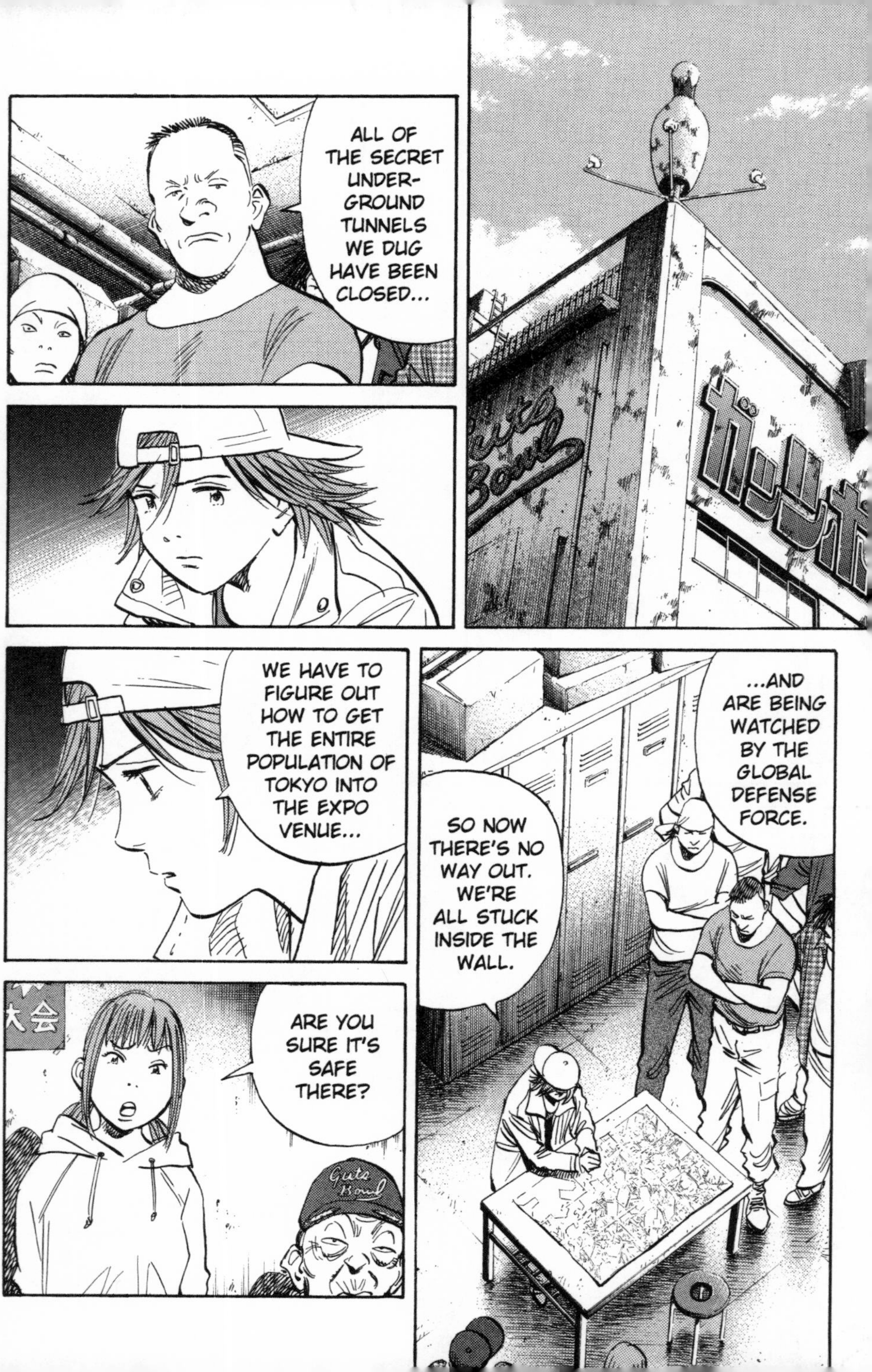
ALL OF THE SECRET UNDER-GROUND TUNNELS WE DUG HAVE BEEN CLOSED...
...AND ARE BEING WATCHED BY THE GLOBAL DEFENSE FORCE.
SO NOW THERE'S NO WAY OUT. WE'RE ALL STUCK INSIDE THE WALL.
WE HAVE TO FIGURE OUT HOW TO GET THE ENTIRE POPULATION OF TOKYO INTO THE EXPO VENUE...
ARE YOU SURE IT'S SAFE THERE?

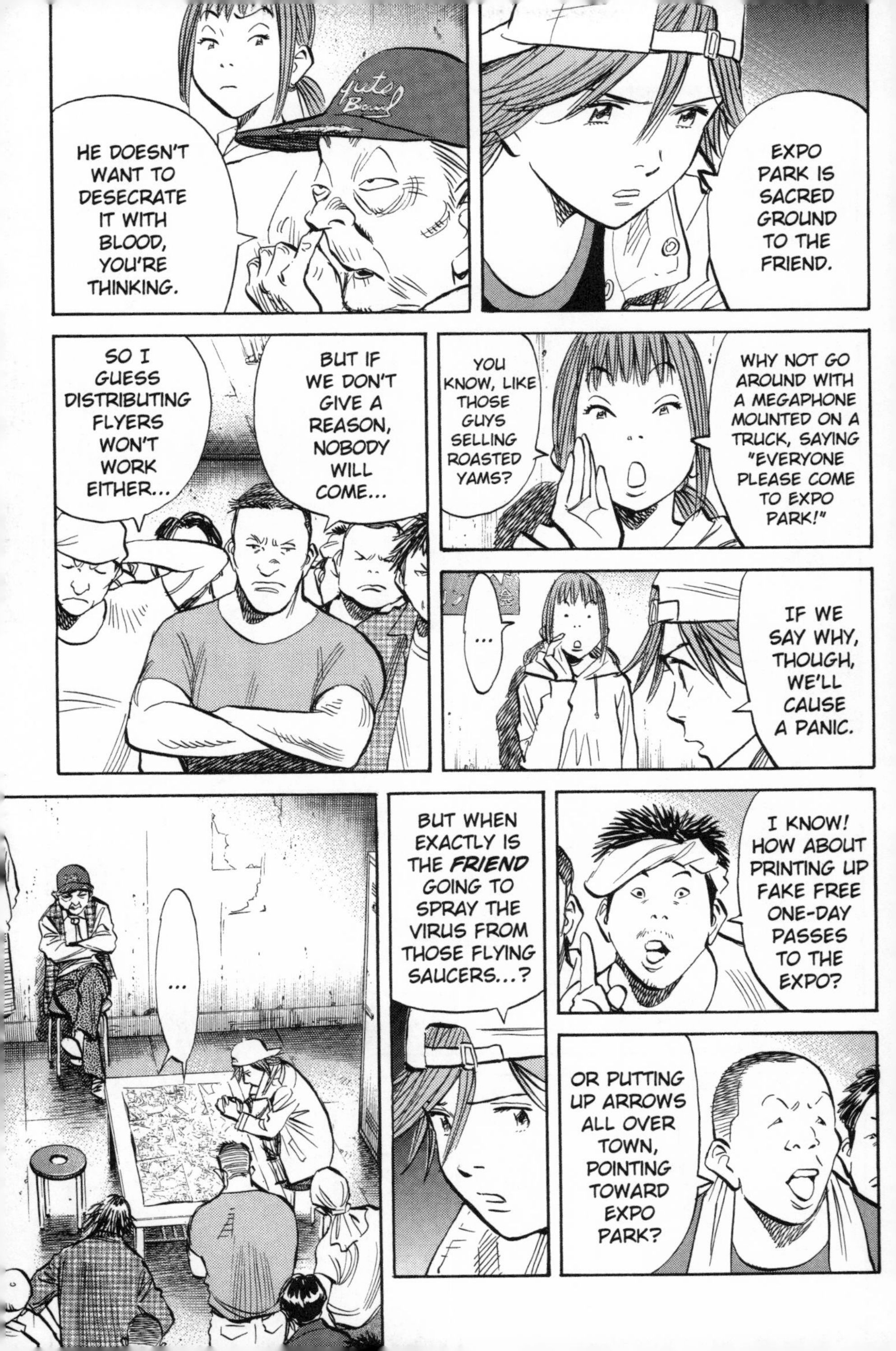
EXPO PARK IS SACRED GROUND TO THE FRIEND.
HE DOESN'T WANT TO DESECRATE IT WITH BLOOD, YOU'RE THINKING.
WHY NOT GO AROUND WITH A MEGAPHONE MOUNTED ON A TRUCK, SAYING "EVERYONE PLEASE COME TO EXPO PARK!"
YOU KNOW, LIKE THOSE GUYS SELLING ROASTED YAMS?
IF WE SAY WHY, THOUGH, WE'LL CAUSE A PANIC.
...
BUT IF WE DON'T GIVE A REASON, NOBODY WILL COME...
SO I GUESS DISTRIBUTING FLYERS WON'T WORK EITHER...
I KNOW! HOW ABOUT PRINTING UP FAKE FREE ONE-DAY PASSES TO THE EXPO?
OR PUTTING UP ARROWS ALL OVER TOWN, POINTING TOWARD EXPO PARK?
BUT WHEN EXACTLY IS THE *FRIEND* GOING TO SPRAY THE VIRUS FROM THOSE FLYING SAUCERS...?
...

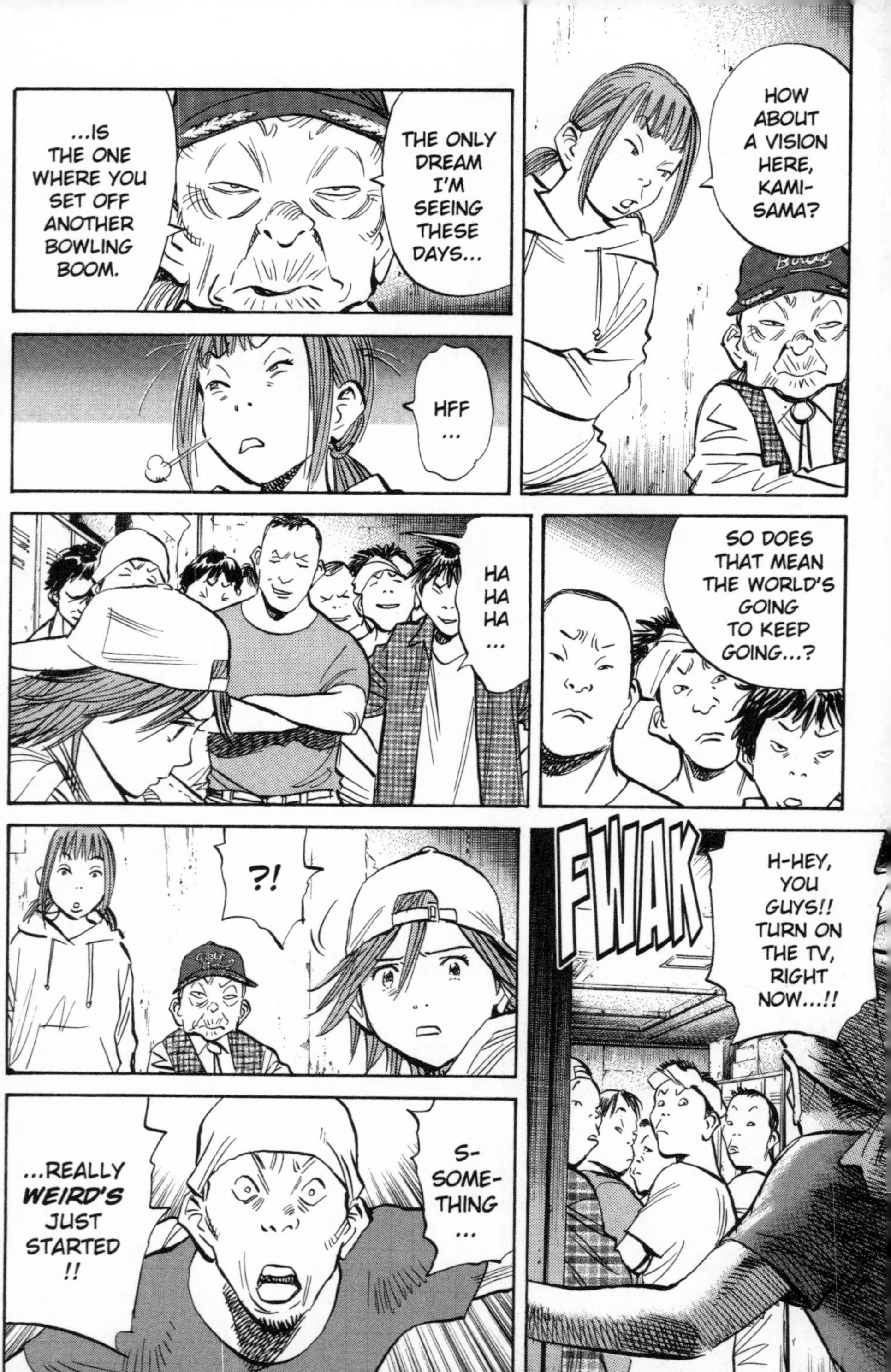
HOW ABOUT A VISION HERE, KAMI-SAMA?
THE ONLY DREAM I'M SEEING THESE DAYS...
...IS THE ONE WHERE YOU SET OFF ANOTHER BOWLING BOOM.
HFF ...
SO DOES THAT MEAN THE WORLD'S GOING TO KEEP GOING...?
HA HA HA ...
FWAK
H-HEY, YOU GUYS!! TURN ON THE TV, RIGHT NOW...!!
?!
S-SOMETHING ...
...REALLY *WEIRD'S* JUST STARTED !!

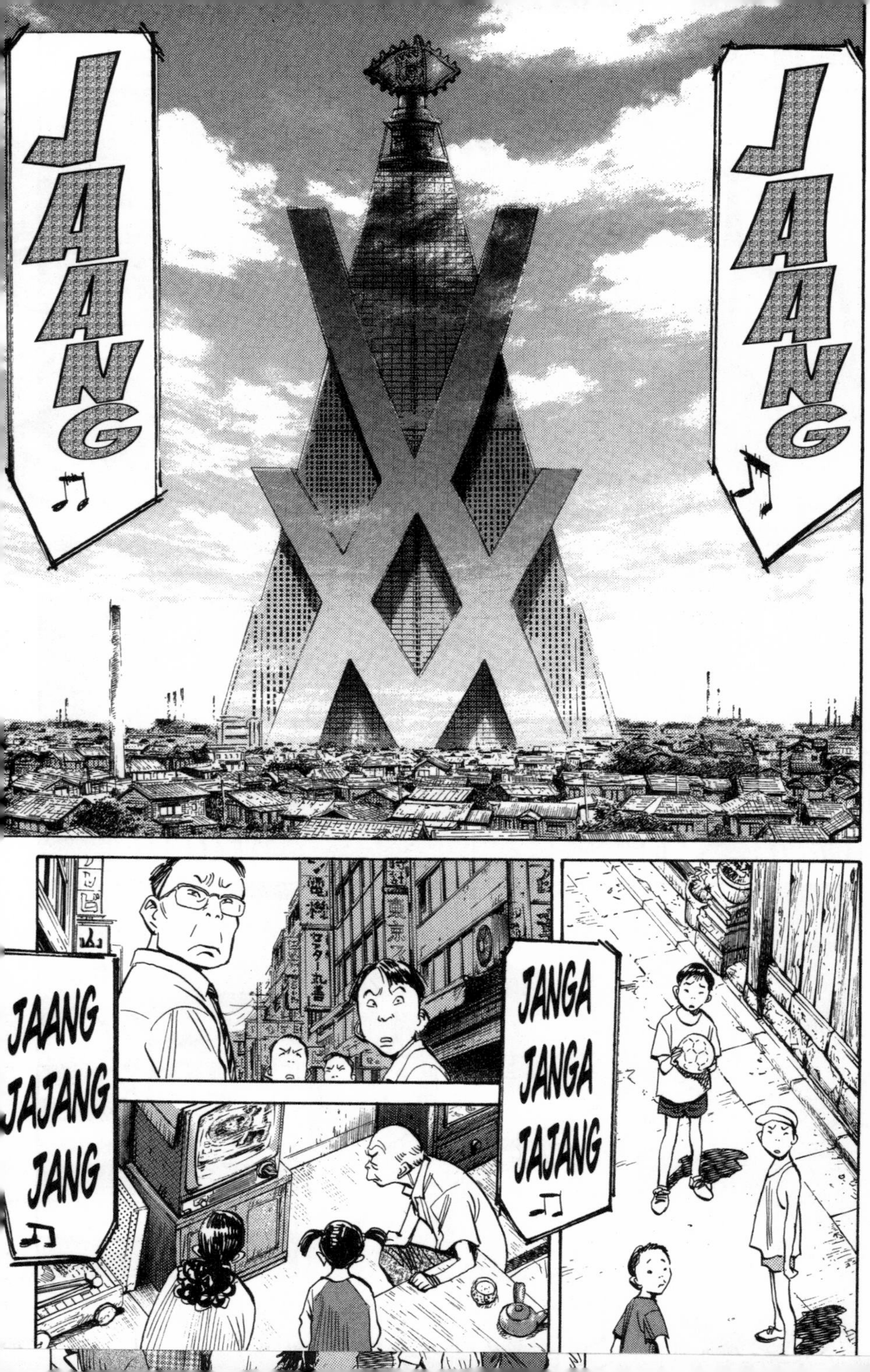
JAAANG ♫
JAAANG ♫
JANGA JANGA JAJANG ♫
JAANG JAJANG JANG ♫

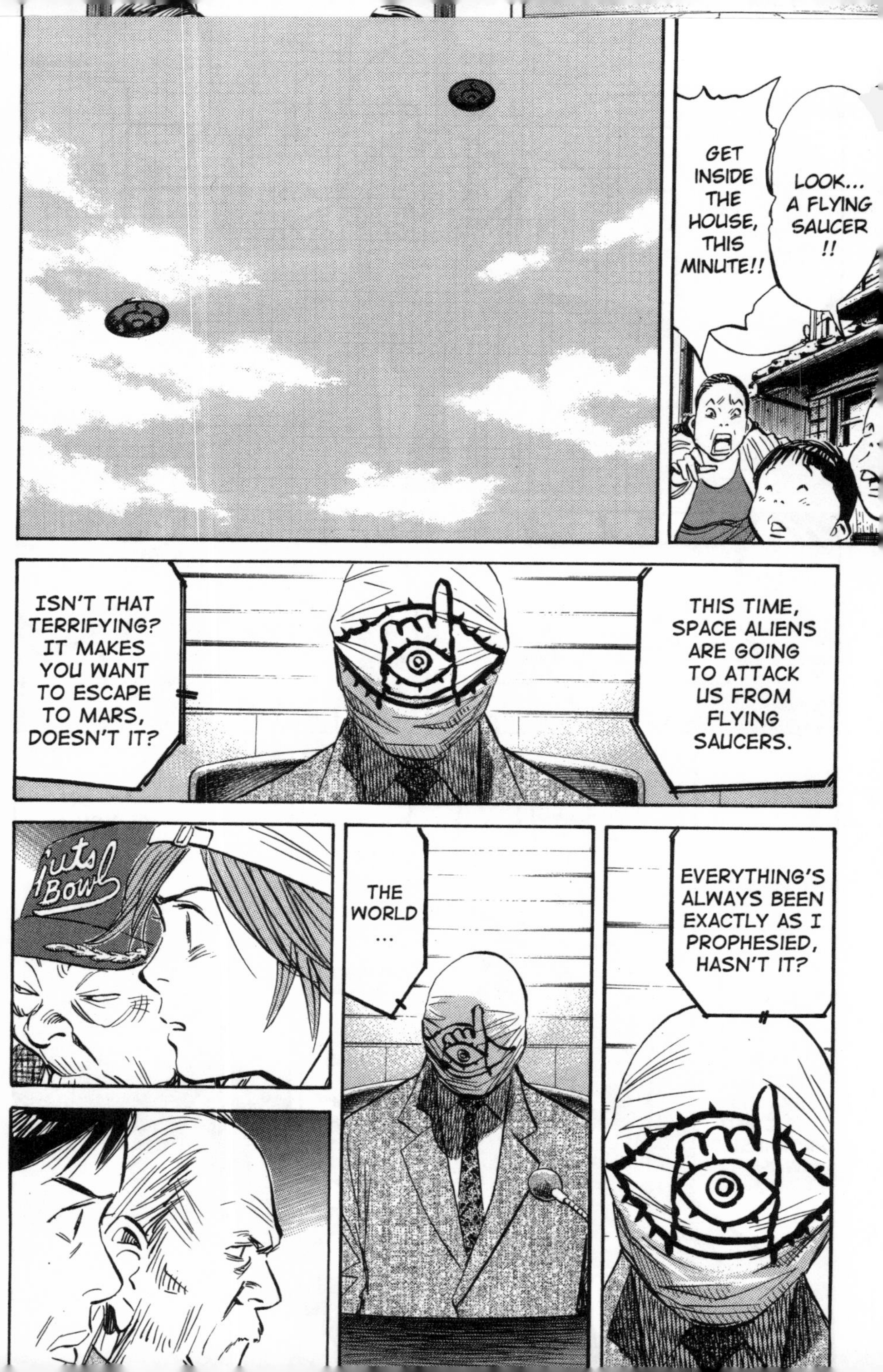
LOOK... A FLYING SAUCER!!
GET INSIDE THE HOUSE, THIS MINUTE!!
THIS TIME, SPACE ALIENS ARE GOING TO ATTACK US FROM FLYING SAUCERS.
ISN'T THAT TERRIFYING? IT MAKES YOU WANT TO ESCAPE TO MARS, DOESN'T IT?
EVERYTHING'S ALWAYS BEEN EXACTLY AS I PROPHESIED, HASN'T IT?
THE WORLD ...

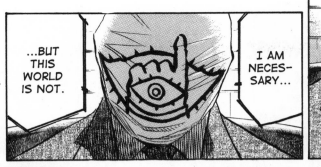

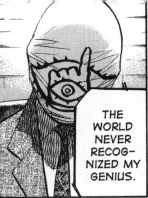

THE WORLD NEVER RECOGNIZED MY GENIUS.
I AM NECESSARY...
...BUT THIS WORLD IS NOT.
THE "PROPHECIES" WERE ALL LIES.
I DID IT. I DID ALL OF IT.

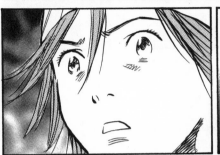

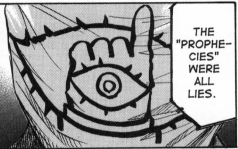

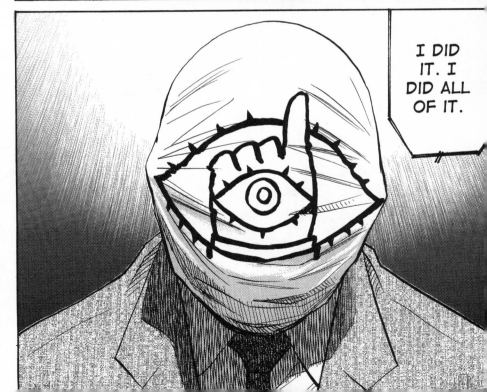

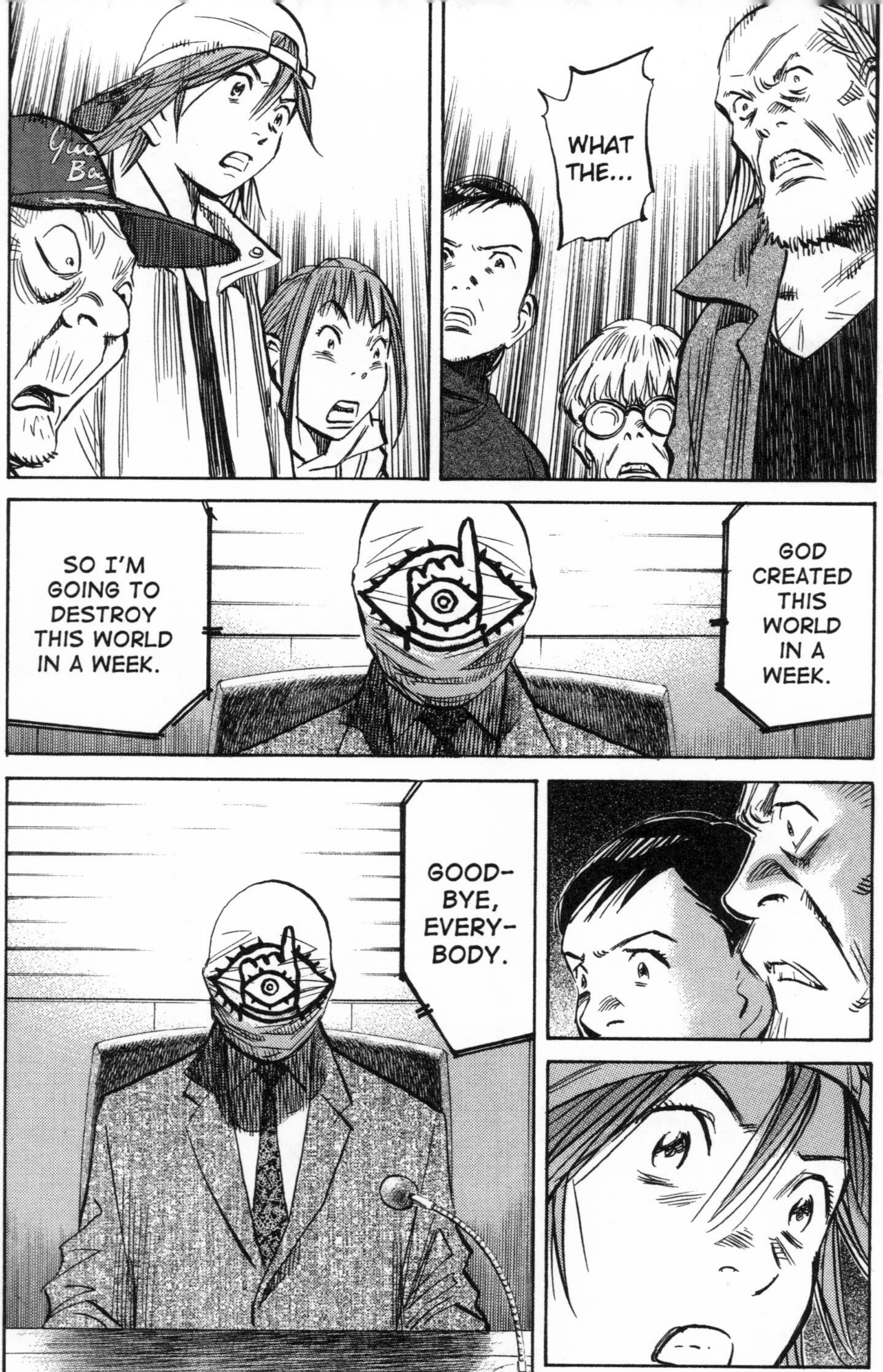
WHAT THE...
GOD CREATED THIS WORLD IN A WEEK.
SO I'M GOING TO DESTROY THIS WORLD IN A WEEK.
GOOD-BYE, EVERYBODY.

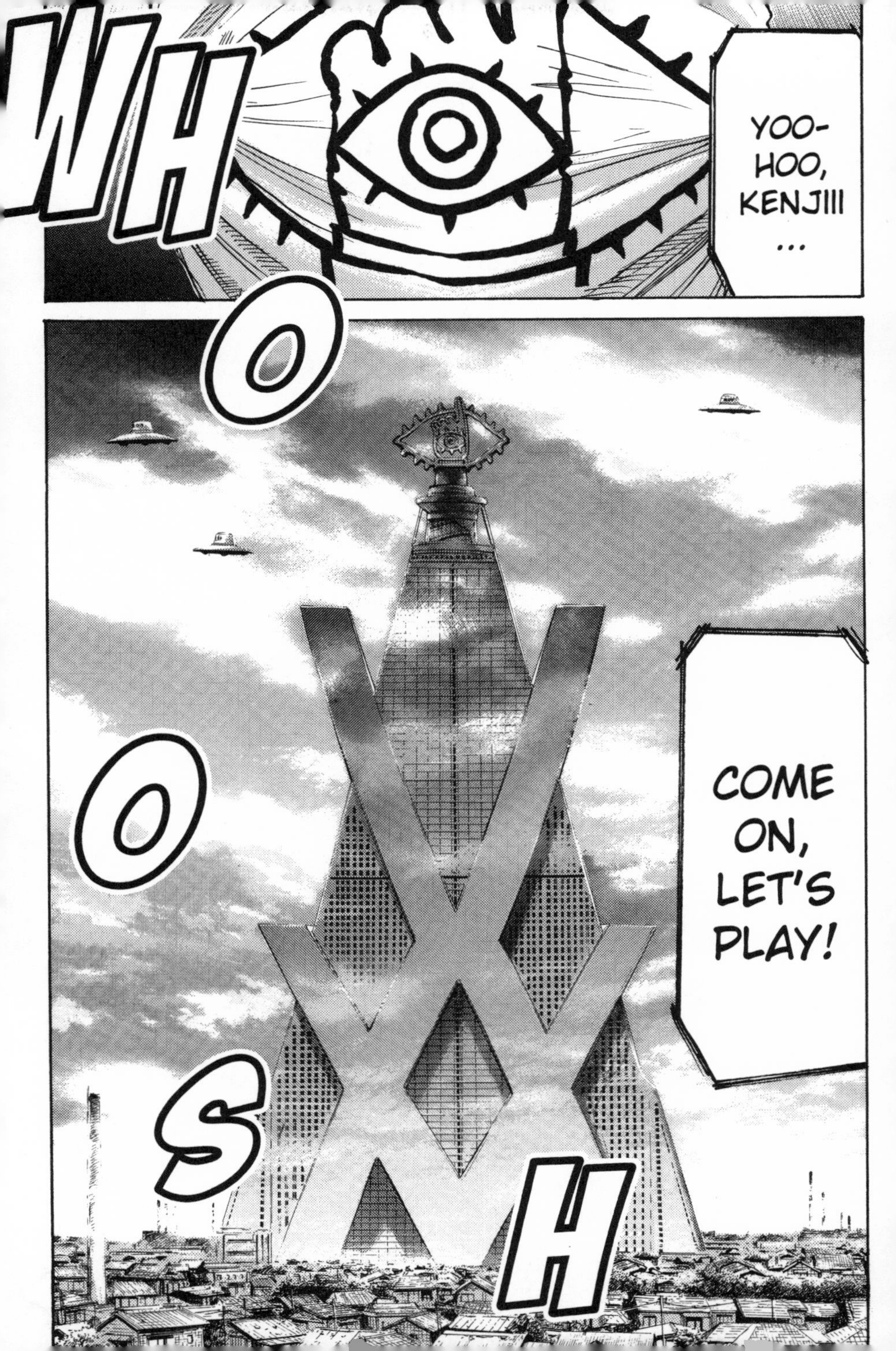
YOO-HOO, KENJIII...
WHOOOSH
COME ON, LET'S PLAY!